AF361527

NIKOLAI GOGOL

Performing Hybrid Identity

Nikolai Gogol

Performing Hybrid Identity

YULIYA ILCHUK

UNIVERSITY OF TORONTO PRESS
Toronto Buffalo London

ISBN 978-1-4875-0825-8 (cloth)   ISBN 978-1-4875-3787-6 (EPUB)
ISBN 978-1-4875-3786-9 (PDF)

Library and Archives Canada Cataloguing in Publication

Title: Nikolai Gogol : performing hybrid identity / Yuliya Ilchuk.
Names: Ilchuk, Yuliya, author.
Description: Includes bibliographical references and index.
Identifiers: Canadiana (print) 20200307800 | Canadiana (ebook)
    20200307878 | ISBN 9781487508258 (hardcover) | ISBN 9781487537876
    (EPUB) | ISBN 9781487537869 (PDF)
Subjects: LCSH: Gogol', Nikolaĭ Vasil'evich, 1809–1852 – Criticism
    and interpretation. | LCSH: Ethnicity in literature. | LCSH: National
    characteristics, Ukrainian, in literature. | LCSH: National characteristics,
    Russian, in literature.
Classification: LCC PG3335.Z8 I43 2020 | DDC 891.73/3—dc23

University of Toronto Press acknowledges the financial assistance to its
publishing program of the Canada Council for the Arts and the Ontario
Arts Council, an agency of the Government of Ontario.

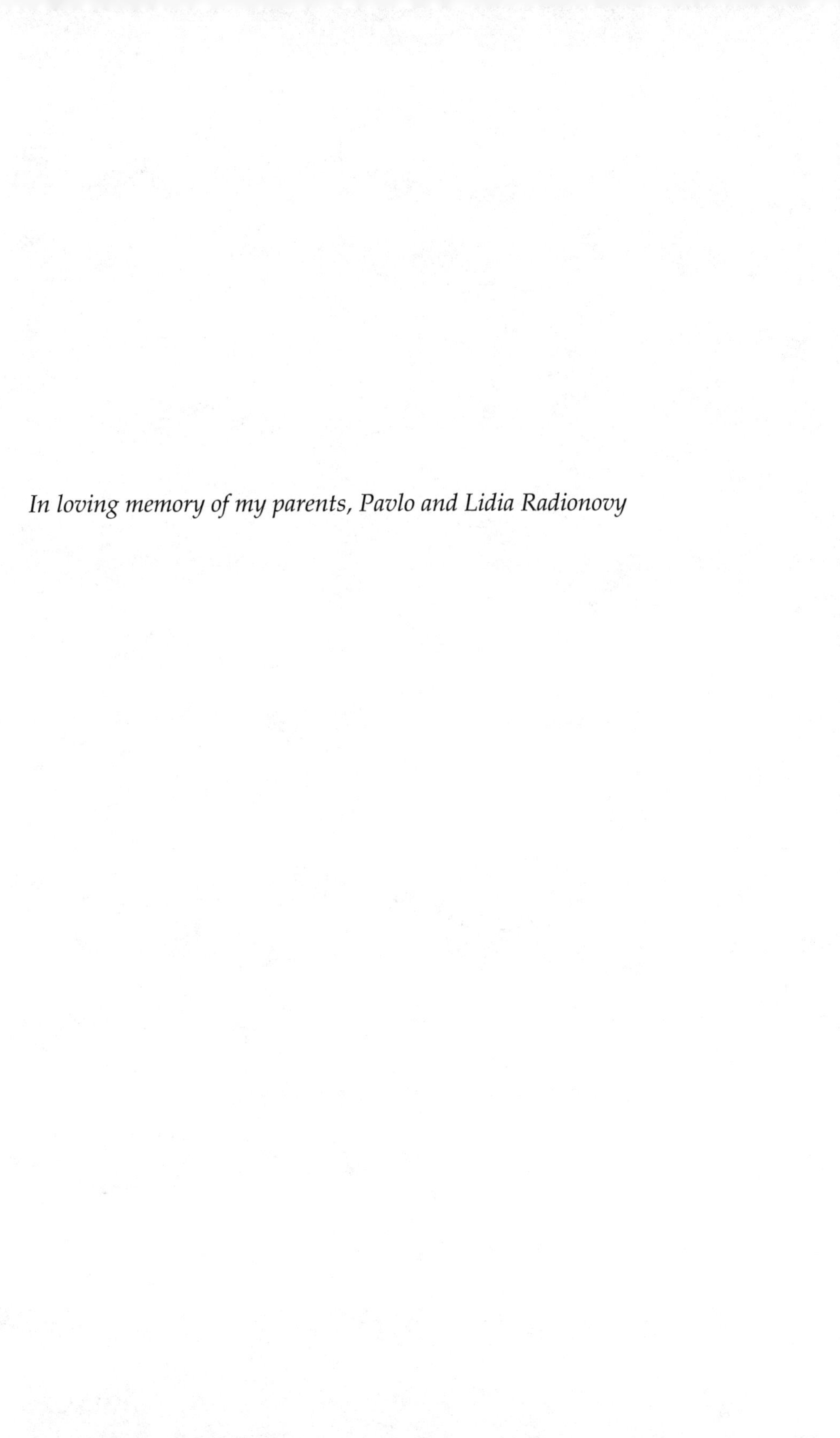

In loving memory of my parents, Pavlo and Lidia Radionovy

Contents

Note on Transliteration

The transliteration of Russian and Ukrainian names used in the book conforms to the Library of Congress transliteration system (without diacritical marks). The softness in names like Даль, Дельвиг, etc. is reproduced with "'," with the exception of Гоголь and Бульба, which are transliterated as "Gogol" and "Bulba" throughout the text. Russian last names ending in -ий, like Вяземский, Сенковский, etc., are transliterated as Viazemskii, Senkovskii, etc. Ukrainian last names ending in -ий, like Котляревський, Яновський, and others, are transliterated as Kotliarevs'kyi, Ianovs'kyi. Geographical names are given according to the official form accepted in the country where they are currently located. Thus, Warszawa appears in Polish transliteration pattern, and Kyiv, Nizhyn, etc., in Ukrainian. However, in the Bibliography I follow the Russian spelling "Kiev" as a place of publication if a book was published before 1991. In quoting from Russian and Ukrainian I have used the Cyrillic alphabet if I needed to show the unique hybrid language of Gogol. In some short quotes, integrated in the analysis, the original Russian text has been transliterated. In quotations from the first edition of Gogol's texts, I have retained his idiosyncratic orthography. Unless otherwise noted, all translations from Russian and Ukrainian are my own.

Tables

Illustrations

Acknowledgments

The intellectual and personal debts to be acknowledged by the author of this book are too numerous to list. Many colleagues and friends have read early parts and drafts of the book and gave me valuable comments. First of all, I would like to express my sincere appreciation to Marcus Levitt for advising me throughout the entire writing process. His numerous readings of the drafts and his thoughtful suggestions have enhanced the manuscript in many ways. Gabriella Safran has been my mentor and the most attentive and critical reader of the manuscript. She has inspired me to think of Gogol's hybridity in broader cultural terms. Her inexhaustible energy and brilliant sense of humour restored my sometimes-waning internal resources and motivated me to develop my own voice and writing style to reach many types of audience. I owe a debt of intellectual gratitude to Tamara Hundorova, George Grabowicz, Serhii Plokhii, Oleh Ilnytzkyj, Marko Pavlyshyn, Roman Koropeckyj, Robert Romanchuk, Taras Koznarsky, Valeria Sobol, and Amelia Glaser for the many conversations we have had and the works they have published, all of which contributed considerably to my own modest input in Gogol studies. My heartfelt thanks to Stanford colleagues Monika Greenleaf, Nariman Skakov, Lazar Fleishman, and Alexander Matthew Key for reading critically various drafts of the manuscript, which improved the final results substantially. I thank my friends-historians, Andriy Zayarnyuk and Ostap Sereda, for reading and commenting on chapter 1. Their comprehensive knowledge of nineteenth-century imperial history has helped me solidify the historical framework of my study. Among the institutions that supported my research on Gogol is Harvard Ukrainian Research Institute, which awarded me with a Shkliar Fellowship in 2015 during which I wrote the first chapters of my book. For professional advice, I have turned to Frederick White, who responded with the immense energy, enthusiasm, and generosity of spirit that are only his. I cordially thank series editor Stephen Shapiro, who provided me with invaluable guidance and assistance in the process of assembling and producing this book. Other friends whose encouragement and support I have relied upon are Olga Solovieva, Anastasia de La Fortelle, Anzhelika Khyzhnya, Ilya Vinitsky, Vitaly Chernetsky, Iryna Odrekhivska, Tina Carroll, Galina Shvedova, Lyubov Shchitka, Halyna Soloviy, Liudmila Mykhalchuk, Yuliya Volkhonovych, Orysia Prokopovych, Khrystyna Hertsyk, and many others.

Finally, I express my sincere gratitude to my husband, Serhii, who helped me with a digital part of the project. Your patience, support, and faith in me were a constant inspiration in writing this book.

Thank you all for making this book happen.

NIKOLAI GOGOL

Performing Hybrid Identity

Introduction

Works of literature do not simply reflect or are not simply caused by their contexts. They have a productive effect in history. This can and should also be studied. To put this another way, the only thing that sometimes worries me about the turn to history now as an explanatory method is the implication that I can fully explain every text by its pre-existing historical context. But the publication of these works was itself a political or historical event that in some way changed history. I think that if you don't allow for this, literature is not much worth bothering with.

– J. Hillis Miller[1]

Сочинение мое, если когда выйдет, будет на иностранном языке, и тем более мне нужна точность, <чтобы> не исказить неправильными именованиями существенного имени нации.

– Nikolai Gogol, letter to M.V. Gogol[2]

"Do not rely on my works." These words from Gogol's "Author's Confession" capture the fate of his texts, which after numerous revisions abound with ambiguities, discontinuities, and gaps. The same can be said of Gogol's national identity. He created a riddle regarding what kind of national "soul" he possessed – Ukrainian or Russian – leaving clues in the variants of his texts.[3] Rewriting, destroying, and restoring the original texts, Gogol engaged in a performance of his hybrid identity. Bilingual in Russian and Ukrainian since birth, Gogol deliberately played with hybrid discourse in his early works. In the late 1830s, however, he became preoccupied with making his literary language more standard and accessible to a Russian-speaking audience. He rewrote his major texts several times – at times eliminating Ukrainian elements and neutralizing regional forms, while in others restoring these elements. As the result of frequent and inconsistent editing, Gogol's texts were transformed into a multilayered palimpsest in which previous hybridized elements remain palpable beneath the normalized Russian discourse. As Roman Koropeckyj and Robert Romanchuk have wittily noted, even if it seems that "Gogol has 'forgotten' the Ukrainian language, it has not forgotten him,"[4] and Ukrainianisms continued to slip into the fabric of his late, so-called Russian, texts.[5] The history of reworking and editing of Gogol's texts runs parallel to his constant vacillations between preserving his hybrid identity and Russianizing it. Trying to negotiate his identity on the borderline of two languages and cultures, he developed a uniquely dialectical worldview and a heightened sensitivity to flux and transition. Such hybrids as Gogol, according to Mikhail Bakhtin, have been "profoundly productive historically: they are pregnant with potential for new world views, with new 'internal forms' for perceiving the world in words."[6]

At first Gogol's hybridity was viewed as neither unusual nor threatening to the empire, because Russian national identity was a rather inchoate concept before the Polish Uprising of 1830–1. When Gogol entered the Petersburg literary scene in the early 1830s, he was perceived as an *in-between* literary actor who could translate Ukrainian "otherness" for the metropolitan audience. In the mid-1830s, imperial ideology regarding national identity started to change. Gogol was caught between two ideological camps – the cosmopolitan Russian émigré society in Italy and the nationalistic Slavophiles in Moscow – and he began revising his Ukrainian tales and adding more Russian flavour to *Dead Souls*. This self-revisionism was Gogol's artistic response to the rising nationalism in Russian society. Many critics of the time regarded Gogol's balancing between the pro-Western and pro-Russian intellectual groups as his innate "Little Russian slyness." In this book, I dispute the idea that Gogol had internalized a colonial mode of behaviour and study his cultural hybridity from several angles: as a problem of his unconventional cultural behaviour, visual self-fashioning, multi-ethnic narrative performance, and hybrid Russian-Ukrainian language. Gogol returned a colonial gaze, having created a hybrid literary language and identity that mimicked and mocked the pretensions of the dominant culture to fix him as a monolingual Russian. He saturated the Russian language with innovative potential for verbal play, indeterminacy, and de-automatization.

Gogol's hybridity brings up the question of his subtle, implicit resistance to imperial homogenization. His self-translations inevitably required the negotiation of different languages within the self, generating powerful experiences for the writer himself and for the increasingly monolingual Russian society. Thus, all his texts contain an unresolved tension between the standard Russian idiom toward which he consciously aimed for the sake of his fame as an imperial writer and his hybrid Russian-Ukrainian voice that was always a source of his creative use of language. Since not all forms of resistance are intentional and visibly oppositional, the question to what extent Gogol's hybrid language was a deliberate or natural phenomenon becomes irrelevant. As Édouard Glissant has persuasively shown, in the colonial situation where open political struggle is practically impossible, language adopts indirect tactics of evasion and camouflage.[7] In Gogol's hybrid use of language, these strategies diversified and undermined the sameness of imperial assimilation, replacing the homogeneity and authoritativeness of the Russian discourse with playful heterogeneous counterpoetics.

The theoretical framework of this study is informed by the concepts of hybridity and mimicry as developed in the works of Frantz Fanon, Robert Young, and Homi Bhabha, and in recent revisions of postcolonial hybridity by Satoshi Mizutani, Anne McClintock, Rey Chow, and Ania Loomba. A term borrowed from the natural sciences, hybridity originally referred to the natural intermingling and mixing between two or more pure species; later, it received a broad application in the social sciences. In classical postcolonial studies, Frantz Fanon first applied hybridity in 1968, describing the psychological impact of French colonialism on colonized Antilleans. According to Fanon, the black man, recognizing that a white colonizer does not share his self-image, finds himself fraught by a state of "corporeal malediction."[8] This becomes a defining moment for the identity formation of both the white colonizer and the black colonized. In this encounter, the colonized Antillean loses his/her sense of inherent selfhood, while the French colonizer acquires a sense of superiority, civilization, and whiteness. In modern postcolonial theory, the colonial relationship has been revised from being seen as hierarchical and oppressive for the colonized to being understood as mutually affecting both the colonizer and the colonized. The difference of this approach from the earlier studies of colonialism is in a new understanding of the growing agency of the colonized, who from a passive, speechless subaltern has become a subject capable of speaking back to the centre. In the 1990s, Homi Bhabha theorized the capacity of the colonized to mimic the colonizer's discourse by subverting the power hierarchy and returning the colonial gaze to the centre. Since the colonizer and the colonized are locked in a relationship of hierarchical individuation, every attribute of authority can be reappropriated by the colonial double. In this reappropriation and restructuring of colonial discursive space, the contingent sites of meaning, or *in-between* spaces, emerge, making identities porous and multifaceted. Thus, the ambivalent nature of representation became one of Bhabha's most important additions to postcolonial theory. It makes any position in the colonial fantasy open to inversion, or "mimicry." As in Lacan's models of the representational mirror that operates by means of a spatial splitting and the threat "your money or your life" that stands for the subject's submission to language, in Bhabha's model colonial self-identification takes place in the interlocutory spaces between self and *other*.[9] The internal conflict between the subject's narcissistic demand for completeness and its avowal of difference produces a split at the site of enunciation and prevents identity from completion. In Bhabha's view, the incompleteness and indeterminacy of colonial identities do not need to be solved, but rather to be acknowledged and celebrated. By divesting hybridity of its categorical colonial connotation, Bhabha thereby makes it a precondition for inclusiveness, dialogism, and subversion.

This concept of hybridity, however, has lately been criticized for its relativism, idealism, "formal fetishism," and ahistoricity. Bill Ashcroft, Gareth Griffiths, and Helen Tiffin discern "replicating assimilationist policies by masking or 'whitewashing' cultural differences" in Bhabha's use of hybridity.[10] Another group of scholars reproaches Bhabha for legitimizing a teleological explanation of imperial penetration[11] and for universalizing the colonial encounter.[12] Ania Loomba, for instance, notes that in Bhabha's theory the hybrid subject emerges undifferentiated, homogeneous, and unaffected by splitting identification. Terry Eagleton, on the other hand, points at the risk of hybridity becoming a kind of transcendentalism instead of being an antidote to the transcendental view of history.[13] Rey Chow finds Bhabha's formulation of hybridity as a mode of resistance problematic because the latter locates it in the ambivalence of the imperialist's speech itself, rather than viewing it as initiated by the hybrid or subaltern subject.[14] Similarly, Anne McClintock argues that in Bhabha's theory of hybridity it is a discourse rather than a concrete historical agent that "desires, dreams, and does the work of colonialism while also ensuring its demise." Such a "formalist fetishism," she continues, "effectively elides the messier question of historical change and social activism."[15]

Despite the critique of hybridity, it does remain a useful tool for analytical intervention. As recently shown in a study of the Eurasian subject by Satoshi Mizutani, it is necessary for scholars to critically engage with hybridity. Mizutani stipulates that "the question of colonial ambivalence should require an immanent critique of history, particularly its contradictions that emerged through concrete social processes of the colonial encounter."[16] A restoration of agency and autonomous subjectivity to the hybrid subject can "reinstall history as an open-ended process, devoid of teleology, and as an equally indeterminate mode of thinking about social change in time."[17] Following Mizutani's proposition, I view hybridity as a specific social and historical phenomenon characteristic of the emerging Ukrainian subject that existed in various camouflaged modes in the nineteenth century and that Gogol's use of hybrid language, ambivalent cultural behaviour, and textual revision perfectly exemplify.

In this book, hybridity is examined at the individual as well as at the group level with its focus on Nikolai Gogol as a very idiosyncratic case of the transition from a denationalized Ukrainian to a more nationally oriented identity. The choice of this approach to identity formation is crucial in my study because Ukrainian intellectuals of Gogol's time were engaged in complex identification with both imperial and national cultural modes. Since hybridity takes on a different valence when it is studied from an individual or a social perspective, only a dual perspective can prevent us from viewing Ukrainian intellectuals as those who unconditionally internalized colonial self-representation as an inferior, ethnic *other*. In previous research on Gogol, this model of internalization has dominated.[18] It inferred that Gogol assimilated others' objectification and made it a part of his own subjective reality. However, the "sly Ukrainian" model of identity was a projection of Russian society's expectations. The process of internalization with its clear-cut differentiation between outer and inner, however, is not sufficient to account for an individual's transformational experience. If viewed as strategic and positional, Gogol's hybridity was not exclusively circumscribed by external influences. His identity was a subject for constant reconsideration and change. It was developed through ambivalent, transgressive movements and escaped identification in terms of "either/or." The focus on the performative aspect of hybridity that this book assumes offers a more nuanced perspective on Gogol's identity formation, which calls into question the essentialism prevalent in much of Gogol studies.

It should be noted that, unlike in Western Europe and the United States, where hybridity signals the preoccupation of Western society with race, in the study of Russian-Ukrainian relations it can be applied in other contexts as well. First, it exposes the conflation of imperial, national, and ethnic identities and provides an alternative to the essentialist categories of "pure" and "authentic" national identities in the nineteenth-century Russian Empire. Second, it captures the frustration of Ukrainian intellectuals who had to create in the imperial language and, in response to this homogenizing practice, produced the narrative masks of ethnic Ukrainian narrators. And finally, it problematizes imperial knowledge and challenges the continuity of imperial control over Gogol's canonization and the dissemination of his works in present-day Russian and Ukrainian societies.

A few words should be also said about the hybrid nature of Russia's colonization of its internal colonies, particularly of Ukraine, which facilitated the formation of hybrid identities. Russia's hegemony in Eastern Europe had always hinged upon its aspiration of becoming the super-agent of domination. In the eighteenth century, when the Russian Empire emerged as a subject of global history by exerting its power and control over Poland, Ukraine, the Baltic provinces, Finland, and Bessarabia, it colonized these territories and people in the name of the European civilizational project. Much in this ambition of Russia had, and still has, depended on Ukraine's presence and participation in the imperial project. In the Russian political imagination, the relationship between the two has been envisioned as mutually beneficial, yet hierarchical. The colonial model of the relationship between Ukraine and the Russian Empire has been disregarded by most Russian scholars. In Ukrainian nationalism, the dominant model that is applied to describe the Russia-Ukraine relationship is the colonial one: Russia had always been an expansion-oriented and centralized state, while Ukraine has been in flux, multi-vectored, and more prone to democratic forms of social structure.

Many scholars contend that Russia was not a classical colonial empire because it expanded only within its own continent; particularly, Russia's policies in the Caucasus, Central Asia, Siberia, and Asia can hardly be considered colonial. Recent attempts at revising the relationship between Russia and its internal colonies have produced some interesting concepts: those of "internal colonization" (Alexander Etkind),[19] "self-colonization" (Boris Groys),[20] and the ideological internalization of external colonialism in Russian hegemonic attitudes about Ukraine (Stefan Rohdewald).[21] What is missing in the internal colonization theory is the history of the external colonization of Ukraine: the liquidation of the Hetmanate's autonomy, the establishment of the imperial system of provincial administration, the appointment of a Russian governor-general as the monarch's representative, the subsequent impoverishment of all Ukrainian estates, and the further Russification of the cultural elite. According to Etkind, Ukrainians were blended into the empire, forming cultural-political differences of "other-but-self," because the Ukrainian population was "ethnically similar to that of the Mother Country." Ethnic and racial differences in the Russian Empire, in his view, were not formative, because the geographical and economic homogeneity of imperial space "outweighed all other differences – ethnic, linguistic, religious – melting them in a shared imperial pot."[22]

The prominent Ukrainian historian Yaroslav Hrytsak is also cautious about applying the term "colony" to Ukrainian territories under the Russian Empire or Soviet Union, because the Little Russian and later Soviet Ukrainian elite, in his view, had accepted the idea of imperial advancement in their region and formed the core of imperial and Soviet administrations. He has proposed viewing Ukraine's case as a "modernization with internal colonization." Ukraine was caught between two extremes as both the core of Russian and Soviet imperial projects and the centre of anti-imperial and anti-Soviet resistance, which together encompassed a wide variety of colonial experiences.[23]

As an attempt to reconcile internal and external colonization, Michael Khodarkovsky has productively applied the notion of a "hybrid empire," arguing that Russia's expansion to the west was both continental and colonial in nature.[24] During the Soviet period and today, Russia has maintained that it has come together as a country and managed to keep its territories because it has been a peaceful unifier, unlike oppressive European empires. This narrative also persists in today's military conflict between Russia and Ukraine. Because of the "frontier" position of Ukraine, it is still often perceived by Russians not as a sovereign state but an extension of Greater Russia.

It is important that, as early as the 1830s, Russian intellectuals acknowledged that the Russian Empire had succeeded in assimilating the Ukrainian elite but failed in Russianizing the masses. In his review of Dmytro Bantysh-Kamenskii's *History of Little Russia* (1822), the Russian Romantic critic Nikolai Polevoi described the relationship between the Russian Empire and Ukrainians by using the European model of colonization:

> We treated [Ukrainians] as conquerors treat colonized lands. We Russianized their aristocracy, gradually replaced local rights with our own laws and customs, eliminated the most recalcitrant, and we ourselves mixed with the alien common people [Germans] but failed to Russianize them … they [Ukrainians] do not and cannot have political independence ["samobytnosti" – could also mean: originality or identity], but again, they are ours but not us …[25]

Indeed, of all Russia's colonies, Ukraine had the most complex and problematic relationship with the metropole. The three-hundred-year existence of Ukraine in the empire led to the material exhaustion of the region, its "provincialization in terms of the loss of quality, narrowing of horizons, [and] distortion of intellectual and artistic production," in George Grabowicz's apt observation.[26] The career opportunities and advancement of Ukrainians in the empire denationalized their intellectual elite and delayed Ukraine's cultural, social, and economic development for decades. By and large, the notions of internal or self-colonization, which are applied widely by scholars to the Russian, Soviet, and even post-Soviet contexts, blur the subject/object opposition and whitewash Russia's colonization of the neighbouring territories, which had a tangible, long-lasting negative effect on people's lives and the development of culture.[27]

Nikolai Gogol vs Mykola Hohol

The perspective on the hierarchical or colonial relationship between Russia and Ukraine to a large extent has determined scholars' approaches to Gogol's identity. The degree to which he should be considered a Russian or Ukrainian writer continues to be argued by scholars on both sides of the issue, with a broad range of combinations. Gogol's alleged "Russianization" has been discussed as the only path he could have chosen in making a career in Russian society. But this process could run parallel to developing hidden subversive strategies through his hybridized literary language. If we consider that even Gogol's late texts contain a considerable number of Ukrainian elements or are grounded in Ukrainian cultural and linguistic traditions, the division of Gogol's oeuvre strictly into Ukrainian (from 1830 to 1836) and Russian (from 1836 to 1852) periods seems problematic.

Ever since Vissarion Belinskii proclaimed that Gogol had undergone transformation from a provincial Ukrainian author to a "Russian national poet," this view became dominant in Gogol studies. Many contemporary scholars still disregard the writer's own bi-national self-identification in order to protect his status as a solely Russian writer. In the early twentieth century, Russian critics cloaked the idea of Gogol's "Russianness" in the concept of "all-Russianness" (*obshcherusskost'*). First, Dmitrii Ovsianiko-Kulikovskii endowed Gogol with the special status of all-Russian (*obshcherus*).[28] In the 1930s, Nikolai Trubetskoi accentuated the word "Russian" in Gogol's "all-Russianness," arguing that, like many other Ukrainian intellectuals, Gogol contributed to the development of Russian culture and "lost over time any specific Great Russian or Ukrainian identification."[29] In post–Second World War scholarship, Gogol's preoccupation with Ukrainian history and culture was reduced to a purely pragmatic intention to capitalize on the literary fashion of the time.[30] Even when his Ukrainianness was finally legitimized as a scholarly topic in Soviet academia, it was limited exclusively to studies of Ukrainian folk sources in his works. One of the major Russian Gogol scholars, Iurii Mann, claimed that Gogol appealed not to Ukraine as such, but to the "authentic national foundations of the Slavic world."[31] The scholar thus reduced "Ukraine" in Gogol's early works, *Evenings* (1831–2) and *Mirgorod* (1835), to the abstract notion of the "Slavic world," which corresponded to the romantic idea of *narodnost'* that existed in Russian critical thought in the 1830s. Mann drew parallels between the place of Ukraine in the literary imagination of Russian Romantics and the perception of the Middle Ages in that of European Romantics – that is, as a repository of the "authentic spirit." In contemporary Russian scholarship, there is a strong tendency to politicize the problem of Gogol's national identity. Vladimir Voropaev, for example, insists that Gogol always remained a Russian patriot and a staunch monarchist. He calls scholars who study the influence of Ukrainian culture on Gogol's legacy and identity the "separatist-traitors, Gogolian Andriis [the character in Gogol's *Taras Bulba*]."[32] His rejection of Gogol's Ukrainianness reveals the insecurity of many Russians about their own imperial identity, since much of it depends on non-Russian territories and cultures, especially on Ukraine, and since losing control over the empire (and over interpretations of Gogol's oeuvre) threatens their own sense of Russianness.

Some Western scholars have also discounted the role of Ukrainian ethnicity in Gogol's identity formation. In his comprehensive study *The Creation of Nikolai Gogol* (1979), Donald Fanger avoided any discussion of the significance of the writer's Ukrainian origin, thereby placing Gogol outside and above his historical and cultural context. Even Gogol's confession in a letter to his mother that he had written *Evenings* "in a foreign language [i.e., Russian]" was interpreted by Fanger as the writer's striving to create something "qualitatively new" for the Russian public in prose fiction, "something that embraced the whole stylistic spectrum."[33] Another scholar, Boris Gasparov, finds it "futile to characterize Gogol as an ardent Ukrainian patriot, a champion of its land and people" because "Gogol always wanted to write about Little Russia in Russian, for the moral benefit of the Russian society and state."[34] Recently, Anne Lounsbery has questioned the importance of the tension between Gogol's Ukrainianness and Russianness altogether. In her opinion, this tension "reveal[s] much about the complex and sometimes antagonistic relationship between two cultures in Gogol's day," but not about the hybridity of Gogol's identity itself.[35] She compares Gogol's "Ukrainianness" with Pushkin's "Africanness," suggesting a similar peripheral role in the formation of the former writer's outlook.

Thus, the very possibility of simultaneous engagement with the imperial, Russian national, and Ukrainian national modes of identity during Gogol's time is denied. Iurii Barabash has criticized this argument by pointing to the fact that

> The Russified "moor of Peter the Great" could have hardly remembered his native language, to say nothing of passing it to his offspring ... Gogol's [language] situation was different. Cossack Ukraine, ethnic origins, ancestors, customs, and language – all these were not a distant history, not only lived in the family legend or genetic memory, but were close, within a distance of one or two generations, literally in his everyday life.[36]

A diametrically opposite view of Gogol as a Ukrainian author making his way in a "foreign" Russian culture has dominated diasporic Ukrainian studies. One of the first attempts to claim Gogol as a Ukrainian writer was made by George Luckyj. In his book *Between Gogol' and Ševčenko: Polarity in the Literary Ukraine: 1798–1847* (1971), Luckyj argued that "the substratum of Gogol's art and philosophy was exclusively Ukrainian, as much as his humor and his liking for poking fun at authority and petty careerism."[37] Similarly, Petro Holubenko discerned "Ukrainianness" not only in relation to Gogol's ethnicity but also at the core of his "moral," "psychic," and "creative" mindset. Gogol's Ukrainian identity, in Holubenko's opinion, was always a solid monolith without any admixture of "Little Russianness" or "foreign" Russian influence.[38] Overall, these attempts to reclaim the neglected Ukrainian elements in Gogol's works and to locate the writer within a Ukrainian national context resulted in a one-sided picture of the writer's active engagement and participation in Russian culture. This approach failed to appreciate not only Gogol's contribution to Russian literature but also his hybridity as a cultural mode of making his Ukrainianness visible.

Another popular trend in studying Gogol's complex national identity has been to divide the writer into two personalities: "Mykola Hohol" from 1829 to 1836 and "Nikolai Gogol" from 1836 to 1852.[39] This approach fixes Gogol's national identity in terms of binary oppositions – a writer who was more Ukrainian in one period of his life and more Russian in another. Aiming to undermine the "Russocentric view of Gogol," Edyta Bojanowska sees him as straddling the line between "Russianness" and "Ukrainianness." A sensible middle course in the arguments about Gogol's dual national identity has been proposed by George Grabowicz, who places Gogol on the border of Russian and Ukrainian cultures. He believes that if in the aesthetic, psychological, and existential senses Gogol is inscribed ("vpysuiet'sia") into Ukrainian culture, in historical and cultural terms he is part of Russian literature and culture.[40] The duality of Gogol's national identity is a proven fact, yet it would be more correct to present the problem not by dividing Gogol into the Russian Nikolai Gogol and the Ukrainian Mykola Hohol, but by viewing him as a hybrid – as Nikolai Hohol or Mykola Gogol – and by introducing his hybrid idiom as a valid cultural medium, because the effect of Gogol's "two-souledness" was a radical expansion of the expressive range of Russian language and culture.

An original solution to the problem of Gogol's hyphenated national identity has been proposed by Oleh Ilnytzkyj. In his view, Gogol is a "post-colonial writer" who emerged not from a "Russian" experience but out of the conjunction of three cultures – the imperial, the Russian, and the Ukrainian.[41] However, Gogol contributed not only to an "imperial literary institution," as Ilnytzkyj suggests, but to national Russian literature as well, and to deprive his works of their proper Russian component would be unfair. Another scholar, Peter Sawczak, has effectively applied the concept of "minority" linguistic practice to Gogol, taken from Gilles Deleuze and Félix Guattari's analysis of Kafka's distorted German.[42] Even though the scholar presents Gogol as one who made the hierarchical purity of Russian language unattainable, the transposition of linguistic hybridity onto national identity is not straightforward and requires an integrated approach that includes the examination of Gogol's hybrid language, self-fashioning, narrative performances, and textual revisions.

That Nikolai Gogol's national identity can be defined as a hybrid "Russian-Ukrainian" or/and "Ukrainian-Russian" has been a less common idea in Gogol studies than the other approaches discussed above. Articulated by the Soviet critic Nikolai Piksanov in the 1930s,[43] this idea has remained largely unexamined. In the 1990s, the Russian-Ukrainian scholar Iurii Barabash attempted to avoid the vicious circle of "either/ or" for Gogol's national identity. In his book *Pochva i sud'ba. Gogol i ukrainskaia literatura: u istokov* (Soil and fate: Gogol and Ukrainian literature; at the beginnings) (1995), the scholar identified Gogol's entire oeuvre as a Russian branch of Ukrainian literature. The duality of Gogol's national identity was a tragic rupture between *pochva* (his native soil) and *sud'ba* (his destiny as a Russian national writer). He moved back and forth between Russian and Ukrainian self-identifications, during which the vector toward Russian imperial consciousness dominated. It could be said that Barabash remains an advocate of the traditional view of Gogol as the exponent of an "all-Russian" identity. His belief that Gogol, despite his lifelong bonds with Ukrainian culture, perceived himself as part of all-Russian culture because he allegedly believed that

Russian and Ukrainian cultures could coexist on equal terms without absorbing each other, is rather wishful thinking. Not only was Gogol aware of the tension between the two cultures, he also deliberately juxtaposed them and manipulated other people's perception of his national identity.

One of the most productive recent rereadings of Gogol's oeuvre through the prism of postcolonial studies has been made by Roman Koropeckyj and Robert Romanchuk.[44] The scholars placed Gogol in a creolized space of the "Little Russian literature," which simultaneously gave birth to the imperial Russian and national Ukrainian literatures. According to the scholars, Gogol, together with other Ukrainian writers such as Narizhnyi, Somov, Pogorel'skii, and Kvitka-Osnov'ianenko, created the Little Russian prose which was characterized by shared literary and linguistic features (peculiar humour and naïve spontaneity, depictions of Little Russian scenes, antiquarian historicism, *skaz* narration, and insertions of Ukrainianisms).

My book on Gogol's hybrid performance differs from all previous studies. With its multidisciplinary scope, it presents a historical overview of the socio-ideological development of the Russian imperial and Ukrainian national cultures, a cultural study of identity as being performed and always on display, a literary and linguistic analysis of the polyvalent meaning of Gogol's texts (assisted by the Digital Humanities "bag of words" method), and, finally, a discussion of publication history and translation practices as part of Gogol's reappropriation by the contemporary Russian and Ukrainian societies. These approaches are reflected in the structure of this book. Chapter 1 studies the assimilation of Ukrainian intellectuals in the Russian Empire, which varied from preservation of their regional identities to complete dissolution in the imperial culture. The participation of Ukrainians in empire-building has problematized the very idea of a pure Russian national identity. Ukrainians formed the avant-garde of state and religious institutions as imperial subjects, while carving up space for the public and private performance of their Ukrainianness. To this end, they worked out various strategies of ethnic defence and disguise (literary mystifications, fictitious authorship, and pseudonyms) and developed workaround theories ("diversity in unity," "two Rus' nationalities," and the "two-in-one Rus' nation") to reserve a place for Ukrainian national identity in the larger imperial project. The hybrid notions of "twin-souled," "mixed-blood," "half-blood," "mongrels," "crossbreeds," and "turncoats" widely circulated among Gogol's generation of Ukrainians, indicating their awareness of the lack of adequate resistance strategies. Ukrainian writers of the 1820s–1830s practised the intentional hybridization of the

Russian literary language. They undermined the very idea of a refined language based on the linguistic norms of the cultural elite and created a powerful democratic literary tradition of Little Russian prose, which could be read as a case of the diaspora writing home.

Chapter 2 examines Gogol's ambivalent self-fashioning within Russian imperial space during the formative years of his career. The negotiation of his identity entailed continual change and adjustment of his visual and oral performance. Having started his literary career as a Romantic poet under the guise of the Russian "V. Alov," Gogol quickly realized the benefits of his Ukrainian ethnicity and creatively used his *otherness* in his first collection of short stories, *Evenings on a Farm near Dikan'ka* (1831–2), which were published under the name of a fictitious Ukrainian editor-narrator, Rudy Pan'ko. This narrative mask played with the common perception of Ukrainian culture as suitable only for the amusement of the imperial audience. In Gogol studies, it has become a commonplace to consider Gogol "sly" by nature and to place responsibility for this colonial stereotype exclusively on the writer himself. This chapter provides a corrective to this approach and examines the intricate power distribution in colonial discourse that produces a racialized perception of the *other*. The other aspect of Gogol's self-fashioning – a transition from the mere reproduction of the cultural code of the *honnête homme* to the visual coding of his ethnicity – is discussed in one of the sections of the chapter. As early as 1830, Gogol realized the provocative potential of fashion and used it as both an adaptive and a differentiation strategy. The motif of the totalizing power of dress for social status also appears in Gogol's early texts. Choosing clothing items from a closet, which at some points were selected to deviate from normative expectations (dressing "to be different") and at others to match particular situations (dressing "to fit in"), became the leitmotif of Gogol's texts in the early period.

Chapter 3 establishes the link between Gogol's hybridized literary language and the narrative performances in his early tales, *Evenings on a Farm near Dikan'ka*. As a bilingual in both Russian and Ukrainian, Gogol used the whole range of his verbal repertoire in these early texts. His idiosyncratic language operated as a creative agency that made his ethnic identity visible and provided him with a space for performing his hybridity. The larger theoretical question of the chapter is how to reconcile the existence of a "linguistic habitus" with the idea of reflexive awareness. Gogol's creative use of a hybrid language – lexical doublets, code-switching and code-mixing, transpositions, pidgin, glosses for Ukrainian words and idioms unfamiliar to the Russian audience, insertions of Yiddish and German, ethnic commentary and translation – presupposed the insertion of the *other* in his discourse and constituted performative speech acts. Gogol's language performances were spontaneous, internally motivated acts that involved a high degree of unpredictability and creativity in both form and message. The language performance is intrinsically connected with narrative performances in *Evenings*. In previous critical literature, the opposition between the two types of narrators has been projected onto Gogol's dual national identity. I approach the narrative construction of national identity as a form of textual filiation and argue that Gogol's narrative act was culturally *performative* because it did not presuppose a dominant narrative voice and ideological position but rather created a dialogic, double-voiced structure that delivered different messages to Russian and Ukrainian audiences.

Gogol's language views and practices are analysed in chapter 4 in the context of the language debates of his time and in the framework of Bakhtin's "heteroglossia" and contemporary postcolonial theory concerning cultural hybridity. I have identified the influence of Gogol's discursive "multivocality" ("raznogolositsa") on Bakhtin's concept of heteroglossia, which the latter originally theorized as the "in-betweenness of languages" ("mezha iazykov"). Later, Bakhtin's ideas about heterogeneous, polyphonic discourse laid the foundation for Homi Bhabha's postcolonial theory of hybridity. Gogol's "deliberate verbal nonsense," the insertions of the discourse of *others*, and transpositions between Russian and Ukrainian not only allowed him to cross language borders to narrate Ukrainian culture but also to undermine the Russian literary language's norms. Chapter 4 demonstrates how attitudes toward the use of Ukrainian elements in Russian-language texts changed from favourable in the 1820s to negative in the late 1830s and the 1840s, and how those changes prompted Gogol to edit his hybrid discourse and to work on the synthesis of heterogeneous elements into a new universal language ("vsemirnyi iazyk"). The chapter concludes with an analysis of Gogol's speech masks in his letters, which corroborates the complex textual dialectic between personal and social identity being shaped in his communication with different groups of addressees. In order to assess all five volumes of Gogol's letters, I have applied a stylometric analysis to identify the formal variables across all of the letters and to visualize the results in dendrograms (diagrams that reveal taxonomic relationships between the elements).

In chapter 5, the textual differences between the draft and first published versions and between the first and subsequent redactions of Gogol's works are examined by means of digital comparison and visualization. Special attention is given to the two redactions of *Taras*

Bulba (1835 and 1842) and to the draft and final versions of *Dead Souls* (1842). The new redactions captured Gogol's concern with the deleterious impact of materialism, technological and commercial innovation, and foreign cultural influence on local societies. Gogol's revision of his works was not merely an attempt to fix the text in its ideal material form. The new versions created a "Janus-faced" text looking backward and forward simultaneously. Read as equally important variants of one and the same text, the opposing redactions change our perception of the text as a *textus* to that of a *textile* and reveal Gogol's palimpsestic mentality. Applying Derrida's definition of the palimpsest to Gogol's rewritten and revised texts, one can say that they resonate not with the Romantic notion of the mirrored or doubled self but with the "post-Romantic notion of the *spectralized* subject. It represents the mind as a textual structure actively haunted by its encrypted traces."[45]

The last chapter presents the posthumous history of publication of Gogol's texts in Russia and their translations into Ukrainian in Ukraine. The scholarly and academic publications of Gogol's *Complete Works* prioritize the textological principle of "the author's final will" (i.e., rejecting earlier drafts and prioritizing the latest textual variants) which was adopted in Soviet textual criticism. This method, however, distorted the texts and bowdlerized ideologically charged or improper passages. I show how modern publications and translations of Gogol's texts have become a political enterprise, revealing the tension in contemporary debates in Russia and Ukraine over Gogol's "true" national identity. Ukrainian translations of Gogol's texts, on the other hand, especially those of *Taras Bulba*, have contributed to a political reading of the writer's inherently double-voiced texts. Since the mid-nineteenth century, Ukrainian translators of *Taras Bulba* have created a "third" version of the text by replacing the "pan-national" idea of "Rus'" and "Rus'ian identity" with a narrower nationalist concept of Ukrainianness. The new version of the tale, which combines the first and second redactions by omitting the "tsar" and the "Russian soul," is now being taught in contemporary Ukrainian schools. By silencing Gogol's original disparity in the use of ethnonyms, post-Soviet translations of *Taras Bulba* reduce the complex myth of Cossack Ukraine to a few national qualifiers toward which Gogol himself was quite indifferent.

Finally, this book develops novel computer-assisted methods of textual analysis. To examine the various redactions of Gogol's works, I have used Beyond Compare software to create side-by-side visualizations (see Appendix 2) and WCopyfind (see Table 3) for determining the similarity rate between the redactions or drafts of the same text. These tools can help us understand Gogol's rewriting process and bring out the multilayered complexity of the texts, which is not apparent in a linear reading. In all of the existing academic editions (including the ongoing one being prepared by the Institute of Russian Literature of the Russian Academy of Sciences, 2001–), Gogol's first published versions and unpublished drafts are placed under the rubric "Variants," not as coherent texts but as commentary on the changes made to the canonical version. A computer-generated comparison of Gogol's versions of his texts could infuse scholarly editions with powerful analytic capability. In a synoptic edition, readers can interact with the original texts published in the first editions of Gogol's works and in later editions and uncover different layers of meaning. A "3-gram" comparison with WCopyfind is an especially useful tool for identifying what two dissimilar texts have in common and for showing the depth of revisions Gogol made in the new versions of his texts. The digital analytical tools that I utilize for the close and distant reading of Gogol provide a magnifying glass to view the changes. I can highlight differences on a micro level (sentence or paragraph) and also visualize the editing principle on the level of composition (e.g., the principle of doubling of significant events that Gogol used in the second redaction of *Taras Bulba*). Such a combination of close and distant readings of the text can facilitate self-reflective critical practices by revealing patterns one would not otherwise have seen.

With multiple versions and editions of Gogol's tales, it is no longer relevant to ask where one version ends and the other one begins, since Gogol's "text" becomes inclusive of all its variants and its "corrections." If there are such things as Gogol's "true" identity and "final" text, they can only be grasped in the relationship among all the variants of his texts. So, how can one establish continuity among all these variants of Gogol's texts? How can one connect all these facets of his identity? What can serve as the link, the cohesive element, and the gathering place in the dynamic process of identity formation? With these and other questions, this book examines the extremely complex link between Gogol's hybridized literary language and his performance of identity.

Chapter One

The Negotiation of Ukrainian Identities in the Russian Empire

Ukrainian intellectuals took an active part in building the Russian Empire and creating imperial culture. Some of them adopted an "all-Russian" (*obshcherusskaia*) identity; others capitalized on their ethnic distinctiveness and maintained their regional identity as "Little Russians" (*malorossy*).[1] In the eighteenth century, dual identification of Ukrainians was still possible because of the weakness of the Russian nation-building project.[2] The Ukrainian regionalism of the period was even encouraged by the imperial government, as long as it helped boost the formation of a long-desired public space. The Russian imperial authorities could work with the Ukrainian elite on terms of mutual collaboration and benefit because they wanted to expedite absorption of the newly acquired territories of the former Hetmanate into the empire. However, this period of cooperation with Ukrainians did not last long, and soon regional distinctiveness became a mark of potential disloyalty to the empire. After the Polish Uprising of 1830–1, the Russian government adopted the doctrine of Official Nationality, which made the ethnic and cultural distinctiveness of Ukrainians incompatible with the ethnolinguistic model of Russian national identity.[3] In order to maintain their dual identity, members of the Ukrainian elite resorted to strategies of ethnic defence, disguise, and resistance. This chapter traces several scenarios of how Ukrainian intellectuals adapted in the imperial culture through the subversive practices of hybridization.

The collaboration of the Ukrainian intellectuals with imperial authorities began with Teofan Prokopovych – a rector of the Kyivan Academy during the Hetmanate and later a leading imperial ideologist during the reign of Peter I. In his sermons, Prokopovych coined the term "all-Russian emperor" and promoted the idea of loyalty to the empire, which became paramount in recruiting the Ukrainian elite into imperial service. Being himself a man of multiple political affiliations,

Prokopovych managed to appeal to a broad stratum of society, urging Ukrainians to show loyalty to the emperor.[4] Through his sermons and speeches, he shaped an audience that felt inspired by his appeal to join the new imperial fatherland. Contemporary historians still cannot agree on whether the former Cossack elite understood "fatherland" in the same imperial sense that Prokopovych tried to invest in it.[5] For the descendants of the Cossack *starshyna*, loyalty to the *patria* had remained palpable even after the subjugation of the Hetmanate, but the borders of the *patria* expanded in the late eighteenth century, and Ukrainians were slowly coming to terms with new reality. Konstantin Kharlampovich and Zenon Kohut have pointed out that the ease with which Ukrainians occupied the highest posts in imperial and church administration indicates that they eagerly switched allegiance and enjoyed their new privileges.[6] By the end of the reign of Peter I, former Cossacks appointed to government positions accounted for half of the non-noble imperial intelligentsia and doubled the number of Russian noble appointees.[7] This was possible because the Ukrainian elite was better educated and had established strong political connections in the upper circles of European society.[8] Ukrainians created their "party" at court during the reign of Elizaveta Petrovna and her morganatic husband, Oleksii Rozumovs'kyi. Son of a rank-and-file Ukrainian Cossack, Rozumovs'kyi appointed his Ukrainian protégés, Oleksandr Bezborod'ko (1747–99) and Victor Kochubei (1768–1834), to high state positions. In their turn, Bezborod'ko and Kochubei helped to integrate the newly colonized Little Russian provinces into the Russian Empire and to secure employment for people of Cossack descent in St Petersburg.

The growing influence of the Ukrainians at court and in imperial administration horrified Russian hereditary nobles, making them feel unsettled about their own status. The offensive label "Little Russian opportunists" ("malorossiiskaia prolaza") was applied to Ukrainian immigrants.[9] This attitude survived through the 1830s, when Aleksandr Pushkin expressed his contempt for Ukrainians who obtained quick promotion in the government administration in his poem "My Genealogy" (1830).[10] Some important Ukrainians in imperial administration provoked society with their unconventional social behaviour. For example, Bezborod'ko, who had been granted the title of "Prince" (it should be noted that there was only one other "prince" in the course of Russian imperial history who did not inherit his rank – the Russian Mikhail Kutuzov) and appointed grand chancellor, could not (or pretended to be unable to) master the Russian language and social manners. He persisted in speaking *surzhyk*[11] and telling obscene Ukrainian jokes at court. Bezborod'ko used his high position strategically and founded one of the first educational institutions in the Left Bank of the Dnieper (Dnipro) River, the Nizhyn Lyceum (where Gogol received his college degree). With his protection, young Ukrainian graduates gained employment in Petersburg state offices.

According to Zenon Kohut, Ukrainians were able to keep their regional identities because of the following factors: "the Ukrainian gentry's dominant role in the imperial administration of Little Russia; the survival of Ukrainian customary law; the occasional restitution of certain legal and military formations traditional to Little Russia; and an interest in the history and folklore of Ukraine that helped nurture the idea of a Little Russian fatherland."[12] Alexei Miller believes that, unlike other minorities such as Jews, Lithuanians, and Poles, whose status as separate nationalities was rarely questioned, Ukrainians were denied institutionalization as distinctive nationalities because they were integrated into Russian society on the principle of individual equality.[13] Ukrainians could maintain both ethnic, *maloross* (Ukrainian) and imperial, *rossiianin* (Russian) identities – a privilege that no other minority in the empire enjoyed. The Cossack *starshyna* was adaptive to new imperial realities because they had lost their local influence and had transferred their loyalty to the central power, which at the time promised them better political and social benefits. At first, imperial ideology allowed them to adopt an identity that "was much broader, looser, and more flexible than the exclusionist, ethno-culturally based Polish type."[14] In the eighteenth century, the imperial policy directed at integrating minority groups was predominantly non-national and did not impose a change of identity on its subjects.[15]

With the introduction of Russification policies by Catherine II, the situation began to change. One of the most effective assimilationist acts was her decree of December 1763. On paper, it guaranteed temporary preferences to the Cossacks, but in practice, the *starshyna*'s original rights were not adequately converted into the existing Table of Ranks, and to a significant extent the Ukrainian nobility lost its former social privileges. Only a few of them were able to retain their noble status in the empire, since the two lowest ranks in the Cossack hierarchy were excluded from the conversion.[16] In 1802, the integration of the *starshyna* into the Russian nobility further slowed down as it became harder to register the patents required from Ukrainians to obtain an imperial title. The Heraldry Committee rejected 441 family emblems as "defective."[17] Cossacks' service in the Hetmanate was no longer a sufficient ground for claiming noble status in the empire. According to Oleksiy Tolochko, "Ukrainian offices were not mentioned in the Charter to the Nobility, and the Heraldry Office maintained that only those who had been granted proper Russian military or civil ranks were eligible for admission to the *dvorianstvo*.[18] In practical terms, this meant that the Ukrainian gentry could no longer send their offspring to the imperial capital to pursue state and military careers. Moreover, the property rights of Ukrainian landlords on their estates were compromised; now they had to prove their right to control the land and the serfs they had received under the Polish crown.

Just this kind of downgrading in status happened to Nikolai Gogol's own family. His great-grandfather, Ostap Gogol, was awarded the title of colonel for his service to the Polish king Jan III Sobieski.[19] Ostap's son, Gogol's grandfather Afanasii, did not have the required documents to prove his noble status in the Polish-Lithuanian Commonwealth; therefore, he married Tetiana Lizohub (a great-granddaughter of Hetman Skoropads'kyi) and obtained a noble title and estate. In 1835, the old dispute about Gogols belonging to the noblemen of ancient standing (*stolbovye dvoriane*) recommenced when Maria Ivanovna Gogol found out that their name was missing in the heraldic registry.[20] She asked her son to collect all necessary evidence of their inherited nobility, but Gogol had shown little interest and concern in the reduction of his family's noble status. In 1849 he assured his mother that "this thing [the *stolbovye dvoriane* status] is all my eye. One just needs a piece of bread, and who cares whether he is a *stolbovoi* nobleman or a regular nobleman, whether he is registered in the sixth or in the eighth book."[21]

Overall, the Ukrainian gentry considered the reduction of privileges in imperial society a humiliation. They distrusted the imperial administration's true intentions and began developing both open and concealed oppositionist strategies. For example, the prominent poet Vasyl' Kapnist (1758–1823), a descendant of Cossack aristocracy, remained politically engaged in developing Ukraine as Russia's most advanced colony. He was elected as marshal of the nobility of Myrhorod County (1782–1823), the Kyiv Governorate (1785–1823), and the Poltava Governorate (1817–22), and established close connections with the former Cossack nobility of Left-Bank Ukraine, especially with the secret Novhorod-Sivers'kyi circle led by the former general Andrii Hudovych. This circle comprised the oppositionist Ukrainians who cherished ideas of federalism for the East Slavs as an alternative to the Russian monarchy. In 1791, this circle delegated Kapnist to seek military and financial support in Prussia to restore the Cossack Hetmanate, but these plans were never realized. At the Petersburg court, Kapnist advocated greater autonomy for the recently colonized territories of Little Russia. In 1788, he compiled and submitted to Catherine II "A Statute for the Recruitment and Organization of the Cossacks" (1788) proposing to recruit Cossack regiments in Little Russia.[22] These regiments, composed of independent Cossack foremen, would not be subordinated to Russian generals.[23] In his literary works too, Kapnist managed to encode a strong oppositionist message while seeming to affirm his imperial loyalty. His "Ode on Slavery" (written in 1783, published in 1806) painted a gloomy picture of the economic deprivation of Ukraine after Catherine II's extension of serfdom to its territory in 1783.[24]

Taken together, the abolition of the Hetmanate, the establishment of the imperial system of provincial administration, and the appointment of Governor General Piotr Rumiantsev (1761–96) as the monarch's representative led to the impoverishment of all Ukrainian estates and in the long run to the Russification of the entire region. Imperial practices of pragmatic tolerance and cooperation with Ukrainians in the eighteenth century gave way to an attitude of superiority toward them, and Ukrainians began losing their political and social power in the centre. From the late eighteenth century onward, they were slowly swallowed up by the imperial apparatus and eventually became invisible in many social spheres – high culture, politics, and economics. As Andreas Kapeller has observed, in the social hierarchy of the empire, "the Ukrainians of the Hetmanate with their Cossack elite were regarded by Moscow as belonging to the steppe population" and faced two alternatives: "either they achieved recognition as nobles or they were demoted to the status of peasants or aliens (*inorodtsy*)." Even though the Cossack *starshyny* chose the first alternative and "gradually became 'Little Russians,'" in the nineteenth century the tsarist authorities "became steadily less willing to recognize the nomadic elites as equal partners."[25]

In order to balance "between assertions of Russo-Ukrainian unity and insistence on Ukrainian political distinctiveness,"[26] Ukrainian intellectuals employed subtle strategies of cultural resistance. The careers of Gogol's precursors – the Ukrainian Russian-language writers Vasyl' Narizhnyi (1780–1825) and Orest Somov (1793–1833) – showcase two cultural and discursive modes of negotiating hybrid identity.

A descendant of the impoverished Ukrainian gentry, Narizhnyi worked all his life in imperial administration, first as a clerk in the Caucasus, then as an expeditor of the Ministry of Interior Affairs, and later as a contractor in the Mining Department. Working closely with the emerging classes of merchants and manufacturers across the Russian Empire, Narizhnyi heard many stories of corruption in local administration. This experience furnished him with material for his satirical writings. His Ukrainian ethnicity was also one of the decisive factors in the formation of his critical outlook on Russian society. In his early novel, *Rossiiskii Zhilblaz, ili pokhozhdeniia Kniazia Gavrily Simonovicha*

Chistiakova (Russian Gil Blas, or the adventures of Prince Gavrila Simo-novich Chistiakov), Narizhnyi created a gallery of social vices personi-fied in grotesque characters from the Russian gentry. The plots of his late tales, *Bursak* (The Seminarian), *Dva Ivana ili strast' k tiazhbam* (Two Ivans, or a passion for litigation), *Zaporozhets* (The Zaporozhian), and *Garkusha* (Harkusha), were taken from the Cossack past and the every-day life of Ukrainian landowners. With Romantic fashion on the rise in the 1820s, Ukrainian material served not only as a locus of Ukrainians' nostalgia for the past but also as a source of exoticism and entertain-ment for the Russian audience.

In Narizhnyi's Ukrainian tales, the encounter between Russian and Ukrainian cultural codes produced a "polyphonic" effect which Mikhail Bakhtin attributed to the writer's excellent knowledge of the "demo-cratic literary traditions of the Ukrainian baroque" (travesty, burlesque, fairy tales, *vertep*, school interludes, and orations).[27] Similarly, the insertion of peculiar Ukrainian words and expressions in his Russian-language texts signalled the writer's orientation toward the middle-brow Ukrainian audience. The Ukrainian lexicon was often accompa-nied by Narizhnyi's translations and comments in the footnotes. These Ukrainianisms embraced terms and notions that were absent in Rus-sian, and included words for: professions (*paseshnik, shinkar', kramar'*); social ranks (*polupanok, povytchik, ataman*); wedding traditions (*boiarin, vesel'ie*);[28] clothes (*ochipok, svitka, postoly*); flora and fauna (*korov'iak, busel*); Ukrainian folk demons (*upyr', iarchuk, vovkulaka*); and other realia of Ukrainian life (*khovtur, khabar, oseledets'*). Another group of words that demonstrate cross-cultural interaction are lexical doublets in Ukrainian and Russian. They indicate the author's continuous work of self-translation between the two languages: "houses": *domy* (Russian) – *khaty* (Ukrainian) – *budynki* (Ukrainian); "hell": *ad* (Russian) – *peklo* (Ukrainian); "mother": *mat'* (Russian) – *maty* (Ukrainian); "father": *otets* (Russian) – *bat'ko* (Ukrainian); "to understand": *ponimaesh' – razumeesh'*; "to hurry": *speshit'* (Russian) – *pospeshat'* (Ukrainian); "to recognize": *uznat'* (Russian) – *poznat'* (Ukrainian). Used in close proximity to one another, Ukrainian doublets expanded the semantic repertoire of the Russian literary language. For the Russian audience, Ukrainianisms represented a repository of the genuine Slavic spirit that the Russian language of the early nineteenth century was lacking. Even though the use of the Ukrainian words was legitimate in Russian literature of the time, owing to the Romantic demand for local colour, the effect they produced on the audience was often disturbing. Russian review-ers criticized Narizhnyi's novels for containing too much "locality" which was incomprehensible for the Russian audience. This is evident in the observations of one anonymous critic who cited the abundance of Ukrainianisms as the major flaw of Narizhnyi's Russian language.[29]

However, Ukrainian words *per se* did not make Narizhnyi's language a hybrid. What made it such was morpho-syntactic calquing from Ukrainian: the use of Ukrainian instead of Russian endings in the plural form of nouns; verbs governed by a Ukrainian preposition and nominal case; the use of verbal aspect more typical to Ukrainian; the use of the reflexive form of verbs instead of the non-reflexive; and many other hybrid forms that emerge as the result of linguistic creolism.[30] Narizhnyi's odd use of Russian was also noticeable in his heavy syntax based on multiple adjectival constructions, which was a key feature of the Ukrainian Baroque rhetoric that also figured in Gogol's syntax. In a sense, these ungrammatical elements disrupted the discursive conventions of the Russian literary language by turning against its structures. By upsetting linguistic conventions and by enriching Russian with Ukrainian elements, Narizhnyi created a unique hybrid discourse that simultaneously appealed to the metropolitan and colonial audiences. This "mid-language" signalled the presence of the *other* in metropolitan discourse and imparted a sense of belonging to the Ukrainian-speaking community in St Petersburg.

The oeuvre and narrative mask of another Ukrainian writer, Orest Somov, also provided Gogol with an example of how to negotiate his identity with the empire. Somov's career presents a typical case of colonial mimicry: his strategic cultural behaviour allowed him to assume the position of a domesticated *other* and also to act as intermediary between the imperial centre and the Ukrainian periphery.[31] Somov was born in Kharkivs'ka province and graduated from Kharkiv University – one of the first higher education institutions in Sloboda Ukraine, a historical and administrative region with the centre in Kharkiv. During his studies, Somov contributed to the first Ukrainian journals (*The Kharkiv Democritus* and *The Ukrainian Herald*). He continued sending them his writing even after his relocation to St Petersburg in 1817. In the capital, he met the Ukrainian writers Prince Mykola Tsertelev and Vasyl' Tumans'kyi, who ushered him into their Petersburg literary circle. As a mark of his acceptance by leading Russian poets, in May 1818 Somov was elected a member of the Free Society of the Lovers of Russian Letters and began to adapt himself into imperial society.[32] In the same year, Somov shared his first impressions of Russia's capital in the poem "Pis'mo ukraintsa iz stolitsy" (Letter of a Ukrainian from the capital), in which he glorified the military deeds of the Russian tsar and summoned his fellow Ukrainians to support their monarch's endeavours. A few years later, however, Somov articulated his anxiety of assimilation in the poem "Toska po rodine" (Homesickness) (1821). This text reflected the psychological trauma of the lyrical subject after his encounter with the reality of a new imperial dwelling. This stands in striking contrast to his idyllic Ukrainian home and makes the poet regret that no return to it will be possible in his lifetime. The poet-migrant exists in the liminal space which Homi Bhabha has defined as the "third space of enunciation" – a space where hybrid identity is formed. This space is governed by an "estranging sense of the relocation of the home and the world – the unhomeliness – that is the condition of extraterritorial and cross–cultural initiations."[33]

Somov's aesthetic views were formed by the national Romanticism, which found its realization in his texts through the symbolic geography and representation of the national community, the production of national character, as well as through the images of the *others*. In his programmatic essay "O romanticheskoi poezii" (On Romantic poetry) (1823), Somov distinguishes between *narodnost'* (nationality) and *mestnost'* (locality) as the spirit and body of the Russian nation and as inseparable facets of Russian identity. When speaking of the rich history preserved in ethnic folk traditions, Somov unites local diversity with the amorphous category of Russianness:

> And there are so many diverse peoples merged under the single name Russian, or dependent on Russia, or not separated from us by other lands or wide seas! There are so many diverse manners, mores, customs offering themselves to a searching eye within the scope of Russia in the aggregate! Without even mentioning those who are in the strictest sense Russian, we have the Little Russians with their sensual songs, and the warlike sons of the Quiet Don, and the courageous settlers of the Zaporozhian Host – all united by their faith and their fiery love for the fatherland, and bearing the same distinctive features in mores and appearance. And what if we cast our gaze to the outlying regions of Russia inhibited by the ardent Poles and Lithuanians, the peoples of Finnish and Scandinavian origins, the inhabitants of ancient Colchis, the descendants of the settlers who witnessed the exile of Ovid, the remnants of the Tatars who once menaced Russia, the variegated tribes of Siberia and the islands, the nomadic descendants of Mongolians, Laplanders, and Samoyeds ...?[34]

Somov's differentiation between ethnic Russians and other nationalities of the empire is based on a discursive hierarchy established in the Romantic tradition that reflected varying degrees of involvement in the empire: first came Ukrainians, with their "distinctive features in mores and appearance," then the people on the western borders – Poles,

Lithuanians, and Finns – and, finally, the numerous tribes in the Eastern and Southern regions of Russia.

A new occasion to fashion himself as a loyal imperial subject arose for Somov during the 1830–1 Polish Uprising, in response to which he wrote a sixteen-page booklet, "Golos ukraintsa pri vesti o vziatii Varshavy" (The voice of a Ukrainian upon hearing the news of the taking of Warszawa). Written in the Ukrainian burlesque tradition, the poems in the booklet were published under the pseudonym Porfirii Baiskii. While showing off his imperial patriotism, Somov, nevertheless, managed to promote Ukrainian culture. The first poem presented a fulsome declaration of the Russian people's love for the tsar, and the second, "Pesn' na usmirenie Varshavy" (A song on the pacification of Warszawa), exemplified a typically chauvinistic attitude. But the last poem in the booklet was written entirely in Ukrainian and accompanied by a four-page glossary. This was a moment when Somov tried to establish himself as a Ukrainian writer and at the same time to promote imperial patriotism.

If during the first half of the 1820s Somov modelled his literary career as a Russian Romantic poet, in the second half of the decade he created under the mask of a fictitious Ukrainian writer, Porfirii Bogdanovich Baiskii (from the Old Slavic verb *baiati*, meaning "to narrate"). He began publishing prose fiction under the pseudonym Baiskii after the Decembrist Revolt of 1825, when he was accused of being a member of the Decembrist society and had even been briefly arrested. Whether the alias of Baiskii was a means of self-protection or an attempt to establish himself as a Ukrainian writer is hard to tell; information about the fictitious narrator is scanty. Only at the end of the 1820s did the persona of Baiskii take on more flesh in Somov's correspondence with the Ukrainian scholar Mykhailo Maksymovych. The main aspects of his fictional biography paralleled Somov's own; eventually, Baiskii even figured as a real person in Somov's correspondence with friends.[35] In a letter to Maksymovych (24 December 1830), he apparently camouflaged a case of writer's block in a disguised message: "Baiskii gives his countryman his regards, he will send his tribute to 'Dennitsa,' only no earlier than February, *because he is so busy plus there is a damn cholera in Volchans'k* [the words in italics are in Ukrainian] (where Porfirii Bogdanovich lives). Somov will also send you something during January."[36] This is the only commentary Somov provides on his fictitious author-narrator Baiskii. By drawing parallels between his own and Baiskii's origin and biography, Somov created a space for a regional Ukrainian identity that coexisted with the "all-Russian" one.

Somov's appropriation of the history of Ukraine as a part of Russian culture was realized in his first Ukrainian tale, *Gaidamak* (The haidamak: a Little Russian *byl'* [memorate], 1826; The haidamak: chapters from a Little Russian novella, 1827–30). In the literary version of the popular legend about the noble Ukrainian bandit Harkusha, Somov-Baiskii mixed historical facts from the Cossack past with ethnographic details of Ukrainian *byt*, folk humour, and superstitions. The chapters, which are written in literary Russian, bear epigraphs in Ukrainian from Kotliarevs'kyi's *Aeneid* and Mykola Tsertelev's collection of Ukrainian *dumas* (epic ballads). The text is also interspersed with Ukrainian proverbs and words translated into Russian in the footnotes.[37] This mixture of different elements and language codes, according to Koropeckyj and Romanchuk, reproduces "the entire continuum of Little Russian idiolects."[38]

Following Walter Scott's Romantic representation of the national past, Somov drew material from the historical epic tradition of the Cossack Ukraine, especially from the *History of Rus' People*. In the first version of *Gaidamak*, published in the almanac *The Polar Star* in 1825, the opening scene at a Ukrainian fair presents a gallery of various social types: a dissipated *chumak* (tradesman), a profiteering merchant, a cunning gypsy, a free-spirited *haidamak*, and a blind bandura player – each associated with a particular voice or sound.[39] Before Harkusha makes his first appearance, readers are introduced to various opinions about him among the locals who are gathered at the house of the district judge, Pan Ladovich. First, the Jew Hershko brings news of Harkusha's mysterious arrival at the fair. In the liminal space of the fair, the uncanny appearance of Harkusha in Somov's tale and the interference of the "devil in a red *svitka*" (robe) in Gogol's "Sorochintsy Fair" bear a close resemblance: their facial features are marked as "alien" (both have dark-skinned faces and piercing eyes "like fire") and both appear in disguise (Somov's Harkusha as a *chumak*, Gogol's devil as a gypsy). The guests who are gathered at Ladovich's house heatedly argue about Harkusha's identity, and in order to relieve the tension, the host invites a blind bandura player to distract the audience.[40] The bandura player sings a historical *duma* about Bohdan Khmel'nyts'kyi's battles and the glorious history of the Hetmanate, creating a framework for the reception of Harkusha as a legendary figure in the tale. Within the uniformly Russian text of Somov's tale, the Ukrainian voice of the bandura player is presented unaltered:

> [narrated in Russian] He [Pan Ladovich] brought a blind bandura player into the guest room … and politely invited his guests to listen to the joyful

songs of the ancestors and old folk narratives ... The singer narrated about the rapid attack of hetman Khmel'nitskii on Poland's ally Moldova ... and concluded his song by appealing to the glory of the Hetmanate:

[narrated in Ukrainian]
Back then we had honour, glory,
Military feats!
[Ukraine] did not let anyone make fun of it,
It trampled on its foes.

[narrated in Russian] Loud sounds of approval and delight rang out in the room. Among them one could hear nostalgic sighs about the old Hetmanate, Khmel'nitskii's times, truly heroic times, when the developing life of the people blossomed, when Cossacks, hardened in battle and matured on the battlefield, fought energetically and cheerfully with their numerous enemies of different tribes and won them all; when Little Russia felt the sweetness of freedom and national independence and threw off the yoke of the treacherous oppressor [i.e., Russia] who promised it equal rights; but hard experience showed that sorrow was the lot of the conquered.[41]

It is interesting that Gogol's narrator in "The Terrible Revenge" almost literally reiterates Somov's bandura player's *duma*, although he renders it in Russian in a compressed form:

In the town of Glukhov, people gathered around an old, blind bandura player and had been listening to him play his instrument for over an hour. No other bandura player had ever sung so well and such marvellous songs. First, he started about the former Hetmanate in the time of Sagaidachnyi and Khmel'nitskii. Oh, it was a different time: Cossackdom stood tall, trampled enemies with its horses, and none dared mock it.[42]

Nina Petrunina and Iurii Mann have studied the mutual influence between Somov and Gogol but limited their focus to the borrowing of plots and motifs.[43] However, the most important result of the interaction between the two writers was the creation of the discourse that referred back to their Ukrainian home. Both Somov and Gogol wrote for the descendants of the Ukrainian Cossack *starshyna* who resided in St Petersburg and had almost lost connection to their homeland and to Ukrainian folklore and history. Their tales appealed to diasporic Ukrainian identity by making a particular kind of connection to Ukraine. Somov collected and preserved Ukrainian folk legends and traditions "so that they won't be lost for future archaeologists and poets," and instead of compiling a collection of original stories he "decided to disseminate them in various tales [of his own]."[44] Gogol not only used folklore as a setting and source of the miraculous but made it the foundation of the narration, bringing together the grotesque, hyperbole, irony, and laughter.[45]

When in the late 1830s Ukrainian intellectuals wanted to prove their loyalty to the monarchy and professed an unequivocally Russian identity in public, they adopted one or another type of colonial identity, which manifested itself in the phenomena of *malorossiistvo* (Little Russianness) and mongrelization. *Malorossiistvo* became a workaround to preserve a separate ethnic identity within the empire, but it gradually acquired more and more negative connotations. At first, it signified simultaneously an indivisible unity and a basic difference between Russia and Ukraine, which were in accord with the imperial discourse of the "triune unified Rus'" and the "tri-lateral united Russian nation" (comprising Great, Little, and White Russias). The second meaning of *malorossiistvo* was linked to Gogol's generation of Ukrainian writers who worked in the Russian Empire but who cherished their recollections of Cossack Ukraine. Toward the end of the nineteenth century with the Ukrainian national movement on the rise, the term *malorossiistvo* took on a somewhat negative connotation. From a mode of assimilation in the empire as regional "others," it gradually came to mean a form of a conformist interaction with the empire and was used critically to remind the Ukrainian elite about its responsibility toward its suppressed national identity and culture.

The second type of colonial identity, mongrelization, is associated with Ukrainian intellectuals' discourse of deceit and ethnic impurity, which captured their feelings of guilt for having abandoned Ukrainian national identity and for their inability to develop proper resistance strategies. Thus, Mikhail Shchepkin, a famous Russian actor who started his career in provincial Ukrainian theatres and who mastered Ukrainian to perfection, called himself a "turncoat" in a thank-you note to Sreznevs'kyi for promoting his theatrical performances in Ukraine: "Accept gratitude not from a pure Ukrainian [maloross], but from a turncoat [pereverten']." Later, Mykhailo Drahomanov called Mykhailo Maksymovych a "mixed person" ("mishana liudyna") for his "eclectic philosophical views and excellent networking skills."[46] In the 1850s, both Kostomarov and Kulish referred to Gogol and other representatives of the Russified Ukrainian gentry as "apostates." Ironically, a few decades later, Kostomarov and Kulish became the target of similar criticism from the more nationalist-minded Ukrainian intellectuals of the turn of the century, such as Serhii Efremov and Borys Hrynchenko.

The Ukrainian national poet Taras Shevchenko commented bitterly on the participation of Ukrainians in their own colonization in his poem "Rozryta mohyla" (A ransacked grave) (1843):

And the Muscovite
Is ripping apart my dear graves ...
Let him ferret, let him dig;
He is robbing them like a thief.
Meanwhile the turncoats
Are growing up
And will help the Muscovite to rule
And to strip their mother's
last patched shirt.
Help them, half-men,
Torture your mother.[47]

Shevchenko often encoded the idea of betraying the national identity via the motif of changing original clothing for a new imperial garb. In a letter to Osyp Bodians'kyi (1 November 1854), Shevchenko expressed his fear of passing as a Muscovite if he were to portray himself wearing an imperial uniform in exile: "I am sending you my self-portrait as a useless Ukrainian [hetmanets'] ... I was afraid to depict myself as a Muscovite [moskal'] because I did not want to scare you with my portrait in a Muscovite overcoat, or, God forbid, in a uniform."[48] Shevchenko's refusal to cover up his Ukrainian identity with imperial dress was later articulated in his refusal to write poems in Russian, as had been suggested by the Russian critic Vissarion Belinskii: "You've given me a sheepskin coat; / Alas, it does not fit me."[49]

Therefore, in the 1840s many Ukrainian intellectuals found themselves in a challenging situation. They were caught between the national Russian and emerging Ukrainian national ideologies and could not publish in their native language in the empire. The publishing situation became even more difficult after the arrest of the leaders of the Brotherhood of Saints Cyril and Methodius, Mykola Kostomarov, Taras Shevchenko, and Panteleimon Kulish, in 1847.[50] As Nikolai Fabricant has argued, the Russian government's anti-Ukrainian policies intensified after 1847. The minister of internal affairs, Count Lev Perovskii, ordered the withdrawal from sale of Shevchenko's *Kobzar* (Minstrel), Kulish's "Povest' ob ukrainskom narode" (A tale of the Ukrainian people), *Ukraina* (Ukraine), and *Mikhailo Charnyshenko*, and Kostomarov's *Ukrains'ki balady* (Ukrainian ballads) and *Vitka* (Branch). The decree banned publication not only of original books in Ukrainian but also of collections of Ukrainian folk songs and almanacs, which had been legal in the first half of the century.[51] The minister of public education, in his turn, ordered the censors to prevent the reprint of Ukrainian works in new editions.[52] The censors meticulously supervised the activity of the Ukrainian intellectuals by spying and organizing denunciations of them. "Not only were the printing of ordinary Ukrainian books and the writing of scholarly articles about Ukraine in Russian forbidden, but even the very words Ukraine, Little Russia, and Hetmanate were now considered illegal. If Ukrainian books made their way into the world from time to time, it was with great difficulty."[53]

If Gogol's generation – Somov, Sreznevs'kyi, Maksymovych, Bodians'kyi, and Burachek – had espoused loyalty to the tsar and developed dual national identities, the following generation of Ukrainian intellectuals – Shevchenko, Kulish, and Kostomarov – held federalist views (i.e., an autonomous state for Ukraine within the federation of Slavs) and tended to cultivate their Ukrainian national identity. The former cohort viewed "all-Russian" identity as the common ground for a merger of the two consanguineous Great and Little Russian nationalities. This strategy left little room for them to profess their Ukrainian identity. They considered Little Russians a separate people, but one unimaginable apart from Great Russians. They also believed that a new imperial identity was a joint creation of both Great and Little Russians. The latter group clearly understood the differences between Great Russians and Ukrainians and criticized the denationalized Little Russian gentry for their lack of patriotism and for the adoption of an all-Russian identity. Nevertheless, the two generations of Ukrainian intellectuals shared a common view of the historical role of the Cossack legacy in the development of Ukrainian identity. Gradually, by the 1840s, the old model of a separate "Little Russian" identity stopped satisfying both groups because it was grounded on the pre-modern idea of the nation; now the rising nationalism across Europe posed new demands on national societies. As Oleh Ilnytzkyj rightly sums up, "Ukrainian 'Little Russianness' and Russian 'All-Russianness' can … be seen for what they were: complementary syndromes, transitional forms of identity and cultural practices; both were accommodations with the empire."[54] The new alternative models of Ukrainian national identity realized by the next generation of Ukrainian intellectuals – the ideas of "two Rus' nationalities" (Kostomarov) and the "two-in-one Rus' nation" (Kulish) – were yet another compromise with the empire's demand for national homogenization.

In the 1840s and 1850s, Kostomarov and Kulish developed the further course of the hybridization of Ukrainian identity. Nikolai/Mykola

Kostomarov's bi-ethnic origin and ambiguous social status played a key role in his hybridization.[55] Born in Russia to a father of ancient Russian noble lineage and a Ukrainian peasant mother, Kostomarov learned Ukrainian only when he entered the University in Kharkiv. As a student of Slavic history, the young Kostomarov was influenced by Gogol's Ukrainian tales, Maksymovych's collections of Ukrainian folk songs, and Sreznevs'kyi's collection of *Zaporozhian Antiquities*. His early literary works *Sava Chalyi* and *Pereiaslivs'ka nich* (The Pereiaslav night), written in Ukrainian, were intended to elevate vernacular Ukrainian to the status of a literary language. In his "Review of Literary Works Written in Ukrainian" (1842), Kostomarov expressed his love for the Ukrainian language and described his project of cultivating it in his literary works. In 1845, his own research on Ukrainian history shaped his nationalist ideas and prompted him to join the Brotherhood of Saints Cyril and Methodius. In collaboration with other members of the Brotherhood, Kostomarov wrote a manifesto entitled *Books of Genesis of the Ukrainian People* (1846), which combined a Ukrainian nationalist narrative with a Christian Socialist agenda. Like many other national narratives, it was founded on an eschatological interpretation of history.[56] The first version of Kostomarov's manifesto did not propose any political agenda. Only in the third redaction did he formulate his federalist views and propose to transform the Russian Empire into a federation of autonomous Slavic states.

After the Brotherhood was suppressed in 1847, with the mass imprisonment and exile of its members, Kostomarov recanted his previous views. During an interrogation, Kostomarov said that the Ukrainian nationality was about to disappear: "if Providence has decided that the Little Russian nationality is giving way to the Russian, then one should not strive to resurrect it." He asserted that the emergence of societies like the Brotherhood signalled the dying agony of the Ukrainian national movement.[57] In the 1860s, Kostomarov reconciled his "duality" by advocating federalism, but never again promoted the political autonomy of Ukraine within the Russian Empire.[58] There is no consensus among scholars whether Kostomarov repudiated his earlier nationalist agenda or stayed loyal to it. David Saunders and Serhiy Bilenky have argued that Kostomarov was interested in the Ukrainian question throughout his entire life, whereas Marko Pavlyshyn has emphasized that Kostomarov "abandoned his advocacy for the full development of Ukrainian literature and culture" and promoted the idea of "complementarity of Ukrainians and Russians as peoples different in character and culture, yet united by destiny."[59]

In any event, in the 1860s Kostomarov continued to question the foundations of Russian nationalism. In his essay "Dve russkie narodnosti" (The two Rus'ian nationalities) (1861), he depicted Russians and Ukrainians as two autonomous entities that developed simultaneously as "nationalities" (not as "nations"), which was in line with Herder's Romantic nationalism. If Russia was formed out of a melting pot of peoples and, therefore, required an authoritarian form of governance, Ukraine conserved the traditions of humanism, personal freedom, and federalism, which Muscovy had purposefully eradicated in its pursuit of "amalgamation, fusion, a strict state, and a social form that swallow the personality."[60] However, Kostomarov emphasized the organic unity between the two and the inevitability of their future joint development, because Ukraine had demonstrated an "incapacity for state life and, therefore, required Russians for the common task of creating a state."[61]

In his polemics with both Polish and Russian nationalist thinkers in the 1860s, Kostomarov defended the right of Ukrainians to have a separate culture and identity. In 1861, Kostomarov wrote two essays, "Pravda poliakam o Rusi" (The truth to the Poles about Rus'), addressed to the Polish nationalist Franciszek Duchiński, and "Pravda moskvicham o Rusi" (The truth to the Muscovites about Rus'), written for Russian Slavophiles. If in the former essay Kostomarov rejected Duchiński's claim of the Poles' historical right to Rus' (Ukraine), in the latter he argued with the Slavophiles against the civilizing mission of Novgorod, which had allegedly colonized Kyivan Rus'. In both essays, Kostomarov vouched for the "Southern Rus'ian," or Ukrainian, nationality against the Polish and Russian disdain for smaller Slavic nationalities. Although Kostomarov's concept of "two Rus' nationalities" did not aim to challenge the idea of an all-Russian identity, in reality it worked to reconcile some of the internal paradoxes created by the notion of having a dual identity without eliminating the distinctions between the Ukrainian and Russian aspects of this identity.

Another case of hybrid identification can be found in the oeuvre of Panteleimon Kulish, the founder of the modern Ukrainian orthography (*kulishivka*) and Gogol's first biographer. In his "Povest' ob ukrainskom narode" (A tale about the Ukrainian people) (1846), Kulish advanced the idea of a merger between "Southerners" (Ukrainians) and "Northerners" (Russians) in a "two-in-one Rus' nation," united by a common civilizing mission. Ironically, the idea of a bifurcated Russian-Ukrainian nation became emblematic of Kulish's own personality, which was cited by the later generation of Ukrainian nationalist intellectuals to illustrate the weakness of national identity among Ukrainian Populists.[62] In many aspects, Kulish followed Gogol's path. Like Gogol, he was a descendant of the high-ranking Cossack elite but could not transfer his status in the empire and as a result could not pursue a state career. Like Gogol, Kulish was also ushered into Petersburg cultural society by Piotr Pletnev, who was branded by him as a colonial subject – a "half-monster" ("poluurod").[63] Thanks to Pletnev's protection, however, Kulish received a grant from the Imperial Academy of Sciences to conduct linguistic-ethnographic research in Central Europe, where he learned several other Slavic languages and dialects (Polish, Czech, Slovak, and Slovenian). Like Gogol, Kulish was accepted by Petersburg society and recognized as an accomplished writer. His friendship with high-ranking Russian officials protected him from tsarist censorship and helped him to get a quick release from exile in Tula, where he was sent for his participation in the Brotherhood of Saints Cyril and Methodius.[64]

During his entire career, Kulish alternated between the Russian and Ukrainian languages. In 1843–5, he published his first novel, *Mikhailo Charnyshenko, or Little Russia Eighty Years Ago*, and the first five chapters of the future *Black Council: A Chronicle of 1663* in Russian, and a historical chronicle in verse entitled *Ukraine* and a short story, "Orysia," in Ukrainian. The first historical novel in Russian, *Mikhailo Charnyshenko* shows a conflict between an ex-Cossack father and his son over their different understanding of the Ukrainian past and the imperial present. The novel begins with a minor episode in Russia's history, when Peter III announced a military campaign against Denmark in 1762. The Russian army was about to take the field in order to conquer the Duchy of Schleswig, but a military coup at the imperial court erupted, which brought Catherine II to power. The protagonist of the novel – a young clerk, Mikhailo Charnyshenko – joins the Russian army hoping to bring home glory and honours. In his effort to match his Cossack ancestors in military accomplishments, Mikhailo enters into open conflict with his father, who curses him for joining the imperial army. Mikhailo's enlistment receives an ambiguous interpretation in the novel: some characters consider fighting in the Russian army an anti-Christian enterprise, while others see in the forthcoming war an opportunity to obtain desirable military training. Moreover, the narrator shows the father as stubborn and bitter in his attitude toward imperial authority. The father's hostility to Russian rule is motivated by the state's inadequate recognition of his merits and the promotion of less deserving Cossack *starshyna*. He is also a passionate collector of Cossack antiquities and believes that one can serve Ukraine best by preserving its past. The father's obsession with collecting things of the past, which is shown as a compensatory mechanism for personal loss (the death of his wife) and for the dissolution of Ukrainian identity, is contrasted with the son's active search for adventure. As a rebellious Romantic, Mikhailo is dissatisfied with mundane reality and seeks the picturesque and sublime in foreign lands. Driven by his sensual instincts, he does not understand that national self-consciousness and patriotism are incompatible with fighting in the Russian army. The violation of his father's will brings Mikhailo various military and personal troubles: the loss of his beloved Katerina, the destruction of his house by fire, his father's insanity, and, finally, his own death. Scholars have interpreted the novel differently: as retribution against a prodigal son; as a case of historical relativism; and as an archetypal conflict between the patriarchal way of living and Cossack liberties, or between feminine and masculine sources of Ukrainian identity.[65]

In 1846, Kulish began working on the Ukrainian version of *The Black Council*, explaining his choice of language by the fact that Russian felt like a foreign language for him.[66] Finally, in 1857, two versions of the novel were published, in both Ukrainian and Russian, targeting two different audiences and further distancing literary Ukrainian from Russian.[67] Mykola Zerov in his essay "Kulish: 'Chorna rada'" argued that the Russian redaction of the novel was written first and then translated by the author into Ukrainian. Several differences between the versions of *The Black Council* support Zerov's hypothesis: the Russian text is more verbose and written in an "old-fashioned discourse," and each chapter opens with a Ukrainian epigraph from folk sources.[68] When translating the novel into Ukrainian, Kulish presumably thought that the Ukrainian epigraphs were redundant and deleted them. The hybrid nature of the two publications may be seen in the Russian introduction to the Ukrainian version of the novel, entitled "O dukhovnom soedinenii iuzhnoi Rusi s severnoi" (On the spiritual union of southern and northern Rus'), and in the author's essay "Ob otnoshenii malorossiiskoi clovesnosti k obshcherusskoi: Epilog k 'Chernoi rade'" (On the relation of Little Russian literature to all-Russian literature: Epilogue to *The Black Council*). Supporting the right of Ukrainians to write in their native tongue, Kulish, nevertheless, argued for maintaining the high status of the Russian literary tradition. While accounting for the need for a separate Ukrainian literature, he cautiously warned that this should not happen "to the detriment of the all-Russian one."[69] In his view, the Ukrainian literary tradition could be developed as regional within the larger Russian literature. Kulish sent copies of the essay to the Russian Slavophile writer Sergei Aksakov and to the Polish Romantic writer Michał Grabowski, thereby performing his self-appointed role as intermediary between Russian and Polish nationalists. In his letter to Aksakov, Kulish stressed the common ground of Russian Slavophilism and

Ukrainian and Polish nationalism and called for a union of all Slavic nations under Russia's leadership. After the suppression of the January Uprising (1863), Kulish was appointed to state service in Warszawa to implement Russification policies in Poland. However, when he communicated with his Polish friend Grabowski, he assured him that Ukrainian intellectuals needed other Slavic friends precisely to offset Russia's predominance.[70] Kulish's strategic interaction with both Russian and Polish nationalists shows how he searched for a space for the emerging Ukrainian nationalism.

Although Kulish believed in the destructive impact of Russian colonization and in the urgency of a comprehensive Ukrainianization of the masses, he held contradictory views on the Ukrainian past and future at different periods of his life. In "The Tale about the Ukrainian People" and *The Black Council*, Kulish glorified the Cossacks for opposing Muscovy and preserving the "spirit of the people." In his three-volume historical study *Istoriia vossoedineniia Rusi* (The history of the reunion of Rus') (1874–7), Kulish described the dissolution of Cossackdom and the reunion with Russia as a historical necessity rather than an ultimate ideal. He endowed the notion of "reunion" with programmatic meaning: that "Old Rus'" (Ukraine) had always striven to reunite with "New Rus'" (Muscovy) on equal terms, and that reunion only exposed their *eternal* bifurcation. In the 1880s, however, he began to criticize both the Cossacks, who, he thought, had not developed sufficient civic maturity and political wisdom, and the Ukrainian intelligentsia, which had participated in imperial policies that denationalized the Ukrainian people.[71] In his collection *Khutorna poeziia* (Homestead poetry) (1882), Kulish called Ukrainian Cossacks "barbarians," a "nation without direction, without honour or respect," who could only boast about their unyielding character, and who, in fact, neglected cultural values. He blamed Ukrainian Cossacks and peasants for their revolts, which had ruined Ukrainian culture and statehood. In his 7 July 1892 letter to Marusia Vovk-Karachevs'ka, Kulish pronounced a ruthless verdict in his evaluation of the Cossacks whom he had previously glorified: "our national ideal is not in the Cossacks" but in a "firm legislative and executive power, that is an absolutism with its harsh despotism."[72] According to Kulish, Ukrainians would benefit if they stayed in the empire because it provided security and prestige. He urged his fellow Ukrainians to leave politics to the Russians, since the latter had already proven their strong state-building skills, which the former lacked, and to focus solely on the development of Ukrainian culture. Thus, Kulish considerably altered his idea of "Ukrainianness," reducing it to strictly cultural terms. With his literary works about the past of Ukraine, Kulish contributed to the "return" to Ukraine launched earlier by Narizhnyi, Somov, and Gogol. By portraying Ukraine as the site of historical, collective, and personal trauma after the loss of national culture and statehood, Kulish established a new relationship with Ukrainian history that nurtured his sense of national identity. Myroslav Shkandrij rightly sums up Kulish's oeuvre by saying that he was "a prime example of an intellectual caught in the crossfire of discourses, constantly evaluating and shifting his position, leaning first toward one tradition then another, mapping the boundaries of discursive conflicts."[73]

Kulish's historical, philosophical, and aesthetic views reveal the attempt of a desperate, frustrated, and alienated colonized subject to restore dignity and a sense of national selfhood to his people. His critical attitude toward the Ukrainian intelligentsia and Cossacks and his sceptical view of Ukraine's independent political future may be viewed as Ukrainian identity-building *in process* rather than as a fixed "Little Russian" or "all-Russian" mindset per se. Another way to think about Kulish's cultural project for Ukraine is by reading it in a psychoanalytical framework, as Nila Zborovs'ka has proposed in her monograph *Kod ukrains'koi literatury. Proekt psykhoistorii novitn'oi ukrains'koi literatury* (The Ukrainian literary code: an attempt at a psychohistory of modern Ukrainian literature) (2006). The scholar has pointed to the changes in the cultural paradigm that Kulish experienced when he tried to overcome the dichotomies of Romantic thinking by developing critical realism, which in psychoanalytical terms may be explained in terms of the Oedipus complex and the search for an authoritative, archetypal father.[74] According to Zborovs'ka, Kulish began his literary career by paying tribute to the Romantic "fathers" of the Little Russian tradition and writing in the fashion of Kvitka-Osnov'ianenko's sentimentalist prose and Gogolian fantastic realism. Later, he engaged in a heated polemics with Taras Shevchenko over the Ukrainian national myth. Thus, Kulish's "Oedipus conflict" with Gogol signified a struggle with the Romantic-mythological view of the Cossack past, while Kulish's anxiety about Shevchenko's influence was realized in his replacement of "national fanaticism" with moderate patriotism buttressed by critical thinking. Instead of continuing Shevchenko's concept of tearful and gloomy "heart," he proposed a union of "reason and heart" as the foundation for a national equilibrium. For Kulish, Ukrainian Romanticism was associated with the elemental power of *haidamachchyna*, named for the *haidamaks*, paramilitary Cossack bands whose uprisings had been brutally crushed; the term suggested unconscious and uncontrollable wrath and an instinctive desire for revenge. The *haidamachchyna*, according to Kulish, could only be countered by the organized cultural resistance of critically thinking individuals. Therefore, Zborovs'ka concludes, the symbolization of Kulish's psychic system follows the path delineated by Sigmund Freud in his *Lectures* as the transition from the Romantic principle of pleasure to the realist principle of fact, which is the most important advance in the development of the individual ego (and national subject).[75]

Kostomarov and Kulish had the misfortune to labour in the highly charged atmosphere of heightened Russian nationalism. After the Polish Uprising of 1861–3, even a moderate Ukrainianophilism prompted suspicion: the Russians thought of the Ukrainian national movement as a Polish ploy, while the Poles considered it part of Russia's imperialist scheme to undermine Polish influence on Right-Bank Ukraine (which was part of the Polish-Lithuanian Commonwealth until the Russo-Polish war [1654–67]). In response to this political situation, Ukrainian intellectuals developed politically moderate programs of Ukrainian culture-building without compromising the all-Russian project: Kostomarov's idea of Ukrainian literature as literature for home use ("literatura dlia domashnioho vzhytku") and Kulish's homestead philosophy ("khutorna filosofiia"). These were compromises meant to foster Ukrainian cultural distinctiveness and to counter restrictive imperial policies regarding the Ukrainian language and culture.

The relationship between the national and personal narratives of Ukrainianness produced by nineteenth-century Ukrainian writers remains largely understudied. It is still unclear whether the Cossack myth of Ukraine created by such different writers as Narizhnyi, Gogol, Shevchenko, and Kulish generated one or several different national narratives, and whether their solidarity, cultural similarities, and engagement with the myth of Cossack Ukraine can be summed up into a coherent story that could have provided the foundation for a future national movement. One of the most common arguments in nationalism studies is that personal narratives essentially mirror national historical narratives.[76] However, this principle stumbles when one deals with the cases of multiple loyalties and multifaceted national identities. The self-identification of Ukrainian intellectuals in nineteenth-century Russian imperial culture can be best captured with the term "ambivalence." Literally meaning "strength on both sides," "ambivalence" equipped them with tools to resist the homogenizing power of the imperial state and to work on nation-building, but at the same time it forced them to develop various strategies of ethnic defence and contradictory theories of Ukrainianness. The most important aspect of this ambivalence was the disruption of homogeneous Russian imperial culture and the classical colonial model of engagement between the centre and the periphery.

Ukrainian intellectuals had to invent various strategies of ethnic disguise, which captured the antinomies of their national and cultural *in-betweenness*. As Taras Koznarsky has rightly pointed out, they were "expected to live in conflict between the adopted normative form of self-representation and a supposed hidden agenda," which naturally led to "a compartmentalization of one's identity into functional, performative modes of self-perception and self-representation ... enacted according to a particular social situation."[77] The coexistence of several models of Ukrainianness has always been problematic for both the Russian imperial and Ukrainian national projects, because it uncovered many transit zones in culture, which from the outside looked monolithic, but which upon closer examination was composed of many, sometimes conflicting, versions of nationhood.

Another phenomenon that signalled the emerging agency to negotiate one's own ethnic-cultural difference in the empire was the proliferation of fictitious editors and narrators "from the people" – Antonii Pogorel'skii (Aleksei Perovskii), Rudy Pan'ko (Nikolai Gogol), Ieremiia Halka (Mykola Kostomarov), Porfirii Baiskii (Orest Somov), Hryts'ko Osnov'ianenko (Hryhorii Kvitka), Is'ko Materynka (Osyp Bodians'kyi), and Kobzar Darmohrai (Taras Shevchenko).[78] Ukrainian popular narrators exceeded the limits of Romantic literary fashion because they presented a distinctively Ukrainian model of culture: if in the Russian hierarchy (God–Tsar–aristocracy–people) the poet resided close to the top, in the Ukrainian one (God–people) he was one of many who could be subjected to mockery and derision by the audience. The Ukrainian literati emerged from middle-class estates and maintained stronger ties with the peasant community. They were perceived by their contemporaries as possessing a stronger sense of group identity than that available to the Russian elite. The Russian dissident writer Alexander Herzen used Gogol's case to comment on the ties between the Ukrainian nobility and the peasantry:

> not being from the folk by birth, like Kol'tsov, Gogol belonged to the people in his tastes and cast of mind. Gogol was completely immune to any foreign influences ... He was more sympathetic to the folk than to court life, which was more natural for Ukrainians. Even after a Ukrainian has become a nobleman, he has never broken off from his own people as quickly as the Russian one.[79]

Whether or not Herzen was correct about Ukrainian gentry's strong ties to the folk, it would be fair to say that they developed a stronger sense of group identity based on a shared goal: to preserve and popularize

Ukrainian culture in the empire. This common task laid the groundwork for the future formation of Ukrainian national identity.

As this chapter has demonstrated, the "in-between" existence of Ukrainian intellectuals and the promotion of a unique Ukrainian culture in an imperial setting can problematize the postcolonial idea of split identification. Postcolonial theory prioritizes a deterministic view of the colonized as those who, while trying to escape their ambivalence, can only alternate between a set of fixed oppositions. As Homi Bhabha notes, since this world is dependent upon "the concept of 'fixity' in the ideological construction of otherness," the colonial subject, too, remains "fixed" in this world's discursive tension.[80] However, if we assume that the strict determination of subjectivity is based solely on a determination of social space, we will overlook the vital significance of subjective freedom and will not be able to find an explanation for the growing nationalism that was nurtured and promoted by Ukrainian intellectuals of the nineteenth century, who, however, by and large, remained Russified and sceptical about the political independence of Ukraine.

Gogol's Self-Fashioning and Performance of Identity in the 1830s

Gogol's self-representation in the 1830s can be studied from different angles – as a deliberate strategy of Romantic self-creation, as a product of discriminatory social discourses imposed by elite Russian society, or as a result of the exchange and negotiation of cultural and symbolic currencies between imperial and colonial agents. All these aspects of Gogol's public performance can be combined in the concept of hybrid self-fashioning, which brings together Stephen Greenblatt's idea of self-fashioning and Homi Bhabha's theorization of mimicry and hybridity. According to Greenblatt, self-fashioning implies that identity is constructed and manipulated both in text and life. Initially, self-fashioning meant "the forming of the self," i.e., the literal shaping of a person's physical appearance; only with time did it begin to include the expression of manners and conduct of the elite, their crafted appearance and stylized speech. The degree of an artist's control over his/her own self-fashioning is irrelevant in modernity, because individuals now become subjects in the course of power negotiation. Modernity neither brings freedom to design one's own self nor represses subjectivity; instead, modern subjectivity emerges from a "complex circulation between the social dimension of an aesthetic strategy and the aesthetic dimension of a social strategy."[1] The most important conclusion of Greenblatt's theory is that self-fashioning inevitably produces an *other* against which self is defined. This production occurs "at the point of encounter between an authority and an alien" and always entails "some experience of threat, some effacement or undermining, some loss of self."[2]

Gogol's self-fashioning in the early 1830s was marked with ambivalence and constant shifting of the reference point. Having entered Russian culture as an entertaining "Ukrainian jester" (a "malorossiiskii zhartovnik" as defined by Osip Senkovskii), Gogol capitalized on Russian society's need for a colonial *other*. The fictitious persona of the

Ukrainian simpleton Rudy Pan'ko in his early work *Evenings on a Farm near Dikan'ka* (1831–2) brought Gogol recognition and acceptance by imperial society as such a character. But the literary persona of Pan'ko paradoxically became the *other* through whose gaze he derived his sense of Ukrainian identity. This is where the concept of colonial mimicry becomes useful to describe the ambivalence of national identification. Traditionally, mimicry has been applied to describe the assimilation of colonial subjects in a metropolitan centre. As a mechanism of the control over representation, mimicry has been treated as a negative outcome of colonial power: it assimilates colonial subjects by suppressing their ethnic, class, gender, and other differences. Homi Bhabha, on the contrary, has emphasized the subverting effect of mimicry: through the internalization of values and norms of the dominant culture, the colonial subject emerges as a "partial," "incomplete," and "virtual" copy of the colonizer. Colonial mimicry thus undermines the pretension of the dominant culture to educate and improve the always imperfect colonized, and, thereby, acquires *agency*: it can only produce an effect of "otherness" but has nothing to do with the "other."[3]

Studying Gogol's self-fashioning within the framework of colonial mimicry helps to overcome the essentialist approach to cultural identity, which claims unlimited access to the writer's psyche, often regarded as mysterious and fragmented by nature. First, the Russian Symbolists discovered that Gogol was a "riddle." In 1909, in his speech on the occasion of Gogol's centenary, Andrei Belyi bitterly admitted that "we do not yet know what Gogol is."[4] In the 1960s–1970s, the idea of Gogol's unstable identity received various psychological interpretations positing that it was rooted in a fundamental fear of having his identity defined. Andrei Siniavskii linked Gogol's problematic identity with the inability to control his artistic creation. Victor Erlich suggested that "Gogol was a thoroughly unspontaneous man who barricaded himself behind a set of contrivances"; it was "his irrational fear of premature exposure, of rebuff and ridicule" that prompted him "to hide his pathologically vulnerable self behind a screen of rhetoric."[5] Hugh MacLean and Simon Karlinsky defined Gogol's problematic sense of identity in psychoanalytical terms and identified it as a theme that operates on several levels in his writing.[6] The unlimited access to a writer's psyche that this approach presumes seems unproductive for studying the fluidity and multiplicity of Gogol's cultural identification. Post-structuralist theory can better account for the production of identities, which is never complete, always in process, and always constituted within, not outside, representation. Gogol reappropriated cultural values, attitudes, and behaviours of the Russian cultural elite and reified them in his self-representation.

Social mobility, adaptation strategies, and networking skills were definitive factors in casting Gogol as "an outsider within" imperial culture in 1828–32. Gogol spent the early years of his career in St Petersburg establishing connections with different social groups: his former classmates and Ukrainian expatriates, Russian middle-brow writers and editors, and the so-called literary aristocrats.[7] Although Gogol's immediate goal was to gain membership in the circle of literary aristocrats, he could not fulfil his ambitious plan until the fall of 1830.[8] His frustration with the Russian capital had been growing. In his first letters to his mother, Gogol complained about feeling alienated in the capital:

> I will tell you also that Petersburg seemed to me completely not as I expected … In general, each capital is characterized by its people that casts an imprint of nationality on it, but in Petersburg there is no character of any kind: foreigners who settled here have become assimilated and no longer resemble foreigners, whereas the Russians have been foreignized [obinostranilis'] … There is an unusual emptiness in it, there is no spirit in the people, all around one sees only civil servants who are serving time, all talk about their departments and ministries, everyone is depressed and buried in insignificant occupations in which their life passes by uselessly.[9]

Disconnected from his native Ukraine, Gogol began to seek a community that would appease his nostalgia and bring a taste of the culture he left behind. In these early years, Gogol maintained his closest connections with former Ukrainian classmates whom he ironically called his "trough-mates" ("odnokorytniki"). It was a group of about twenty-five graduates (including Nestor Kukol'nyk, Mykola Prokopovych, Oleksandr Danylevs'kyi, Tymofii Pashchenko, Kostiantyn Bazili, Evhenii Hrebinka, and Apollon Mokryts'kyi) from the Nizhyn Lyceum, who had just arrived in the capital to pursue careers in the imperial administration.[10] Gogol's early literary and intellectual circles have been thoroughly researched by Panteleimon Kulish and Vladimir Shenrok and recently systematized by Oksana Suproniuk in a biographical encyclopedia. She followed Vadim Vatsuro's approach to the study of Pushkin's "literary milieu" ("literaturnaia sreda") and applied it to Gogol's contacts (about 480 total) during his school years.[11] Through their collaborative literary activities in journals and almanacs, Russian Romantic writers of the 1820s–1830s developed a sense of group identity that not only facilitated their professionalization as literary folk but also created a public space for political, ideological, and artistic polemics.[12] Similarly, the group of young Ukrainian literati to which Gogol belonged established lifelong artistic connections, although they did not compete with each other for the status of professional writers. Just as during their school years in Nizhyn, they held regular meetings in St Petersburg in the early 1830s, which often included the joint reading of periodicals and the recounting of literary anecdotes. The young Ukrainian literati imitated and mocked the high salon culture of St Petersburg. Their demonstrative literary dilettantism was democratic in spirit as they strove to achieve artistic autonomy without relying on the old institution of patronage. The Ukrainian literati's gatherings bore the flavour of a communal, friendly spirit that was significantly different from the elitist atmosphere of the salons. The all-male company resembled a *bratiia* (brotherhood) and professed a mock-monastic lifestyle of Ukrainian seminarians. *Bratiia* designated a group of poor students who earned their living by performing interludes and school dramas in public spaces. This tradition originated in seventeenth-century Ukrainian culture and was still very active at the end of the eighteenth and the beginning of the nineteenth centuries when Gogol's father, a graduate of the Kyiv-Mohyla Seminary, wrote his Ukrainian comedies. Unlike Russian habitués of the salons, who cultivated good taste and manners in everything (from how to pick up a dropped handkerchief to how to write a poem), Gogol's cohort appeared rather ignorant of the concept of good taste. The Ukrainian literati named their mock almanac *Parnassus Manure* and collectively decided whose verses deserved to be published and whose – to be burnt.[13] They did not follow the aesthetic standards of Russian Romanticism and were, thereby, less confined by existing codes of the cultural behaviour of the Russian elite.

Gogol appeared to be the driving force behind these meetings. He invented literary nicknames for each participant – "Balzac," "Dumas," "Hugo," and "Jules Janin" – and wrote funny couplets about them.[14] Some habitués of these gatherings later fashioned more conventional literary and poetic personae by imitating European Romantics and exploring fashionable literary topics.[15] For example, Vasyl' Liubych-Romanovych began his literary career as a translator of Mickiewicz and Byron; later he became interested in Slavic history and wrote several articles on Russian medieval history. Andrii Borodyn became known for his translations of Shakespeare, Shelley, Byron, and Moore. Nestor Kukol'nyk, who had a lifelong interest in the Renaissance Italian poet Torquato Tasso, made him a role model in his literary career. The mask of Tasso, which exemplified an ideal poet creating for art's sake, won Kukol'nyk popularity in the court. His self-fashioning corresponded to the Romantic elitist impulse to transform one's self into an aesthetic plot. Obviously, Gogol was aware of the trend and also invented an appropriate literary persona. At first, he strove to become a Romantic poet and published his first text, the idyll *Hanz Küchelgarten* (1829), under the pseudonym "V. Alov." Gogol pinned all of his hopes on this poem, but when the critics of *The Moscow Telegraph* and *The Northern Bee* gave it harsh reviews, he purchased all available copies, burnt them, and took a trip to Lübeck, Germany, in the spring of 1829.

Upon his return to St Petersburg from Lübeck, Gogol began to seek career guidance from the middle-brow writer Faddei Bulgarin, whose growing popularity inspired him to undertake to write stories for a broader readership. According to Bulgarin, at the end of 1829, Gogol came to him praising his literary works and hoping to get a post in the Third Department.[16] Bulgarin's supervisor in the Third Department, Maksimilian von Fok, allegedly granted Gogol a sinecure in which he only showed up to collect his wages. Most likely, Gogol received a position in the Third Department thanks to Bulgarin but did not work there or worked there only briefly.[17] However, Bulgarin might have influenced Gogol in another important way. Born as Tadeusz Bułharyn to a family of Polish revolutionists, Faddei Bulgarin changed his name together with his political allegiance once he moved to Russia. He spent most of his life in St Petersburg "using his otherness to play one side off against the other"[18] and became notorious for his adaptability to political circumstances. For his acceptance in the ranks of Russian writers, Bulgarin was obliged to his associations with both the Decembrists and Tsar Nicholas I, who first arrested him and then enlisted him to serve state interests. In 1826, Bulgarin began to work as an agent in the Third Department to monitor literary life in Russia. As a reward, he was permitted to publish his journal, *The Northern Bee*, and he used his connections with the Third Department to his advantage. This rapid rise of an alien in the Russian capital apparently attracted Gogol, who was in a similar position. As Melissa Frazier has observed, just as Bulgarin "used his own Polishness as a springboard into Russian literature, beginning his literary career in St. Petersburg with the publication ... of 'A Short Survey of Polish Literature' (1820) ... so Gogol used his well-researched Ukrainianness in much the same way ... gaining acclaim in the Russian literary world with his representation of Ukrainian local color in *Evenings on a Farm Near Dikan'ka*."[19]

Like Bulgarin, Gogol also modified his last name, "Gogol-Ianovskii," by eliminating the Polish part, "Ianovskii," which was the first name of Gogol's paternal great-grandfather (Ian) plus the Polish suffix -ovski.[20] At the end of the eighteenth century, Ian's son (Gogol's grandfather), Opanas Dem'ianovych, had added "Gogol" to "Ianovskii." He had a pragmatic reason for combining Ukrainian and Polish ancestry in his last name: the Gogol-Ianovskiis could only claim noble status in the empire via the "Gogol" line. According to family legend, the Gogols traced their Cossack origins back to a sixteenth-century colonel from Mohyliv, Ostap Gogol, who was rewarded with noble status for his exemplary service to Polish King Jan III Sobieski. Opanas Dem'ianovych's claim to nobility via the Gogol lineage received official recognition in the late eighteenth century. This act was a response to Catherine II's edict "Letter of Grant to the Nobles" (1785), which regulated the transfer of the noble status only to those Little Russians who could prove their aristocratic origins in the Polish *szlachta*.

Back at school, Gogol had only used the "Ianovskii" part of his last name.[21] During his first two years in St Petersburg, he signed his correspondence with the hyphenated name Gogol-Ianovskii. All of his creative works of the same period were published anonymously, or under pseudonyms (Alov, Ianov, Glechyk, 0000, and Rudy Pan'ko). In January 1831, Gogol finally dropped "Ianovskii" and became "Gogol." In his correspondence with family and friends, he was so persistent in this change that he even asked his mother not to address him as "Ianovskii" because this part of his last name "had gone somewhere."[22] While working as a tutor in Longinov's family, Gogol asserted that "Ianovskii" was a Polish invention and he asked the children to call him "Mister Gogol."[23] His letter to his mother of 16 April 1831 can shed light on his true motive for getting rid of the Polish part of his last name: his sister Maria was being courted by a Polish man, and Gogol was concerned that in the current political climate (during the November Rebellion) "Poles have now become suspect";[24] the name "Gogol" clearly foregrounded the family's Cossack origin. The name change also signifies that Gogol was an active subject who manipulated his own authorial myth.

That Gogol actively sought acquaintance with middle-brow writers demonstrates his understanding of the changing literary market in the 1830s.[25] The rise of commercial book printing brought about the expansion and diversification of the readership and offered literati immediate remuneration for their creative efforts. In these new conditions, literary salons and almanacs could no longer meet the demands of Russia's more democratic reading public. Moreover, the differentiation of roles in the literary marketplace led to writers' new social status: from the closed network of familiar associations the writer emerged as a public figure. These changes in imperial literary institutions impelled Gogol to consider a career choice: to be a salon writer for a tiny group of well-educated aristocrats or a writer for a broad national audience. Gogol's acquaintance with Orest Somov, who had managed to bridge the two literary camps – elite and middle-brow – helped determine his subsequent literary career. Somov was one of the few Ukrainian writers of the time who was accepted as an insider in the circles of the literary aristocrats. In the 1830s, Somov performed the duties of the assistant editor both for Pushkin's *Literary Gazette* and for Anton Del'vig's almanac *The Northern Flowers*. Simultaneously, Somov actively collaborated with the Ukrainian expatriate community in St Petersburg: he collected Ukrainian folk songs and published works of Ukrainian writers such as Ivan Kotliarevs'kyi and Mykhailo Maksymovych in *The Northern Flowers*. Somov impressed the young Gogol with his exploration of Ukrainian topics in his stories and with his fictitious Ukrainian literary persona, Porfirii Baiskii. Thanks to Somov's introduction, Gogol became acquainted first with Del'vig, poet and chief editor of *The Northern Flowers*, and, later, with the leading Russian literati Vasilii Zhukovskii and Piotr Pletnev, who immediately began to promote the promising young author. They secured Gogol employment as a history teacher in the Patriotic Institute for Noble Maidens and as a tutor in several aristocratic families; at the same time, they encouraged him to pursue a literary career. In one year, Gogol published a pedagogical essay, a philosophical dialogue, two fragments from the tale "The Terrible Boar," and an excerpt from his unfinished historical novel *The Hetman*. Gogol also wrote an essay on Pushkin's historical drama *Boris Godunov* (1830) with the hope of gaining Pushkin's attention. Finally, on 20 May 1831, the two writers met in Pletnev's house.[26]

Gogol's social skills and talent gradually opened the doors of many prestigious salons and associations both in St Petersburg and in Moscow. By 1832, Gogol had made appearances in several fashionable Petersburg salons (Khitrovo's, Pletnev's, Smirnova's, and Repnina's) and become acquainted with major Russian writers and artists.[27] Gogol was noticed chatting with court noblemen and with one of the Grand Dukes.[28] That Gogol maintained relationships with various social strata provided him with a great degree of freedom in his self-presentation and social behaviour. "Calculation" became a key word with which Gogol later described his desire to mimic established social codes. In a letter to Smirnova, Gogol confessed that he had always tried to control "what could and could not be said to each" of his friends and confreres.[29] Nevertheless, Gogol had relatively infrequent interactions with members of Russian polite society, and they offered him no tenable social position. As Michael Holquist has put it, Gogol "never quite overcame the gap that separated the muddy Ukrainian village outside Poltava where he was born from the glitter of Saint Petersburg. He always felt uncomfortable among the brilliant circles … in a place where hostile critics sometimes ascribed his outlandish style to his not being a native speaker of Russian."[30]

His ambiguous status in polite society resulted in a sense of non-belonging which later became an existential problem for him. Commenting on his second "escape" from Russia after harsh reviews of his comedy *The Inspector General* in 1836, Gogol formulated his ideal of a writer's existence in society as follows: "a poet … [l]ike a silent monk … lives in the world *without belonging to it*."[31] For Gogol, life's deceptiveness was intrinsically connected to the impermanence of worldly authority; that is why he tried to avoid fixation as a certain type of writer, or even as a person in the broader sense.

Gogol as the Colonial Other

Gogol became famous as a writer thanks to his mask of the fictitious Ukrainian editor-narrator Rudy Pan'ko, which enacted a stereotype of Ukrainian culture suitable for the amusement of the imperial audience. In contemporary Gogol studies, the persona of Rudy Pan'ko has been discussed within the framework of the powerful tradition of *malorossiiskie povesti*, which produced a variety of masks of simple-hearted Ukrainian narrators. One of the earliest artistic realizations of this type of colonial behaviour can be found in Ivan Kotliarevs'kyi's *Malorossiiskaia Eneïda* (Little Russian Aeneid, 1798; 1809; 1842) and Hryhorii Kvitka-Osnov'ianenko's *Malorossiiskie povesti* (Little Russian tales, 1834–7). In his travesty of Virgil's *Aeneid*, Kotliarevs'kyi developed a model of Ukrainian identity that allowed him to mock the imperial centre "without direct risk."[32] Kvitka-Osnov'ianenko's narrators also spoke and acted "à la muzhik," which, according to Marko Pavlyshyn, only "reaffirmed a local noble identity: it looked as if the gentleman knew the peasant vernacular idiom so well that he could imitate it but he resided on an incomparably higher cultural level which allowed him to look condescendingly at peasants."[33]

With regard to Gogol's narrative mask, it is important to examine the role of patronage in fixing Gogol as a sly Ukrainian writer and his own response to this colonial stereotype. The view of Gogol as colonial *other* by Russian society in 1830–1 played a crucial role in the development and later reception of his fictional mask of Pan'ko. When scholars discuss the problem of Gogol's authorship in *Evenings*, they usually put too much emphasis on his pragmatic reasons to conceal his authorship and hide behind this mask, disregarding the benefits that the publication of Gogol's tales brought to the literary aristocrats.[34] There are several telling indications that Gogol was ready to publish the tales under his real name before May 1831. First, Gogol had already established his authorship, having used his real name in the essay "Zhenshchina" (Woman), which was published earlier that year. Second, at the end of 1830 and the beginning of 1831, Gogol had already finished the first book of *Evenings*, but he did not publish any of the tales in *Literary Gazette* and *The Northern Flowers*, reserving them for publication in a separate book. Third, in March of 1831 he requested a large amount of money from his mother to finance the publication of his "piglet" ("porosia"), which in all likelihood referred to the finalized manuscript of *Evenings*. The legend behind the creation of Rudy Pan'ko was recorded by Panteleimon Kulish, Gogol's first biographer, later, after Gogol's death; it sheds light on the role of the colonial patron, Piotr Pletnev, in capitalizing on the popular device of the folksy editor-narrator:

> By May 1831 he [Gogol] had completed several tales that were to form Book One of *Evenings on a Farm near Dikan'ka*. Not sure how to go about publishing these tales, Gogol turned to P.A. Pletnev for advice. Pletnev wanted to shield the young man from the pull of literary parties and to protect him from the preconceived notions of people who had met Gogol personally or had read his first literary experiments and had not received a favourable impression. For these reasons he advised Gogol to observe a strict incognito on this first occasion, and he invented a subtitle for the tales that would arouse the public's curiosity. Thus the tales appeared as having been edited by the beekeeper Rudy Pan'ko, who was supposed to live near Dikan'ka, which belonged to Prince Kochubei.[35]

As follows from Kulish's account, Gogol initially did not conceive of the stories within the framework of the fictitious editor-narrator Rudy Pan'ko. Pan'ko's title and the mask were suggested by Pletnev and served the interests of the literary aristocrats who hoped to win over the reading audience from such middle-brow writers as Faddei Bulgarin and Osip Senkovskii. The beginning of the 1830s had seen a rapid decline of the literary aristocrats' popularity owing to the emergence of a mass audience. Pletnev believed that Gogol's tales, oriented toward this new audience, could help the literary aristocrats increase the circulation of their publications. As a reward for serving the interests of his patrons, Gogol gained access to the Russian literary elite. The result of this mystification was quite unexpected both for the patron Pletnev and for the client Gogol. What Pletnev helped to create became a brand name for Gogol and affected his further identification as the colonial *other* in Russian society. Gogol's "passing" as a blabbering Dikan'ka beekeeper was so successful that the difference between the mask of Rudy Pan'ko and the empirical writer remained unnoticed for several years. To a certain extent, this was due to the suggestive nature of the autobiographical legend behind Rudy Pan'ko. The name "Rudy Pan'ko" was formed like a Ukrainian *prizvis'ko* (a nickname that reflects its bearer's profession or origin). The odd name "rudy" (a Ukrainian word for "red-haired") is associated in folklore with secret knowledge possessed by people of certain professions, particularly by beekeepers; "Pan'ko" (Pan'-ko) was formed from Gogol's grandfather's name Panas (in Ukrainian) and the suffix -ko attached to the contracted root. This was in accord with the old Ukrainian and Russian tradition of taking a grandfather's name. For example, Peter I, while travelling in Europe, used the fictitious name Mikhailov, which referred to his grandfather Mikhail.[36] The act of naming has always been a powerful device in literary mystifications. The fictitious name has often served not so much to conceal as to highlight a writer's personal legend. The use of the toponym "Dikan'ka" in the title also corresponded to the Romantic fashion of foregrounding the author's place of origin. Many Ukrainian writers before and during Gogol's career encoded their place of origin into their pen names. Gogol's family estate, Dikan'ka, was a legendary place, famous for its *dikii les* (wild forest) in which a remnant of the Cossack army had hidden from imperial forces after the abolition of the Zaporozhian Host. Therefore, the name of the fictitious narrator actualized Gogol's personal myth as a Cossack descendant.

As much dependent on the metropolitan audience's reception as Gogol himself in his real life, Rudy Pan'ko presents a stylized *suplika* in the preface to *Evenings* to play to metropolitan readers' expectations of him as an entertaining Little Russian:

> What oddity is this: *Evenings on a Farm near Dikan'ka*? What sort of evenings? And thrust into the world by a beekeeper! Goodness! As though geese enough had not been plucked for pens and rags turned into paper! As though folks enough of all callings and types had not dirtied their fingers with inkstains! And now some whim's possessed a beekeeper to drag himself in their footsteps! Really, so much printed paper has proliferated nowadays that it takes some time to figure out what to wrap in it.[37]

The meta-literary device of the *suplika* (from Latin "supplico" [sub+plico], i.e., to "kneel," to "plead" with someone) emerged in sixteenth-century Ukrainian officialese and rapidly became a subversive narrative device in Ukrainian prose fiction.[38] By using this popular narrative device, Gogol created a meta-mockery which, on the one hand, entertained the metropolitan audience with Pan'ko's semi-grammatical language, but, on the other, parodied the very device of *suplika* and the audience's colonial stereotypes of him as a semi-literate Ukrainian.

As Roman Koropeckyj and Robert Romanchuk persuasively demonstrate, Pan'ko's "Preface" to Book One of *Evenings* exemplified a sort of a double talk, the "'innocent' game of distancing and identification" with colonial discourse.[39] It could be also said that the fictitious persona of Pan'ko simultaneously became Gogol's second self and his anti-self. Acting "like himself" and "like someone else" became intricately linked in Gogol's persona. Here we deal with a phenomenon of camouflage as a mode of sociability; it unravels the very texture of subjectivity and becomes a form of social masking.[40]

Published anonymously, Gogol's *Evenings* launched a mythopoetic process by which the author's personality was constructed in readers' minds out of the projection of a literary image onto his biographical self. Soon after the publication of *Evenings*, the purely fictional device was extended beyond the fictional text and blurred the boundaries between Pan'ko and Gogol himself. The void that emerged between the absent author and the text created a space for what Michel Foucault termed "the author function."[41] The ascription of an author's name to literary discourse rather than to a concrete real-life person makes authorship a contingent affair. If the author-function, according to Foucault, is a social construct projected onto an author's verbal products and serving some ideological purpose, then Gogol's Rudy Pan'ko is not just a fictitious editor and narrator, but a projection of the literary aristocrat's colonial desire for the *other*.

In the absence of the author's name, readers began constructing their image of the author to match their stereotypical notions of Ukrainians. For about three years – from the publication of Book One of *Evenings* in 1832 to the publication of the "sequel," *Mirgorod*, in 1835 – the actual name of the author was kept secret. Some of the more informed readers like Vladimir Odoevskii and Nikolai Iazykov learned the author's identity from hearsay. In 1832, Odoevskii wrote to his friend Aleksandr Koshelev: "Recently, 'Evenings on a Farm. Little Russian Tales' came out in print. People say that a young man named Gogol wrote them."[42] Less informed readers, like the minor writer Nikolai Mukhanov, could not guess who was hiding behind the guise of Pan'ko: "Here appeared two books, *Evenings on a Farm*, [I] do not know whose, but everybody praises them."[43] Even when Gogol eventually revealed his identity to the public, the book was still associated not with him, but with Rudy Pan'ko. Three years after the publication of *Evenings*, Odoevskii still credited the success of the book to the "novelist Pan'ko" whose simple-hearted personality captured the spirit of the book. The reductive identification of the author with his fictional persona needed an audience for the performance of identity, but the audience's perception threatened to replace the author with the image it extrapolated from the fictional text. The reception of Gogol as Rudy Pan'ko proved that, in collaboration with the author, the imperial power could fix his ethnic "difference" as the most memorable and knowable feature of an individual, having reduced everything else about the individual to those features.

As much as Gogol's mask of a semi-literate Ukrainian beekeeper was a collective project of the colonizer and the colonized, his public reception as the colonial "other" was largely shaped by his "patrons."[44] Introducing Gogol's first publication of the Ukrainian tale "Bisavriuk, or St John's Eve" (1830) in the journal *Annals of the Fatherland*, the editor Pavel Svin'in described him as an exotic Ukrainian author through a contrast between the Russian and Ukrainian peoples:

> Malorossiiane [Ukrainians] more [than Russians] resemble a magnificent Asian people ... by their appearance, frame, slender stature, laziness and carelessness ... Malorossiiane ... do not have such an ungovernable character as the adherents of Islam do; their phlegmatic carelessness protects them from blustering emotions, and often the fiery and audacious European intellect sparkles from their bushy eyebrows; ardent love of their Motherland clothed in primal simplicity fills their breasts.[45]

The presentation of Ukrainians as exotic *others* helped the Russian elite overcome their own sense of inferiority vis-à-vis their Western European peers. Svin'in's comparison of Ukrainians with Asians was symptomatic of nineteenth-century Russian nationalist discourse. The important difference from Asian people in Svin'in's account is that the "Little Russian people" often demonstrate an "audacious European intellect" which makes them, reversing Homi Bhabha's definition of the hybrid subject, "almost the same, but not quite." This combination of sameness and otherness also marked Gogol's relationship with his patrons – Svin'in, Pletnev, Pushkin, and Smirnova. They applied one of the most popular colonial stereotypes, "slyness," to Gogol when promoting the writer on the literary market. Pletnev, for example, called "slyness and careerism" ("khitrost' i prolaznichestvo") the defining qualities of Ukrainians.[46] Later, during Gogol's rising literary success, Pushkin characterized him as a "cunning Little Russian" ("khitryi maloros") who had taken advantage of Pushkin's best ideas for his own literary plots.[47] He referred to himself as the "godfather" of Gogol's comedy *The Inspector General*.[48] The myth of Gogol "stealing" from Pushkin was further perpetuated in the mid-1830s when Gogol achieved wide public recognition.[49]

Aleksandra Smirnova (born in Ukraine), a court lady and a close friend of Gogol, also promulgated an image of Gogol as a stubborn and sly Ukrainian. In her diary and correspondence, she repeatedly called the writer a *khokhol*, a derogatory term for a Ukrainian. Smirnova's first encounter with Gogol occurred in 1830 in the house of Princess Elizaveta Repnina (also known as Warette), where the writer worked as a tutor for Repnina's daughter Maria. Reproaching Repnina for not letting her talk to the "shy *khokhol*," Smirnova presented Gogol within the framework of proprietorship: "From a distance I saw Warette's *khokhol*."[50] Smirnova's amusement at seeing an "authentic *khokhol*" turned immediately into a desire to "tame" him. Her repeated attempts to domesticate the "stubborn *khokhol*" are all documented in her diary.[51] In the passage quoted below, she renders a curious discussion that occurred in the 1840s among herself, Ivan Aksakov, and Gogol:

> [Aksakov asks] – Aleksandra Osipovna, tell us how you met Nikolai Vasil'evich.
>
> [Smirnova says] – I am bored with you, Ivan Sergeevich! Leave me alone! I do not remember at all. What does it matter to you?
>
> [Gogol says] – Well, listen to me. I taught a lesson to a lady, a very boring lesson. I am not a good teacher … My poor student was yawning when Aleksandra Osipovna and the student's sister came in and immediately recognized the *khokhol* in me. We [Ukrainians] are twins with Great Russians, but apparently every *khokhol* has a special physiognomy, as well as every Muscovite. Aleksandra Osipovna instantly noticed that the sky of the Northern Palmyra [St Petersburg] burdens and depresses the *khokhol*. She already knew that P.A. Pletnev had welcomed me, and that V.A. Zhukovskii and A.S. Pushkin were favourably disposed toward the *khokhol*. The next day she ordered Pletnev to bring the *khokhol* to her … A.S. Pushkin said: "Aleksandra Osipovna, shelter the *khokhol* and scold him when he becomes depressed," and Vasilii Andreevich mumbled [to me]: "Do you see, brother, that Pletnev was right when he railed at you for your foolishness: you did not want to come and now you are happy that you came and will be grateful that we grabbed and brought you, the *khokhol*."[52]

At first glance, this account seems to demonstrate how Gogol "played up" to the domesticating colonial discourse. But Gogol's recollection in the passage above is double-framed; it is Smirnova's daughter who recorded her mother retelling Gogol's story of his entrée into high society. Although Smirnova's accounts have proved to be an accurate source of information about Gogol, her recollection of a conversation that happened thirty years earlier (the account was written in the 1850s) cannot be literally taken as the writer's own perception of himself.[53] Without discrediting the authenticity of Smirnova's recollections, I want to stress the ironic tone of Gogol's reported speech and the repetition of the word *khokhol* seven times within a short passage. These show how Gogol understood Smirnova's manipulation and mocked her use of the colonial stereotype. In neither his literary texts nor his essays and letters had he ever used the derogatory *khokhol* to designate himself or other Ukrainians. By repeating *khokhol* after Smirnova, Gogol mimicked colonial discourse and transformed it into mockery.

Memoirs of Gogol after the publication of *Evenings* are full of descriptions of his appearance and character in the spirit of colonial representation of Ukrainians. Russian memoirists repeatedly portrayed Gogol as sly, lazy, and stubborn. One of the first mentions of Gogol's ethnic appearance was made by Aleksandr Nikitenko, an ethnic Ukrainian who would later become one of Gogol's strictest censors. He wrote on 22 April 1832: "[I] was at a party at the house of Gogol-Ianovskii, the author of the tales of the beekeeper, red-haired Pan'ko, which are quite entertaining, especially, for a Ukrainian. He is a young man about twenty-six years old, of pleasant appearance. However, there is some *slyness* in his physiognomy which makes one *distrust* him."[54] Even in the late 1840s, Gogol's image was perceived in racial terms. Thus, Nikolai Berg, anticipating their first meeting in 1848, immediately recognized the *khokhol* in Gogol's "cunning Ukrainian" look and smile: "In Gogol's entire figure there was something unfree and clenched in a fist … His glances darted here and there were almost always glances from under the brow, slantwise, in passing, as if *cunningly* … One who is acquainted with *khokhols'* physiognomies a little bit could recognize the *khokhol* immediately. At once I grasped that this was Gogol [emphasis added]."[55]

Branded as a "sly Ukrainian" in the 1830s, even in his late years Gogol was often treated with a grain of contempt. Throughout his entire career, he strove to overcome the dubious status of an "outsider within." The halo of otherness surrounded Gogol throughout his life, especially in the second half of the 1840s when Russian society became increasingly chauvinistic.[56] Sergei Aksakov recorded a biased opinion of Gogol's personality circulating among the Slavophiles in the 1840s. It was largely based on his ethnic performance as Rudy Pan'ko:

After dinner Gogol had a long conversation with Grigorii Ivanovich [Kartashevskii] about art in general: about music, theatre, and the peculiarities of Ukrainian poetry; he was talking surprisingly well! Everything was so new, original, and true! And what was the result? Grigorii

> Ivanovich, this intelligent, educated and insightful man, a man of high
> moral standards, told me and Vera that Ukrainian people are shallow and
> that Gogol himself is the kind of *khokhol* he presents in his tales.[57]

Gogol's entrée into the field of Russian letters in the early 1830s demonstrates how both the colonizer and the colonized became involved in colonial patronage and the negotiation of power. The discourse of power produced a racialized representation of Gogol as the *other*, but it was expressed not exclusively in terms of coercion or constraint, but in broader cultural terms, among which the power to represent someone in a certain light was the most important one. Although Russian society imposed its stereotypical presumptions about Ukrainians as sly, lazy, and stubborn people on Gogol, he did not completely assume this objectification and did not make them a part of his own subjective reality. If taken as the dominant identity politics, such a narrow behavioural conceptualization of Gogol's identity would neglect the attitudinal component and result in underestimation of the complex relationship between his identity and self-identification. As a creative agent, Gogol made his identity into a performance and thereby influenced the discursive practices of the dominant culture.

In the 1830s, Russian culture was still bound to "the ideology embedded in the language, behavior, self-image, art, and ethics of Russia's cultural elite."[58] Despite the increased popularity of Slavophile ideology, which called for a return to national roots in language as well as in dress, Russian society still judged a person's appearance and manners in accordance with the code of the *honnête homme* of the previous cultural epoch. In keeping with the social and cultural codes of his rank, a Russian aristocrat was expected to display familiarity with the accepted code and to create a unique performance of identity, which included the visual fashioning of the body and appropriate social behaviour (movements, gestures, manners).[59]

When Gogol entered imperial society, he fully embraced the power to control his public appearance and oral performances. His letters and the memoirs of his friends documented how meticulous he was about his clothes and hairstyle and how rigidly he controlled the representation of his image in portraits. At a very young age Gogol realized the provocative potential of fashion and used it as a means of both adaptation and differentiation. The combination of dandiacal attire together with an ambiguous hairstyle, which appeared around 1832, revealed his desire to provoke the audience. Even before his migration to St Petersburg in 1828, the eighteen-year-old graduate from a provincial

Ukrainian town began to inquire about Petersburg fashion. In a letter of 1827 to his older school friend Herasym Vysots'kyi, who had moved to the capital, Gogol inquired about the latest fashion trends and entrusted him to order a tailcoat for him:

> May I ask you about a favour: could you order a tailcoat for me at the best tailor in St Petersburg? Find out how much an excellent custom-tailored fashionable tailcoat costs. I am dying to have my tailcoat done by the end of [October] or by November 1. Write to me, please, about fashionable fabrics suitable for vests and trousers. What colour of tailcoats is fashionable? I would like very much to have a blue one with metal buttons made; I have plenty of black tailcoats and I am bored with them.[60]

Upon his arrival in St Petersburg, Gogol began to smarten himself up with the necessary accoutrements of a Russian dandy: a suit, a hat, a pair of gloves, and a fur collar for his coat. Throughout his life, Gogol maintained an acute sense of style and used fashion to make statements, different at different stages of his career. Pavel Annenkov left an informative account of Gogol's dress during the writer's early years in St Petersburg. Gogol always aimed to impress society with his bizarre attire: "Usually, he put on a bright motley tie, fluffed up a tall curly quiff [of hair], cloaked himself in some white, extremely short and loose high-waisted frock coat with puffed sleeves, all of which made him look like a rooster."[61] Smirnova and Pletnev observed that even in the late 1840s, when Gogol underwent his spiritual crisis and became a religious devotee, he rid himself of many pleasures but not his fashionable clothing. In 1848, Pletnev wrote that Gogol's "foppish appearance bordering on daintiness" conflicted with his new image of a writer-prophet. While travelling abroad in the 1830s, Gogol constantly ordered new suits and vests. Later in his life, however, he confessed to Smirnova that his wardrobe included only the minimum of items (one suit, three ties and vests, and a change of underwear) "necessary to be clean."[62]

At first, Gogol merely emulated the dress code of Russian dandies, which had changed drastically since the beginning of the nineteenth century. If, in the eighteenth century, dress (official or civil) designated a certain social rank and prescribed a proper behaviour, in the 1830s, fashion, as well as everyday behaviour and public rituals, was becoming freer and more symbolic. Caught in a transition from the middle-class Ukrainian milieu to Petersburg high society, Gogol masked his lower background status by incorporating fashionable particulars into his modest attire. He only possessed one frock coat (most Russian gentlemen owned three)[63] and emphasized his belonging to the artistic caste by wearing a huge golden chain on his vividly coloured vests.

In Gogol's day, Russian fashion was becoming more democratic and idiosyncratic. Bright ties, vests, accessories – all these new fashionable details had appeared in Russia after the Napoleonic Wars, when Russian officers had become acquainted firsthand with new European fashions. The traditional court dress-coat (*mundir*) gradually gave way to the fashionable frock coat (*siurtuk*). Russian intellectuals used new ways of dressing to express their liberal political views.[64] A new aesthetics of theatricality was manifested in the proliferation of fops and dandies. With the new fashion trends, impoverished Ukrainian noblemen, like Gogol himself, received the opportunity to demonstrate their membership in one or another social group, without necessarily belonging to it (Figure 1). *Petits-maîtres* (fops) and *flâneurs* (saunterers) imposed new fashion codes on the rest of Russian society. In 1831, Gogol satirically depicted this tendency in his story "Nevsky Prospect":

> O Creator! What strange characters one meets on Nevsky Prospect! There is a host of such people as, when they meet you, unfailingly look at your shoes, and, when you pass by, turn to look at your coattails. To this day I fail to understand why this happens ... At this blessed time, from two to three in the afternoon, when Nevsky Prospect may be called a capital in motion, there takes place a major exhibition of the best products of humanity. One displays a foppish frock coat with the best of beavers, another a wonderful Greek nose, the third is the bearer of superb side-whiskers, the fourth of a pair of pretty eyes and an astonishing little hat, the fifth of a signet ring with a talisman on his smart pinkie, the sixth of a little foot in a charming bootie, the seventh of an astonishment-arousing necktie, the eighth an amazement-inspiring mustache ...[65]

Thus, imperial fashion became a commodity that circumscribed the self. It also showed that identity was something apart from one's self, something that must be displayed and fashioned. As early as 1830, Gogol began to realize the power of fashion. The motif of the totalizing power of dress in securing a social status first appears in his unfinished tale "A Terrible Boar" (1830). In this tale, the frock coat metonymically signifies imperial power that imbues fear and veneration in the locals. The story begins with the description of the uniform of a new teacher, Ivan Osipovich, who arrives from St Petersburg to work in the

Figure 1. Portrait of Gogol by Goriunov (1835)

Ukrainian countryside. The teacher's frock coat establishes an invisible presence of the faraway imperial authority:

> The frock coat in general (not to mention blue ones), be it made only not of a gloomy-coloured cloth, produces a stunning effect in villages: whenever it shows up, hats from the most sluggish heads fall into hands, and imposing faces, armed with black and gray mustaches, reverently bow to it from the waist. There were three frock coats in the village, including the sexton's *chlamys* [short cloak], but our fellow's frock coat outshone all the rest.[66]

In another tale, "Christmas Eve," the ritual of exchanging indigenous clothes for new imperial dress reveals the important ideological context. At the end of the eighteenth century, the former Cossack *starshyna* was subjected not only to political subjugation but also to the Russian nobility's dress code.[67] In the tale, this symbolic change of clothes is played out in the episode when the Cossacks, preparing to meet with the tsarina, order Vakula to change from his peasant-like dress into the appropriate court attire: "Put on a dress similar to that which we are wearing."[68] Once Vakula is dressed in court attire, he wants to show off his proficiency in the "literate language" ("gramotnyi iazyk"), i.e., Russian. At the same time, the Cossacks, who are also in court dress, intersperse their speech with Ukrainian words and phrases,[69] thereby making a political statement about their free spirit and demonstrating their defiance to imperial authority. This is clear from the reaction of their "teacher," Count Potemkin, when he remarks to himself during the Cossacks' meeting with the empress that they "speak not at all in the way he taught them."[70] That the Cossacks use Ukrainian language on purpose is also corroborated by Vakula. Listening to the Cossacks makes Vakula wonder why "this Cossack, who could speak such good, correct Russian, was talking to the tsarina in the most uncouth language, just like a peasant. 'The wily fox!' he thought to himself, 'I bet he has a special reason for doing that.'"[71]

In Gogol's works of mid-career, change of clothing could serve as an important historical action associated with switching allegiance and treason. In the historical novella *Taras Bulba* (1842), Taras's and Andrii's different behaviour after changing their Cossack attire for European dress indicates the instability of the connection between national identity and allegiance. Andrii betrays his faith and nation as he immerses himself in the material reality of Western civilization, associated with flesh, physical beauty, and lust. His conversion to Catholicism is paralleled by his shedding his modest Cossack dress for European-style knightly armour. A Jewish character, Iankel', expresses his delight at seeing Andrii in new attire to Taras in chapter 7: "His shoulder straps are golden, his sleeve cuffs are golden, his breastplate's golden, his hat's golden, his belt's golden – gold everywhere, all over! He sparkles with gold like the sun in spring, when all the little birdies are in the garden twittering and the grasses smell all nice. And the governor even gave him his best horse – worth at least two hundred gold ducats!" Taras Bulba is perplexed with Andrii's new dress and asks Iankel': "'But why would he be wearing foreign armour?' – 'Because it's better, that's why!'" Iankel' replies.[72] When it is Taras's turn to dress in foreign attire in order to ransom his eldest son, Ostap, from prison in Warszawa, he completely fails the identification test because of his firm Orthodox convictions and Cossack code of behaviour. Having had his hair and mustache dyed black and putting on noble dress and a *iermolka* ("he put on his crown a little black hat"), Taras wants to pass as a foreigner who has come to entertain himself by watching the Cossacks' execution. But when the Polish warden provokes him by saying that "the Cossacks are dogs, not human beings" and that "no one respects their faith," Taras reveals his inability to "pass" as someone else, quite opposite to the transformation process that Andrii has undergone earlier and to the mimicry of the Jewish Iankel', who needs to survive among Poles and Cossacks.[73]

In the 1830s, Gogol's self-fashioning generated uncertainty concerning his representation as a Russian dandy. This was manifested in two aspects of Gogol's self-representation – his ambivalent hairstyle and his provocative behaviour in St Petersburg salons. It was no mere chance that around 1832, the year of the publication of Book Two of *Evenings*, which marked Gogol as an entertaining, sly Ukrainian author, a curious detail appeared on his head – a tuft of hair elevated over his forehead, which Gogol's contemporaries unanimously called the *khokhol* (Figure 2). The literal meaning of *khokhol* is a long lock of hair left on top or on the front of an otherwise clean shaven or shortly cropped head – a hairstyle that was typically sported by Ukrainian Cossacks. Another meaning of the word appeared in the late eighteenth century and was applied by Russians to any inhabitant of Left-Bank Ukraine.[74] Nowadays, Russians use the word *khokhol* pejoratively to refer to any Ukrainian, pretty much in the same way as it was applied to Gogol in the 1830s–1840s. Although the term had lost most of its initial connotations by the turn of the twentieth century, for Russians it still denotes a disloyal Ukrainian who can easily betray the Russian-Ukrainian fraternal relationship.

This *khokhol* figured in descriptions of Gogol's appearance during the 1830s by Mikhail Longinov, Pavel Annenkov, and Sergei Aksakov. Longinov recalled a "khokholok" on the top of Gogol's head in 1832 when the writer was tutoring him.[75] Annenkov mentioned "the tall, curled, and whipped-up tuft of hair" on Gogol's forehead, making him look like a rooster.[76] Aksakov retrospectively recorded his impression after first meeting with Gogol in 1832, emphasizing the *khokhol* in his hairdo.[77] It was perceived as something exotic, deviating from what was defined as the "norm" in Russian society, a mark of Gogol's Ukrainian *otherness*. This is especially evident in Aksakov's memoir, in which *khokhol* is used both in its direct meaning (the hairdo) and metonymically as the derogatory ethnonym of a Ukrainian: "Gogol's appearance then was absolutely different and unattractive: a *khokhol* on his head, clean-cut temples, shaven mustache and chin, big and stiff collar – all imparted a completely different expression to his face. We saw something *khokhol*-like and cunning in it."[78] By making a verbal pun – using *khokhol* to designate both the Cossack hairstyle and the ethnic slur – Aksakov created a racial stereotype of Gogol as an untrustworthy *other*.

Figure 2. Portrait of Gogol by Venetsianov (1834)

So, by fashioning his *khokhol*, did or did not Gogol try to make a statement about his Ukrainian ethnicity? The scholar Richard Gregg believes that he did.[79] I believe that Gogol's hairdo in Venetsianov's portrait (Figure 2) looks quite dissimilar to the traditional haircut of Ukrainian Cossacks (see, for example, the portrait of Hetman Petro Kalnyshevs'kyi in Figure 3). In this portrait, Kalnyshevs'kyi, already an eighty-one-year-old man, has a long, white *chub* or *oseledetes'* (the Ukrainian terms for this peculiar Cossack hairstyle) on top of his clean-shaven head. Gogol's "quiff" was a foppish hairstyle among his Russian and Ukrainian contemporaries (see the portrait of the Russian poet Evgenii Baratynskii, made in the early 1830s, Figure 4), which looked quite different from the Cossack haircut. Therefore, Gogol's *khokhol* was, rather, a discursive construct revealing Russian society's fantasy of domesticating a "stubborn," "sly" Ukrainian (*khokhol*). Thanks to his ambiguous haircut, Gogol was expected to look and act according to his "eccentric" Ukrainian nature.

It is important that neither in the years preceding the publication of *Evenings* nor in the 1840s had Gogol sported such an ambiguous haircut. His classmates depicted the young Gogol of the 1820s with his hair plastered closely to his head,[80] while already in 1836 Vera Nashchokina recalled Gogol wearing a *skobka*, a long bob traditional for Russian peasants (which in the 1830s became popular among Slavophiles).[81] In 1842, Longinov, who ten years earlier had been impressed with Gogol's exotic *khokholok*,[82] hardly recognized Gogol, who now had a haircut "à la *muzhik*."[83] In the portraits of Gogol in the 1840s,

Figure 3. Portrait of Petro Kalnyshevs'kyi (1771) by an unknown artist

Figure 4. Portrait of Evgenii Baratynskii by Chevalier (early 1830s)

Figure 5. Portrait of Gogol by Moller (1840)

for instance, by Fyodor Moller (Figure 5), his appearance lacks any provocative detail.

He has a mustache and longer hair and is dressed in comfortable home clothing – a velvet dressing gown and a shirt without a tie – which indicated his free status as a man of letters. In the 1840s, Gogol's appearance and fashion resembled that of the Slavophiles, with whom the writer began to share ideas concerning a renewal of Russian national identity.[84] Thus, it was only in the early 1830s that Gogol had an ambiguous haircut that differentiated him from the Russian literary aristocrats.

Gogol's contemporaries were fascinated with his superb adaptability and social skills. He was fond of playing roles and manipulating his public image depending on his artistic and ideological goals, which was in tune with the theatricality of everyday behaviour of the Romantic age. The model of social behaviour that Russian high society expected from its members is exemplified in Chichikov's interaction with the landlords in *Dead Souls*. While preparing for the ball, he practises the facial expressions and social skills that he needs to demonstrate there.[85] Being constantly on the wing, Chichikov adapts his style of communication to each new landowner while negotiating purchase of the dead souls. The most representative case of him switching between his own and his interlocutor's speech manner is his verbal "battle" with Nozdrev in chapter 4. Nozdrev refuses to sell the souls and instead proposes to stake the dead-soul bargain on a game of cards. Once Chichikov sees the cards in Nozdrev's hands, he tries to distract Nozdrev with his usual verbal repartee. In the beginning of the scene, Chichikov's responses are twice as long as Nozdrev's, demonstrating his masterful art of persuasion. Once he realizes that Nozdrev can outplay him, he shortens his rejoinders and switches to gambler's jargon in order to withstand Nozdrev's frantic pressure.

Not only adaptability to the accepted societal norms and codes but also the ambivalence of Gogol's jokes and anecdotes characterized his oral performances in society.[86] He deliberately intensified his marginality by failing to master society "talk" and took part in social interaction by challenging it with inappropriate jokes. Gogol's contemporaries were shocked by the obscenity of his jokes, which they attributed to "the exclusive peculiarity of his Ukrainian mentality."[87] His repertoire consisted of both Ukrainian[88] and international[89] anecdotes that the writer creatively reworked every time to fit the occasion. Gogol's stories were considered to be "unique, but sometimes not entirely in good taste,"[90] "almost always quite obscene," and "never fit to print."[91] It should be noted, however, that spicy jokes were in fashion among salon attendees of the time, and Gogol obviously imitated older fellow poets, particularly Zhukovskii, in trespassing beyond the norms of "good taste." Gogol's oral performances differed from Zhukovskii's in terms of both repertoire and his inimitable manner of performing.[92] According to Kurganov, unlike Zhukovskii, who entertained his listeners with the same collection of stories and from whom they knew what to expect, Gogol always took his listeners by surprise and "employed a more subtle and calculated strategy than Zhukovskii" in his oral performances."[93] Gogol's risqué jokes were tolerated because he was accepted into the Russian beau monde as a Ukrainian jester, and as such was excused for jokes for which other society people could not have been. Compare, for example, the reaction of society to Odoevskii's and to Gogol's indecent jokes, as recorded by Vladimir Sollogub: "[Odoevskii] … told ladies the most indecent things in the most innocent way, completely sincerely and without any ulterior motive. In this sense, he was not at all like Gogol, who had the gift of narrating the most salacious jokes without provoking anger from his female listeners; whereas poor Odoevskii was angrily cut short, Gogol, meanwhile, always transgressed deliberately."[94]

Gogol purposely subverted the requirements of the *honnête homme* imposed upon him, no matter how idiosyncratic that norm would seem. In a sense, Gogol became a burlesque model of the *honnête homme* who strove to participate in polite society by at once imitating and ridiculing its codes. Gogol's bizarre hairstyle, non-conventional dress, and eccentric verbal behaviour made him stand out from among Russian aristocrats of various ideological orientations and shaped his public image as the *other*. "Almost the same, but not quite," Gogol took advantage of the ambivalence of his position to transform mimicry of the imperial centre into mockery and thereby undermined its control over his self-fashioning. Thus, the colonial mimicry allowed him to assert his ethnic and cultural difference and at the same time to subvert the colonial project of his "domestication."

Hybrid Language and Narrative Performance in *Evenings on a Farm near Dikan'ka*

When Gogol's first collection of short stories, *Vechera na khutore bliz Dikan'ki* (Evenings on a farm near Dikan'ka, 1831–2), was published, it "amazed" the Russian audience not only with its exotic Ukrainian folklore but also with the stories' idiosyncratic Russian language.[1] Major critics espied in Gogol's Ukrainian tales everything that Russian culture lacked at the time: the expression of nationality, authentic characters, vivid storytelling, bold imagination, and a taste of "local colour." But they rarely attempted to explain why there were so many Ukrainianisms in Gogol's Ukrainian tales. The answer may be found in the bilingual environment of Left-Bank Ukraine, in which Gogol developed his language proficiency. After the incorporation of the Hetmanate as the Little Russian Governorate into the Russian Empire, Ukrainian landowners became increasingly Russianized, but they continued to use Ukrainian in the private sphere, which naturally led to non-symmetrical diglossia in all strata of Ukrainian society. Landowners used Ukrainian as their speaking medium and the *prosta mova* (a hybrid mix of old Ukrainian, Russian, and Church Slavonic) as their formal language; students were educated in Latin and Greek but wrote their school plays in vernacular Ukrainian; peasants spoke vernacular Ukrainian but were trained to read and write in Church Slavonic at parochial schools. Functional diglossia was also typical of the Russian cultural situation in the early nineteenth century. The Russian literary elite commonly used French for correspondence and society talk. However, the bilingualism of native Russian writers was essentially different from that of their Ukrainian peers. The chief difference was in the value and prestige of the second language. The "additive" bilingualism of the Russian elite developed because both languages – Russian and French – were considered equally valued and useful. Russian polite society required all educated noblemen to speak both languages fluently, which resulted in their equal proficiency in both.[2] The Russian-Ukrainian bilingualism of the Ukrainian landlords, on the other hand, created an obstacle to their assimilation into Russian society. However, once the imperial administration was established in Left-Bank Ukraine, the offspring of former Cossack *starshyna* acquired government positions and rapidly became Russianized by necessity. For them, Russian was associated with the "high" language variety, which carried cultural and social capital. Thus, Russian gradually superseded Ukrainian in all social spheres.

Throughout his life, Gogol remained an active speaker of the Ukrainian language. Gogol's letters from his school years and records collected by his biographers testify that from 1818 until his death in 1852 he was constantly accompanied by Ukrainian-speaking servants: first by Simon, who worked for Gogol while he studied at the Poltava district school and the Nizhyn Lyceum, then by Yakym Nimchenko while living in St Petersburg in 1828–36, and, finally, by Semen Hryhor'iev in his later years. In their memoirs, Mikhail Shchepkin, Osyp Bodians'kyi, Pavel Annenkov, and Sergei Aksakov captured moments when Gogol fluently spoke Ukrainian with his servants. His written proficiency in Ukrainian can be corroborated by his 1837 letter to the well-known Polish poet of Ukrainian origin Jósef Bogdan Zaleski. Written almost ten years after leaving his native Ukraine, Gogol's letter demonstrates an excellent knowledge of Ukrainian, including the use of the idiomatic expressions:

Дуже, дуже було жалко що не застав пана земляка дома. Чував що на пана щось напало не то соняшниця не то завійниця (хай присниться їм *лисий дідько*) та тепер спасибі Богу пан буцімто кажуть зовсім здоров. Дай же Боже, щоб на диво на славу усій козацькій землі й давав би чернецького хліба всякій болезні і злидням. Хай і нас би не забував, писульки в Рим слав. Добре було як би і сам туда коли-небудь примандрував. Дуже, дуже близький земляк, а по серцю ще ближчий чим по землі. Микола Гоголь.

What a great, great pity that I did not find you, my fellow countryman, at home. I heard that you were attacked by some kind of illness, something like *sonyashnytsia* or *zaviinytsia* (let them both see a bald-headed devil in their dreams), but now, thank God, according to what I've heard, it looks as if you are already quite all right. I pray to God that you will be able to kick out all kinds of illness and misery, to the glory of the Cossack land. Do not forget us and send us some letters to Rome. It would be great if some day you might come there personally. Your very, very close fellow countryman, and even more close to you in my heart than by homeland alone. Mykola Hohol.[3]

Both of Gogol's parents operated in two languages, Russian and Ukrainian, throughout their lives. His father, Vasilii Afanas'evich Gogol, wrote comedies in Ukrainian and lyrical poems in Russian. In his correspondence, he constantly switched between the two languages. His texts, written in a mix of Russian and Ukrainian, abound with lexical, grammatical, and orthographic forms peculiar to Ukrainian. Even when translating Ukrainian words into Russian, Vasilii Gogol remained within the limits of the Ukrainian grammatical system. For example, his Russian explanations for the Ukrainian glosses "kuchma" as "shapka vsia **s** ovchiny sdelannaia" (a hat made out of sheepskin) and "knish" as "pirog **s** odnogo testa" (a pie made out of one dough) were both rendered with the preposition "s" (according to the Ukrainian grammar) instead of "iz" (as in Russian). Gogol's mother, Maria Ivanovna, also operated with two different language codes. She wrote letters in a pidgin, *surzhyk*, to her family members, and in normative Russian to members of Russian society. The transposition of Ukrainian grammar onto Russian affected her use of Russian in vocabulary ("kopitsa," "shynok," "vecherial," "karbovanets'," etc.); grammar ("s Luben," "za korovy," "v tetin'ky," "negodiat'sia dorobyty," etc.); and phonology (reproduced by means of the *iaryzhka*, e.g., "nikhto," "nesovetuvala," "probuvat'," "vzhe," "v Antoshky," "boliat'," "pishesh," etc.).[4] At the same time, Maria Ivanovna's letters to the Aksakovs were written in a more standardized Russian. Her clear understanding of language etiquette showcases the aspirations of the Ukrainian landowners to be assimilated into Russian society as equal educated nobles.

Gogol's own letters and early drafts of *Evenings* exhibit several types of hybrid formations resulting from Ukrainian phonological spelling patterns.[5] These ungrammatical forms served to reproduce the peculiarities of the Ukrainian manner and place of articulation of sounds.[6] Gogol's contemporaries noticed the absence of vowel reduction in unstressed position in the writer's speech, which is characteristic of Ukrainian pronunciation. Ivan Turgenev left an interesting record of Gogol's speech: "Gogol talked a lot, with animation, rhythmically rapping out each word ... He spoke on *o* [but] I did not notice other peculiarities of Little Russian pronunciation, unpleasant to the Russian ear."[7] Turgenev pointed to the major distinctive feature of Gogol's Ukrainian pronunciation – the absence of vowel reduction; its other "peculiarities" did not grate upon his ear as ethnic markers. Vera Nashchokina also discerned the lack of vowel reduction in Gogol's speech: "[Gogol] spoke [Russian] with a Little Russian accent, slightly emphasizing *o*."[8] It is also probable that Gogol pronounced the fricative [ɦ] (which is peculiar to Ukrainian) in Russian words where the plosive [g] was required. Although there is no documented evidence of Gogol's pronunciation of this phoneme, his spelling of words like "khalstukhi," "v ispukhe," "nekhoditsia" (instead of "gal-stuki," "v ispuge," "negoditsia") in his correspondence of the period and in the drafts of *Evenings* support this hypothesis.[9] Not only were Gogol's pronunciation and spelling in line with the norms of Ukrainian rather than Russian, but his syntax also violated basic rules of Russian grammar with the Ukrainian morphosyntax. The presence of idiomatic Ukrainian expressions and some inherently Ukrainian morphological structures (particularly, verbal aspect, coordination between verbs and the appropriate case of nouns, the use of active instead of passive forms of verbal adverbs, the use of reflexive personal pronouns instead of reflexive verbs with the suffix -sia, etc.) testifies that his language competence was formed in a Ukrainian-speaking environment. Ukrainian hybrid forms were still present in Gogol's writing as late as the 1840s despite his conscious effort to conform to Russian norms; this shows the enigmatic ways in which their first acquired language has a protracted effect on speakers during their entire life.

As a bilingual, Gogol was subject to a complex cognitive operation while mastering Russian.[10] As Andrei Belyi brilliantly formulated it, "Gogol concocted his language out of a motley mixture in which Russianisms, Ukrainianisms, and Polonicisms sometimes pass into the grammar, but are not validated by any grammar at all; the fate of such a striking motley is to become three quarters of the Russian literary language and even to transform that very language in which Gogol at times felt himself a foreigner."[11] As a result of the intervention of various heterogeneous elements in the major language, not only are its dominant values and meanings destabilized but the very way in which the language works is altered. Paraphrasing Deleuze and Guattari, we can say that Gogol's hybrid discourse was not an *entente cordiale* between two different languages but a "minority" practice within the dominant language. The tension occurred not between "major" Russian and "minor" Ukrainian, but between the normative use of Russian and what Gogol's hybrid language made of it. Gogol created his own variant of Russian that "truncated" its usage on the semantic, syntactic, and stylistic levels. Gogol's contribution to Russian literature was ultimately in destabilizing the norms of the literary language and appropriating it figuratively.[12]

Compared to his classmates – the playwright Kukol'nyk, the poet and translator Bazili, and the editor and professor of Russian

Prokopovych – Gogol displayed more cross-language features that pertain to bilingual speakers. His classmates recalled how Gogol persistently refused to improve his speech: "Gogol ... gave up for lost working on his conversational speech. He often used to say some words and the whole class burst out laughing. Once one of our teachers rebuked him about that and Gogol responded, 'How can you prove that I speak incorrectly?'"[13] During his school years, Gogol perceived his non-standard idiom as the marker of his uniqueness; his awkward Russian was a standing jest among his Nizhyn classmates.

Gogol's language practices present an interesting case of the reflexive awareness of an idiosyncratic hybrid discourse. If he and his classmates were equally exposed to the same language practices during their education and obtained a solid knowledge of standard Russian, how did it happen that only Gogol preserved a striking ignorance of its rules and continued to make grammatical errors even in his late texts? According to Pierre Bourdieu, all speakers of the same speech community are equally exposed to the same repetitive practices that shape their "habitus," or way of being in the world.[14] However, Bourdieu does not take into account that even within the same speech community, distinctions can be made among varieties of the language associated with different social settings. The very mechanism by which habitus operates, according to Bourdieu, does not allow individuals to do away with the ideological associations of their own ingrained ways of speaking, since these associations result from a slow process of being socialized into normative and acceptable language use. In fact, proficiency achieved during early years in the family *can* influence the structuring of school experience and produce an effect on further language development. Thus, reflexive awareness allows for potentially rich linguistic variation as a dimension of social practice. Considered in this light, Gogol's idiosyncratic Russian can be explained by the fact that during his pre-school years he was equally exposed to both Russian and Ukrainian languages more deeply and more systematically than his other classmates and that both languages shaped his language consciousness and were always simultaneously activated in his language practice. Gogol's reflexive awareness of his hybrid language can thus problematize Bourdieu's theory.[15] Judith Butler has essentially corrected Bourdieu's theory of language practice by foregrounding performativity and its power to resist and challenge social norms. In *Excitable Speech*, she has argued that "the speech act, as a rite of institution, is one whose contexts are never fully determined in advance, and that the possibility for the speech act to take on a non-ordinary meaning, to function in contexts where it has not belonged, is precisely the political promise of the performative."[16] Thus, the "non-ordinary" meaning is a potential of speech performance that can break with the social context in which it occurs. It could be said that the regional discourse developed by Gogol in his early tales was a performative act of his hybrid identity. Through hybridized language, Gogol could express a sense of belonging to his local Ukrainian language and culture and could also create a mid-language that helped him achieve his transition into a Russian writer.

In the early 1830s, Gogol inhabited the language of his new Petersburg territory as a foreigner. He entered Russian literary culture as one who was challenged to overcome the difference between his own Ukrainian variant of Russian and the Russian of the Petersburg elite. As Andrei Siniavskii wittily noted, Gogol could not even imitate contemporary writers, especially Pushkin, because he was "too provincial and burdened with a foreign, Little Russian language element."[17] Gogol felt himself a foreigner in Russian and expressed his frustration in a letter to his mother (24 July 1829) in which he confessed: "If my work is ever to be published, it will be in a *foreign language*; and I need to be even more precise in order that I not distort the [characteristic] noun[s] [*nomen substantivum*] of the nation with incorrect naming."[18] This "foreignness" of the Russian language has been interpreted by Gogol scholars as one of his numerous mystifications. Since the entire letter was written in Russian, the "foreign language" was allegedly used to obfuscate his future creative plans. However, another of Gogol's "confessions" about his mother tongue can confirm this early statement about Russian as a foreign language. In 1839, on his way from Rome to Vienna, Gogol stopped in Trieste, a seaport in the northeastern part of Italy inhabited by Slovene immigrants. As Gogol describes the Slovenian language to his mother (in his letter of 26 September 1839), he emphasizes that it sounds like Russian but is even closer to Ukrainian. What is more important, he identifies Ukrainian as "our" language: "Trieste is an active commercial town, half of which is inhabited by Italians, another half – by Slavs who *almost* speak in Russian – in a language very close to *our* Ukrainian."[19]

The defamiliarizing effect that the imperial language produced on the colonial Ukrainian subject, which Gogol himself had experienced upon his arrival in St Petersburg, is playfully presented in one of the tales from *Evenings*, "Christmas Eve." The protagonist, blacksmith Vakula, is preparing to join the Zaporozhian Cossacks in their meeting with Empress Catherine II. Trying to show off their proficiency in

Russian, Vakula and the Cossack corrupt it to the extent that it becomes pidginized:

"Что ж, земляк," – сказал приосанясь запорожец и желая показать, что он может говорить и по-русски. "*Што, балшой город?*"

Кузнец и себе не хотел осрамиться и показаться новичком, притом же, как имели случай видеть выше сего, он знал и сам грамотный язык.

"*Гоберния* знатная!" отвечал он равнодушно: «нечего сказать, *домы балшущие*, картины висят *скрозь* важные. Многие *домы* исписаны буквами из сусального золота до чрезвычайности. Нечего сказать, чудная пропорция!" [emphasis added]

"Now then, fellow-countryman," said the Zaporozhian [Cossack], drawing himself up, hoping to show off his knowledge of Russian, "*Bih city, izn't it?*"

The blacksmith also did not want to shame himself and show himself a complete greenhorn, and anyway, as we have already had occasion to see, he too knew the educated language.

"It's a splendid *provance!*" he replied in a nonchalant manner. "There's no denying it: the homes are *mity* big, you see some decent pictures hanging right through 'em. Many homes are extremely *decerated* with letters of gold leaf. No gainsaying it; the proportions is marvellous!"[20]

In Vakula's distorted Russian, Gogol mocks Ukrainians' attempts to use Russian as a means of self-affirmation as new imperial elite. He "defamiliarizes" Russian and makes it sound as odd and amusing to Ukrainians as Ukrainian sounds to many Russians. The above episode figures the partial presence of the colonized's tongue within the dominant language. Thus, the hybrid use of Russian sheds light onto Gogol's own statement about his "foreignness," which was both the reality of a bilingual speaker and a mode of writing in a colonial situation. Vakula's and, by extension, Gogol's Ukrainian-inflected Russian demonstrates that language is not only a means of communication but also a channel through which social identity comes to life. Social actors, especially marginalized and subjugated ones, do not necessarily consent to become native speakers of the imperial language; sometimes their struggle to master the dominant language impedes learning literacy in general. From this perspective, colonial speakers of their own and of imperial languages face not only affective and cognitive challenges in mastering both languages equally, but also ideological dilemmas of allegiance, competence, and authenticity.[21] Thus, oral and literary language practices are often used by hybrid subjects like Gogol as strategies of resistance, self-assertion, and divergence.

Hybrid Forms in Gogol's Texts

The question of which grammatical mistakes were generated by an unconscious process of language mixing and which arose from Gogol's deliberate hybridization is irrelevant in postcolonial studies of basilectalization. Gogol's hybrid form of Russian was developed out of the close contact between a Ukrainian non-standard variety of Russian and vernacular Ukrainian, which was not codified yet in the early nineteenth century. The process of basilectalization analysed by sociolinguists in other non-European varieties of creole and pidgin can be also applied to Gogol's hybrid language, which acquired a *basilect*, different from the *acrolect* – the educated variety of the lexifier.[22]

The first edition of Gogol's *Evenings* (1831–2) exhibits a variety of lexical and morphological loans from Ukrainian. In the first group of hybrid elements, Ukrainian words are interspersed in the Russian-language text without translation in the footnotes or in Pan'ko's Ukrainian-Russian "Lexicon" that accompanied the edition. These are predominantly Ukrainian verbs and adverbs that are absent in Russian (I provide the standard Ukrainian spelling and closest Russian equivalents in parentheses):

1 Verbs:
    "спознаться с" (to get along) (Ukrainian "спізнатися с," Russian "сойтись с"); "захолонуло" (to be paralysed from fear) (Ukrainian "захолонуло," Russian "похолодело");
    "смерзнуть" (to get cold) (Ukrainian "змерзнути," Russian "замерзнуть");
    "скидать" (to take off) (Ukrainian "скидати," Russian "снимать");
    "сбираться" (to get together) (Ukrainian "збиратися," Russian "собираться");
    "накласть" (to put) (Ukrainian "накласти," Russian "наложить").
    Verbs with the cumulative-distributive prefix по-: "понапугали," "поприставали," "пороняли," "поразобрало," "повлезали," etc., which in Russian belong to the low register but in Ukrainian to the neutral.

2 Adverbs and adverbial prepositions:
    "наперед" (Ukrainian "наперед," Russian "в начале");
    "нанизу" (Ukrainian "нанизу," Russian "внизу");
    "гуртом" (Ukrainian "гуртом," Russian "вместе");
    "неначе" (Ukrainian "неначе," Russian "как будто");
    "по-за" (Ukrainian "по-за," Russian "за").

Table 1. Examples of calquing from Ukrainian in Gogol's Ukrainian tales

Evenings	Ukrainian	Russian
"темно, хоть в глаза выстрели" (it is pitch-dark)	темно, хоч в око стрель	темно, хоть глаз выколи
"запорожец … ничего не работал" (The Zaporozhets was not doing anything)	запорожець … ничого не робив	запорожец … ничего не делал
"хоронить[a] концы [в воду]" (and no one is the wiser)	ховати кінці [у воду]	прятать концы [в воду]
"тут не можно пропустить одного случая" (one should not omit one occurrence)	тут не можна пропустити одного випадку	тут нельзя пропустить одного случая
"тетушка … имела лет около пятидесяти" (the auntie was about fifty years old)	тітонька мала років майже п'ятдесят	тетушке … было лет около пятидесяти
"озираясь на стороны" (looking around once in a while)	озираючись на сторони	озираясь по сторонам
"того ж году" (the same year)	того ж року	в том же году
"спичку тебе в язык" (thorn in your tongue, idiomatically meaning "shut your mouth")	"шпичку тобі в язик" (thorn in your tongue, idiomatically meaning "shut your mouth")	"спичку в глаз" (thorn in your eye, idiomatically meaning "to swindle someone")

[a] *Khoronit'* in Russian has only one meaning, "to bury," whereas in Ukrainian the equivalent *khovaty* has two meanings – "to bury" and "to hide." In this idiom, Gogol used *khoronit'* in the meaning of Ukrainian *khovaty*, i.e., "to hide."

Calquing from Ukrainian also occurred as one-to-one morphemic substitution – the result of the transposition of Ukrainian grammar onto Russian. This phenomenon can be explained by the fact that the two related languages often use the same part of speech but differ in the way they put them together in a sentence. In Table 1, one can see examples of Gogol's mixing of the Ukrainian and Russian language forms.

The transposition of Ukrainian grammar onto Russian morphology generated various hybrid forms and mistakes in the following categories:

a   Case or/and ending: "о полночи" (Ukrainian "**о** північі," Russian "**в** полночь"), "гостьми" (Ukrainian "гістьми," Russian "гост**ями**"), "в церкве" (as declined from Ukrainian "церква"), "Вечер накануне Ивана Купала" (Ukrainian "Вечір напередодні Івана Купала," Russian "Вечер накануне Ивана Купал**ы**"),

"до царицы" (Ukrainian "**до** цариці," Russian "**к** царице"),
"моя доню" (Ukrainian "моя дон**ю**," Russian "моя доч**ка**"),
"давай магарычу" (Ukrainian "давай магарычу," Russian
"давай магарыч"), "с радости побежала" (Ukrainian "з радості
побігла," Russian "от радости побежала")

b Gender: "обеим пленникам" (Ukrainian "обом полоненним,"
   Russian "обоим пленникам"), "под обеими глазами" (Ukrainian
   "під обома очима," Russian "под обоими глазами")

c Verbal forms: "слышило" (Ukrainian "чуло," Russian "слышало"),
   "исповедается" (Ukrainian "сповідається," Russian "исповедуется"),
   "брезгает" (Ukrainian "гидує," Russian "брезгует")

d Reflexivity: "вареник выплеснул из миски, шлепнул в сметану"
   (Ukrainian "вареник виплеснув з миски, шубавснув в сметану,"
   Russian "вареник выплеснулся из миски, шлепнулся в
   сметану"); "спокой себя" (Ukrainian "заспокой себе," Russian
   "успокойся"); "зашелохнет" (Ukrainian "зашелохне," Russian
   "пошевелится")

Most of the hybrid elements are consistent throughout the speech of
Gogol's Ukrainian folk storytellers and serve to characterize them
as semi-literate provincial residents. The fictitious editor-narrator
Pan'ko manifests his playful attitude to Russian grammar in the opening of the Preface to Book One, in which he warns his readers that
he is not very familiar with reading and writing ("я грамоту … кое-
как знаю"). Here, Gogol cleverly manipulates the Russian stereotype
about uncivilized, uneducated Ukrainians through the misspelling
of words and orthographical mistakes.[23] It is noteworthy that Gogol
wrote Pan'ko's Preface to Book Two without any grammatical mistakes. In the Preface to Book One, most of the verbs with the negative
particle "не" are written together, breaking the grammatical rules of
normative Russian of the time ("невидал," "неплачь," "неизвольте,"
"неносил"); furthermore,

1 adverbs, adjectives, and nouns are also written together with the
   negative particle "не" and "ни" ("неслишком," "нислова");
2 or, vice versa, adjectives are separated from the particle "не" when
   they should be written as one word ("сладость не описанная");
3 the spelling of adverbs does not conform with the rules of Russian
   grammar: some, such as "вовсе," are written separately (as "во
   все"), thereby becoming other parts of speech (a preposition and a
   noun), while others are hyphenated: "во-свояси," "на-бекрень,"
   "на-стороже."

Other misspelled words reflect the phonemic nature of Pan'ko's regional language ("слышило" instead of "слышало"; "раскащик" instead of "разсказчик"; "имянно" instead of "именно"; "к **щ**астью" instead of "к **сч**астию"; "на **щ**от этаго" instead of "на **сч**ет этого," etc.).[24] In addition, in Pan'ko's text half of the verbs in the second person singular present tense end in 'ъ' (e.g., "расскажешъ," "упросишъ"), according to the Ukrainian spelling, instead of 'ь' ("расскажешь," "упросишь"), as in Russian orthography. Evidently, Pan'ko's preference for sound over letter accounts for his misspelling of Russian words. Another strategy of creating hybrid discourse is to provide Russian glosses for Ukrainian words and idioms unfamiliar to the metropolitan audience, and Pan'ko accompanies his prefaces to Books One and Two with glossaries of Ukrainian words (about 130 entries). This demonstrates not only that the text itself activates the process of language variation, but also that its discourse is directed toward the *other* – a metropolitan Russian reader.

The hybridization of the speech of the two other major narrators, Makar Nazarovich, the narrator of "Sorochintsy Fair" and "A Night in May," and Foma Grigorievich, the narrator of "St John's Eve," "The Lost Dispatch," and "The Bewitched Place," deserves special discussion. Makar Nazarovich, a gentleman ("panich") from the town of Gadiach, represents a Russified Ukrainian, someone who, like the writer himself, studied the grammar and literary conventions of Russian Romanticism, whereas Foma Grigorievich, a Dikan'ka sexton, is an authentic Ukrainian, whose knowledge of folklore is deeply rooted in the local tradition. The competition between these two narrators for narrative and ideological authority is evident in their different use of Ukrainian.

Foma Grigorievich's speech is the most hybridized among the narrators in *Evenings*. As an oral folk storyteller, he incorporates various Ukrainian words and idiomatic expressions without translating them into Russian because he assumes that his audience belongs to the same Ukrainian community as himself. Instead, Pan'ko serves as mediator between the Ukrainian narrator Foma Grigorievich and the Russian audience, providing translations of peculiar Ukrainian expressions in footnotes. In the examples below, one can see that Pan'ko's Russian translations are quite literal. They not only create a comic effect, but also neutralize the original connotation of the expressions in Ukrainian.

1   Да, расскажу я вам, как ведьмы играли с покойным дедом в *дурня** (I'll tell you about the time the witches played Jackass* with my old grandfather) [emphasis in original].
    **То есть в дурачки* (That is, Fools).[25]

2 *Люлька-то у меня есть, да того, чем бы зажечь ее, чорт-ма** (I've got myself a pipe, but damn-all* to light it with) [emphasis in original].
    **Не имеется* (Nothing).[26]
3 *Дывысь, дывысь, маты, мов дурна, скаче.** (Look, look, Mama is jumping about like a madwoman!*) [emphasis in original].
    **Смотри! Смотри! мать, как сумасшедшая, скачет!* (Look, look, Mama is jumping about like a loony!)[27]

Ukrainian words and expressions penetrate Foma Grigorievich's discourse during code-mixing. They are usually italicized in his text, as in this passage from "St John's Eve":

"Плюйте ж на голову тому, кто это напечатал! *бреше, сучий москаль.* Так *ли* я говорил? *Що то вже, як у кого чорт-ма клепки в голові!* Слушайте, я вам расскажу ее сейчас."

   (Spit on the head of the man who printed it! *He tells lies, a damned Russian. Are these really my words? He hasn't a scrap of wit in his head!* Listen and I'll tell you the real story now.)[28]

The switching from one language to another within a paragraph is used to differentiate between the audience that shares Foma Grigorievich's idiolect and the audience that does not.

In sharp contrast to Pan'ko and Foma Grigorievich stands the gentleman narrator Makar Nazarovich with his mediated depiction of Ukrainian culture. In his use of language, he remains within the cultural codes of the imperial centre. Makar Nazarovich's arsenal of Ukrainian elements is limited to the use of Russian-Ukrainian doublets ("кружка" – "кухоль" (mug), "ад" – "пекло" (hell), "сорванец" – "шибеник" (scamp), "жена" – "жинка" (wife), "девушка" – "дивчина" (girl), "спешить" – "поспешать" (to hurry), "узнать" – "познать" (to know), "любимый" – "любый" (beloved). Because the original Ukrainian word appears in close proximity to its Russian equivalent, the use of Ukrainian becomes redundant. In the examples below, Russian translations that accompany Ukrainian words present functionally undifferentiated lexical items and thereby erase the hierarchy between the original and its translation. The Ukrainian words retain their material texture, but once they enter the single, homogeneous space of the Russian language, they lose their essence.

Другой цыган, ворча про себя, поднялся на ноги, два раза осветил себя искрами, будто молниями, раздул губами трут и, с **каганцом** в руках, обыкновенною малороссийскою **светильнею**, состоящею из разбитого черепка, налитого бараньим жиром, отправился, освещая дорогу [emphasis added]

(The other gypsy, grumbling away to himself, rose to his feet, struck two bright showers of sparks, pursed his lips to blow on the tinder, and brandishing a *kaganets*, the usual form of illumination in Little Russia, consisting of a potsherd filled with melted mutton fat, set off on his way)[29]

В **мирской сходке**, или **громаде**, несмотря на то что власть его ограничена несколькими голосами, голова всегда берет верх и почти по своей воле высылает, кого ему угодно, ровнять и гладить дорогу или копать рвы [emphasis added]

(At the village council, or *gromada*, where his power is limited to a couple of votes, the headman somehow always gets the upper hand and sends out whomever he wants to do jobs like levelling roads or digging ditches)[30]

In their choice of Russian and Ukrainian, Gogol's major narrators – Pan'ko, Foma Grigorievich, and Makar Nazarovich – differ in one important respect: while Pan'ko modifies the grammatical norms of Russian as if they were processed through the consciousness of a non-native speaker of Russian, Foma Grigorievich as a Ukrainian speaker corrupts Russian with peculiar Ukrainian locutions, and Makar Nazarovich does not violate Russian grammar at all; when he uses Ukrainian in the songs performed by the characters in "A Night in May," he does this for the sake of local colour. Overall, the untranslated Ukrainian words, phrases, and quotes in each discourse create a metonymic gap between the metropolitan Russian audience and the Ukrainian storytellers.

Narrative Performances in *Evenings*

Gogol's hybrid language, fully realized in *Evenings*, also necessitated a diversification of narrative voices. In Gogol scholarship, the variety of narrators in the tales is often reduced to the clash between the two major ones – a Russified urban gentleman and a Ukrainian villager. Scholars sometimes use this opposition between narrators to characterize Gogol's dual national identification.[31] Thus, Koropeckyj and Romanchuk have identified Gogol's "Russianness" with Makar Nazarovich's fancy language, while assigning "Ukrainianness" to Foma Grigorievich's knowledge of local traditions and linguistic codes.[32] The scholars credit "the appearance of a retrospective first-person narrator," i.e., Makar Nazarovich, and "the elegiac register" in the opening passage of "Sorochintsy Fair" to "Gogol's ritual Russianizing."[33] One should not ignore, however, that Makar Nazarovich also demonstrates a superb knowledge of Ukrainian literary and folk traditions, which is evident in his use of the Ukrainian epigraphs and in rendering the folk songs performed by the characters in "A Night in May."[34] Edyta Bojanowska has also analysed the competition between the Russified narrator Makar Nazarovich and the local Ukrainian Foma Grigoriev-ich as concomitant with Gogol's own oscillation between two modes of his identity. At the same time, she emphasized that "the actual author [Gogol] has more in common with Makar Nazarovich than with any other person in the stories. Like Makar, he is a Russified nobleman from the Poltava region."[35] However, in my view, reducing the story's narra-tive structure to the "absolute disjunction between Ukrainian and Rus-sian worlds"[36] cannot explain the polyphonic nature of Gogol's narra-tive and the hybrid nature of his identity. Certainly, the clash between the two narrators in Book One does denote a certain tension between the Russian and Ukrainian sides of Gogol's identity, but the concepts of "competition" and "national contrast" between the two narrators can-not fully account for the play of national affiliation in the book. The tales are authored not by the two narrators but by several different ones. Book One features Makar Nazarovich and Foma Grigorievich as the literary narrator and the oral storyteller. In Book Two, there are two identifiable authors or/and narrators, the familiar Foma Grigorievich and a new one, Stepan Ivanovich Kurochka, the author and narrator of "Ivan Fedorovich Shpon'ka and His Auntie," as well as the two anony-mous authors of "Christmas Eve" and "The Terrible Revenge" and a blind bandura player who is an oral narrator of part of "The Terrible Revenge." Therefore, the opposition between Russified and Ukrainian narrators is only the surface of a more complex problem of the narra-tive authority in *Evenings*, which appears more unstable and dynamic.

The construction of national identity in a narrative text cannot be limited to the representation of identity through fictional characters and narrators. As a form of imaginative identification expressed in a text through symbols and discourses, national identity in a narrative text builds upon individual and collective fantasies of the past. In my approach to Gogol's narrative and national performance, I stress the contextual nature of the storytelling in *Evenings*, which occurs on mul-tiple levels and communicates different messages to the imperial Rus-sian and colonial Ukrainian audiences. Only by appealing simultane-ously to both communities could Gogol unify them for the duration of the reading act and create what Homi Bhabha has called "a form of living the locality of culture." This idea of the locality of culture is more complex than that of "nation," as it is "more hybrid in the articulation of cultural differences and identifications than can be represented in any hierarchical binary structuring of social antagonism."[37]

The world of Dikan'ka pulsates with different sounds and discourses; the authoritative word in local Dikan'ka culture is collective, produced by the crowd (as in the tale "Sorochintsy Fair," where the noise of a fair reveals the emergence of the collective body) or passed from the older to the younger generations (e.g., from a grandfather to his grandsons, as in Foma Grigorievich's tales). The fact that some stories are presented as orally performed narratives and others as written texts, however, does not reduce the opposition between oral and written discourses to the mode of their production.[38] Each of the stories in *Evenings* has its own individual author, as in the written tradition, yet only some of them (like those told by Foma Grigorievich, i.e., "The Lost Dispatch," "St John's Eve," and "The Bewitched Place") resonate with orality and transmit the collective memory of the past. Therefore, it is not so much the primacy of the oral word over the written but rather the narrators' proximity to the national past and their embeddedness in the local community that establishes their narrative authority.

In order to challenge a hierarchical view of Gogol's narrators it is necessary to examine the multilayered structure of *Evenings* through its series of narrative performances. This approach is informed by the application of speech act theory to the study of narrative, as developed in the works of such scholars as Judith Butler, Barbara Smith, and Terry Threadgold. The concept of performativity originates in John Austin's *How to Do Things with Words* (1976). Austin viewed utterances not in terms of their meaning (words do not "constate" things) but in terms of their effect (words "do things") – either those intended by the speaker or those perceived by the listener. Narratives also can be viewed as performative speech acts, since "[t]hey not only connote certain kinds of meanings ... but also they perform identities and rehearse, enact and change social realities and norms."[39] In the 1980s, Barbara Smith applied Austin's analysis of performative utterances to the study of narratives.[40] In her essay "Narrative Versions, Narrative Theories" (1980), she proposed shifting the focus from narrative as a structure to narrative as a performative utterance which is not confined to specific "referents" or "signifieds." According to Smith, it would be more correct to describe individual narratives "not as sets of surface-discourse-signifiers that represent ... sets of underlying-story-signifieds, but as the verbal acts of particular narrators performed in response to ... sets of multiple interacting conditions."[41] These conditions are 1) an awareness of contextuality (cultural, social, and the strictly "physical" settings in which the tales are told); 2) the dynamic relationship between the narrative structure and the meaning; and 3) responsiveness to the factors that constitute a particular narrative.[42] If traditional narratology focuses on the study of narrative structure as a set of relationships internal to a context-free text,[43] Smith's approach stresses the contextuality within texts, as distinct from the textuality of texts and the contextuality around texts. Stories as narrative performances are not only framed by their context, but themselves construct a wider social and cultural context. The emphasis on the performative function of storytelling may help us avoid the binary oppositions of Gogol's narrators in which a narrator is interpreted in terms of his counterpart. Moreover, it can bring back to the discussion the presence of actual authors and readers, which from the point of view of contemporary narratology might seem outdated, but from the point of view of Gogol's own understanding of narrative art is essential, as it takes into account his desire to communicate appropriately with his audience.[44]

Narrative performances happen on several levels in *Evenings*: extra-textual (in the genre of "evenings"); metanarrative (in Pan'ko's prefaces, introductions, and footnote comments on the stories); and intratextual (in the acts of storytelling or dramatic presentation). "Evenings," i.e., stories which are told at evening gatherings, are based on a "simple interchange of storytellers" whose stories are "framed by the introduction and afterword ... justifying the very occasion of their narration."[45] This genre was the most prolific in Russian and Ukrainian literature of the early nineteenth century[46] because it could connect the local and metropolitan communities through the medium of oral storytelling. The local Dikan'ka community that gathers together at Pan'ko's house can share its knowledge about the past and cultural traditions with metropolitan readers who can only appreciate the entertaining side of Ukrainian folklore. Gogol's narrative exhibits many features of oral performances: the *skaz* storytelling, the narrators' playful remarks and requests to the audience, comments on the manner of performance (e.g., the kind of voice and dialects used by the storytellers). According to Koropeckyj and Romanchuk, the oral mode of narration in *Evenings* "is situated ... somewhere between performance and lecture."[47] The scholars attribute this to the use of a *skaz* narrative that "not only inscribes the transition from an 'oral' culture, the object of an ethnographic gaze, to a 'literate' one, structured by the market," but also "makes the reader into the implicit or complicit subject of the prose, (retrospectively) constructing the reader as the 'proper' audience."[48] This synergy between place and time of narration creates a community of performers and listeners. The events take place either in Dikan'ka or in the villages and towns located in close proximity. The chronotope of the "evening" designates both the time of the events in the story and the time of telling "on the eve" ("nakanune") of holidays (St John's Eve or Christmas Eve), when demonic forces become active and disturb the human world.[49]

Pan'ko's role in Gogol's dual-voiced narrative is to single out the local listeners who have knowledge of the Ukrainian past from educated metropolitan readers. Quite cunningly, in his Preface to Book One he invites his implied Petersburg readers to visit Dikan'ka but forgets to provide any directions.[50] In the Preface to Book Two, he enumerates his local Dikan'ka listeners, whom he calls "my fellow-villagers" ("zemliaki moi"): Foma Grigorievich, Stepan Ivanovich Kurochka, Zakhar Kirillovich Chukhopupenko, Taras Ivanovich Smachnen'kii, Kharlampii Kirilovich Khlosta, and Osip (whose last name Pan'ko forgets, owing to his old age), which reinforces the differentiation between his local listeners and the distant metropolitan audience. The Russian audience appreciates the tales within the framework of an exotic "singing and dancing tribe," whereas the local Ukrainian community can apprehend an encoded message about their national past beneath the seeming "cheerfulness" of the plots.

The "Russified" narrator Makar Nazarovich depicts this "singing and dancing" Ukraine as something familiar and pleasing to the metropolitan audience. Romanchuk and Koropeckyj suggest that, "like the character of Mr. Interlocutor in the minstrel show, in blackface but dressed in formal tails and without a trace of black dialect … [he] acts as something of a master of ceremonies who quite literally brackets the show with his own introduction … and epilogue."[51] In fact, it is the variegated narrative and discursive components of "Sorochintsy Fair" that require such a master of ceremonies. The plot of the story itself includes elements of both Russian literary and Ukrainian folk and popular sources: a sub-plot reminiscent of popular eighteenth-century Ukrainian tales; theatrical performances; folk trickery; a satiric portrayal of naïve superstitions; and an embedded tale about supernatural forces. Although Makar Nazarovich's participation as a narrator is minimal in the storytelling, his role in orchestrating the scenes is crucial. Both stories that Makar Nazarovich narrates are divided into short chapters,[52] like acts in a play, and are framed by an introductory and/or concluding note by the omniscient narrator.[53] Like a stage director, Makar Nazarovich observes and provides remarks apropos of the scenes and actions of the characters without being involved in the events. His almost perfect literary discourse suggests a degree of formal education and familiarity with the literary conventions of the time. "Sorochintsy Fair" opens with a conventional lyrical digression about the beauty of Ukrainian nature and ends with the narrator's intimate reflections upon the cruelty and transience of time. Such a visual description is unusual for the folk storytelling tradition but is familiar to the educated Petersburg reading public educated on Karamzin's sentimentalist prose fiction. Makar Nazarovich's metatextual commentary on the plot development and his appeals to readers' experience reveal the power of the narrating subject. Remaining detached from the audience, he figures as a monologic author, because even when he asks the audience, "Do you know what a Ukrainian night is like? Oh no, you do not know!"[54] the question is rhetorical, and he answers it himself.

Unlike Makar Nazarovich's literary narration, Foma Grigorievich's storytelling is a unique act of communication with the audience, which encourages a dialogic response and presupposes knowledge of the Ukrainian past. Interaction with the audience is the driving force of his storytelling. At the onset of "The Lost Dispatch," Foma Grigorievich tries to please his audience with another "old true story." His listeners' active aesthetic response inspires his storytelling:

> So, you want me to tell you some more about my old grandfather? By all means, why not amuse you with another of his little stories? Ah, yes, the good old days! What exuberance fills the heart when you hear about the things that went on long, long ago, longer than any of us can remember! ... No, the worst ones are the womenfolk, the young women and girls; the moment they catch sight of you it's all: "Foma Grigorievich! Foma Grigorievich! Do tell us one of your scary stories about the old days! Go on! Tell us, please! ..." and on, and on, and on ... Not that I mind telling them, of course, but if only you could see them later on in their beds! I know for a fact that every one of them will be atremble under her blankets, just as if she's in a fever, and ready at the drop of a pin to hide her head in her sheepskin coat. All it needs is for a rat to scratch the cooking pot, or for her to stumble on the poker – and Lord help us! She's scared clean out of her wits. The next day you'd think nothing had happened, they're at it again: tell us a scary story, go on, do.[55]

Unlike Pan'ko, who constantly seeks to please his "dear readers," Foma Grigorievich tries to argue with the audience, which he does through a series of questions. Foma Grigorievich anticipates his listeners' questions ("You might ask why they lived like that?")[56] and reproaches them for being inattentive ("Nobody's forcing you to listen; it was you who begged me to tell the story. So, you'd better listen properly!").[57] He also responds to their scepticism about plot twists ("Now don't tell me people get such ideas into their heads for no reason!");[58] anticipates their loss of attention ("Wait a second, that wasn't the end of the matter");[59] puts his listeners to shame for laughing at inappropriate moments ("You may laugh, but let me tell you it was no laughing matter for our fore-fathers");[60] and builds on shared life experiences ("Well, when a young man and a pretty girl live near one another ... you don't need me to tell you what that leads to").[61] Foma Grigorievich's superb skills of story-telling demonstrate that it is not a simple act of revealing the "truth," but a performative act aimed at producing an effect on the audience.

Through the genre of his tales, *byl'* (a "memorate," to use the folklor-istic term), Foma Grigorievich is also cast as a communal storyteller. A *byl'* presents a popular folk belief in demonology (goblins, mermaids, ghosts, charmed treasures, etc.) and usually implies a participant's tes-timony, which is treated as a real fact.[62] This is precisely the attitude to the fictional material that Foma Grigorievich demonstrates. He does not question his grandfather's involvement with the supernatural; on the contrary, he verifies the truthfulness of his own narrative art by referring to his grandfather's fame as a storyteller. His other references to authoritative members of the village – "honest elders" ("chestnye starshiny"), his aunt, and other villagers[63] – have an important function in demonstrating how the devil interferes in people's lives. Foma Grig-orievich begins and ends all his stories by pointing at the real presence of the devil in this world. Overall, his narrative performance suggests a relational identity determined by social network and kinship within the Ukrainian village community that still espouses the ideal of free-dom and heroism of the Cossacks. At the same time, Foma Grigorievich invites readers into sharing a national memory.

The narrative performances in *Evenings* do not so much serve to rep-resent Ukraine as a fixed ethnic community as become an articulation of what Homi Bhabha has called "a dialectic of various temporalities," which integrates modern, colonial, postcolonial, and native in the act of enunciation.[64] This performative activity that is connected to the struggle for liberation and justice is best illustrated by the last narrator, the blind bandura payer of "The Terrible Revenge." He appears in the epilogue of the tale and sings an epic song (*duma*) which explains that the origin of the sorcerer's curse on the Cossacks is for breaking their oath of Christian brotherhood. I believe that the blind bandura player is the anonymous storyteller whom Pan'ko mentions in the Preface to Book Two and whom he praises for his high art of storytelling: "We had another storyteller, too, but he (and it's not a thing to mention with the night setting in) used to dig up such fearful stories it made your hair stand on end."[65] Pan'ko's comment that follows ("I intentionally did not put him in this book"), however, problematizes this hypothesis.

Only reconstructing the changes in the narrative between the draft version and the final text of "The Terrible Revenge" can reveal similarities between the style and poetics of the bandura player of the epilogue and those of the rest of the tale.

Textual evidence in support of this interpretation can be found in the earlier drafts of the tale. The 1831 draft version of "The Terrible Revenge" shows that Gogol initially planned to attribute the tale to the fictitious editor Rudy Pan'ko.[66] The draft begins with Pan'ko's introduction, in which he mentions his fellow Dikan'ka raconteurs Foma Grigorievich and Taras Ivanovich Smachnen'kii. Further, the first line of his introduction is rendered with the grammatical mistakes and in the colloquial mode characteristic of Pan'ko's prefaces in the collected volume of *Evenings*: "*Has* you heard the story about a Blue Sorcerer?" This is then followed by a more lyrical mode: "Well, gentlemen, when are we going to visit Kiev? I am sinful before God. We need, indeed we need to worship the holy places ... How beautiful the places are there!"[67]

Pan'ko's unexpected invitation to the villagers to visit Kyiv and the formal way of address, "gentlemen," apparently sounded false to Gogol. In his view, Pan'ko could not be the author of a Romantic horror story because he had already declared his belonging to the traditional world of Dikan'ka.[68] Since Pan'ko's introduction to "The Terrible Revenge" did not accord with the overall tone of the tale, Gogol dropped it in the final version, and the tale emerged without an identifiable author-narrator. In the final story, Gogol added the embedded tale performed by the blind bandura player, which can be interpreted as a *mis-en-abîme* mirroring the overarching narrative structure of the entire tale. This new addition to the story also entailed some important changes in the plot and the narrative. Initially, "The Terrible Revenge" consisted of twelve chapters ending with the appearance of the mysterious horse rider in the Carpathian Mountains, seeking revenge for the sorcerer's murders. The ending in the draft version revealed the voice of a personalized narrator grumbling at God for not punishing the villain: "Did God stop looking at our sinful earth, or is there no punishment for such an unprecedented crime?"[69]

In the final version, however, Gogol eliminated this and all other traces of personal narration, while enhancing the epic mode. He ended the story with the mysterious horseman assassinating the villain and added the historic song about the two sworn brothers, performed by the blind bandura player. This song reverses the order of the events, subjecting the plot to a different logic of causation: the bandura player's story now precedes the events in the main story about the evil sorcerer and becomes its beginning. Thereby the main story has turned into an epilogue. This reversal colours the main story with the bandura player's view of the Ukrainian past. He is not a typical omniscient epic narrator who resides in universal time and space; he recounts a communal view of the past grounded in the national consciousness. Blind bandura players have always been venerated in Ukrainian culture for their public performance of the *dumy*, which became especially popular after the abolition of the Hetmanate in the second half of the eighteenth century. Traditionally, blind minstrels encoded hidden messages about the past in their *dumy*. In the nineteenth century they were persecuted by the imperial police.[70]

In "The Terrible Revenge," the bandura player's song reiterates the Ukrainian folk motif of *zlopomsta* (an evil revenge), referring to the murder of the Cossack Ivan by his sworn brother Petro. The plot of the song is based on real historical figures and events.[71] It relates how, during the rule of the Polish King Stephen, the two Cossacks, Ivan and Petro, lived like brothers and shared all their possessions together. As a gift for victory in a campaign against the Turks, the king granted Ivan a plot of land in the Carpathians. Ivan decided to share it with his sworn brother Petro. The greediness of the latter led to the death of Ivan and his son and to the ultimate decay of the Cossack Republic. The song ends with the justice of Heaven when God calls Ivan to judge Petro's sin and to devise a punishment for his brother. Ivan requests that Petro's descendants never be happy, and that the greatest criminal in his lineage be thrown into the abyss together with all his descendants. Shocked by such a cruel request, God nevertheless satisfies Ivan's wish but for his vengefulness deprives him of entry into Heaven. He must sit eternally on his horse above the abyss and watch the terrible revenge taking place.

The apocalyptic finale of the first part of "The Terrible Revenge," in which a mysterious horseman tortures the sorcerer to death and keeps frightening the people, thus serves as the dénouement of the story performed by the bandura player. The eternal horseman in both stories appears to be the same figure, i.e., Ivan, serving out God's punishment. Moreover, by connecting the beginning of the decay of Cossack Ukraine in the song with its aftermath in the main story, the bandura player's song sheds light upon the myth of "cursed" Ukraine. The song about the strife between the two sworn brothers recapitulates the history of the fall of Cossack Ukraine as outlined by the protagonist Danilo in the first part of the tale.[72]

Although the national Ukrainian myth created in the tale includes concrete historic details, it is presented in the song as being recurrent throughout history. This is conveyed in the bandura player's manner of performance, reminiscent of Boyan, the folk narrator of *The Lay of the Host of Igor*:

"The Terrible Revenge":

The old man also sang cheerful songs and followed the people with his eyes, as if he could see. His fingers, with ivory plectra attached to them, were flitting about like a fly over the strings, which seemed to play by themselves.[73]

The Lay of the Host of Igor:

Boyan did not [really] set ten falcons upon a flock of swans but he laid his own vatic fingers on the live strings, which then twanged out by themselves a paean to the princes.[74]

This striking similarity between Gogol's bandura player and Boyan establishes continuity between medieval and modern Ukrainian history. The underlying message of *The Lay of the Host of Igor* is to forgive quarrels and to unite with the rest of the Orthodox Christians, which also becomes a central theme in "The Terrible Revenge."

The blind bandura player recounts a glorious era in the history of Ukrainian Cossacks: "the former Hetmanate at the time of Hetmans Sagaidachnyi and Khmel'nitskii … it was a different time: Cossackdom stood tall, trampled enemies with its horses, and no one dared mock it."[75] Then he switches to the rule of Stephan Báthory, the king of Poland and Transylvania, who began to enlist Ukrainian Cossacks and consequently initiated strife among them. By making comparison between the two periods in Cossack history, the bandura player hints that the internal division that plagued the Cossacks was the result of one unforgivable sin, of a "terrible revenge." The concluding paragraph depicts the profound effect of the message on the listeners. The word "terrible" refers both to the past event and to the tragic consequences for future generations of Ukrainians. It could be said that the bandura player's song figures as the *mise-en-abime* in the tale in two senses: it paraphrases the outer work, the first half of the tale, and at the same time it unifies the community by reviving their historic memory through the moral message ("the people that gathered around – the old ones having hung their heads, the young ones having raised their eyes at the old man – … [were] thinking about the terrible events of yore").[76]

The bandura player's song also prompts the Ukrainian audience to see a causal relationship between the "terrible events of yore" and the present: "When the blind man came to the end of his song; he put his fingers back to the strings of his bandura and started to sing comic songs about Khoma and Erioma, about Stkliar Stokoza."[77] Russian comic songs were part of the bandura players' repertoire, being performed at the beginning and end of the performance.[78] In Gogol's tale, these comic songs about Khoma and Erioma and Stkliar Stokoza frame the main story and serve as a diversionary move to hide the political implications that surround the song about Cossack Ukraine. The first song is a popular Russian comic one about the twin brothers Foma and Erioma, who do things backward. In the spirit of carnivalesque play, the song overturns the hierarchy of official culture. In the context of the bandura player's performance, it is used to attune the listeners to the concealed political content of the historical song. The second song about Stkliar (glass-cutter) Stokoza exists in neither Russian nor Ukrainian folklore. Stokoza also does not figure as a character in Russian or Ukrainian literary sources. The Ukrainian historian Ivan Sen'ko has hypothesized that the glass-cutter Stokoza alludes to Peter I, who began colonizing Ukraine in the early eighteenth century. The scholar has discovered a popular legend circulating about a tsar who got lost in a Glass Kingdom and whose place was occupied by the Anti-Christ who ruled Russia from then on.[79] The contrast between the tragic events in the bandura player's epic song and the disharmoniously comic ones serves to shock the audience:

> When the blind man came to the end of his song; he put his fingers back to the strings of his *bandura* and started to sing comic songs about Khoma and Erioma, about Stkliar Stokoza ... But all his listeners, old and young, remained spellbound, and stood there for a long time yet, their heads bowed, pondering this terrible tale of times long past.[80]

As Bojanowska has persuasively demonstrated, the bandura player's comic songs have the same function in Pan'ko's repertoire as *Evenings* in Gogol's entire oeuvre: for the imperial audience they create the illusion of humorous and light entertainment, whereas for the Ukrainian audience they revive the memory of a lost national past.[81] The bandura player's performance causes the differentiation of the audience, which also operates in the other tales in *Evenings*. His songs are addressed, first of all, to Ukrainians who have the memory of the Cossack past and can confirm the veracity of the story. Among all of the narrative performances presented in *Evenings*, only the one by the bandura player can unify the Ukrainian audience, and in this capacity the bandura player can be considered Gogol's ideal narrating subject. This narrator appeals to the universal truth associated with Christian Orthodox values and thereby provides an alternative to the opposition between the bookish gentleman Makar Nazarovich, associated with Russian culture, and the village storyteller Foma Grigorievich, personifying Ukrainian culture, because he reaches beyond ethnic and imperial identification. Within this conceptual framework, the interpretation of Gogol's "Russianizing" tendency in *Evenings* runs the risk of overgeneralization.

The principle of contextuality of narration is played out differently in the tales, yet always in accordance with the expectations of the projected audience. Pan'ko's performance is simultaneously addressed to the metropolitan readers in the "big world" and to his local Dikan'ka listeners and produces a two-level narrative structure. Makar Nazarovich, a sophisticated urban narrator, interacts only with the implied readers who belong either to Russian society or to the Ukrainian literary elite. Foma Grigorievich constructs an active audience for his accounts, asking them to participate in his sharing of the common past and folk belief. The quintessential moment in the entire collection is the unifying act that the bandura player's performance produces on listeners, transforming them from a crowd into a community.

Chapter Four

Heteroglossia, Speech Masks, and the Synthesis of Languages

As a true Romantic, Gogol believed in a strong link between language and identity. Being influenced by the German Romantics' view of language as a universal abstract system, he developed his own interactionist ideas of language. Gogol's knowledge of German Romantic aesthetics has been analysed by many scholars. During his first years in St Petersburg, Gogol read Humboldt, Novalis, Schelling, and Herder, whose works were translated and popularized by the members of the Society of Lovers of Wisdom (1823–5).[1] The problem that German Romantics tried to resolve – that is, the extent to which language users can display their identities without affecting the language system that shapes those identities – largely informed Gogol's own views and language experiments. According to the Romantic philosophy of language, individuals, being agents of free will, can manipulate language as they wish in their expression of personal meaning, which makes individual language practice highly unpredictable and idiosyncratic. This stipulates that an utterance, as an act that instantiates the relationship between a speaker and a listener, assigns a significant role to individual users in changing the language system and helps the users establish their subjectivity. The ideas of subjectivity, intersubjectivity, and identity, as expressed fully through language, became a cornerstone of their emerging theory of language. Thus, Schleiermacher distinguished between "grammatical" interpretation, in which "the person ... disappears and only appears as the organ of language," and "technical" interpretation, in which "language with its determining power disappears and only appears as the organ of the person, in the service of their individuality."[2] Gogol, similarly, juxtaposed the "poetic" and "prosaic" uses of language that can often intrude into each other's territory and produce new meaning.[3]

In his *Essays on the Origin of Language* (1772), Herder made another important discovery about the intersubjective nature of language. He argued that it was language, rather than a transcendental schema, that structured human consciousness. From the moment of its origin, language is bound with both cognition and communication, which Herder illustrated with the example of an individual's encounter with a sheep. A person cannot make sense of the sheep until it bleats; the sound it produces makes an imprint on the human mind as a mark by which it will be recognized again and as a word signifying its distinctive activity. The "speech act" that the sheep initiates alters the perception of the listener and gives the sheep itself an identity within that world. Therefore, Herder concluded, we experience the world as a series of encounters with "sounding acts" rather than with things themselves. Importantly, these acts occur in the human mind prior to the agents that produce them.[4] Therefore, after the German Romantics, identity began to be treated not as something singular, fixed, and intrinsic to the individual, but as a dynamic interaction of the social, historical, and political contexts of an individual's lived experiences.

Throughout his literary career, Gogol's hybrid language had a strong interactional and performative potential; it was an "act," or a form of doing language.[5] Comprising several idiolects, Gogol's literary language was a polycoded structure in which Ukrainianisms and idiolects formed one pattern of reference for Russian readers and another for Ukrainian ones. Gogol existed in a linguistic continuum between Ukrainian and Russian and not only generated various kinds of hybrid-language phenomena but also captured the heteroglossia of Ukrainian culture, which, according to Bakhtin, saved Russian literature from agelasm (that is, from becoming too serious, rigidly regulated, and ritualized by the state). It is significant that the hybrid discourse of two Ukrainian-Russian writers, Vasyl' Narizhnyi and Nikolai Gogol, provided Bakhtin with the material for his pioneering theory of heteroglossia and polyphony. In the 1935 version of *Discourse in the Novel*, Bakhtin mentioned only one aspect of "heteroglossia," "mnogoiazychiie" (multi-language-ness), which creates the internal conflict stemming from the presence of "alien speech in a foreign language" ("chuzhaia rech' na chuzhom iazyke").[6] Later, in the fragment "Heteroglossia as a Precondition for the Development of Novelistic Discourse" and in two presentations of 1940 and 1941 at the Institute of World Literature, Soviet Academy of Sciences ("Discourse in the Novel: Toward the Question of the Stylistics of the Novel" and "The Novel as a Literary Genre"), heteroglossia began to signify the "in-betweenness of languages" ("mezha iazykov").[7] Both laughter and heteroglossia, discussed as preconditions of the novel, originate, according to Bakhtin, in Gogol's prosaic heteroglossia.[8]

In his analysis of Gogol's Ukrainian tales, Bakhtin identified devices and features similar to those that he found in Rabelais's medieval carnivalesque discourse. One of them, the *coq-à-l'âne-stil*, borrowed from Leo Spitzer's analysis of Rabelais, is present in the nonsensical verbal play in Gogol's works. Spitzer illustrates this verbal absurdity, which is capable of destabilizing the semantic, logical, and spatio-temporal connections, with the French proverb "sauter du coq à l'âne" (literally meaning "to jump from the rooster to the donkey"),[9] while Bakhtin chooses a Ukrainian idiom, "v ohorodi buzyna, a v Kyivi diad'ko" (there is an elder bush in the garden and an uncle in Kyiv), to characterize Gogol's hybrid discourse. Initiated by Rabelais in the medieval burlesque tradition, according to Bakhtin, deliberate verbal nonsense ("narochitaia slovesnaia bessmyslitsa") constituted a cornerstone of Gogol's poetics. His creative language undermined norms and habitual relationships and gave a temporary break from all stable semantic connections, and thus necessitated the construction of the new world.[10] Bakhtin considered Gogol's mixing of discourses a crucial stage in the formation of the novelistic genre and a truly transnational phenomenon which subverted all previous national rhetorical traditions and created a modern literature. Heteroglossia and polyphony are often viewed by Bakhtin scholars as "other-language-ness" or "many-voicedness." However, in Bakhtin's initial theorization, the former concept meant the presence of "another national language" in the discourse of the dominant language and was explicitly applied to Gogol's use of Ukrainian in Russian-language texts.[11] After being criticized by his opponents for ignoring the class struggle in Gogol's oeuvre,[12] Bakhtin considerably revised the idea of heteroglossia, impregnating it with ideology that, he believed, was inherent in any language regardless of its contact with others.

In Bakhtin's late theorization of heteroglossia, it was transformed from a cross-language to an intralinguistic phenomenon that signalled the coexistence of several socio-ideological languages within one "national" language. The important stage in this process was the internal stratification of the national language into socio-ideological discourse through the penetration of dialects and sociolects into it. Therefore, the heterogeneity of the Russian literary language resulted from the contest between different dialects, among which the Ukrainian language played a crucial role. During Romanticism, heteroglossia brought many mixed-language phenomena into literary prose and activated double-voicedness of discourse by appealing to two or more speakers and expressing two or more intentions: the direct intention of a character or a narrator and the refracted intention of the author. For Bakhtin, Gogol was a *passeur* who crossed language borders back and forth to narrate

Ukrainian culture. The metaphor of crossing language borders can be related to heteroglossia and hybridity, but there are some nuanced differences between the two. It is known that Homi Bhabha borrowed his idea of the hybridity of colonial identity from Bakhtin's theory of "organic" and "unintentional" heteroglossia.[13] However, Bakhtin's earlier concept of the "in-betweenness of languages" ("mezha iazykov") can better inform Gogol's crossing the border of Russian and Ukrainian, which led to the semantic shifts, unusual collocations, neologisms, and new compounds – all of which deterritorialize and reterritorialize discursive and social systems of the imperial culture. "In-betweenness" conveys a sense of openness and flexibility, and features uncertainty, fluidity, and temporal and spatial restlessness better than "hybridity." So, if "hybridity" refers to a "single mix" in which the entities are mixed and boundaries are blurred, "in-betweenness" additionally has the idea of inter- and multi- that allows for a coexistence of multiple entities. In terms of directionality, "in-betweenness" is more ambiguous because it does not emphasize the one-directionality, whereas "hybridity" implies directionality.

Gogol's own understanding of heteroglossia was far from the idealized treatment evident in the work of literary theorists from Bakhtin to Todorov and Kristeva, who espied in contesting voices the affirmation of a unity composed of differences (formulated by Kristeva as "the *other* within us"). Gogol's use of heteroglossia, which he called "raznogolositsa" (heterology), varied from neutral to negative in his texts. In his early tales, such as "A Teacher" and "Sorochintsy Fair," multi-voicedness figures as background noise. In the former tale, babble and heterology ("treskotnia i raznogolositsa") are followed by a series of italicized insertions of peculiar Ukrainian colloquial forms and expressions. In the latter tale, the polyvocal speeches ("raznogolosnyie rechi") deaden each other, so that one cannot hear any distinct individual word arising above the multivocality.[14] In another Ukrainian tale from *Evenings*, "Christmas Eve," the arguing voices of the two mean old ladies, Tkachikha and Pereperchikha, compete for audibility. A similar use of heterology can be found in *The Inspector General* (in the verbal contest and mirroring speech patterns of Anna Andreevna and Maria Antonovna and of Bobchinskii and Dobchinskii) and in *Dead Souls* (the society ladies' disseminating gossip in unison or the non-individualized voices of the *zemsky* court).[15] Even when multi-voicedness is mentioned in Volume 2 of *Dead Souls*, it is presented ironically, through the perspective of the idealistic, detached Tentetnikov (a literary precursor of Goncharov's Oblomov), who envisions his reformed estate as a "zvukosoglasnyi khor" (a chorus in harmony) of people's voices who can find agreement with each other and with the landlord.[16]

Insertion of the *Other*: Jewish and German Speech in Gogol's Early Texts

One of the sources of heteroglossia in Gogol's early texts was the Yiddish and German language elements. They produced parodic laughter in a masquerade of discourses that bore foreign-sounding but recognizable syntactic forms. The distorted form of the foreign languages made the very the structure of the Russian language visible. Before Gogol, Jewish and German characters had been ridiculed for their looks and conduct, but very rarely for their speech. The uncertainty of the Jewish voice expressed by means of Russian was linked to the dubious position of Jews in the Russian Empire: if Jews wanted to prove that they were part of the Russian community, they needed to speak a comprehensible Russian.[17]

The analysis of Gogol's use of Yiddish cannot be divorced from the discussion of his representation of Jews in *Taras Bulba*. Such scholars as Dubnow, Zaslavskii, Gorev, and Nakhimovsky have claimed that Gogol established a model for the anti-Semitic treatment of Jews in Russian literature.[18] Most recently, Leonid Livak in *The Jewish Persona in the European Imagination: A Case of Russian Literature* (2010) has discerned in Gogol's Iankel' "the main reference point for the depiction of the jews" in Russian literature.[19] Thus, he has disregarded the socio-historical construction of Jews as *other* in the Russian Empire and placed responsibility on Gogol for creating the myth of "the jews" as a universal Other, grounded in the Christian exegetical tradition of anti-Judaism. Elena Katz, however, has argued that "Gogol expressed elements of Judeophobia in his writings but was not a Judeophobe, whereas Dostoevsky's Judeophobia is not reflected in his literary works."[20] According to Gary Rosenshield, in Gogol's early stories, "the Jews are implicated along with Poles and Russians in the spiritual decline of the age" and "appear no worse than the Russians, who are presented as Judases, betrayers of their own Orthodox faith."[21] In *Taras Bulba*, however, the Jewish characters are used not so much for comic relief, but as a foil in the creation of the heroic identity of the Cossacks. While following the Romantic representation of Jews, Gogol created such individualized portrayals of Jewish characters that they problematize the statements of Gogol's alleged "anti-Semitism." Gogol's Jews were depicted in tune with Ukrainian and Polish Romantic traditions in which they were perceived not so much as the *other* but as familiar subjects, for they had been part of Ukrainian and Polish communities for centuries. For example, in Narizhnyi's novel *Russian Zhilblas*, the Jewish Ian'ka is a positive character who supports the family of the protagonist Chistiakov in times of hardship. Ian'ka, like all other Russian characters in the novel, speaks in an elevated normative Russian. The Russian critic Faddei Bulgarin wrote a negative critique of Narizhnyi's novel, claiming that "the Jews" cannot be [depicted] as people of virtue," which testifies to the democratic tradition of the representation of Jews in Narizhnyi's prose fiction. In *Pan Tadeusz*, by the Polish writer Adam Mickiewicz, the Jew Jankiel is also portrayed as a sympathetic character who gets along with everybody in the village and is respected for his moral outlook and human values.

In *Taras Bulba*, the main Jewish character, Iankel', likewise, speaks a flawless Russian, interspersing it with Ukrainianisms and Polonicisms, which demonstrates his complete assimilation into the local community. At the same time, the speech of other Jewish characters whom Taras meets in Warszawa is presented as "foreign and incomprehensible" and is unmarked graphically. Elements of Yiddish slip into the fabric of Iankel''s speech in the form of interjections ("ai-ai," "vakh-vakh," "oi-oi," and the original Yiddish exclamation "oi vei ist mir" as an expression of dismay). Yiddish embedded into the Russian discourse of *Taras Bulba* is unitalicized and untranslated, just like the use of Ukrainian. The few examples of Yiddish speech can be explained by Gogol's lack of communication with Jews in the early 1830s. Although scanty, these elements serve to individuate Iankel''s speaking manner and differentiate it from the rest of the "silent" or non-speaking Jewish characters. Peculiar Ukrainian and Polish expressions are inserted into Iankel''s speech to underscore his intermediary status among both the Orthodox Cossacks and the Catholic Poles. Trying to persuade Taras that he is not the Cossacks' enemy, Iankel' uses Ukrainianisms: "We have never yet *hobnobbed* [*sniukhivalis'*] with the enemy … And as for the Catholics, we want nothing to do with them, *may the devil visit them in their dreams* [*pust' im chert prisnitsia*]! To us all Zaporozhians are like our very own brothers" (emphasis added).[22] The expression "may the devil visit them in their dreams" is a literal translation of the Ukrainian idiom "khai nasnyt'sia im lysyi did'ko," which Gogol used in his letter to Zaleski.[23] But when describing the state of the Poles in besieged Dubno, Iankel' uses a Polish expression: "Далибуг, я не узнал!" (I swear to God, I did not recognize you) (emphasis added).[24] Iankel''s switching of linguistic codes is paralleled by his fluid perception of the border between "us" and "them," because he is caught between the Cossacks and the Poles and must camouflage himself in order to survive. When pretending to be a Pole while escorting Taras in Warszawa, Iankel' asks for entry into a Polish prison, repeating "It's us!" four times ("It's us! It's me! It's your own [svoi] people").[25]

It is important to note that Gogol presents the "foreignness" of the Jewish characters' speech through the perception of Ukrainians. When the Jewish characters talk to each other, supposedly in Yiddish, the narrator, who acts as a focalizer of Taras's point of view, calls Iankel''s Yiddish a "tarabarskoie narechiie" (savage gibberish), "neponiatnyi iazyk" (incomprehensible language), or "po-nemetski" (in German). The difference between rendering Iankel''s speech and that of the rest of the Jews lies in the degree of their otherness as registered in the Cossacks' minds. In chapter 11, for example, the Jewish community of Warszawa is presented through Bulba's eyes. He does not understand a word the Jews say to each other, but manages to develop a feeling of trust regardless of their eccentric verbal behaviour:

> The three Jews began speaking in German. Bulba strained his ears, but could only catch the word "Mordechai," which the men often repeated ...
>
> Finally, the crowd was shouting so loud that the Jew standing watch had to motion to them to keep quiet. Taras began to worry for his safety, but then remembered that Jews always discussed matters in the street, and that the devil himself could not understand their language.
>
> A few minutes later the Jews came crowding into the room. Mordechai walked up to Taras, patted him on the shoulder, and said, "When man and God want to do something, then it will be done!"
>
> Taras looked at this Solomon, the likes of whom the world had never seen, and a glimmer of hope sparked within him. Mordechai's appearance did somehow inspire hope.[26]

Taras entrusts his own and Ostap's fate to the Jewish intermediaries and does not blame them for not fulfilling their promises to ransom his son:

> Finally, late in the evening, Mordechai and Iankel' returned. Taras's heart stopped. "Well? Any luck?" he asked with the impatience of a wild steed ... Mordechai started talking so incoherently that Taras could not understand a word. "Oh, Your Excellency!" Iankel' gasped ... "It is completely impossible ... !" Taras looked the Jew in the eyes, but no longer with impatience or anger.[27]

German speech in Gogol's works is marked both grammatically and graphically, creating the impression of being spoken by a native speaker. A German character, Schiller, in "Nevsky Prospect" is ridiculed as a "real German in the full sense of the word": he sets a goal, say, "saving fifty thousand in the course of ten years," and "never under any circumstances does he increase his expenses" in order to fulfil his goal. The rigid syntactic constructions (repetition of "I have" and "I am" and the improper use of Russian idiomatic expressions) underscore Schiller's Germanness: "How dare you kiss my wife? ... I don't want to wear horns! ... I have been living in Petersburg for eight years. I have a mother in Swabia and an uncle in Nuremburg. I am a German and not a horned ox."[28] In another episode, the narrator literally translates a conversation between Schiller and Hoffman in German into awkward Russian for Pirogov, "whose knowledge of German was confined to 'Gut Morgen.'"[29] But when Schiller speaks directly to Pirogov, his Russian betrays him: "What is an officer! I am a Swabian officer. Me myself will be an officer [Мой сам будет офицер]: a year and a half a cadet, two years a lieutenant, and I am now tomorrow an officer. But I don't want to serve. I *does* this with the officer [Я с офицером сделает так]: phoo!"[30] In a dialogue with his wife, Schiller mixes German and Russian in one sentence: "'*Gehen Sie* to the kitchen [na kukhnia].'"[31] The use of untranslated German speech is relatively perfunctory, marking the German voice as foreign for a short textual moment. In most cases, the ungrammatical elements in the German characters' speech are not italicized because Gogol wanted to indicate the German profile of St Petersburg and its residents. Notably, in the feuilleton "Petersburg Notes of 1836," Gogol depicted the city as an "orderly man, a German par excellence."[32]

In the first draft of *The Inspector General*, the insertion of a German word into the speech of a German character – Khristian Ivanovich Gibner, a district doctor – was a means of creating social satire. In his conversation with the clerk Rastakovskii, Gibner used the German verb *gibt* in its conjugated Russian form *otgibaiu* to veil his begging for a bribe: "Вы мне *гибт* теперь, а я вам после назад *отгибаю*" (You *gibt* me [bribe] now, and I will *giben* it back later).[33] In the final version of the comedy, Gogol deleted the episode. Gibner now cannot speak a word of Russian; he only makes incomprehensible sounds ("partially resembling 'i' and somewhat 'e'"). His "muteness," as a literal realization of the semantics of the Russian ethnonym for "German" (i.e., *nemets*, a mute person), has a detrimental effect on his patients' health. As the welfare commissioner Zemlianika puts it: "They are simple people: if they die, they'll die anyhow; if they recover, they recover anyhow. And it would be difficult for Khristian Ivanovich to interview patients; he does not know a word of Russian."[34]

If with Ukrainianisms it is hard to tell whether Gogol used them strategically or if they were the result of the natural interference between two closely related languages, with the use of Yiddish or German in the Russian text it is clear that they were chosen deliberately for comic effect. The presence of marked foreign words in Russian discourse ultimately produced a defamiliarizing effect that legitimized the presence of an ethnic *other* in Russian culture. They became a metonymic device of creating difference and polyvocality. As Bakhtin rightly noted, "external multi-language-ness strengthens and deepens the internal contradictoriness of the literary language itself," ultimately eroding the "system of national myth that is organically fused with language."[35]

Gogol and the Language Debates of the Time

The critique of Gogol's hybrid language in many respects continued the early nineteenth-century debate about the national Russian language between the so-called *novatory* (innovators) and *arkhaisty* (archaists), with Nikolai Karamzin and Aleksandr Shishkov at their respective heads.[36] The *novatory* believed that the Russian language should be open to borrowings from Western European languages. Therefore, they took the colloquial idiom of the educated Russian nobility as the model for the literary language. However, with the development of Romanticism in the 1810s–1820s, many Russian writers were dissatisfied with the conceptual monotony, stylistic limitations, and lack of nationality of the salon idiom that the *novatory* advocated. One of the Romantic poets of the period and an archaist, Vil'gel'm Kiukhel'beker, complained that the rich Russian language was being reduced to the polite language of the few, "un petit jargon de coterie."[37] Unlike the *novatory*, the *arkhaisty* considered Church Slavonicisms and Russian vernacular locutions the main sources for the vocabulary and style of the modern Russian language. For the *arkhaisty*, the colloquial speech of middle-class Russians – particularly of non-francophone nobles, clergy, landowners, and petty bourgeois residing in the Western outskirts of the empire (especially in Ukraine) – became a vehicle for nationalizing the Russian language. In the 1820s, with the rising interest in regional folklore, the Russian literary language began incorporating a variety of previously inadmissible linguistic elements: colloquialisms, professional jargon, and regional dialectisms.

One of the reasons for the diversification of the Russian literary language was the emergence of a middle-class audience from recently acquired Western provinces of the empire, contemporary Ukraine and Belarus, the population of which was multilingual and generally better educated than their peers in the rest of the empire. This orientation toward a provincial, non-Russian literary audience inevitably led to the broadening of the concept of the national language. The cultural multilingualism of the Western provinces, on the one hand, and social separation between the Europeanized elite and the carriers of traditional Russian culture, on the other, produced, according to Victor Zhivov, a "constant semiotization and ideologization of linguistic and cultural behavior and did not contribute at all to the establishment of a single, universal literary language."[38] Precisely because of the lack of uniformity within Russian culture, Romantic writers celebrated the growing interest in collecting dialects from the imperial corners.[39] They believed that Slavic vernacular dialects preserved a primordial national spirit that was missing from both the bookish Church Slavonic and the francophone Russian of the upper class.

Ukrainianisms played a significant role in the process of democratization of the Russian literary language in the 1820s–early 1830s. Since they were associated with Slavic antiquity, they gained a high cultural currency. This positive attitude toward a moderate use of Ukrainian (often accompanied with Russian glosses) was still evident in the early reception of Gogol's tales. The favourable reception of Gogol's Ukrainian tales, in Stephen Moeller-Sally's view, signalled the "ongoing frustration" of Russian intellectuals over the question of Russian nationality. At this moment, Ukrainian culture was seen as "a deeply rooted plant onto which modern Russian identity could be grafted, and the vigorous efforts of Ukrainian writers to sustain a living connection with their origins were held in sharp contrast to the superficial and derivative efforts of Russians in their own native field."[40] It should be emphasized that Ukrainian elements were permitted in Russian only if they were used to define the Russian national character. For example, the Russian critic Nikolai Nadezhdin called Ukrinianisms "idiotismy" (idiomatic locutions) and wrote that only their translation into Russian legitimized their use in a literary work. He noted that Ukrainian writers of the period "fell into two opposing extremes: they either completely smoothed out all of the local idiotisms of the Ukrainian dialect or preserved it completely untouched," and that, fortunately, Gogol "managed to occupy the golden mean" between them.[41] In his praise of Gogol's literary language, Nadezhdin stressed his talent of "translating the national motif of the Ukrainian dialect into, so to speak, Muscovite notes, without losing its original physiognomy."[42]

Taras Koznarsky has summarized the nature of discussions about the status of the Ukrainian language in the empire in the title of his article "Neither Dead nor Alive: Ukrainian Language on the Brink of

Romanticism." Despite the fact that Ukrainian tales were praised for their colourful language and ethnographic material useful for the development of Russian literature, the growing popularity of Ukrainian literature "alarmed both Russian critics and administrators, who began to see in these developments not only unproductive and anachronistic vexations, but also a culturally and ideologically subversive agenda that had to be discouraged."[43] The more Ukrainian intellectuals of the 1830s–1840s pursued the idea of Ukrainian as a language worthy of high literature, scholarship, and linguistic codification,[44] the more ardently Russian critics insisted on its status as a regional dialect. Polevoi blamed Ukrainian writers for deviating from the mission of Russian culture by artificially creating a "false Ukrainian literature."[45] When Taras Shevchenko's *Kobzar* was published in 1840, Polevoi grew anxious about Ukrainian literature reaching the realm of "artful" poetry: "How can people with talent occupy themselves with such trifles [as artificial Ukrainian poetry]? … It is a pity to see how Mr. Shevchenko deforms thought and the Russian language, playing at it *a là khokhol*!"[46] Thus, a positive attitude toward the occasional insertion of Ukrainianisms co-occurred with a negative perception of the Ukrainian language in general, which was called variously a "Little Russian dialect" ("malorossiiskoe narechie"), "spoiled Polish" ("isporchennyi pol'skii"),[47] a degenerated Old Slavic language,[48] or a hybrid Old Slavonic "mixed with German, Latin, and Polish words."[49]

After 1832, when Sergei Uvarov – minister of education and advisor to Nicholas I – developed the principles of "Official Nationalism" based on the triad of "Orthodoxy, autocracy, and nationality," the standard use of the Russian language without any admixture of ethnic or foreign elements was imposed more rigorously. Any deviation from linguistic correctness, not to mention the use of Ukrainian proper, was taken as a sign of disloyalty to the empire. If in the 1830s Ukrainian elements were perceived as an embodiment of the true folk spirit of the Russian nation and corresponding to the principle of *narodnost'* (nationality), in the 1840s they alarmed censors as deviating from the imperial idea of Russianness. This shift in the attitude toward Ukrainian language and culture also affected the reception of Gogol's *Evenings* and *Mirgorod*. One of Gogol's early critics, the well-known Vissarion Belinskii, denied the very existence of Ukrainian culture as an autonomous phenomenon. He called Ukrainian a "prostonarodnyi iazyk" (an uncultured, or lower-class, language) and advised Gogol to write exclusively in Russian.[50] Clearly, Belinskii voiced the general trend in Russian society that the epoch of liberal philo-Ukrainian tendencies in Russian culture was over and giving way to Great Russian chauvinism.[51] The differentiation between Russian and Ukrainian languages became subject to political classification, which entailed more rigid censorship and editorial practices, as Gogol's case clearly exemplifies.

How did it come about that Gogol's hybrid language was criticized simultaneously by his literary adversaries (Polevoi, Bulgarin, Grech, Senkovskii, Masal'skii, and Zagoskin) and by his allies (Pushkin and Dal')? The answer may be found in the imperial desire to cast the colonized as partially present in the dominant discourse. Gogol's mistakes in Russian were attributed to his Ukrainian ethnicity and thereby marked him as incapable of achieving perfection in the Russian language. In their reviews, Russian writers and critics meticulously listed examples of Gogol's "ungrammaticalities." Nikolai Polevoi identified "hundreds of such mistakes in the beekeeper's book."[52] Another critic, Nikolai Masal'skii, compiled a long list of ungrammaticalities and awkward phrases from the speech of the Ukrainian characters and presented them as Gogol's own errors, disregarding the fact that the writer often used non-normative Russian and Ukrainian as a means of characterization. Paradoxically, writers who were not the best connoisseurs of Russian or whose native tongue was not Russian but who were eager to assert their political reliability also engaged in denouncing Gogol's hybrid use of the language. The Polish-Russian writers Bulgarin and Senkovskii insisted on Gogol's "illiteracy," often resorting to overt misrepresentations and falsifications. In 1842, Senkovskii published a feuilleton in which he falsely accused Gogol of the incorrect use of the genitive form of nouns in the recently published *Dead Souls*, although Senkovskii's examples of the misused genitive endings betray his Polish origin.[53] Bulgarin also wrote in his reviews that Gogol "corrupted" Russian by his use of colloquialisms and Ukrainianisms: "Among us writers, there are some who for the sake of originality corrupt and torture Russian ... Let us take a look at a book entitled *Mirgorod*, a book so much praised in the journals. There are such phrases that Oedipus himself could not interpret. [Everything] is distorted and corrupted in the extreme."[54]

Not only Gogol's enemies but also his older friend Pushkin spoke ironically of Gogol's flawed proficiency in Russian. In his 1830–1 notes, Pushkin wrote: "I have been printing [my works] for sixteen years already and critics have found only five grammatical mistakes in my poems (and they were right); I have always been grateful to them and have always corrected the marked mistake. I write much worse in prose, and speak even worse, almost as badly as Gogol writes."[55] In the 1840s, the Russian writer and lexicographer from Sloboda Ukraine, Vladimir Dal', described the stunning effect that Gogol's language produced on him in terms of mixed delight and criticism: "Greedily you swallow up the whole [story] to the end, then you read it again and still do not notice that he is writing in a wild language. You try, pedantically, to figure it out, and you see that one absolutely should not write or talk like this. You try to correct it – you spoil it. You cannot touch a word. *What if he would write in Russian?* [emphasis added]."[56]

Overall, the meticulousness with which Gogol's contemporaries scrutinized his language to verify its conformity with the rules of Russian grammar was unprecedented. Gogol's unique feeling for language and his expanded use of non-standard colloquial forms and expressions were all attributed to his flawed Ukrainian origin. Later in the 1840s, Russian society grew even more suspicious of Gogol's hybridized language because it became associated with the satirical depiction of Nicholas I's Russia.[57] These critical reviews of his language prompted Gogol to eliminate many Ukrainian elements from the first editions of *Evenings* and *Mirgorod*. The extent to which Gogol was aware and anxious about his imperfect Russian can be seen from his letter to Pletnev, in which he complained that he had failed to improve his Russian style:

> No matter how hard I have been trying to polish my style and language, the most important tools of the writer, they are still more ungainly than the worst writers have demonstrated, so that even an inexperienced schoolboy has the right to laugh at me. All that has been written by me is remarkable only from a psychological perspective but can in no way serve as a model of belles-lettres, and any teacher who advises his pupils to learn the art of writing from my works would be insufficiently prudent.[58]

In all objectivity, Gogol's confession reflected a typical perception among bilinguals – a sense of "impurity" or of linguistic decadence and a lack of confidence in their proficiency. Caught between Ukrainian, the regional Ukrainian form of Russian, and proper literary Russian, Gogol was coming to embrace the pragmatic benefits of writing in standard Russian.

Gogol's "Speech Masks" in His Letters

Gogol's letters are an invaluable means of showing an interactionist conception of language and his deliberate use of hybrid linguistic resources with Ukrainian and normative Russian language with Russian addressees. The analysis of Gogol's "speech masks" requires an empirical approach that would take the syntactical nuances and meanings of a "language in practice" more seriously. The idea that Gogol used certain speech patterns in his correspondence with different addressees emerged when the writer's letters were published in their entirety in 1907–9. The literary critic Vladimir Kallash, who compiled the first complete edition of Gogol's works and letters, accused the writer of manipulating his public image:

> Gogol's letters introduce us to an enormous intricate labyrinth: what a wonderful combination of the most intimate sincerity and spontaneity with some explicit signs of natural cunning [prirodnaia khitrost'] – cunning that was lurking in his soul since childhood together with his strange, early practicality and ability to play on the most secret strings of the human soul! In them [letters] one can find servility and reverence toward powerful people, a genius's pride and self-confidence, and a realization of his own high predestination ...[59]

However, Gogol's speech masks – i.e., the situational use of language characterized by a radically different manner of speaking – cannot be treated as unique, given recent research in interactionist theory of personality and politeness theory in sociolinguistics. Nowadays cultural anthropologists define as normal an individual's ability to mimic the verbal and non-verbal behaviour of others without always being completely aware of it. Such an interactional synchrony occurs involuntarily, especially among those who, like Gogol, tend to see themselves as more dependent upon the reaction of others. In natural speech acts, matching verbal and non-verbal communication usually happens sequentially: a speaker's behaviour is followed in kind by the listener when s/he becomes a speaker.[60] The mimicker constantly changes his or her speech patterns, utterance duration, loudness, articulation, speech rate, silence duration, etc., in order to participate in communication.[61] It was quite typical for Romantic writers to imitate the naturalness and spontaneity of living conversation with an imaginary interlocutor, which required masterful adjustment to the interlocutor's verbal style.[62] Therefore, Gogol's discursive adjustment to his interlocutors and correspondents may be understood as his playful use of style, including careful selection of the genre of the utterance, compositional devices, and language vehicles. The medium of letters can challenge the popular misconception about Gogol's moral values when talking about his social skills.[63]

The writer's epistolary legacy encompasses five out of fourteen volumes of his complete works, making him one of the most prolific letter writers in the history of nineteenth-century Russian letters. Gogol's performative use of language is different in his letters to family and friends than in his literary texts.[64] In the letters, he could practise direct persuasion, trying to get an immediate response from his addressees that would show his impact on them. He could preach about morals, instruct an audience how to read his texts, request financial aid from the tsar, and make confessions to his spiritual advisers. After the publication of *Selected Passages from the Correspondence with Friends* in 1847, which was partially based on Gogol's correspondence with actual friends, Gogol did not publish any new prose fiction, making letter-writing his main literary medium.

To this day, we have access to 1,350 letters from Gogol to 107 correspondents and 450 to Gogol from 83 correspondents. Given the high number of words in Gogol's letters (571,425 words in his letters compared to 437,020 in all of his fictional texts), "distant reading" is an appropriate method to aggregate and analyse the letters as "big data" and to test the hypothesis of Gogol's varying use of language in response to different groups. In order to classify and compare Gogol's letters across gender, age, familial relationship, ethnicity, and profession, I used "Hierarchical Cluster Analysis" (HCA) and software "stylo" in R for stylometric analysis. These tools help us to identify, across all of the letters, formal variables that take on stylistic content. By combining computer-assisted methods with traditional humanistic reading, one can get a fuller picture of the evolution of Gogol's epistolary style.[65]

The first dendrogram (Appendix 1, Figure 9) demonstrates the clustering of Gogol's early letters, which, with a few exceptions, fall into three main groups: letters to his family (mother and uncle Kosyarovs'kyi); letters to his new Russian acquaintances (Zhukovskii, Pushkin, and Dmitriev); and letters to Ukrainian classmates (Vysots'kyi, Danilevs'kyi, and Prokopovych) and associates (Maksymovych and Tarnovs'kyi). Gogol's correspondence with his Ukrainian friends and acquaintances shows more stylistic and topical homogeneity because only in these letters could he express his nostalgia for home and his dissatisfaction with Petersburg life and use a mix of Russian and Ukrainian. A close reading of Gogol's early letters from the 1820s to the first group – his parents and uncle – confirms the machine-generated grouping: letters to family members are shorter in length, full of grammatical errors, and childish in tone, which was typical of a child who had been sent away from his country home to a gymnasium in the city. On the thematic level, these letters reveal a recurrent motif that will appear in Gogol's adult letters – the need to find an intimate soul and communicate with it. The young Gogol captures every detail of his impressions of city life. For example, an excerpt from his 1820 letter to his parents lists all the "important people" with whom he has become acquainted: "last Sunday I had dinner at Ivan Alekseevich's; the next day I saw Ivan Dmitrievich; on my return from the garden with Gavril Maksimovich, Ivan Dmitrievich showed his house to us." This technique of enumerating the full names of minor, insignificant personages would be fully realized in *Dead Souls*.[66] Gogol's childhood letters from the school period begin to show some elements of preaching and at the same time his sincere desire to "converse in a written form" (as expressed in a letter written immediately after his father's death on 23 April 1825).[67] He often copied lines from the letters of his addressees and responded to questions raised in those letters, as if launching into an imaginary conversation with them.

In the 1820s, Gogol's letters to his family exhibit a high ratio of Ukrainianisms and hybridized Russian-Ukrainian forms: "сюды" (here), "позычил" (borrowed), "прыймете" (will accept), "влюблен у вас" (in love with you), "разов" (times), "мета" (goal), "халстухи" (neckties), "шлахбаум" (turnpike); oddly formed neologisms: "уроченное время" (a set time), "не поразскажете ли чего-нибудь животрепящаго" (wouldn't you tell me something exciting), "жить в разрознении" (to live separately), "несбытодумие" (unrealistic thinking); and various orthographic mistakes.[68] The stylometric analysis of all Gogol's correspondence, without the division into three periods, indicates that the letters to his mother are clustered as a clear outlier at the highest position because of their unique lexical-syntactical content compared to the normative Russian language that he used in his correspondence with members of Russian society. Gogol's letters to his mother abound in marked hybrid forms and regionalisms.[69] At the same time, his letters to his intimate Russian friend, the poet Vasilii Zhukovskii, exhibit fewer ungrammatical elements.[70]

In general, one can see in Gogol's letters to his Ukrainian friends a tendency to use more peculiar Ukrainian forms of verbs (especially the use of the non-reflexive form in place of the reflexive as in Russian) and more proper Russian grammatical forms in correspondence with his Russian acquaintances. For example, he writes "я соскучил" (I miss [you]) to the Ukrainian interlocutors Smirnova and Maksymovych and "я соскучился" (I miss [you]) to the Russians Aksakov and Repnina. Furthermore, Gogol never swears in his letters to his mother or to Russian correspondents but completely neglects propriety of style in his letters to his Ukrainian classmates. For example, in his letters to Maksymovych, Gogol refers to the "devil" ("the devil knows," "to the devil") several times, which at the time was considered vulgar. He also tends to use peculiar Ukrainian grammatical elements in these letters: the vocative case ("Чувствительно благодарю вас, земляче" [I sincerely thank you, my fellow countryman]); syntactic Ukrainianisms ("мне пришло в думку" [it came to mind], "покамест не додаст" [until s/he adds], "что тебе потребно" [what you need]); hybrid colloquial phrases ("мы такое удерем издание" [we will make such an edition], "одно по боку" [to hell with him/her], "другому киселя дай" [kick him with a knee from behind], "что за безалаберщина деется" [what a hodgepodge is going on]); and archaic Church Slavonic word forms ("зане скудельный состав мой часто одолеваем недугом и крайне дряхлеет" [because my weak constitution is often affected by sickness and gets enfeebled]).[71] Corresponding with his classmate and editor Mykola Prokopovych, Gogol uses spicy jokes in the tradition of the burlesque school humour practised in the Nizhyn Lyceum.[72] At the same time, he expresses his intimate, friendly feelings to Prokopovych via the idiosyncratic use of the diminutive forms: "Что такое писатоночки?" (what are you writing right now?),[73] "Что вы делон<о>чки, мои краснотоночки?" (how are you doing, my red one? ["krasnen'kii" (a red one) was Pro-kopovych's school nickname; in Ukrainian "krasnen'kyi" also means "a handsome boy"]),[74] "Пиши повестоночки или стишоночки, если стишоночки, то пришли их в твоем письме кусоночки" (write tales and verses, if you have any verses, send some excerpts in your letter),[75] "Прощай, мой жизненочек" (good-bye, my life).[76]

Gogol's excellent knowledge of the conventions of the familiar letter is evident in his brief correspondence with Alexander Pushkin. In his letter to Pushkin from 13 May 1834, Gogol instructs the leading Russian poet on how to talk to the minister of education, Sergei Uvarov, about him. First, Pushkin needs to inform the minister that the writer Gogol "is hardly alive." Then, to add verisimilitude to such a dubious fact, Pushkin has to

> blame the dying Gogol for not following the doctors' advice, and when the minister becomes engrossed in his thoughts about the unfortunate writer's fate you need to change the topic, and start chatting about the weather, thereby changing the topic so that the minister himself will come to the suggestion to save [Gogol] by giving him a professorship not in freezing Petersburg but in southern Kiev.[77]

Pushkin without hesitation accepts Gogol's proposal and even adds his own nuances: "I absolutely agree with you. I will lecture Uvarov today, and in passing will mention the death of *The Telegraph* and your own. From that topic I will smoothly and craftily approach the topic of his own immortality. Maybe we will fix the matter up."[78] The imaginative performance that Gogol delegates to Pushkin indicates his acute aware-ness of the cultural code of behaviour established in familiar Peters-burg society and Pushkin's excellence at enacting this code. Society expected highly aestheticized behaviour of "playing styles" from the Romantic artist.[79] But here Gogol lays bare the very mechanism of exercising style by assuming a highly individualized stance and demonstrating how cultural conventions can be both restrictive and liberating.

During 1836–48, Gogol lived abroad (in France, Austria, Germany, and Switzerland, 1836–9, and Italy, 1839–48), only visiting Russia twice for short stays (fall 1839–spring 1840 and fall 1841–spring 1842). Living as an immigrant, Gogol actively corresponded with his family, friends, and editors, which resulted in three out of the five volumes of his letters. His first impressions of the foreign travel experience are typical of Russians' attitudes about Western culture and are nostalgic about home. The most detailed account of Gogol's émigré experience can be found in his correspondence with his female addressees: his mother, 72 letters; Smirnova, 65; Sheremeteva, 44; Anna V'elgorskaia, 38; his sisters, 30; Sofia Sollogub,16; Maria Balabina, 12; Elagina, 4; Raevskaia, 3, for a total of 284; and male addressees: Zhukovskii, 50; Pletnev, 40; Shevyrev, 40; Iazykov, 40; Aksakov, 34; Danilevs'kyi, 33; Ivanov, 33; Pogodin, 31; A.P. Tolstoy, 26; Prokopovych, 20; Rosset, 11; Shchepkin, 8; Annenkov, 6; Konstantinovskii, 6; Viazemskii, 5; Samarin, 4; Odoevskii, 2, for a total of 389 letters written during this period.

The number of female addressees and the frequency of Gogol's correspondence with them increased drastically during the years he spent abroad. Overall, these letters were more deliberately constructed, with knowledge of the addressee's manner and style in mind. Gogol's use of jocular forms of expression in them – jokes, scenes described, cultural commentary, proverbs, and literary quotations – was meant to entertain his female friends and relatives. In this respect, Gogol's unconventional comic devices and performative techniques in the letters addressed to his former student Maria Balabina are the most interesting in his epistolary legacy. Twelve of Gogol's and four of Balabina's letters have come down to us. One of Gogol's letters to her is written as a humorous sketch, played out between Gogol and a French waiter who served him a dinner on his trip from Lausanne to Vevey in October 1836.[80] Another is written by Gogol from Balabina's point of view as an instruction about how to write to him properly.[81] Gogol's letters to Balabina are full of sensual imagery and references to his nose.[82] In the only letter written entirely in Italian, Gogol emerges as a playful suitor who hides behind the language of love; it would be impossible for social reasons to express his feelings in Russian. He asks the ancient statues and columns why his beloved Maria Petrovna forgot to respond to him. Gogol's secret "language of love" echoes the Hellenistic epigrams preserved in the Greek Anthology. The playfulness of voice and perspective of the

Hellenistic epigram required readers to reconstruct their imagined setting and context. Similarly, Gogol introduces Maria Balabina to classical art, as well as to the art of reading between the lines:

> The Coliseum is inclined against your kindness. Therefore, I do not come to him, because he always asks me: "Tell me, my dear man [chelovechishche] (he always calls me by this name), what is my lady-love Maria doing now? She swore on the altar to love me forever, but, in the meantime, she is silent and does not want to know me, what does this mean?" And I respond: "I do not know." And he says: "Tell me why she no longer loves me?" And I respond: "You are too old, mister Coliseum." Having heard this, he frowns with his eyebrows, his forehead becomes angry and brown, his cracks – those wrinkles of antiquity – seem dark and threatening, so that I feel fear and escape, frightened.[83]

In the second, mid-life group of letters, written between 1836 and 1846, the addressees are more clearly grouped by gender, age, and occupation (Appendix 1, Figure 10). Thus, the letters to his mother and to his best female friend, Smirnova, share more stylistic features in common, owing to Gogol's lasting relationship with both women. The same could be said about another pair of correspondents – Zhukovskii and Aksakov – with whom Gogol discusses not only his everyday concerns but also his creative plans and intellectual ideas. Letters to his younger sister Elizaveta Gogol and to Maria Balabina are clustered together because here Gogol adopted a mentoring tone with both young women and actively participated in the arrangement of their lives. Gogol's letters to his "spiritual Godmother," Princess Sheremeteva, occupy a special place in the mid-life corpus because of the high number of religious words and topics in the letters. This in no way suggests that Gogol communicated on spiritual subjects only with Sheremeteva, but the ratio of words such as "God," "Lord," "sin," "soul," "salvation," etc., proportional to all other words, is significantly higher in his letters to her compared to the same group of words in his letters to other correspondents.

In the mid-life letters, Gogol's letters to the Russian poet Iazykov are a clear outlier. The most intensive period of correspondence between Gogol and Iazykov occurred from 1841 to 1846, during which they wrote forty-six and thirty letters to each other respectively. During these years, Gogol worked on finalizing his magnum opus, *Dead Souls*, and struggled to produce the second volume of the novel. Iazykov, similarly, had experienced writer's block, but his creative crisis lasted longer and was deeper than that of Gogol. Gogol considered Iazykov his mentor, but it was the former, in fact, who provided the latter writer with spiritual support and encouragement.

Gogol's late-period letters (Appendix 1, Figure 11) are grouped by machine algorithm into similar clusters: the young female addressees (Gogol's youngest sisters, Olga and Anna, whom the writer instructed about their life choices); his Russian colleagues – writers and critics (Shevyrev, Pletnev, Zhukovskii, and Pogodin) – with whom Gogol had corresponded about literary and publishing matters; and his "spiritual" addressees (his mother, Smirnova, Anna V'elgorskaia, his confessor Matvei Konstantinovskii, the artist Aleksandr Ivanov, Count Aleksandr Tolstoy, and Sheremeteva, who is an outlier in this group, as in the corpus of mid-life letters). Gogol's late letters start to show more variability of speech patterns as he mastered social conventions and became more concerned with the improvement of the moral condition of Russian society. In the second half of his life, Gogol tended to adjust to the recipients of his letters even more. According to Todd, Gogol used various patterns of coercion: combinations of accusation, humble confession, instruction, illustration, pleading, and encouragement. He cast himself in different epistolary roles: the "prophet dishonored in his own country, merciless social critic, dislocated artist, penitent sinner, impatient missionary."[84]

To sum up, Gogol's late letters demonstrate a complex textual dialectic between personal and social identity. He treats communication between correspondents as a co-construction of each other's identity. By means of modality and interdiscursivity, Gogol promotes a well-polished self-image: he appears sensitive, romantic, spiritual, thoughtful, and humorous with one group of addressees; moralistic, critical, expository with another; and with yet others, playful in employing colloquialisms, inventive and with a fine taste for language. His choice of language elements and topics depends on the interlocutor's needs and on the communicative situation. Gogol's speech masks, which he developed in his early correspondence and in *Evenings*, activated a self-reflexive process of shaping and reshaping his identity. In his concurrent engagement with different social and ethnic groups, Gogol had to constantly reposition himself as a member of polite society, in one situation, and as a colonial *other*, in others. Having realized the power of language to fashion himself simultaneously as the "same" and "other," from a "subject of the politics of recognition" Gogol became a hybrid subject. Homi Bhabha explained the distinction between the two in an interview with *Journal for Advanced Composition*:

> The politics of recognition assumes – whether it's in the Hegelian master-slave model or in any other model of a kind of mutual culturally relativistic

recognition – that there are these kinds of in-place subjects in and through whom the process of recognition happens. The question of hybridization is precisely to draw attention to the way in which the process of negotiation is continually placing and replacing the members of that act of cultural or social or political interaction. First of all, the "subject" of hybridization is a different subject than the subject of the politics of recognition. The subject of hybridization is an enunciatory subject. In the enunciatory subject – which is a subject in performance and process, the notion of what is to be authorized, what is to be deauthorized, what difference will be signified, what similarity or similitude will be articulated – these things are continually happening in the very process of discourse-making or meaning-making. They are not subjects which are already given to that process of enunciation.[85]

Therefore, in society's "reading" of Gogol – of his visual and verbal behaviour in salons – he was constructed by a politics of recognition that tended to clearly demarcate self/other boundaries in his identity. A verbal performance produces the subject of a proposition (*énoncé*), while the "subject of enunciation" has a greater potential for enacting hybridity, which is discursively embedded and culturally positioned. The hybrid subject, thus, can deliberately enact multiplicity within the space of enunciation because it is directly engaged with constituting the self so that difference is articulated by destabilizing cultural relations available in the written language.

From Heteroglossia to the Synthesis of Languages

Gogol's "minor" use of Russian created new possibilities for language play. By means of confusion over the original meanings of Russian idioms or their conflation with Ukrainian ones, Gogol's hybrid formations destabilized the normative use of the literary language. The examples in Table 2 which are taken mostly from the late works, show how Gogol modified Russian idioms, appropriating them for his own creative purposes. In sentence 2, the phrase "kak mukhi vyzdoravlivaiut" (recuperating like flies), which belongs to Zemlianika, the superintendent of charities from *The Inspector General*, who masks his corruption in the city hospital, is a reversal of the original saying, "dying like flies." Obviously, Gogol intentionally makes the character slip in order to emphasize the absurdity of Russian reality and the hypocrisy of the local authorities. In sentence 7, "[Nozdrev] had been anxious to get hold of a bulldog for a long time," the narrator talks about Nozdrev's passion for hunting and dog breeding. He uses a standard idiomatic

Table 2. Gogol's modification of Russian idioms in *Dead Souls* and *The Inspector General*

Standard use in Russian[a]	Gogol's modification of Russian idioms
1. нахлобучить шапку на голову (to pull a hat down over one's eyes)	нахлобучиваются на город сумерки (dusk falls down on a town) (*Dead Souls*)
2. мрут как мухи (die like flies, i.e., in copious quantities)	Как мухи выздоравливают (recuperate like flies) (*The Inspector General*)
3. войти в силу (to come into force)	Собакевич вошел в самую силу речи (Sobakevich became eloquent) (*Dead Souls*)
4. на тебе нет лица (you have no face – you look awful)	сам на себе лица не увидишь (you won't see your own face) (*Dead Souls*)
5. ни аза в глаза (not to know the first thing)	не знать ни аза (not to know the basics) (*Dead Souls*)
6. кудрявый слог (flowery style)	написано кудряво (written in a flowery language) (*Dead Souls*)
7. точить зубы (to sharpen one's teeth – to have a grudge against someone)	Давно острил зубы на мордаша ([Nozdrev] had been anxious to get hold of a bulldog for a long time) (*Dead Souls*)
8. потрафить (to please, to be lucky) идти на лад (things are looking up)	потрафить на лад (to get good luck – a redundant phrase) (*Dead Souls*)
9. седьмая вода на киселе (second cousin twice removed)	я ему дядюшка, как он мне дедушка (I am an uncle to him as he is a grandfather to me) (*Dead Souls*)
10. в пух и прах (smash to pieces)	все распушено было в пух (the whole fabric [of Chichikov's money scam] came crashing to the ground (*Dead Souls*)
11. зарубить на носу, вбить себе в голову (to make a mark on one's nose – to get an idea into one's head, mark it well)	зарубить себе в голову (to make a mark in one's head) (*Dead Souls*)
12. полюби-ка нас в черне, а в красне-то и всяк полюбит (Love us when we are poor, because everybody will love us when we are rich)	Полюбите нас черненькими, а беленькими нас всякий полюбит (Love us when we are black [sinful], because everybody will love us when we are white [impeccable]) (*Dead Souls*)
13. все, что родится, то и годится (whatever is born will be of use)	Один умер, другой родится, а все в дело годится (One dies, another is born, but all will be of use) (*Dead Souls*)
14. дурак на дураке сидит и дураком погоняет (an idiot is on top of another idiot and whips him with an idiot)	Мошенник на мошеннике сидит и мошенником погоняет (a swindler is on top of another swindler and whips him with a swindler) (*Dead Souls*)

[a] All examples are taken from Vladimir Dal´'s *Tolkovyi slovar' zhivogo velikorusskogo iazyka* (Explanatory dictionary of the living Great Russian language) (1880).

expression but endows it with a different meaning. In Russian, "tochit'
zub" unambiguously means "to have a grudge against somebody." In
Gogol's modified use it signifies "to crave something."

Gogol's range and variety of verbal puns surpass the language repertoire of other Russian writers of his time. Some of his most popular language devices for the creation of a comic effect include puns
based on polysemanticism; the merging of homonyms; the pairing of
stylistically different but semantically similar words ("sbruia i dospe-
khi" [harness and armour]); and juxtapositions of semantically different words as if they were synonyms ("doekhal i otdelal" [reached and
finished]), "zhmuril i khlopal" (was screwing his eyes and blinking).
These contextual synonyms led to a convergence between normative
Russian and vernacular idioms, which reflected the non-hierarchical
use of discourses in Gogol's texts. The best illustration of the punning
juxtaposition of words may be found in the characterization of Nozdrev
in *Dead Souls*. As the narrator writes, "Nozdrev to a certain extent was
istoricheskii chelovek [a historical person]. Every meeting he attended
resulted in a funny *istoriia* [episode]."[86] By connecting a serious idiomatic expression, "a historical person," with the comic homonym "a
funny episode" (both of which may be expressed in Russian by "istoriia"), Gogol lowered the serious original idiom to the level of a comic
pun. Another device, creating a figurative meaning out of a direct use
of language, is achieved by transposing the professional jargon peculiar to a personage's speech onto his physical appearance or speech
manner. Thus, Gogol borrowed the word "perederzhka" (brawl) from
thieves' jargon to describe both Nozdrev's illicit gambling tricks and
his notorious side-whiskers that get pulled by angry fellow gamblers.[87]
This example demonstrates how the narrator appropriates a peculiar
word of "other's speech," adding a polyphonic overtone to a neutral
statement.

Gogol's lexical puns also reveal his desire to highlight the creative
potential of words by laying bare their etymological meaning: "The village of Manilovka [the "alluring village"] could lure few by its location."[88] Another category of puns is based on internal rhyming between
words of the same part of speech that only seem etymologically related:
"[he] settled temporarily at the place of a peaceful and meek host
[mirnogo i smirnogo]";[89] "Everything was down and neglected [opush-
cheno i zapushcheno] in the peasant's as well as in his lord's house-
hold."[90] Punning contrasts and juxtapositions occur not only between
the roots of the words but also in prefixes and suffixes that combine
with the same root: "Засим начал он слегка поворачивать бричку, –
поворачивал, поворачивал, и, наконец, выворотил ее совершенно

набок" (Then he started to turn the carriage around a little – and kept on doing so until it capsized onto its side).[91]

The juxtaposition of homonyms and the use of putative tautology (i.e., synonymic pairs of a verb and a noun or an adjective and a noun with the same root) constitute the stylistic "fingerprint" of Gogol's late works. The next example showcases both the tautological repetition of "chitateli" (reader) and a homonym, "prichitaiushchie" (identifying themselves), and a merger of homonyms of "iazyk." Within the limits of one passage, "iazyk" appears in three alternating meanings: as a style (1), as the Russian language (2), and as a tongue (3). In the third occurrence, Gogol creates one more verbal pun by merging two meanings of "vystavit' ego" – the physical (to stick out one's tongue) and figurative ones (to show off one's Russian language):

… если слово с улицы попало в книгу, не писатель виноват, виноваты **читатели** и прежде всего **читатели** высшего общества … Вот каковы **читатели** высшего сословия, а за ними и все **причитающие** себя к высшему сословию! А между тем какая взыскательность! Хотят непременно, чтобы все было написано **языком** (1) самым строгим, очищенным и благородным, словом, хотят, чтобы русский **язык** (2) сам собою спустился вдруг с облаков, обработанный, как следует, и сел бы им прямо на **язык** (3), а им бы больше ничего, как только разинуть рот да выставить его.

… if a word from the street has found its way into a book, it's not the writer who's at fault; at fault are the readers, above all the readers of a higher social sphere … Such, then, are readers of the higher social levels, and after them, all who count themselves members of the higher social levels! Yet at the same time, how very finicky they are! They want everything, without fail, to be written in the most austere, purified and noble language (1), in a word, they want the Russian language (2), all on its own, to descend suddenly from the clouds, properly polished, and to settle straight on their tongues (3), and all they would have to do would be to open their mouths and stick out those tongues.[92]

One other peculiar case of transposition from literal to figurative meaning occurs in Gogol's polysemantic use of the word "kulak" (fist). Originating in the slang of the Russian merchant class who profited from lending money to peasants, thanks to Gogol the word entered the Russian language in its figurative meaning as peasants' negative reaction to emerging capitalism. The authorial narrator captures this phenomenon in his portrayal of Sobakevich:

Вот уж, точно, как говорят, неладно скроен, да крепко сшит!.. Родился ли ты уж так медведем или омедведила тебя захолустная жизнь, хлебные посевы, возня с мужиками, и ты через них сделался то, что называют **человек-кулак**? Но нет: я думаю, ты все был бы тот же, хотя бы даже воспитали тебя по моде, пустили бы в ход, и жил бы ты в Петербурге, а не в захолустье.

Here is a case of being roughly cut but strongly stitched, as they say! Were you born a bear, or were you made bearish by the backwoods life, the sowings of grain and the pother and bother with the muzhiks, as a result of which you became what's called a kulak? But no: I think you would always have been the same, even if you had been brought up fashionably and launched into society and lived in Petersburg, and not in the back-woods.[93]

Sometimes Gogol places the newly formed word in opposition to the original homonym, laying bare the inner form of a neologism: "он [Noz-drev] явился веселый, радостный, ухвативши *под руку* прокурора … бедный прокурор поворачивал на все стороны свои густые брови, как бы придумывая средство выбраться из этого дружеского *подручного* путешествия" (he appeared, cheerful and in high spirits, clutching the arm of the Public Prosecutor … the poor Prosecutor was turning his thick eyebrows in every direction, as if seeking to figure out some way of breaking loose from this friendly arm-in-arm journey).[94] The traditional operation of verbal puns is based on a conjunction of homonyms. Gogol, however, complicates this junction even further by combining links from different semantic chains with these homonyms. In the pun from *Dead Souls*, "okhlop'iami lezla khlopchataia bumaga" (the cotton paper was shedding into tatters),[95] the first homonym, "okhlop'ia" (tatters), is combined with the homonymous word "khlo-pchataia" (made of cotton), which has a completely different meaning and is used only for sonorous effect.

Gogol's use of mixed registers was firmly grounded in the synthe-sis of vernacular and Church Slavonic, practised during the Ukrainian Baroque.[96] His last printed book, *Selected Passages from Correspondence with Friends*, employs several traditional Baroque figures and tropes peculiar to the Ukrainian homiletic tradition. Gogol's practical knowl-edge of this tradition was formed during his studies at the Nizhyn Lyceum, where *A Short Manual to Russian Rhetoric*, written by the Kyi-van archbishop Amvrosii (Serebrennikov), was a mandatory text in the school curriculum.[97] Later in his life, in the 1840s, Gogol's friend Aleksandra Smirnova recalled how the writer had read to her some excerpts from texts by the above-mentioned authors. While working on *Selected Passages*, Gogol reviewed texts by the Ukrainian polemicists and rhetoricians Ioannikii Haliatovs'kyi (1620–1688), Lazar Baranovych (1620–1693), Dimitry Rostovs'kyi (1651–1709), and Stefan Iavors'kyi (1658–1722). The works of these Ukrainian scholars created a national rhetorical tradition and stood in sharp ideological and rhetorical contrast to the official imperial ideology developed by their Ukrainian colleague Teofan Prokopovych.

In his *Selected Passages*, Gogol adopted the following Baroque rhetorical figures and devices:

1 Tautology based on the repetition of words with the same root but belonging to different parts of speech (*figura proizvozhdeniia*, or paregmenon): "может слышать всеслышащим ухом поэзии поэт" (a poet can hear with his all-hearing ear of poetry), "безлюднее самого безлюдья" (more solitary than solitude itself), "живой как жизнь" (living as life), "выбирая на выбор" (choosing a choice), "недоумевает ум решить" (mind is perplexed to decide), "дело стоит того, чтобы о нем толково потолковать" (the matter is worthwhile to talk about it sensibly)

2 Repetition of a semantically loaded word (*figura usugbleniia*, or reduplicatio): "Вы очень односторонни, и стали недавно так односторонни; и оттого стали односторонни, что, находясь на той точке состояния душевного, на которой теперь стоите вы, нельзя не сделаться односторонним всякому человеку" (You are very one-sided, and have recently become so one-sided; and you have become one-sided, because being on that point of the spiritual state, on which you are now, one cannot but become one-sided)[98]

3 Parallel syntactical structures: "покажи им пальцем и самые буквы, которыми это написано; заставь каждого … поцеловать самую книгу, в которой это написано" (show them the finger and the very letters with which it is written; make everyone … kiss the very book in which it is written)[99]

4 Epiphora: "Все перессорилось: дворяне у нас между собой, как кошки с собаками; купцы между собой, как кошки с собаками; мещане между собой, как кошки с собаками …" (Everything got quarrelled: the nobles among themselves, like cats with dogs; merchants among themselves, like cats with dogs; petty bourgeois among themselves, like cats with dogs)[100]

5 Anaphora: "Односторонний человек самоуверен; односторонний человек дерзок; односторонний человек всех вооружит против себя. Односторонний человек ни в чем не может найти

середины. Односторонний человек не может быть истинным христианином: он может быть только фанатиком ..." (A one-sided person is arrogant; one-sided person is impudent; one-sided person will turn everyone against himself. A one-sided person cannot find a middle ground in anything. A one-sided person cannot be a true Christian: he can only be a fanatic ...)[101]

In *Selected Passages*, Gogol deliberately modifies set expressions with the purpose of secular persuasion: "Всякому теперь кажется, что он мог бы наделать много добра" (Now everyone thinks s/he could do a lot of good deeds).[102] The original idiom in Russian is "nadelat' mnogo zla" (to do a lot of evil). The invisibly present original meaning exposes the arrogance of an individual who thinks that s/he could accomplish more good things if s/he occupied a higher position in society. This perception, in Gogol's view, is the source of all evil, since one should try to be useful in one's current place in society. Gogol's idea of "poprishche" (the Russian word means both a "profession" and a "walk of life") reverberates with Hryhorii Skovoroda's concept of the "srodnyi trud" (congenial work) which was at the core of the Ukrainian philosopher's ethical doctrine.[103] In other passages, Gogol modifies the standard biblical expression "neissiakaemyi istochnik" (an inexhaustible source) into the folksy phrase "neissiakaemyi kolodets" (an inexhaustible well); invents new words, such as "gramoteia i negramoteia" (scholar and non-scholar); uses the singular instead of the usual plural form of a word when speaking about "chelovecheskogo pokhozhdeniia" (a human adventure); and highlights the inner form of a word by means of tautological word formation; e.g., he writes "obstoiatel'stva obstanovilis'" (circumstances circumstanced) instead of "obstoiatel'stva slozhilis'" (circumstances came together).

Gogol's language experiments demonstrate how he appropriated language for concrete artistic purposes. If, in the Ukrainian tales, Ukrainianisms and hybrid forms were used to reproduce the heterogeneous soundscape of the Ukrainian village, in his second redaction of *Taras Bulba*, the increased occurrence of historical terms in Ukrainian contributed to an epic style; and in his so-called Russian tales, *Dead Souls*, plays, and *Selected Passages*, the combination of high and low registers mixed with professional jargon and archaisms expanded the idea of the normative literary language. In his rather unsystematic but creative use of hybrid forms, Gogol echoed the endeavours of previous Ukrainian intellectuals to create an "interlanguage" that would be comprehensible to all social strata of the Russian empire.

For educated Ukrainians who were competent in four or five languages, or at least trilingual (fluent in Church Slavonic, vernacular Ukrainian, and Russian), multiple language proficiency helped them develop an acute feeling for the inner form of the word. Seventeenth-century Ukrainian philosophers and grammarians discerned etymological connections between Slavic words and their counterparts in Church Slavonic, the classical languages, Hebrew, and modern European languages. They practised multi-discursive writing: Meletii Smotryts'kyi, for instance, catalogued numerous morphosyntactic forms peculiar to the Ukrainian vernacular side by side with the written *slavenorossiiskii* language forms in order to reinforce Ukrainian's connection with living speech; in Ivan Uzhevych's *Hrammatyka slovenskaia* (Slavic grammar) (1643), Church Slavonic and Ukrainian were treated as two variants of one and the same language.[104] The next generation of Ukrainian writers – Ivan Kotliarevs'kyi[105] and later Hryhorii Kvitka-Osnov'ianenko[106] – continued to mix languages, but not as systematically as the previous generation and mostly for the sake of comically portraying Russified Ukrainian bureaucrats. These writers broadened the notion of modern literary language based on the synthesis of various regional forms of Ukrainian – an idea which was in opposition to the perceived purity of the Russian literary language, as well as to the artificiality of the bookish *iazychie* practised in Ukrainian Galicia.[107] The late eighteenth and early nineteenth centuries in Eastern Europe witnessed the rise of nationalism accompanied by the codification of national languages and the delineation of distinct borders between them. This process left no room for the development of regional literatures written in dialects. The language scene in Ukraine at the turn of the nineteenth century was quite different in this regard. Ukrainians used the Russian-Ukrainian *surzhyk* as a "makeshift" bridge between the Ukrainian vernacular of the peasants and the Russian language of the Ukrainian nobility.[108] Originating in Ukrainian-Russian language contacts in the seventeenth and eighteenth centuries, *surzhyk* was fully developed during Ukraine's colonization later in the nineteenth century.[109] The popular use of *surzhyk* signalled the unequal inter-ethnic and inter-linguistic relations between Russian and Ukrainian languages and cultures, but at the same time it united Russianizing Ukrainians into a community of hybrid language speakers. The purity of the Ukrainian language versus a Russian-Ukrainian hybridized discourse became a major concern of Ukrainian intellectuals much later, in the 1860s–1880s.[110]

One of the most unusual features of the ideal literary language, according to Gogol, was "the most audacious transitions from elevated spheres to a low register within the same sentence."[111] This stylistic synthesis was realized in his late texts not only on the lexical but also on the syntactic level. Concluding his quintessential essay "What, After All, Is the Essence of Russian Poetry and What Is Its Peculiarity?" in *Selected Passages*, Gogol outlines the path of the Russian language's transformation into a global or universal language ("vsemirnyi iazyk") by absorbing world traditions and other dialects:

Языку, который сам по себе уже поэт и который недаром был на время позабыт нашим лучшим обществом: нужно было, чтобы выболтали мы на чужеродных наречьях всю дрянь, какая ни пристала к нам вместе с чужеземным образованьем, чтобы все те неясные звуки, неточные названия вещей … не посмели бы помрачить младенческой ясности нашего языка и возвратились бы мы к нему уже готовые мыслить и жить своим умом, а не чужеземным …

The language, which is by itself already a poet, was, not for nothing, forgotten for some time by our best society; we needed some time speaking alien dialects in order to babble away [another Gogol pun, which can also mean "to stir away"] all of the rubbish which stuck to us along with our foreign education, so that all those vague sounds, the inaccurate names of things … would not dare to obscure the juvenile clarity of our language, and we would return to it already prepared to think and live with our own and not with foreign minds …[112]

Taken together, the mixed linguistic elements in Gogol's language – Russian and Ukrainian, vernacular Russian, Ukrainianisms, Church Slavonicism, and the elements of Yiddish and German speech (used for speech stylization and to set apart certain "others" *from* Russian) – paved the way for the emergence of a new global Russian language that could communicate the universal truth throughout the nations. In Gogol's other literary essays from *Selected Passages*, the creation of the ethos is intrinsically connected with the universal logos, because Russian language can absorb the cultural legacy of the ancient world and rejuvenate itself by excavating authentic elements in local cultural traditions. I think that in Gogol's late writing, Russian, as a global language, does not eliminate Ukrainian as a local language but legitimizes it. Gogol's hybrid language in his early texts and the linguistic synthesis of his late works challenge the way we understand "language" and "culture." The tendency to root them in a particular place, to give them a permanent, territorialized existence, and to see in them a natural property of a spatially circumscribed nation was too confining for Gogol. Viewed from the point of view of contemporary cultural theory, Gogol's ideas of language erode the isomorphism of language and place. The weakening of the ties between language and place, however, does not presume that the new global language will destroy localities, but, on the contrary, ensures that cultural experience will be "'lifted out' of its traditional 'anchoring' in particular localities" and reterritorialized into hybrid forms.[113]

Chapter Five

Gogol's Texts as Palimpsest:
Taras Bulba and *Dead Souls*

Gogol's active creative period spanned twelve years, from 1830 to 1842; the last ten years of his life he spent trying to complete the second volume of his magnum opus, *Dead Souls*, and rewriting his earlier texts. Gogol's major works – *Evenings*, *Mirgorod*, tales from *Arabesques* (his so-called *Petersburg Tales*), and *Dead Souls* – all underwent substantial transformation in content and style from the original manuscripts to the published versions as well as from their first to subsequent editions. This chapter presents Gogol's revisions as part and parcel of his shifting historiosophical and ideological views, which cannot be defined solely in national or imperial terms. During this period, Gogol began to link social improvement not with innovation and progress but with the restoration of the pre-modern harmony between individual and society that he believed had existed in Kyivan Rus' and the Cossack Age. According to Grigorii Gukovskii, the idea of wholeness informed Gogol's vision of the Zaporozhian Host's social utopia in *Taras Bulba* and also undergirded his general critique of the fragmentation and stratification of Russian society inflicted by modernity, as depicted in his *Petersburg Tales* and *Dead Souls*.[1] Gogol's synthetic view of history was closely related to his idea of "vsemirnoe preobrazovanie" (universal transformation).[2] An instantaneous synthesis of archaic and modern elements could reconcile inevitable cyclical regressions to a stable centre in the medieval concept of history and at the same time could revise the modern view of history as a linear progression.[3] Gogol's views marked the shift from the Herderian pluralistic and teleological interpretation of history to the dialectial unfolding of history in Hegel's thought. In Gogol's intertwining of archaic and modern worldviews, modernity was not contrasted with the archaic. He exposed the eversameness lurking in modernity and unravelled the healing potential of archaic elements that could neutralize modernity's destructive effect.

This dialectical approach to history as an endless cycle of repetitions and innovations prompted the writer to revise the correlations between local and global, particular and universal, Ukrainian and Russian, in the new versions of his tales.

Editing Gogol's Early Texts

The history of Gogol's revisions begins with the preparation of his *Evenings* for the second publication in 1835–6. By that time, his name as the author of the collection had been revealed to the broader audience, and the Russian critics – Vissarion Belinskii and Faddei Bulgarin – hailed him as a Russian writer.[4] Therefore, Gogol wanted to address the Russian audience in an appropriate literary language and began to change his attitude toward Ukrainianisms. This attitude is already evident in his instructions to his fellow Ukrainian writer Mykhailo Maksymovych. In a letter of 20 April 1834, Gogol asked him to replace peculiar Ukrainian expressions with Russian equivalents:

> There are loads of phrases, idioms and expressions which we, Little Russians, think will be clear for Russians if we translate them literally, but which sometimes destroy half of the original meaning. Almost always a strong laconic passage becomes unclear in Russian because it is not in the spirit of the Russian language; in this case it is better to express it [the Ukrainian word] with ten words, than to conceal it ... Remember that your translation is intended for Russians and, therefore, get rid of all Little Russian idioms and phrases.[5]

Several moments in the letter deserve commentary: first, Gogol suggests that the Ukrainian expressions are richer and more laconic than their Russian equivalents; second, that a direct Russian translation of Ukrainian words and idiomatic expressions destroys their authentic meaning; and, third, Gogol admits that his audience is Russian and, therefore, can understand only standard Russian. It is significant that in the same year Gogol wrote two letters to Pushkin asking him to "mercilessly" proofread the rough copy of his new book, *Arabesques*.[6] Whether or not Pushkin was involved in the editing of Gogol's texts is not as important as Gogol's growing concern over his language's lack of conformity with his status as a Russian national writer.

While rewriting *Evenings* for the second edition, Gogol eliminated ungrammatical elements and Ukrainianisms. He grouped its original two books together and removed the list of misprints as well as Pan'ko's Afterword in which the beekeeper begged the editors to ignore his misspellings. Gogol's corrections, however, were unsystematic; the most intensive editing occurred in the text of the first three tales of Book One. In these texts, the average number of corrections per page reached 2.5; in the fourth tale, "The Lost Dispatch," there were fewer than 2 per page; and the average for Book Two is less than 1.5. While working on the style of the tales, Gogol enhanced the *skaz* elements of Foma Grigorievich's narration and standardized Makar Nazarovich's literary discourse in accordance with the norms of modern Russian. In Makar Nazarovich's tales, Gogol replaced Ukrainianisms and Russian dialectisms with normative lexicon.[7]

The second attempt to "improve" Gogol's style was made during the preparation of the *Complete Works* (1842), in which *Evenings* and *Mirgorod* formed the first volume. Because Gogol did not feel sufficiently confident in his Russian to edit his own works, he authorized his classmate Mykola Prokopovych to do it. By that time, Prokopovych was already a professor of the Russian language and an expert in Russian grammar. Delegating enormous editorial freedom to him, Gogol wrote:

> While correcting the second volume, I beg you to do it as brutally and autocratically as you can: in *Taras Bulba*, there are many mistakes that a copyist has made. He likes the letter "i"; get rid of it wherever it is misplaced. In two or three places I have noticed bad grammar and almost the complete absence of sense. Please, correct everywhere with as much freedom as when you are correcting the notes of your students. If there is a repetition of the same expression, find another one, and do not doubt or think about whether it will be good – everything will be good.[8]

Prokopovych took the writer's advice to correct every mistake literally. The only problem was that his definition of mistakes was too broad: he understood his task not only as correcting Gogol's orthography, grammar, and punctuation but also as polishing his overall style. His correction of the language proceeded in two directions: on the one hand, peculiar Ukrainian lexicon, grammatical forms, and orthography were replaced with their Russian equivalents; and on the other, ungrammatical moments, misprints, colloquialisms, and vulgarisms in Russian were neutralized with more literary forms. Prokopovych's corrections in *Evenings* included: the elimination of inversions; the insertion of additional new words whenever they were missing, from the editor's point of view (especially in the dialogues between the characters, which were often carried on in incomplete sentences); refinement of the spelling in direct speech of the characters, which Gogol had intentionally written in "i-dialect" to emphasize their belonging to oral discourse;[9]

elimination of grammatically marked Ukrainianisms, which were dubious from a linguistic purist perspective;[10] and the merger of the two glossaries of Ukrainian words from Books One and Two into one and placing it at the end of *Mirgorod*, which naturally linked the two cycles. Trying to make Gogol's texts more comprehensible to the Russian audience, the editor added about fifty new Ukrainian words to the lexicon. In preparing *Mirgorod* for publication, Prokopovych standardized the creolized discourse of the narrator and characters, which Gogol had used to satirically capture the Ukrainian gentry's Russianization and assimilation into the empire. In making Little Russian landlords speak more like "Russians," Prokopovych proceeded with the elimination of proper Ukrainian words,[11] Russianized the Ukrainian grammar,[12] and neutralized peculiar colloquial forms and expressions that served to reproduce Ukrainian landowners' vernacular Russian.[13]

Not only Gogol's early texts, *Evenings* and *Mirgorod*, but also his later comedies *The Gamblers* (1842) and *Marriage* (1842) underwent the same type of editing. While revising these texts, Prokopovych disregarded Gogol's idiosyncratic feeling for language and removed professional jargon and colloquial idioms from the texts. Unsatisfied with the fact that the editor deleted various meaningful phrases from *The Gamblers*, in his letter of 26 November 1842, Gogol asked Prokopovych to reinstate the words "rute" and "foska" from the original text:

> Also, in *The Gamblers* there is a very important phrase missing. Particularly, when Uteshitel'nyi keeps the bank and says: "Here, German, take and eat your seven!" After these words you should add: "*Rute*, definitely *rute*. Just the card is *foska*!"[14] By all means insert this phrase. It is a real army and has its own charm.[15]

According to Gogol's biographer Vladimir Shenrok, these words were Russianized forms of the French gambling terms "route" and "carte fausse," which meant, respectively, "to keep the bank on one card" and a deceptive card that one cannot rely on. This episode shows that Gogol's acute feeling for language and his knowledge of regional dialectisms and professional jargon surpassed Prokopovych's sanitized version of the Russian literary language. In the same vein, Prokopovych revised another play by Gogol, *The Marriage* (1842). He replaced ungrammatical forms and lexicon peculiar to provincial idiolect with proper grammatical forms.[16]

Reporting to Gogol about the results of his editing, Prokopovych wrote: "I can guarantee the exactness of my editing of which I am proud: I have become a skilled hand [nabil ruku] at this enterprise and read two proofs by myself; Belinskii read it one more time after me."[17] The unasked-for involvement of Belinskii,[18] who was notorious for his critical attitude to the Ukrainian language, accounted for a large number of corrections, which drastically increased in the tales following "May Night," rising to 3.5 corrections per page. Since Prokopovych's corrections had been sanctioned by the author himself, this version of Gogol's text may be accepted as the most valid text. However, as noted, Gogol was not completely satisfied with Prokopovych's editing. In his letter to him, the writer masked his dissatisfaction in self-criticism:

> The publication of my works came out not as I intended it to be, and, of course, I am the one who should be blamed, because I did not give accurate orders ... Some misprints have crept into the text, but I think they were there because of the bad original and belonged to the copyist, or even to me. Everything that came from the publisher is good, everything from the typesetter – bad. The letters are also nasty. I am very guilty in everything. First of all, I gave you so much trouble, although I meant well. I wanted to awaken you from immobility and get you involved in book publishing; but now I see it was too soon.[19]

In 1850, Gogol initiated a new publication of his works in five volumes. He hired Stepan Shevyrev and Mikhail Likhonin as the editors, but they understood their role in the same way that Prokopovych did earlier. Gogol's acquaintance, the Russian poet and translator Nikolai Berg, recalled that "while editing Gogol's works, Shevyrev corrected the style of his fellow writer who, as it is known, did not overmuch bother about [Russian] grammar. Having corrected, however, he [Shevyrev] ought to have shown Gogol what and how he corrected, of course, if the author had been in Moscow [at that time]. Sometimes it happened that Gogol told him: 'No, leave it as it was before!' For him, the beauty and the power of some vivid expression were more valuable than any grammar."[20] This time, Gogol wanted to check the proofs and worked on them during the last month of his life, in January and February of 1852. He managed to verify the first nine sheets of the first volume (up to the middle of "Christmas Eve"), the first nine sheets of the second (up to the middle of *Taras Bulba*), the first thirteen sheets of the third (up to "Diary of a Madman"), and the first seven sheets of the fourth volume (up to *The Inspector General*).

Since Gogol did not finish his editing, it is hard to determine how much textual damage was done by Shevyrev and Likhonin in the *Complete Works* that came out in 1855. Compared to previous editions, the edition of 1855 had a smaller ratio of changes: 2.5 per page for "Sorochintsy Fair" and "St John's Eve," 2 for "May Night," 1.5 for "The Lost Dispatch," and 0.5 for the other tales. The editors corrected awkward Russian forms and expressions[21] and simplified the syntax in the rhetorical figures, making them sound proper but flat. Overall, the linguistic richness of Gogol's fiction was sacrificed to what was considered clarity and grammatical uniformity. The editors overlooked or misunderstood his creolized language and standardized it with the normative Russian. Significantly, the corrections in 1851 were made on top of Prokopovych's corrections of 1842 so that Gogol's "texts" were increasingly obscured, with new texts layered on top of one another, producing the effect of a palimpsest.

The Second Redaction of *Taras Bulba* (1842)

Of all his texts, Gogol entirely rewrote only *Taras Bulba* (from *Mirgorod*) and *The Portrait* (from *Arabesques*), both of which were published in 1835 (the first redactions of both tales) and 1842 (their second redactions). The second redaction of *Taras Bulba* reflected the refinement of Gogol's ideas of "Ukrainianness" and "Russianness," which were treated not as separate phenomena, as in the 1835 version, but as sometimes overlapping, sometimes merged, and sometimes separate entities. In order to problematize the widely accepted idea of Gogol's alleged Russification in the second redaction of *Taras Bulba*, I take into consideration all of the intermediary drafts of the tale as well as the historiographical and folkloric sources that Gogol consulted while adding historically verifiable details to the second redaction. My analysis of the redactions reveals the work's layering of historical meanings, which I believe to be a source of the tale's ambivalence. In order to examine the differences between the 1835 and 1842 redactions, I have used the software programs: Wcopyfind to calculate the ratio of similarities between narrative events in both redactions and Beyond Compare to visualize side-by-side differences.

Among the most important historical sources from which Gogol drew his knowledge of Ukraine's history for the second redaction of *Taras Bulba* were Koniskii's *The History of the Rus' People, or Little Russia* (the end of the eighteenth to the beginning of the nineteenth centuries), Bantysh-Kamenskii's *The History of Little Russia* (1822), Hrabianka's *The Chronicle of Little Russia: The Samovydets Chronicle* (the end of the seventeenth to the beginning of the eighteenth centuries), Prince Myshetskii's *History of the Zaporozhian Cossacks*, and Boplan's *Description of Ukraine* (1651, 1832).[22] These sources solidified the factual background of *Taras Bulba*, but Gogol's contemporaries regarded his effort as unsuccessful, given the number of factual mistakes and chronological incongruities he made in the second redaction. Kulish was especially critical of Gogol's "falsifications" of Ukraine's history, pointing to the fact that the events depicted in the new *Taras Bulba* had taken place in three different centuries. The chronological diffusiveness of the second redaction, however, was meant to establish connections between the Cossacks and the medieval tradition of Kyivan Rus'. From the first pages of the second redaction, Gogol stressed the historical continuity between the different periods of Cossack history. In the beginning, the narrator talks about "times of war, when battles and skirmishes broke out because of the union with Poland," i.e., no earlier than 1569, when the Union of Lublin transferred lands of Rus' from the Grand Duchy of Lithuania to the Kingdom of Poland. The next paragraph presents Bulba as an original Cossack of the "violent fifteenth century." In the final chapter, Bulba participates in the uprising led by Hetman Ostrianytsia, which took place in 1637. By extending the chronological framework from the sixteenth to the fifteenth century, Gogol wanted to show how the Cossack military proto-state became a key player in the European arena. The narrow national identification of Cossacks as Ukrainians was only secondary to their higher mission as defenders of Orthodox Slavic civilization. Beginning in the 1570s, Cossacks actively sought to exert political power in the region. Their expeditions to Constantinople and Anatolia to fight the enemies of the Christian faith, as depicted in the new chapters of *Taras Bulba*, paralleled the Crusades of the Latin Church in the Middle Ages.[23]

Emphasis on the Cossack-peasant liberational struggle rather than historical precision determined the loose chronology of the second redaction of *Taras Bulba*. Gogol deliberately selected events of national liberation from three different centuries because he wanted to create a national epic of a "cruel age" ("zestokii vek"), in the way it was preserved in people's memory. In this respect, Walter Scott's novelistic approach to history was instrumental for Gogol's method. Scott prioritized the dialectical principle in national development, based not on the rise and fall of dynasties but on a *longue durée* perception of history and on the interconnectedness between global and local social structures. He used this approach in the first three of his "Waverley novels," tying each one to a different period of Scotland's history. In the "Advertisement" preceding the first edition of *The Antiquary* (1816), he wrote: "*Waverley* embraced the age of our fathers, *Guy Mannering* that of our own youth, and *The Antiquary* refers to the last ten years of the eighteenth century."[24] Gogol compressed the events of the three centuries of Cossack history into the plot of the second redaction of *Taras Bulba*. If the first redaction captured the Cossacks at their birth and youth, the second also offered the further development of Ukrainian society and promised the rebirth of a nation under a new form of rule ("one's own tsar"). By expanding the action across the three centuries, Gogol placed the history of Cossackdom within the context of East Slavic Orthodox civilization (or, to use Riccardo Picchio's term, "Slavia Orthodoxa"), in which national history was subordinate to its teleological progress.

Gogol's views on the continuity between ancient and modern history corresponded to the Ukrainian historiographical tradition of the 1830s–1840s. His fellow Ukrainian intellectuals – Mykhailo Maksymovych, Mykola Markevych, and Izmail Sreznevs'kyi – established genealogical connections between the legacy of Kyivan Rus' and the Cossack Age, a link that was missing from Karamzin's *History of the Russian State* (1781–1826). They presented the history of the Ukrainian nation as an ongoing process of building connections between ancient times and modernity and interpreted Cossack Ukraine as an organic extension of Kyivan Rus'.[25] Mikhail Pogodin, the leading Russian historian and Gogol's friend, polemicized with the Ukrainian historians about the origin of the Rus' people and of the Cossacks. He saw an unbridgeable gap between "antiquity" (be it Kyivan Rus' or Muscovy) and modernity (the Russian Empire); he argued that before the Mongol invasion the Dnieper Basin had been inhabited exclusively by Russians, and that Ukrainians, who originated in the Subcarpathian region, did not settle in this area until the sixteenth century. Moreover, Pogodin claimed that the Zaporozhian Cossacks were not native to southeastern Ukraine but constituted a separate Slavic-Turkic tribe.[26] Therefore, he envisioned antiquity as a homogeneous and unified entity based on how it differed from modernity and replaced the idea of historical progress with the eschatological idea of the end of history. Although Pogodin only published his lectures on Russian history four years after Gogol's death, it is very likely that the two friends exchanged their ideas about Russian history during the 1840s. Gogol's engagement with Russian and Ukrainian historiographical traditions resulted in the multiplicity of ideological meanings that emerged in the successive, overlaid versions of *Taras Bulba*.

In addition to his comprehensive study of the Cossack history of Ukraine, Gogol also developed an interest in the "Slavonic question," or Pan-Slavism, which complicated his view of the Cossack engagement with the empire. During his first years of emigration in 1836–7, Gogol became acquainted with Polish dissidents (the Romantic writers and intellectuals Adam Mickiewicz, Juliusz Słowacki, Jósef

Bogdan Zaleski, Piotr Semeneńko, and Hieronim Kajsiewicz) and attended their gatherings in Paris.[27] These Polish intellectuals introduced Gogol to the idea of *zmartwychwstanie* – the resurrection of a nation that has lost its political independence. Like Ukraine, but more recently, Poland had ceased to exist on the map of Europe.[28] It had no political borders, no government, and no officials elected by Poles. The Polish Resurrectionists promulgated a religious doctrine of Poland's mission to embody piety and faith and considered political restoration dependent upon the fulfilment of this divine mandate. By and large, Pan-Slavism, in both the Polish and Russian philosophical discourses of the time, reacted against the common view of Western European intellectuals about the Slavic nations as backward and insignificant. In response to this, Adam Mickiewicz contrasted the disordered, unstable, but amenable character of the Slavs with the rigid and fixed structures of Western civilization. He argued that because the history of Slavs had been written by their conquerors, their great achievements had been disregarded, depriving them of their past and their identity. In his lectures, Mickiewicz depicted Slavic civilization as a *terra incognita* – an anarchic and unmarked geographical space which to some extent recalls Gogol's vision of "Rus'" and his depiction of the Cossacks as an amorphous but active force in European history. Another way in which Mickiewicz might have influenced Gogol's views of history was through his depiction of the sacrificial death of Polish martyrs. Mickiewicz's heroes die for the sake of the redemption of the Poles and for the world's deliverance from Western and Russian despotism.[29] In *Taras Bulba*, the Cossacks are described as a free and unconquerable people who fight for their freedom against enemies on all fronts. Mickiewicz's call for a renewed Christianity that would sacrifice the ideals of nationhood for the sake of universal love and brotherhood also attracted Gogol.

It is significant that Gogol established connections with the Polish nationalist intellectuals two years before his meeting with Russian Slavophiles in Moscow. He had become acquainted with Aksakov, Kireevskii, and Khomiakov during a two-month stay there in December–January of 1839–40. At that time, Gogol did not show any interest in the Slavophiles' discussions, which earned him a reputation as an "empty" ("pustoi," as Kireevskii put it) interlocutor, which in turn sparked displeasure among the writer's sympathizers.[30] The fact that, later in the 1840s, Gogol became involved in the Slavophiles' heated discussions about Russia's mission does not necessarily link his view of the Zaporozhian Cossacks exclusively to Slavophile ideology or to Russian values, as some scholars claim.[31] In Gogol's era, Russian

Slavophiles, Polish *zmartwychwstancy*, and Ukrainian nationalists (the Brotherhood of Saints Cyril and Methodius) all propagated similar ideas about Orthodox brotherhood, *sobornost'*, and the special mission of Slavic civilization as an antidote to Western individualism and materialism. Therefore, Cossack communal virtues cannot be treated as pertaining exclusively to Russian, rather than Polish or Ukrainian, messianism.

By and large, the second redaction of *Taras Bulba* realized Gogol's earlier unsuccessful attempts to create a larger literary form about the history of the Ukrainian Cossacks. In the late 1830s, he had started writing a historical novel called *Getman* (Hetman) and a drama, *Za vybrityi us* (About a shaven forelock), but never finished them. Until August of 1841, Gogol did not plan to rewrite the tale. He had called *Taras Bulba* and "The Old-World Landowners" some of his best creations and had asked Vasilii Zhukovsky to find an opportunity to present them to Nicholas I.[32] In all likelihood, Gogol rewrote *Taras Bulba* after burning the draft copy of *Za vybrityi us* in August of 1841. That the manuscript of the drama had existed in a physical form was corroborated by several of Gogol's friends. One testimony is from the Russian actor Mikhail Shchepkin (as recorded by Panteleimon Kulish):

> In his first visit to Moscow, Gogol told Shchepkin: "Well, M[ikhail] S[emenovich], you will have a great work [rabota]. I have a drama about the shaven forelock à la 'Taras Bulba.' I will finish it soon." M.S. was imprudent when he asked Gogol about this drama in front of others. Gogol denied it and answered that he had never said anything like that; but when leaving the room, he whispered into Shchepkin's ear: "What a windbag! I will never tell you anything anymore."[33]

In late August of 1841, Gogol recited the completed drama to Zhukovskii, who fell asleep during the reading because he had been exhausted by his wife's difficult labour the night before. Gogol interpreted Zhukovskii's reaction as a lack of interest and in the middle of the reading threw the manuscript into the fireplace.[34] A month after this incident, Gogol was already reading fragments of a new version of *Taras Bulba* to Iazykov. That material from the destroyed historical drama had been incorporated into the new version of *Taras Bulba* is evident from the scenes that were borrowed from the remaining fragments of the drama. These include the Cossacks' shame at having their forelock, symbol of the Cossack identity, shaved by the enemy (chapter 7 in the 1842 *Taras Bulba*);[35] the election of a new ataman (*koshevoi*); Taras's meeting with him; the Cossacks' gathering in the square and their demand for a new war; and, finally, the *koshevoi*'s address to the Zaporozhians. Gogol thus "recycled" material from the burned drama in the second redaction of *Taras Bulba*, although he did not have time to fully edit it for the final publication.

The textual changes in the new redaction are summarized in Appendix 2. In the new version, some chapters were supplied with additional factual details and psychological motivation; others were divided into two and expanded with new literary characters and narrative twists. The order in which Gogol rewrote the tale demonstrates his urge to add historical verisimilitude to his depiction of the Cossack epoch. First, he rewrote chapter 5 and the beginning of chapter 6, chapter 1, and chapter 3 (all of which in one way or another portray the Cossacks' customs or their military success). Once Gogol finished the first six chapters of the tale, he asked his younger sister Elizaveta to write out a fair copy. Elizaveta made some mistakes and changes during copying. After her manuscript was ready, Gogol checked it cursorily but was not able to correct all of his sister's mistakes. He only inserted words in the blanks that Elizaveta had left where she could not decipher his handwriting. Among the most important of Gogol's modifications were the insertion of a sentence about the goldeneye ("gogol'") in the last paragraph and the deletion of a phrase in the scene of Taras's burning: "Нет, черт подери всех прислужников черта, не найдутся такие огни, муки и такая сила" (No, the devil take all of the devil's flunkeys, they'll not find such fire, torments and such power).[36]

After finishing the first round of revisions, Gogol proceeded with a more meticulous rewriting of chapters 7 through 12. In order to assess the depth of the textual changes between the redactions, I generated a "3-gram" comparison using the software program WCopyfind. The results show only a 31% similarity between the redactions of *Taras Bulba*, while the similarity between the early and final versions of "Old-World Landowners," "The Two Ivans," and "Vii" constitute 82%, 97%, and 65%, respectively. In order to analyse Gogol's revisions of *Taras Bulba*, I have divided each version into ten narrative events and compared the relevant passages from the second redaction to the same events in the first one. I have named these events for the main action in each part across both redactions of the tale: 1, The arrival of Taras's sons (Ostap's and Andrii's return home after graduation); 2, Going to Sich (Taras's and his sons' journey to the Zaporozhian Host); 3, Sich (life and customs among the Cossacks in the Host); 4, The Siege of Dubno; 5, Andrii's Treason; 6, The Battle at Dubno; 7, The Council; 8, Andrii's execution; 9, Taras in Warszawa and Ostap's execution; 10, The finale.

Table 3. Total number of words in the events and similarity by 3-gram

Events	1835	1842	Ratio (1842/35)	Similarity (%)
1 Arrival	2,978	3,463	1.16	58
2 Going	3,113	3,117	1.00	91
3 Sich	3,082	5,193	1.68	36
4 Dubno	582	1,822	3.13	8
5 Treason	1,292	5,337	4.13	2
6 Battle	978	4,631	4.74	0
7 Council	1,385	4,337	3.13	3
8 Execution	1,243	2,246	1.81	7
9 Warszawa	4,701	5,456	1.16	73
10 Finale	1,840	1,994	1.08	21
Total	21,194	37,596	1.77	31

The ratio of the word count of each event and their similarity by key-words is presented in Table 3.

The ratio of textual changes varies from chapter to chapter; the first chapter and the last two remained more or less intact while the body of the tale was significantly rewritten. While adding seventy new pages to the original version of the tale, Gogol followed the principle of doubling: for example, in the new chapter 3, Gogol made two Cossack councils out of one in the first edition; Andrii's and the Polish princess's responses became twice as long as they were in the 1835 redaction (in new chapter 6); and Bulba's address to the Cossacks was divided into two speeches in chapters 8 and 9 in the new redaction.

By the end of 1841, Gogol produced two final copies of the new *Taras Bulba* – the authorized copy and the unauthorized revised manuscript. Gogol left the first, unedited copy with Prokopovych and took the second copy to Rome, planning to finish proofreading there. Prokopovych made more than five hundred corrections to the tale and published it in the *Complete Works* (1842) without Gogol's final authorization. Because Gogol was abroad during the final stage of proofreading and publication and remained unsatisfied with the published text, we cannot consider the 1842 *Taras Bulba* the final authorized text and need to take into account all existing versions and drafts while interpreting the tale.

The most substantial changes that Gogol made to the second redaction involved its language. It became not only more refined but also more poetically stylized as the writer incorporated elements and tropes from medieval Rus' texts and Ukrainian historical *dumas*. Given the nature of the historical sources, it would be an oversimplification to present these changes in terms of Gogol's unilateral "Russification." If in *Evenings* the hybrid language was generated because of an interference between two language systems, in the 1842 *Taras Bulba* the use of Ukrainianisms was subject to a circumspect creative logic. In the second redaction, Gogol limited Ukrainianisms pertaining to the vernacular register and conflicting with the overall epic tone of the new version. For example, while Prokopovych restored the previously used Ukrainian form "chuesh, bat'ku?" (can you hear me, father?) in Ostap's final appeal, Gogol insisted on the Russian "slyshish'," explaining his choice by the fact that the Russian audience had got used to the normative form.[37]

The tendency to replace grammatical and lexical Ukrainianisms with Russian forms is already visible in Gogol's intermediate drafts for the 1835 version of the tale, which had a higher ratio of grammatical Ukrainianisms, especially in the dialogues of Cossack characters. The Ukrainian "dity" (children) was replaced in several passages by the Russian "deti," the Ukrainian "synov" (sons) with the Russian "molodtsov" (young men), and Ukrainian prefixes and prepositions were replaced with Russian forms (e.g., "sdurel" – "odurel" [got mad]; "po-za" – "iz-za" [from behind]).

At the same time, in the 1842 redaction Gogol added more lexical Ukrainianisms preculiar to the historical epoch of the Cossack Ukraine (see Table 4).[38] The Ukrainian-Russian lexicon ("Malorossiiskie slova, vstrechaiushchiesia v pervom i vtorom tomakh") accompanied *Mirgorod* (in which the tale was published), increased by sixty entries. Gogol also modified the definitions of about thirty words, foregrounding their meaning in Ukrainian, which indicated his desire to provide an accurate ethnic commentary. Therefore, Gogol made the second redaction more ethnically and historically nuanced and, at the same time, replaced grammatical Ukrainianisms with standard Russian forms to ensure conformity with the Russian novelistic tradition.

One of the main sources of the Russificatory interpretations of the 1842 version of *Taras Bulba* is the increased frequency of the modifier "Rus'ian" ("russkii"), which the scholars wrongly treat as a unified category. It seems more accurate to consider the meaning of "russkii" as differing in every single episode of the tale and referring variously to a pre-modern concept of Kyivan Rus'; the national Ukrainian idea of Rus'-Ukraine; or the imperial idea of "all-in-one Rus'," as Oleh Ilnytskyj has persuasively demonstrated.[39] While the

Table 4. Language changes between the draft and the 1835 redaction, and between the 1835 and 1842 redactions, of *Taras Bulba*

Draft 1	1835
Ну, **диты**! Что и как? (602)	Ну, **дети**! Что и как? (284)
Вот, **диты**, смотрите, каких я вам двух **сынов** привел! (603)	Вот посмотрите, каких я к вам **молодцов** привел! (285)
… **диты**, теперь спать **лягай** (604)	Ну, **дети**, теперь **надобно** спать (285)

1835	1842
А поворотись, **сынку**! **Цур тебе**, какой смешной! (279)	А поворотись-**ка**, **сын**! **Экой** ты смешной какой! (41)
Вот это **сдурел** старый! (280)	Смотрите, добрые люди: **одурел** старый! (42)

Draft 2	1842
… а **по-за** ними, **тем часом** … **по-за** пологами засядут в засаду (395)	
А, красные жупаны на **всему воинству**! (408)	А, красные жупаны на **всем войске** (116)

increased occurrence of the modifier "Rus'ian" in the second redaction frequently figures in scholars' interpretations, the addition of several dozen instances of "Cossack" and "Zaporozhian" has never been taken into consideration.

Figures 6 and 7 show the differences in the total use of ethnonyms in the two redactions and their use in the ten narrative events we defined earlier. The disproportional increase of "Cossack" is especially important as it relates to the increase of the total number of words in the ten events. If the chapters grew between 50 and 100% of their initial length, the number of occurrences of "Cossack" and "Zaporozhian" went up to 700–1000% in events 3, 6, and 7.

The variability of the ethnonyms for "Ukraine" occurs because the Zaporozhian Host in the 1842 redaction is shown through the eyes of a contemporary historian-narrator presenting the Ukrainian past to the imperial audience. In the direct speech of the Cossacks, Ukraine is designated as "Sich" (Host) (mentioned 44 times), "Ukraina" (Ukraine) (13 times), "Hetmanshchyna" (Hetmanate) (once) or "russkaia zemlia" (Rus'ian land) (10 times). According to Oleh Ilnytzkyj, in the second redaction the contrast between these categories is unintentional. In the opening passage of chapter 12, for example, "the Cossacks,"

Figure 6. Comparison of the occurrence of "Russ-," "Ukrain-," "Cossack-," and "Zaporozhian-" in *Taras Bulba* (1842)

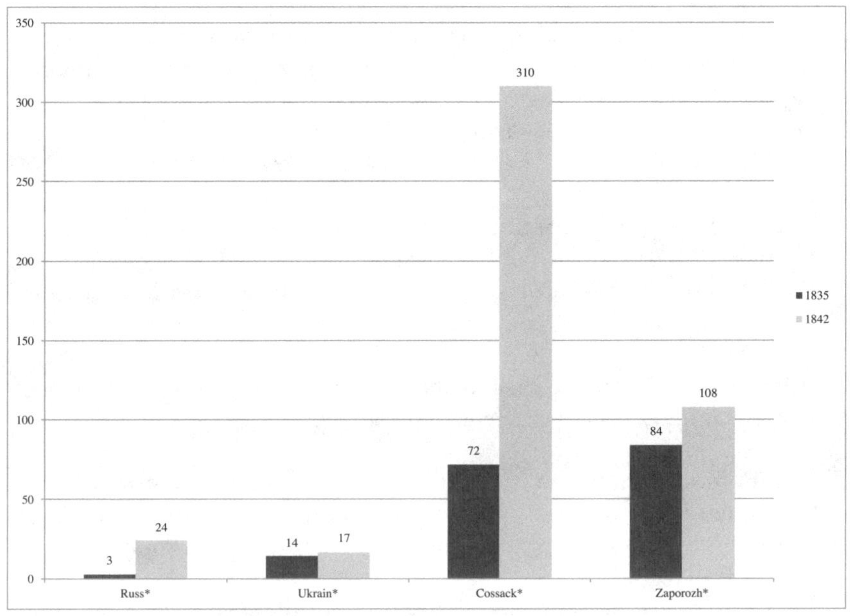

Figure 7. Comparison of the occurrence of "Cossack" by narrative event in *Taras Bulba* (1835 and 1842)

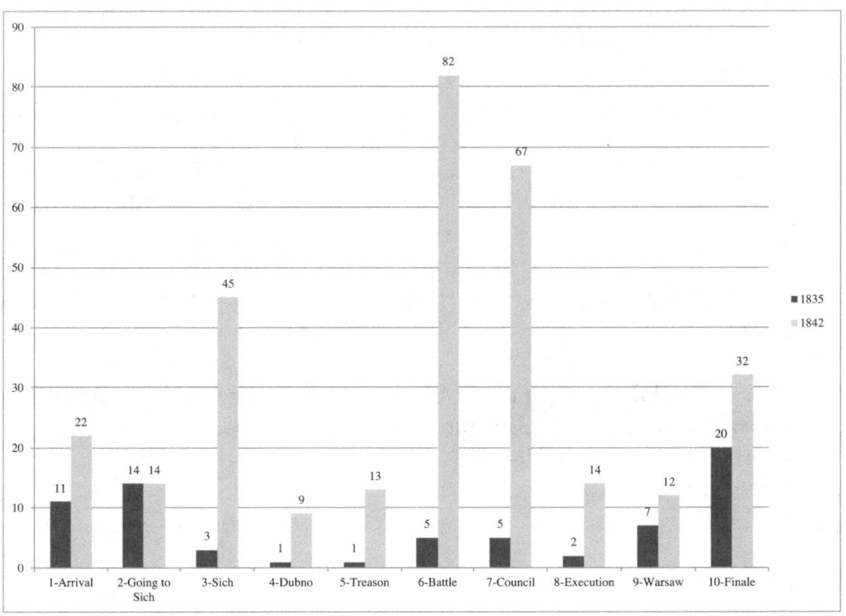

"Ukraine," "nation," and "Rus'ian land" all constitute parts of the Ukrainian national myth:

> Отыскался след Тарасов. Сто двадцать тысяч *козацкого войска* показалось на границах *Украйны* … поднялась вся *нация*, ибо переполнилось терпение *народа* … Нечего описывать всех битв, где показали себя *козаки*, ни всего постепенного хода кампании: все это внесено в летописные страницы. Известно, какова в *русской земле* война …[40]

And yet Taras was to reappear. A hundred and twenty thousand *Cossack* warriors marched across the *Ukrainian* border … The *Cossack people* had finally been tried beyond endurance, and the whole *nation* rose to seek vengeance … There is no point in describing the many battles in which the *Cossacks* distinguished themselves, nor the progression of the campaign. All this can be read in the pages of the chronicles. It is common knowledge how a war for the faith is waged on *Rus'ian land* …[41]

The different variables ("Cossacks," "the people," "Ukraine," and "Rus'ian land") in the passage signify "Ukraine," showing how Gogol attempted to reconcile national memory with the contemporary view of Cossack history.

In fact, many of the so-called Russificatory changes in the ethnonyms and geographical names intensify the relationship between ancient Rus' and Cossack Ukraine. Rus''s relation to Ukraine is established in the Cossacks' invocation to the "russkaia zemlia" (Rus'ian land) in chapter 9. Dying in the battle at Dubno, they do not "enunciate the ideology of [the] Russian nation"[42] but pay homage to the medieval tradition of the glorification of the Rus'ian land. In folk songs and *dumas*, Ukraine was often designated as "Rus'," "the Cossack land," and "the Rus'ian" or "Christian land"; for example, "Do you have a father or a mother in Rus'?" ("The Cossack Death in Kodym Valley"); "To the Rus'ian shore, to the merry land" ("Captive's Weeping"); "She saw him off to the Christian land" ("Ivan Bohuslavets'"); "I will lay my head down in the Christian land" ("Samiilo Kishka"). The Ukrainian writers Taras Shevchenko, Panteleimon Kulish, and Opanas Markovych also used the terms "Southern Russia," "Little Russia," and "Ukraine" interchangeably to designate Ukraine. For example, in his introduction to the almanac *Colourful Ukraine* (1844), Shevchenko alternated between these three terms referencing "Ukraine." He began his book's introduction by describing "Southern Russia," whose history "amazes anyone with its adventures and semi-fictional heroes," then switched to "Little Russia," which "from golden times had had its own composers, painters, and poets," and finished by referring to "Ukraine," for whose "name's glory" he served.[43]

Two other new additions to the second redaction – Taras's speech before the battle at Dubno in chapter 9 and his prophecy about the emergence of "one's own tsar" in chapter 12 – have been interpreted as a transformation of the Cossacks into "ideal Russians"[44] or as the "defender[s] of Holy Russia."[45] The contextualized reading of these ideologically charged passages renders such interpretations highly questionable. The former episode, although culminating in the idea of "tovarishchestvo" (comradeship), obfuscates the real meaning of Bulba's address to the Cossacks. The pragmatic aspect of the speech reflects its dramatic, rather than patriotic, overtones. Prior to the battle at Dubno, a messenger from the Host delivers sad news about a Tatar attack on headquarters and their confiscation of the Cossack treasury, horses, and ammunition. The usual practice in the Cossack army was to start pursuing the enemy immediately, as the narrator mentions in a non-judgmental tone in his introduction to the speech.[46] After giving an opportunity to both sides to express their opinion, Taras proposes to divide the Cossack army into two parts: one under the command of the *koshevoi* would go after the Tatars, while the other under Bulba's leadership would stay to seize Dubno. Thus, chapter 9 begins with Taras realizing how small his regiment is compared to the Polish army in Dubno. He wants to inspire patriotic feelings in the Cossacks but ends up reflecting upon the general decay of morals in the Host, which Gogol may have intended as commentary on the state of the Ukrainian gentry of his day. At the beginning of his speech, Taras reminds the Cossacks about their brotherly obligations to one another. A side-by-side comparison of the draft and final versions of Taras Bulba's speech (Appendix 3) demonstrates that Gogol embellished it with new rhetorical figures. These included repetitions, e.g., "Father loves his child, mother loves her child, child loves his father and mother"; tautological phrases, e.g., "become related by spiritual ties of relation"; and juxtapositions, e.g., "There were comrades in other lands, but nowhere were there such comrades as in the Rus'ian land." All of these have a strong emotive impact on the Cossacks. The second part of the speech is a disjointed, passionate critique of the recent trend among the Cossacks to strive for material enrichment and to serve foreign rulers:

"No, brothers! To love as the Rus'ian soul can love, not with the mind or whatever, but with everything that God has given us, with everything that is inside us – no, nobody else can love like that!" Taras said, waving his hands and shaking his gray head and mustache. "I know how badly things stand in our land. All that men think about is how many haystacks and herds of horses they have, and whether their mead is safely locked away in their cellars. They have taken on the devil knows what heathen habits. They loathe their own mother tongue, one man won't speak to another, men sell their own brothers as beasts are sold on market squares! The favor of the Polish King – and, often enough, not even the favor of the King but the cheap favor of a Polish magnate who will kick them in the face with his elegant boot – is dearer to these men than any brotherhood. But even the lowest scoundrel, the lowest of the low, though he may have scraped and bowed, rolled about groveling in the mud, even he, brothers, has a spark of Rus'ian sentiment which can burst into flame! The poor wretch will pound his fists and clasp his head in his hands, cursing his worthless life, thirsting for any turture to atone for his shameful ways. And may all men know that this is what brotherhood means on Rus'ian soil! And when the time comes to die, not a single one of them will manage to die as we will! Not a single one of them, for these wretches are mice, not men![47]

The illogical phrasing of the second part of the speech reinforces Bulba's accusation of his contemporaries' servility: in one sentence, he reproaches them for adopting "infidel [Muslim] ways," abandoning their own language and betraying each other; while in the other, he blames them for collaborating with Polish magnates. His critique of the Cossacks' forsaking their democratic values and native traditions could be projected onto nineteenth-century Ukrainian gentry who were eager to gain imperial favour by serving the tsar. Finally, Taras predicts the time when even the last villain who is "covered in soot and boot-licking" ("v sazhe i v poklonnichestve") will "curse his vile life" and "redeem his shameful deeds with suffering." Volodymyr Dibrova rightly asks the questions: what kind of "shameful deeds" did the Cossacks perform and who are the "all" in the phrase "Let them all know"? The scholar discerns in the "very unpredictability, wild imagery and occasional babbling" of Taras's speech the "imprint of a classic Ukrainian mind, big on 'sound and fury' and very often 'signifying nothing.'"[48] The structure of Taras's speech seems comparable with that of the letter of complaint written by Ivan Nikiforovich in another tale from *Mirgorod*, "The Tale of How Ivan Ivanovich Quarrelled with Ivan Nikiforovich." Ivan Nikiforovich's discourse is an example of pure verbal play, lacking any corresponding content and reflecting Gogol's general treatment of language as capable of signifying anything. The paradox of Gogol's most ideological passages in *Taras Bulba* is that they capture not only Gogol's own back-and-forth relationship with the Russian Empire but also the unstable meaning of his politically charged discourse.

The conflation of national sentiment and imperial loyalty led to the debates about the other newly added ideologically charged passage in *Taras Bulba*, which predicts the emergence of "one's own tsar" ("svoi tsar'") out of the "Rus'ian land" ("russkaia zemlia"). It is important to quote this passage as it was published in the 1842 version:

> Что, взяли, чертовы ляхи? Думаете, есть что-нибудь на свете, чего бы побоялся козак? Постойте же, придет время, будет время, узнаете вы, что такое православная русская вера! Уже и теперь чуют дальние и близкие народы: *поднимется* из Русской земли свой царь, и не будет в мире силы, которая бы не покорилась ему! ...[49]

> So you thought you'd caught us, you damn Poles? Do you think there is a single thing in this world that will frighten a Cossack? Just wait, the time will come when you will understand the meaning of the Russian Ortho-dox faith! Word has already spread through every nation: one's own czar *will spring* forth from the Rus'ian land, and there will be no power in this world that shall not yield to him! ... (emphasis added)[50]

As Oleh Ilnytzkyj has rightly noted, for those who adhere to the Rus-sificatory interpretation of the tale the words "one's own tsar" and the "Rus'ian land" sound "mutually reinforcing."[51] For example, George Grabowicz sees in Bulba's prophetic vision of an emerging tsar a logical outcome of the Cossacks seen as "a foreshadowing of imperial Russian Orthodox power,"[52] while Myroslav Shkandrij interprets it as the com-ing "Ukrainian salvation" that "depended on the coming to power of the Romanov dynasty in 1613."[53] Bojanowska also reads this scene as a confirmation that Ukrainians will come "[u]nder the leadership of the mighty Great Russian tsar."[54] Arguing against this view, Ilnytzkyj proposes to decouple "russkaia zemlia" from "svoi tsar" and to shift emphasis to the possessive "svoi" (one's own). Ilnytzkyj's argument is that, had Gogol intended to create a paean to Russian nationalism, he could have expressed the idea of Cossack Ukraine's unification with Russia more clearly, as did all other contemporary writers.[55]

I propose to approach Gogol's dilemma of dual national allegiance here by returning to the original grammatical tense form, the perfec-tive future of "podnimetsia" (shall arise), that was changed to the present tense form "podymaetsia" (is arising) in Gogol's *Complete Works* in 1855 and that remains in the latter form in all subsequent pub-lications. I think that editors Likhonin and Shevyrev were disturbed by the notion that the tsar would arise in the indefinite future and replaced it with the less ambiguous present continuous form. But the question remains: if the Romanovs had already ruled Russia for several decades when the final battle led by Hetman Ostrianytsia took place in 1638, as depicted in the finale of *Taras Bulba*, why would Gogol have used the perfective future "will spring forth"? In answering this question I would like to develop further Iurii Barabash's thesis about "one's own tsar" as reflecting "the ancient dream of Ukrainian Cossackdom about *its own* statehood – a direct descendant of the state traditions of Kyivan Rus'."[56] The phrase "svoi tsar" reverberates with the idea of an autonomous ruler established as early as in 1037, when Hilarion in his *Sermon on Law and Grace* polemicized with the patristic tradition of a singular universal empire and declared the right of other minor nations (which Kyivan Rus' was in relation to Byzantium at the time) to political independence and autonomous rulership. In his *Sermon*, Hilarion called Prince Volodymyr "the autocrat of his own land who conquered the neighbouring countries, some of them amicably, some resistant ones – by the sword" ("единодержець бывъ земли своеи, покоривъ подъ ся округъная страны, овы миромъ, а непокоривыа мечемь").[57] Similarly, Bulba's prophecy first puts the unification of all people ("dal'nie i blizkie narody") under the aegis of the Orthodox faith and then foresees the emergence of a local ruler ("svoi tsar"). In this controversial finale, Gogol paid tribute to the traditional ending of Ukrainian heraldic verses, a.k.a. "All sing his praises."[58] Although "tsar" does not figure in Cossack chronicles and folk *dumas* as one of the hetman's titles, in the popular imagination of the descendants of the Ukrainian Cossacks "tsar" without a modifier could mean the highest Cossack authority. For example, Markevych in his comments on the *duma* "Ukraine" contrasted the autocratic Russian tsar and the tsar (i.e., hetman) who was democratically elected by the Ukrainian people: "And therefore Hetman Konashevych did not attack his compatriots; he was a warrior (not a rebel against his rulers), elected by his people to be the Tsar because 'Hetman' is like 'Roi,' 'Król' or 'Rex.' Hetmanate is also an elected monarchical rulership."[59] Furthermore, in the original Cossack chronicles and folk *dumas* written or collected in the eighteenth to early nineteenth centuries, the Russian ruler appeared either as the "royal majesty" ("tsarskoe velichestvo," as in Hrabianka's *Chronicle of an Eyewitness*), or as an "Orthodox tsar" ("We want [to be] under the Orthodox Tsar," as in the *duma* about the Zhvanets' battle), or as a "white tsar" (as in the *duma* about Vyhovs'kyi, who supported the Poles, or Martin Pushkar, who "stood for the Orthodox faith and for the white tsar"), or as an "Eastern tsar" (as in the folk song "The Eastern tsar distrusts Ukraine").

That the two versions of *Taras Bulba* convey different messages to Russian and Ukrainian audiences had been already evident to Gogol's contemporaries. In the Preface to his novel *The Black Council* (1857), Panteleimon Kulish wrote: "In *Taras Bulba* Gogol spoke about Little Russia in a language comprehensible to both tribes [Russians and Ukrainians]; on the one hand, he demonstrated to his native tribe all of the wonderful things it had and still has; on the other hand, he revealed to Great Russians a unique and poetic nation that had only been known through the ludicrous literary representation."[60] However, after Belinskii's verdict that Gogol allegedly abandoned his Ukrainian identity in favour of the Great Russian in the 1842 redaction of *Taras Bulba*, other Gogol critics have interpreted the tale in this key. Igor Vinogradov, editor-in-chief of the bicentennial edition of Gogol's *Complete Works and Letters* (2009) (the publication of which was funded by the Moscow Patriarchate), pointed out that "the changes and insertions that Gogol made between the first and second redactions of the tale demonstrate that his initial idea was to create a parable about contemporary Russia, not a heroic tale of Little Russian history. He rewrote the tale because he wanted to clarify his conception of Russia."[61] Judith Kornblatt also called the modification of the tale in the second redaction a "Russification," which made the tale "one of the most ultra-nationalistic works in all literature … A metonymic relationship between the Cossacks and the Russians through the mediation of Rus'" was realized on various textual levels, including the presentation of the Cossacks "as though they themselves *are* the Russians."[62] Saera Yoon wrote that Gogol deliberately annihilated the "cultural specificity and unique historical experience" of the Cossacks in the new redaction of the tale.[63] In Bojanowska's view, Gogol's overall revising strategy in the second redaction of *Taras Bulba* was "to identify the place of action as 'Russia' and the Cossacks' identity as 'Russian' or 'southern Russian'" by eliminating references to Ukraine and Ukrainians.[64] Notably, in Gogol's time "southern Russia" functioned as an alternative geographical designation for Little Russia.

Gogol's significant textual and linguistic changes in the 1842 redaction of *Taras Bulba* created a hybrid text par excellence. By having Cossacks fight for the Rus'ian land and sacrifice their lives for the Orthodox Russian faith, Gogol did not transform Cossack Ukrainian identity into an imperial Russian one but complicated the idea of Russianness by its dependence on the heroic Cossack myth. In the new redaction of the tale, Gogol modernized the Cossack myth of Ukraine by stressing the Cossacks' contribution to the development of East Slavic Orthodox civilization, which surprisingly satisfied both descendants of the Cossacks and the imperial audience, who saw in the new redaction of *Taras Bulba* Russia's aspirations to become a global power. Partly as the result of unsystematic editing, partly because of Gogol's own hybrid identification with the imperial audience, the 1842 redaction operated differently for the Ukrainian and Russian audiences. Ukrainian translations of *Taras Bulba* made in the second half of the nineteenth century in Eastern Galicia and Left-Bank Ukraine were used to mobilize Ukrainians to resist the oppressive power of the Polish and Russian governments, and this corroborates the fact that the Ukrainian audience did not find that the work contradicted the idea of their national myth.

Textual Changes in *Dead Souls*

While working on *Dead Souls* during 1836–41, Gogol produced several handwritten drafts and three final copies.[65] The first final copy was prepared and edited by Gogol himself; the second (the so-called Rome copy) was produced by two copyists, Pavel Annenkov and Vasilii Panov, and was immediately rewritten by Gogol. This text soon became a draft for the third final copy, in which Gogol made significant changes in anticipation of censorship. This was an unusual practice for Gogol, who almost never proofread the copyists' rewritten texts. In preparing *Dead Souls* for publication, he continued rewriting it, producing an extra layer of text on top of the existing final copy. As a result, Annenkov's and Panov's not quite legible handwriting, coupled with Gogol's handwritten corrections, complicated the publication of the text. The typesetters made on average 4.5 mistakes and omissions per page, totalling more than a thousand mistakes in the entire manuscript. Gogol could not control the publication process from Rome and authorized the final text of the novel without final proofreading.

The submitted final copy of the novel not only had numerous orthographical mistakes and inconsistencies (such as the spelling of "Russian" in some places with one "s" and in others with two) but also carried hidden satirical messages. When submitting the manuscript to the censor in 1841, Gogol did not have any concerns about his satirical depiction of imperial society. In his previous interactions with censors in the 1830s, the writer had relied on the protection of Nicholas I, who held a high opinion of his satirical talent. The writer's confidence in imperial protection is corroborated by Annenkov, who wrote in his memoirs: "When at the end of the story I gave in to an uncontrollable outburst of gaiety, Gogol began to laugh together with me and asked me several times: 'So, how do you like "The Tale of Captain Kopeikin"?' – 'Will it ever be published?' – I asked. 'Publication is a piece of cake,' Gogol replied with confidence. 'Everything will be published.'"[66] After Annenkov's comments, however, Gogol softened the satirical tone. In the winter of 1841–2, he submitted a revised text of "The Tale of Captain Kopeikin" to the censor. His changes in the content of the tale were so significant that it prompted Annenkov to comment that the earlier version surpassed the final text in "power [of style] and maturity."

A comparative analysis of the two versions of "The Tale of Captain Kopeikin" shows that Gogol enhanced the *skaz* manner of the postmaster's storytelling by adding more "fillers," such as "so to speak," "you can just imagine it," "in a certain sense," and "you understand." The "bigwig" was transformed from a polite and sympathetic individual into an irritated government official. Trying to alleviate the responsibility of the top-ranked officials, Gogol deleted the sentence "With his refusal, the minister drives Kopeikin to despair and makes him a robber" from the final draft.[67] But the most significant alteration of the tale involved the episode about Kopeikin's transformation into a "noble bandit," which might have been hinting at the popular legend of the Ukrainian bandit Harkusha.[68] In the early draft of the tale, Kopeikin takes revenge on the repressive state by noble acts of banditry. When hungry Kopeikin receives nothing from the government official, he announces that he will not leave the office. The minister orders Kopeikin arrested, but he escapes and organizes a band of like-minded men who rob only state property. Once Kopeikin accumulates substantial capital, he emigrates to the US and writes to the emperor asking him to show his monarchical mercy and to stop persecution. The emperor is touched to his heart by Kopeikin's letter and establishes a special fund "which had no analogue either in England or in other enlightened states."[69] The final text of "The Tale of Captain Kopeikin" ends when the narrator announces the appearance of the gang in the Riazan' forests and hints at Kopeikin's role as its ringleader. By omitting all the initial details of Kopeikin's banditry, Gogol muted parallels with the legendary Ukrainian hero Harkusha.

The textual changes between the early draft and the final text of the tale show that Gogol wanted to avoid any ambiguities and to present Kopeikin as a noble bandit who suffered from the injustices of the imperial bureaucratic system. Describing the actions of Kopeikin's gang, Gogol specified that it targeted only state property. The aggrieved peasants were supplied with the document for the avoidance of justice. The emperor's reaction to Kopeikin's letter expresses reconciliation. However, even after Gogol softened the social content of the tale, the injustice of the imperial machine remained palpable, and the censorship committee ordered him to eliminate "The Tale of Captain Kopeikin" entirely. Gogol expressed his frustration and intent to fight for the tale in a letter to Prokopovych of 9 April 1842 ("I have decided not to give up on the 'Tale' in any way") and one to Pletnev on 10 April 1842:

> The elimination of Kopeikin has disturbed me deeply. This is one of the best passages in the poem, without which there will be a hole which I absolutely cannot patch up and sew. I have made up my mind to recast it rather than be deprived of it altogether. I got rid of all *generalitet*. Kopeikin's personality is made more palpable so that everyone sees now that he is the reason for all [of his misfortunes] and that he was treated well.[70]

In his letter to the censor Nikitenko, Gogol repeated his willingness to remove references to state officials, but he obfuscated the true importance of the embedded tale. Gogol's begging the censor to publish the tale echoed Kopeikin's own wrestling with the bureaucratic system. At first, Gogol complained that "without Kopeikin he could not publish the novel," but when he exhausted his last arguments he resorted to pleading for the emperor's intervention. In a letter to Odoevskii of 7 January 1842, he asked to him show the manuscript to Nicholas I, and he also asked for financial support (he wrote to Pletnev on 27 March that he was "without a kopeck"). Even though this expression is a standard idiom in the Russian language ("to remain without a kopeck," "not to have a kopeck to one's soul"), Gogol used the word "kopeck" deliberately to suggest an affinity between Kopeikin's fate and his own. After waiting five months for the censor's approval, Gogol contacted other influential censors, Sergei Uvarov and Mikhail Dondukov-Korsakov, saying that he "sacrificed everything, condemned [himself] to a severe poverty" hoping that when the book was published "the Fatherland would not deprive [him] of a piece of bread."[71] Thanks to the protection of the royal authorities, on 3 March 1842 the manuscript was approved for publication on the condition that Gogol changed the title from *Dead Souls: A Poem* to *Chichikov's Adventures, or Dead Souls: A Poem*; deleted "The Tale of Captain Kopeikin"; and removed all references to the monarch, negative characterizations of government officials and the upper classes, all instances of corruption and bribery and of alcoholism among state and military officials, any mention of serfs' disobedience and criminal activities, and, finally, any references to God, prophets, or other holy figures.

Having received this message, Gogol agreed to all of the changes in the main text of the novel in exchange for rescuing "The Tale of Captain Kopeikin." Furthermore, he wrote more lyrical digressions about the Russian mentality in order to compensate for the social critique, which still remained patent even after the revisions of the tale. The final version of the first authorized copy demonstrates how Gogol modified the lyrical digressions or added new ones. For example, the statement about Russians' habit of playing dirty tricks on people ("nagadit' blizhnemu") in the final version applies to one person: it is now a state official endowed "with a star on his chest" who can "play dirty tricks in such a way and on such a scale as a collegiate registrar would" (chapter 4).[72] The new lyrical digressions provided commentary on the Russian mentality in general: on Russians' worship of ranks ("Such indeed is the Russian: he has a powerful passion for rubbing shoulders with anyone who might stand one rank higher than himself, and a nodding acquaintance with a count or a prince he deems preferable to any intimate friendship" [chapter 2]);[73] on the peculiarities of women's education (when describing Mrs Manilova in chapter 2);[74] on Russians' predilection for drinking (chapter 8);[75] on the foreign manners of upper-class readers who cannot say a word in Russian (chapter 8);[76] on the author's resistance to using foreign words in his novel (chapter 9);[77] on the fact that Russians "have somehow not been created for representative bodies" (chapter 10);[78] on the inability of Russians to express their thoughts; and many others.

These new lyrical digressions, instead of enhancing patriotic feelings, deepen the gap between the archaic and modern, the unbounded and bounded space of Russia. Like the use of ethnonyms and geographical names in the second redaction of *Taras Bulba*, the parallel use of "Rus'," "russkii," and "Rossiia" in *Dead Souls* has generated fierce debate about Gogol's real feelings toward imperial Russia.[79] But if in *Taras Bulba* the national referent of such concepts as "Rus'" and "russkii" was arguably limited to "Ukraine" (at least to literate Ukrainians of Gogol's cohort), in *Dead Souls* these words refer to the imperial space of Russia. Gogol's contemporaries were looking for the "Russian Russia" – a socially, morally, and spiritually unified nation – but instead they found in the novel a satirical picture of crude Russian reality that sharply contrasted with the poetic image of Rus' in the lyrical digressions.

The tension between the symbolic space of "Rus'" and the imperial space of "Russia" emerged only at the last stage of Gogol's work on the novel. At the beginning, Gogol had designated the artistic space unambiguously as "Rus'" (sometimes "Orthodox Rus'," both signifying Russia), which he wanted to show "at least from one side" (as put it in his letter to Pushkin, on 7 October 1835).[80] His poor knowledge of the Russian Empire was notorious and ridiculed by his contemporaries, so that his lyrical image of "Rus'" might have been a compensation for his actual lack of experience of the country. A hundred years after Gogol's death, Vladimir Nabokov humorously described the problem:

> … to search for true Russian reality in *Dead Souls* is as futile as to imagine that Denmark is based on one accident in foggy Elsinore. And if you want "facts," then let us inquire what experience did Gogol have of provincial Russia? Eight hours in a Podolsk inn, a week in Kursk, the rest he had seen from the window of his travelling carriage, and to this he had added the memories of his essentially Ukrainian youth spent in Mirgorod, Nezhin, and Poltava? But all these towns lay far away from Chichikov's itinerary.[81]

Nabokov's irony captured Gogol's real fear of representing Russia without knowing it properly. Therefore, at the early stage of his work on the novel, Gogol hesitated to call the geographical space he described "Russia." A year later the geographical and social scale of the novel expanded and received more concrete contours, but the space remained designated as "Rus'." In a letter to Zhukovsky (1836), Gogol wrote: "What a variegated mass [kucha]! The whole of Rus' will appear in it [the novel]!"[82] As he clarified the genre of the future novel in his letter to Pletnev of 1835, this was a "poem" with a "vast," "original" plot; he changed the spatial parameters to Russia (signalled by the terms "Rossiia" and "rossiiskii"). However, "Rus'" and "ruskii" persisted in the lyrical digressions, signifying the symbolical connection of Russia with Rus'. These two designations of Russia are contextually related in *Dead Souls* but do not overlap: the latter evokes the symbolic image of Kyivan Rus', while the former designates the Russian Empire. In eight (out of twenty-two total) occurrences in *Dead Souls*, "Rus'" signifies epic space coinciding with the "Rus'" of the second redaction of *Taras Bulba*, reflecting religious or folk connotations.[83] This is especially manifested in the motif of *bogatyrstvo* (ancient Slavic heroism), for example: "especially at the present time, bogatyrs are beginning to die out even in Rus'";[84] "Rus' … Is it not here that a bogatyr is destined to live, since there is room for him to stretch himself and stride about?";[85] and "he was what in Rus' is called a bogatyr."[86] In the other fourteen uses of "Rus',"[87] it has distinct sociopolitical contours and can be replaced with "Rossiia."[88]

"Rossiia" appears twelve times in the final text of *Dead Souls* and signifies both the geographical territory and the Russian Empire (twice named "the Russian state").[89] The main feature of "Russia," its vast size, is conveyed by frequent mention of different cities and *guberniias*, located mainly in the European part of the empire: Riazan', Kazan', Torzhok, Tsarevokokshaisk, Ves'egonsk, Krasnyi, Tula, Tambov, Kherson, Sol'vychegodsk, Ust'-Sysol'sk, Iaroslavl', the Caucasus, the Volga river, and Kamchatka. Earlier drafts of the novel also included Berdichev and Krakow – cities located in Right-Bank Ukraine and in Poland, which probably appeared too "Western" to fit into Gogol's idea of Russianness and therefore were eliminated from the final version. But, overall, Gogol's choice of geographical sites was rather random and served mainly to demonstrate his improved knowledge of the empire. Significantly, the vagueness of Chichikov's actual itinerary also contributes to blurring the boundaries of the imperial space.

In his study of Gogol's artistic space, Iurii Lotman argued that the alternating use of "Rus'" and "Russia" in *Dead Souls* corresponded to the spatial categories of bounded versus unbounded and "directed" (*napravlennoe*) versus "undirected" (*nenapravlennoe*).[90] "Rus'," according to Lotman, is a bounded space in Gogol's chronotope; it is driven by a goal-oriented, directed movement toward a higher metaphysical plane, whereas "Russia" signifies an unbounded, undirected space, which lacks any goal or orientation. In the novel, "Rus'" indeed has the ability to transform itself and its inhabitants:

> And so, this [Pliushkin] was the species of landowner who was standing before Chichikov! It must be said that such a phenomenon is rarely encountered in Rus', where everything likes to expand rather than to contract, and it is all the more striking by virtue of the fact that in the same neighbourhood lives a landowner who carouses with all the expansiveness of the Russian nature …[91]

In my opinion, the dual terms "Rus'" and "Russia" serve not primarily to describe the space of *Dead Souls* but to integrate archaic and modern concepts of Russia.

At the late stage of his work on the novel, Gogol added the famous passage about the racing Rus'-troika that flies into the distance, with other peoples yielding the way without completely apprehending what goes before them:

> Art not thou too, O Rus', rushing onwards like a spirited troika? Smoking like smoke under you is the road, thundering are the bridges, all falls back and is left behind. The onlooker comes to a stop, struck by the divine miracle: is this not a lightning bolt flung down from heaven? What is the meaning of this awe-inspiring movement? And what manner of unknown power is contained within these steeds, who are unknown to the world? Eh, steeds, steeds, what manner of steeds! Do whirlwinds nest in your manes? Does a keen ear burn in your every fibre? They have heard from on high the familiar song, and at once as one they have strained their

bronze chests, and barely touching the earth with their hooves, all are transformed into merely long straight lines that fly through the air, and on rushes the troika, all-inspired by God! Rus', whither art thou racing? Give an answer. She gives no answer. The bells pour out a wondrous ringing: rent to shreds, the air thunders and is transformed into wind: all that exists on earth flies by, and, looking askance, other peoples and nations step aside and make way for her.[92]

None of the three earlier drafts of the novel concluded with this "troika" image. Having added it at the final stage, Gogol also may have wanted to create expectations for the sequel, Volume 2, which he had begun contemplating already in 1836. Russian intellectuals from both camps, Westernizers and Slavophiles, read the passage through a nationalistic lens. They saw in it a positive view of Russia that neutralized Gogol's satirical representation of the dreadful reality of the Russian Empire depicted elsewhere in the novel.[93]

The satirical representation of Russian society notwithstanding, the notion of the compensatory passage about Rus'-troika seems ungrounded. As Bojanowska has argued, by metonymically connecting Russia to a troika racing nowhere, Gogol created a disembodied idea of it: "[j]ust as the troika that leaves behind all concrete reality, finally to transform itself into abstract lines that cleave the air, Russia becomes the realiora that transcend the coarse realia that overflow the novel."[94] It is significant that the spatial imagery of the troika passage in *Dead Souls* echoes the phantasmagorical vision of Russia presented by Poprishchin in "Diary of a Madman."[95] As a void, Rus' in the final passage of *Dead Souls* is an "open and flat wasteland" with its "flat, lowly cities that stick out imperceptibly among the plains like points or signs." The foreigners who gaze at the troika appear insignificant and unable to comprehend it. Mikhail Epshtein, in his turn, has pointed to the textual parallels between the passage about Rus'-troika and the depiction of the demonic in "Vii" and "The Terrible Revenge," which signifies the symbiosis of apophatic and demonic, sacred and profane in Gogol's art and in Russian culture in general.[96] One could say that the overall effect of Gogol's Rus'-troika passage is so dubious that it can be read as a symbol both of the destructive emptiness of Russia and of its messianic potential.

Gogol's critical view of Russia's power structures in his last years casts light on this highly ambivalent image. Piotr Semenenko, a Polish revolutionary and an émigré, believed that Gogol had to conceal his real attitude to the empire. In their private conversation, Gogol mentioned the empire's lack of spirit and uniformity: "He sees very well that there is no cement that could bind this formless, monstrous building. Power oppresses from above, but inside there is no spirit."[97] Gogol's close friend Aleksandr Ivanov also recorded Gogol saying that "[t]he Russians are in trouble! … Russians, by nature, are deprived of a basis [baza] on which one could safely place and build anything."[98] It seems that even in the 1840s Gogol still believed in the cultural difference between Russia and Ukraine. In his "Author's Will," published in *Selected Passages* (1846), he called himself "a close relative" to Russians, thereby emphasizing his link but not identity with them.[99] As I have suggested, the straddling between being a Russian and looking like a Russian is manifested in Gogol's nuanced use of the categories of "Russianness" in the final version of Volume 1 of *Dead Souls*.

Chapter Six

The Posthumous Publications and Translations of Gogol's Texts

The previous chapter analysed Gogol's editing and correcting the language of his first editions. Repeated writing and revision became Gogol's basic working method in his late period.[1] Anticipating the harsh hand of a censor or the critical reception of his audience, he self-censored ideologically charged or controversial passages in his texts. This chapter surveys the history of Gogol's posthumous publications in Russian that aimed to canonize him as a Russian imperial writer. It also analyses translations of Gogol's texts into Ukrainian, which served to reappropriate the writer as a Ukrainian. New editions not only further corrupted Gogol's original texts but also put his art in the service of ideology. It is crucial to determine how much of his original texts has remained in academic editions; to what extent Gogol's editors have censored his letters; how the ambiguous meaning of "Rus'" was obfuscated in Ukrainian translations of *Taras Bulba*; and how the translation and retranslation of a hybrid writer like Gogol can help map the changing role of ideology in Ukrainian culture in the post-Soviet period.

The Posthumous Publication of Gogol's Works

The academic edition of Gogol's works consists of at least three textual "layers": the initial texts of the first editions; the Russianized texts of the second editions (1836–42); and the combination of the two that occurs in all subsequent posthumous editions. Since the 1890s, editors and scholars have been engaged in cleansing Gogol's texts of the accrued layers of editorial corrections. First, Nikolai Tikhonravov verified the text of Gogol's first publications with the 1842 and 1855 editions and compiled a list of variations. For the tenth edition of Gogol's *Complete Works* (1889–96), Tikhonravov chose the texts published in the 1855 edition (which was based on the 1842 edition with Gogol's revisions). He pointed to Prokopovych's distortions of Gogol's texts and formulated his own editorial principle: "In defining the authenticity and correctness of particular passages we take as the basis either Gogol's own handwritten drafts or his corrections made to the copyist's text, or the first editions of the texts which were published under his personal direct supervision before 1842."[2] A decade later, he launched the eleventh edition of Gogol's *Complete Works* (1900), which for the first time included his early unfinished works, the essays from *Arabesques*, the 1835 redactions of *Taras Bulba* and *The Portrait*, and the uncensored text of "The Tale of Captain Kopeikin." He also adhered to Gogol's original plan of grouping the works into volumes.

Gogol's next editor, Nikolai Korobka, criticized Tikhonravov for his undifferentiated treatment of the edited texts. Korobka pointed at Tikhonravov's own insertion of new words and expressions from the draft versions which Gogol himself had discarded in the final text. Instead, Korobka proposed to consider the text of the 1836 edition of *Evenings* with Gogol's corrections made in 1851 as the "author's final text."[3] This seemed a more reasonable approach than Tikhonravov's republication of the first edition of the tales. However, when Gogol himself proofread his texts for the 1855 edition, he used not the text of the 1836 edition but the text from 1842 that had been "co-authored" with the editor Prokopovych. Hence the editing principle that Korobka proposed could not be realized systematically. The Soviet editors Konstantin Khalabaev and Boris Eikhenbaum realized the limitations of both Tikhonravov's and Korobka's attempts to restore the original text as they began to compile the first Soviet academic edition of Gogol's works in the 1920s. They decided to follow the 1836 edition of *Evenings*, which was entirely edited by Gogol himself, and ignored the corrections made in the 1842 and 1851 editions, which were only partially approved by Gogol. These corrections, in their view, were purely stylistic and technical rather than artistic.[4] The next academic edition of Gogol's works (1937–52), supervised by the editor Boris Tomashevskii, used the first publications as the basis for a reconstruction of "Gogol's text." However, this principle was not consistently applied to all cases of textual variation. Tomashevskii prioritized those corrections made in the 1842 and 1855 editions "which could be attributed to Gogol with certainty."[5]

The latest academic edition of Gogol's works (2001–) follows the principle of the author's final corrections (i.e., made by Gogol or indisputably approved by him in 1851–2).[6] These corrections restored the semantic transformations, lexical changes, and removal of inversions and Ukrainianisms made by previous editors. Importantly, the editors also restored the graphic design of the first edition of *Evenings*, although they used a smaller print for Pan'ko's texts and a larger one for the rest of the book, reversing the original design. It is well known that Gogol paid a lot of attention to the paratext: the author's name (or its absence) on the title page, the book's title, the vignette on the cover page, prefaces, footnotes, appendices, glossaries, list of misprints, etc. Only the editions of 1836 and 1842 of the tales retained Gogol's original graphic design; all posthumous editions have used one typeface, distorting the visual border between the text of the fictitious editor-narrator and those of the other narrators.

Another problem occurred with the reproduction of the Ukrainian epigraphs in "Sorochintsy Fair" and "May Night." All editions of the tales published in Gogol's lifetime transcribed Ukrainian words in the *iaryzhka*, an official tsarist method of rendering Ukrainian using a Russian-based orthography.[7] This led to confusion between the Ukrainian letter "и" in one case and the Russian "ы" in another (both "и" and "ы" render the same Ukrainian sound, a central front middle vowel, the modern reflex of the old central back high vowel "ы" in modern Ukrainian orthography and in the *iaryzhka*, respectively). The editors tried to balance between the modern Ukrainian and the *iaryzhka* transcription of the epigraphs in the first edition, which created some inconsistency. For example, in the epigraph to chapter 5 of "Sorochintsy Fair," the word "хилися" is transcribed in Ukrainian, whereas "журыся" is in the *iaryzhka*; the same spelling occurs in Paraska's song in "Sorochintsy Fair," in which "стелися низенько" is transcribed in Ukrainian, while the next line, "А ты, мылый, чернобрывый," is in the *iaryzhka*.[8]

Since 1842 none of the academic editions have presented Gogol's texts and his idiosyncratic hybrid language as the author intended them. Considering that all attempts to rectify Gogol's texts from the editorial corrections have failed in one way or another, it would be important to reprint the first editions of his texts side by side with the subsequent editions in order to show Gogol's meticulous work on his hybrid language.

Censoring Gogol: Panteleimon Kulish's Publication of Gogol's Correspondence

It was not only Russian imperial ideology that guided the use of Russian in Gogol's texts; Ukrainian intellectuals were also engaged in censoring his texts in edited collections. One of the first publications of Gogol's epistolary heritage was made by his biographer Panteleimon Kulish. He collected materials for Gogol's biography for several decades and received unlimited access to his correspondence through the author's mother and sisters. In 1857, Kulish published Gogol's complete works in six volumes, which for the first time included both redactions of *Taras Bulba* and *The Portrait*, the surviving fragments of the second volume of *Dead Souls*, and, most importantly, 789 of Gogol's letters to various addressees (compared to 1,320 letters in the Soviet academic edition of Gogol's *Complete Works* of 1937–52).

When compiling two volumes of the letters, Kulish experienced intensive pressure from Gogol's most frequent correspondents, Sergei Aksakov and Piotr Pletnev, who did not want to publicize their private letters and who insisted that Kulish disguise the names of all address-ees in order to protect their privacy. After long debates, Kulish agreed to their conditions and published Gogol's letters without the names.[9] At the same time, he suggested that a key to the names be published separately, motivating the need for such a list by a desire to help future researchers. He prepared a booklet with an index containing the names and submitted it to the publisher, but it mysteriously disappeared the day before typesetting. Kulish did not want to believe that it was an accident and accused Aksakov of "deliberate, poorly concealed sabo-tage."[10] The "key" was published only in 1886 by Shenrok in *Index to Gogol's Letters*. While comparing Kulish's publication with the writer's actual letters, Shenrok discovered multiple distortions of the original text which Kulish made in his attempt to "retouch" Gogol's public image according to the existing canon.

Kulish had described his method of selecting what was appropri-ate and what was not in his introduction to the 1857 *Works and Letters*: "Our main objective was to present all available material which was gathered bit by bit and which can be synthesized into an overall pic-ture only after the true acceptance and insight into Gogol's chief idea, which, in the editor's view, rests in his search for the truth and perfec-tion."[11] Kulish's editing of the letters was conditioned by his view of Gogol as his spiritual mentor. He eliminated Gogol's discussions of mundane, practical issues as incompatible with the writer's late reli-gious transformation. The overall compositional order and presenta-tion of Gogol's letters was sloppy. Kulish did not assemble the letters in chronological order. He often left out the addressee, date, place, and closing polite formula, such as "Yours Gogol," "Kiss you and hug you," "God bless you," "Say hi to …," "Adieu, hug you firmly …" etc., which may provide valuable information on Gogol's relationship to his addressees. The most edited texts were Gogol's letters to his mother (16 February 1847), Aleksandr Ivanov (10 January 1844), Aleksandra Smirnova (18 December 1844), Piotr Pletnev (27 September 1839), and Sergei Aksakov (21 December 1844).

For example, in the 1847 letter to his mother, Gogol instructs her on how to instil spirituality in his sisters. Next, he switches to a more practical topic and discusses his family's annual income and expenses in a rather irritated tone. He criticizes his mother for misrepresenting and mismanaging their income: "I can see from the reports that there were 1,600 rubles of income this year. With these funds, living in the countryside you should be the last one to complain." Kulish deleted these sentences and continued with the religious material from the letter (the deleted material is crossed out):

Happy is the one who can see one's mistakes and go over one's accomplished deeds in one's mind in order to find mistakes in them; s/he will achieve perfection and succeed in everything. Troubled is the one who is self-confident and does not analyse his/her past actions, thinking that s/he is smart: s/he will never gain any knowledge and God will abandon him/her. ~~From your debit and credit reports, delivered to me by Liza, despite the fact that they were handled in a slipshod way, with omissions and without detailed explanations how they [the funds] were spent, I nevertheless can see (having done an approximate estimate and striking an annual balance) that during the year, you had an income of 16,000, and if I add to this number the income of a skipped month, one can surmise that the annual income of the estate could reach 20,000 in a given year. Let's assume that about six thousand are allocated for the payment of the mortgage and there are more than ten thousand left for all other expenses. With all these funds, living in the countryside, you should be the last one to complain about circumstances and fill your letters with whining, as was done by some of my sisters, especially by Liza, for five years in a row.~~ In foreign lands I lived without any funds for some time, without having all found, with an effort making my daily bread for the poorest existence, I have relied on God's help to this moment and have seen that the reason for human misery lies in a person him/herself, precisely because of his/her confidence that s/he stints him/herself completely. Precisely from the confidence that s/he has limited his/her needs to an extreme and has not wasted on any luxuries. God save you from such a ridiculous confidence.[12]

In the letter to Aleksandr Ivanov (10 January 1844), Gogol gives the younger artist practical advice about how to get a desirable job decorating the newly built Cathedral of Christ the Saviour in Moscow. Kulish omits these sentences in order to highlight the ideas of asceticism and piety that Gogol says a genuine artist should practise. In addition to deleting information, Kulish also replaces Gogol's original expressions with what he considers more appropriate synonyms or phrases:

~~Meanwhile do not lose~~ your p~~eace of mind~~ [replaced with: "do not worry about other people making much money"], remember that one cannot serve God and Mammon simultaneously; you have chosen a difficult path for yourself, therefore you have to learn how to stand firm on it. ~~You won't die from hunger, but you will be in need, certainly~~. One needs to think about the future, but do not worry about it. This is what a man who has experience ~~in this matter~~ [replaced with "in spiritual matters"] tells you.[13]

In his urge to enhance a picture of Gogol's spiritual crisis, Kulish "builds up" a subtext and magnifies Gogol's mysticism. In a letter to Maksymovych (9 November 1833), he adds the highlighted words to Gogol's letter: "Если б вы знали, какие со мной происходили страшные, **неподвластные пониманию привычному** перевороты!" (If you only knew what awful, **unexplainable by customary logic** transformations happened to me!)[14]

Other similar insertions can be found in Gogol's letters to Smirnova (7 July 1845), Pletnev (20 February 1846 and 24 March 1846), Lvov (20 March 1847), and Father Matvei (9 May 1847), in which Kulish replaces neutral modifiers with more elevated expressions to accentuate Gogol's religiosity. As the result of the editor's censoring and retouching, Gogol emerges as a holy man who is only concerned with his addressees' moral perfection and who does not actively participate in helping his friends and family with everyday concerns and troubles.

The most significant distortions in Kulish's publication of Gogol's letters are the softening or muting of criticism of the empire, in general, and of Petersburg and Moscow societies, in particular. By doing so, Kulish tried to protect his own shaky reputation as an emerging writer in the 1850s. When he returned from exile for participating in the Brotherhood of Saints Cyril and Methodius, he had been able to publish his first work, *Notes from the Life of Nikolai Vasilievich Gogol* (1856), and to reestablish himself in imperial literary circles thanks to the protection of Pletnev and Nekrasov. His editing of Gogol's letters may have resulted from the direct involvement of Pletnev in the publication. In Gogol's letter to Maksymovych (21 December 1833), Kulish deleted the scandalous phrase "It [Kyiv] is ours, not theirs" and replaced "damn" with "unfavourable" in Gogol's characterization of the Petersburg climate:

There, there! To Kiev! To ancient, beautiful Kiev! ~~It is ours, not theirs, isn't it?~~ There and in the vicinity the old deeds of our past were enacted. I work. I try with all my might but sometimes terror paralyses me: maybe I will not be able to finish it. I am tired of Petersburg, but rather, not of the city, but of its ~~damn~~ [replaced with "unfavourable"] climate; it annoys me.[15]

Having eliminated Gogol's unambiguous "It is ours, not theirs," Kulish distanced the writer from the heated polemics of the 1830s between Ukrainian and Russian intellectuals about who had primacy in the development of Russian civilization – "Southerners" (Ukrainians) or "Northerners" (Russians).[16] By emphasizing the Ukrainian origin of Kyiv, Gogol obviously was taking the "Southerners'" side in the polemics. This attitude can be corroborated by Gogol's negative attitude to Moscow, at least in the 1830s. However, Kulish also removed Gogol's criticism of Moscow as a stagnant and uncultured woman in another letter to Maksymovych (12 March 1834) in order to allay the letter's overall critical tone:

> Well, are you going or not? You have fallen in love with ~~this old, fat woman~~ Moscow, from which you cannot hear anything but pickled cabbage soup and foul language. Listen: judge by your impeccable consciousness how it feels for me to be in Kiev all by myself. The land and the country are good, but people are even better.[17]

Kulish also deleted all obscene lexicons that Gogol used to characterize wealthy Petersburg and Moscow youth and literati. In a letter to Iazykov (from 26 October 1844), Gogol, enraged by Pogodin's unauthorized publication of his portrait, called Petersburg and Moscow writers "c***s" and "b*****s." Kulish replaced the foul expressions with the neutral "ignoramuses" ("nevezhdy"). In contemporary academic editions, these words are replaced by ellipses and a footnote saying, "words unacceptable in print" ("nepriniatye v pechati slova"). Kulish's censoring of Gogol's letters, in fact, set a trend of bowdlerizing the classical writers' correspondence, which was also the case in Pushkin studies.[18]

Kulish's systematic replacement of "Rus'" and "russkii" in Gogol's letters with "Rossiia," "rossiiskii," or "velikorusskii" reflected his own idea of a "bipartite Rus'." For him, "russkii" was associated not with the common ethnic-linguistic definition of "Russianness" but with the pan-national idea of "Slavonic." He, therefore, strove to add more ethnic differentiation to Gogol's use of the word. In a letter to Pletnev (5 January 1847), in which Gogol compared the differing attitudes of Russians to each other when abroad and at home and used the phrase "znatnymi russkimi" (wealthy Russians), Kulish changed it to "znatnymi rossiiskimi" (wealthy imperial Russians), even though then and now "rossiiskii" can be only a modifier, not a noun. But when Gogol wrote about himself as a "Russian" (in a letter to Sergei Aksakov from 5 March 1841), Kulish preserved "russkii," because in this case it is meant to combine both "Russian" and "Ukrainian" elements as a primordial Slavic unity.

Clearly, Kulish was unable to ignore the vicissitudes of Gogol's reputation and publish the letters in their original form. There were still many contemporaries of the writer who had a vested interest in creating an appropriate public image of Gogol as well as in protecting their own reputations. Kulish's edition of Gogol's texts and letters clearly divided his oeuvre into "Ukrainian" and "Russian" periods. The editing of the letters served to demonstrate Gogol's mastery of Russian and his loyalty to the imperial state. By eliminating obscene expressions and discussions of mundane subjects and by inserting more words with specifically religious connotations, Kulish distorted the content of Gogol's letters. He projected an image of a Gogol who was preoccupied exclusively with his spiritual quest, with his sinful human nature, and with his unrealized social ideals – the image that the Slavophiles popularized in the 1850s. Kulish's editorial practices thus legitimized the careless editing and publication of Gogol's works practised earlier by his Russian peers.

Translations of Gogol's Texts into Ukrainian

Ukrainian translations of *Taras Bulba* exemplify the attempt to appropriate Gogol's hybrid oeuvre for Ukrainian culture. Why did Gogol's most ideologically charged text capture the imagination of the Ukrainian audience and how was it used to propagate nationalist ideas? What role did Ukrainian translations of Gogol's tale play in the national liberation movement in the second half of the nineteenth century, and how have they been used to reappropriate Gogol as a Ukrainian writer in the twenty-first century?

In semiotic terms, translation always marks some sort of deficiency in the target culture, which may be compensated by appropriating or domesticating what already exists elsewhere. The Ukrainian intellectuals of the late nineteenth century Olena Pchilka and Mykhailo Drahomanov believed that Gogol's tales in Ukrainian could fill the lack of prose fiction in the Ukrainian literary canon.[19] Besides this compensatory function, Ukrainian translations of Gogol's tales had another purpose. By disseminating the idea of all-Russian identity, Gogol's tales helped mobilize the audience in Eastern Galicia against Polish oppression.[20] The publication of the first Ukrainian translation of *Taras Bulba* (1850) occurred two years after the European Revolution of 1848, when the Ukrainian intellectuals in Galicia (who were predominantly from a clerical background) struggled to de-Polonize the elite and to advance

Ruthenian-Ukrainian national culture. The first translator of Gogol's *Taras Bulba* into Ukrainian, Petro Holovats'kyi, was the younger brother of the pro-Russophile scholar Iakiv Holovats'kyi, who together with the other activists Markiian Shashkevych and Ivan Vahylevych formed a circle called the Ruthenian Triad. Its leaders established schools and community organizations across Eastern Galicia but faced various challenges once they started debating what the modern literary language should be for educating the masses. Like their eastern and southern Christian peers, the Ruthenian Triad found it impossible to supplant Church Slavonic with the vernacular Ukrainian idiom. To complicate the language question, the Ukrainians' neighbours – Poles and Russians – lived in territories where Polish and Russian were the dominant languages of the educated elite.[21] Thus the task of Petro Holovats'kyi in translating *Taras Bulba* into Ukrainian was to create a usable literary language, which he identified on the front page of the book as "galyts'ko-rus'kyi iazyk" (Galician-Ruthenian). This language was artificially created as the *iazychie*, i.e., a hybrid bookish idiom based on a mixture of Church Slavonic, Russian, Ukrainian, and Polish. In this way, Galician intellectuals denied the Ukrainian vernacular (which they called "muzhychiia mova," i.e., a "peasant language") the status of a literary language and argued that only the *iazychie* could achieve parity with the literary Russian.[22]

Holovats'kyi preserved Gogol's use of the ethnonym "Russian," yet its spelling showed some variation: when he translated the geographic name he used "Rus'" (Rus'), but when he translated "Russian nobility" as a social class, he rendered it as "russkii" (Russian); in all other cases he used "ruskii" with one "s" (Rus'ian). The nationality word "Russian" was rendered as "rusyn" (Ruthenian) elsewhere, which corresponded to the self-naming of Ukrainians in Eastern Galicia. In some places, Holovats'kyi added new information: in a passage about the Polish influence on the Russian gentry (e.g., "Then Polish influence began to imprint itself on Russian nobles; *the Russian nobility was being formed*") and in Taras's words about the tsar emerging out of the Russian land ("he will emerge *one day*"), which were rendered close to the original, the addition of an adverb of indefinite frequency, "one day" ("kolys'"), imparted a prophetic tone.[23] Holovats'kyi also "corrected" the sensitive passages referencing the Catholics (thus, he replaced "katolicheskiie nedoverki" [Catholic infidels] with "liatskiie nedoverki" [Polish infidels]). The epic mode was enhanced through the addition of an epigraph and epilogue to the tale, which were taken from the popular Ukrainian *duma* on the death of Bohdan Kmel'nyts'kyi[24] and which counteracted the historical diffuseness of the original text. Now, the emerging tsar became associated with the legendary hetman who led Ukrainians of all social strata in their struggle for national liberation.

Between 1850 and 1874 there were no new Ukrainian translations of *Taras Bulba*, owing to the imperial ban on publishing Ukrainian literature. In 1874, a new Ukrainian translation of the 1842 redaction of *Taras Bulba* was made by M. Loboda (real name Mykola Lobodovs'kyi).[25] A village teacher from Ekaterinoslavskaia gubernia, Lobodovs'kyi was an activist of the Ukrainian Populist movement. He used his translation of *Taras Bulba* to disseminate nationalist ideas among the peasants in Left-Bank Ukraine. In it, Lobodovs'kyi replaced all of the ethnonyms and national modifiers of Russianness with "Ukrainian." In 1876, the Volhynian chief of police, Bel's'kyi, and, later, the curator of the Kyiv school district, Iuzefovych, reported to the imperial authorities that Lobodovs'kyi was propagating the dangerous ideas of federalism and autonomy for Ukraine. In his denunciation, Iuzefovych pointed to the replacement of the word "Russian" with the word "Ukrainian" in Lobodovs'kyi's translation and accused him of altering the sentence about the emerging tsar with a prophecy about a Ukrainian ruler. Although the translator had kept the sentence about the tsar unaltered, he added a more seditious line about Cossacks fighting for Ukraine's independence ("za samostiinist' Ukrainy"), but Iuzefovych apparently overlooked this.[26] The denunciation led to the arrest of an entire group of Ukrainian activists (their trial became known as the "Kosach-Lobodovs'kyi's case"), the confiscation of the entire print run of *Taras Bulba*, and the introduction of the new Russificatory policy known as the "Ems Ukaz" (1876).[27] In 1883, Lobodovs'kyi reprinted his translation with some minor changes: he dropped the line about Ukraine's independence, added more emphasis on the free Ukrainian spirit, and replaced the "Russian" with the "Ukrainian" Orthodox faith. It was the first Ukrainian translation of Gogol's text published in Eastern Ukraine; printed in the *iaryzhka*, it best captured Gogol's original hybrid language.

Imperial policy regarding national cultures was relaxed after the revolution of 1905. Several new translations of *Taras Bulba* were made during the first decade of the twentieth century, marking the fiftieth anniversary of Gogol's death in 1902 and the centennial of his birth in 1909. In these pre-revolutionary years, Gogol's tale helped Ukrainian intellectuals counterbalance the support among Ukrainians for the imperial all-Russian project, on the one hand, and the radical Russian nationalist agenda of the Black Hundreds, on the other. Mykhailo Hrushevs'kyi, a prominent historian and a leader of the Ukrainian national movement, referred to Gogol's bicultural identity in his polemics with pro-Russian nationalist opponents as a critique of the colonial model of Ukrainian identity (known as "Little Russianism"). In his programmatic speech "An Anniversary of Mykola Hohol" (1909), Hrushevs'kyi called Gogol one of the "greatest sons of Ukraine," but at the same time he pointed to the weakness of Gogol's national identity, explaining it by the colonial position of the Ukrainian gentry in the empire. Nonetheless, for Hrushevs'kyi, Gogol captured the "Ukrainian life that was dying before his very eyes under new influences, new forms"; he "showered Ukraine with the gorgeous flowers of his creative art" without "even understanding that its [Ukraine's] resurrection was near."[28] Hrushevs'kyi paraphrased Gogol's own phrase about Kyiv but applied it to the writer's belonging to Ukrainian culture ("he is our own, not theirs [the Russians']"). Hrushevs'kyi wanted to reserve a place for Gogol in the Ukrainian national movement because of the positive influence that his Ukrainian tales had exerted on the younger generation.

Echoing the political discourse of the time, early twentieth-century translations of *Taras Bulba* emphasized the national Ukrainian rather than ethnic Little Russian content of the tale. The author of the first twentieth-century translation of *Taras Bulba*, published in 1900, Vasyl' Shchurat, claimed the equivalent effect as the main reason for his translation's appropriateness. In a translator's note, Shchurat broadened the notion of national Ukrainian literature by including in it texts written both in Ukrainian and in other languages which are "organically, ideologically connected with the life of the Ukrainian people."[29] In his view, Gogol's tale was a Ukrainian text to its core; it not only "emerged out of the heart of Ukrainian culture, but also laid the foundation for national Ukrainian literature." Shchurat ended his note questioning the genre of the tale: "what kind of historical tale is *Taras Bulba* …? It is neither a factual-historical novel, like Flaubert's *Salammbô* and Wells's *Ben Goor*, nor a realistic-historical tale, since the pictures of everyday life are taken from different epochs. It is rather a propagandistic [ahitatsiina] tale which arouses people's historical-populist [istorychno-narodni] sentiments."[30] He remained faithful to the Galician tradition of translating the ethnonym "russkii" as either "rusyn" (Ruthenian) or "ukrainets'" (Ukrainian). His translation of Bulba's last words is rendered close to the original, with just one, yet important, replacement of the word "tsar" with the Ukrainian word "volodar" (ruler). Thus, the translator followed a domesticating approach, trying to produce an effect on a contemporary audience which was more consciously nationalist. The work's historical verisimilitude was less important than the powerful national myth of Cossack Ukraine that Gogol's tale promoted because it could guide Ruthenians in seeking national self-determination.

During the Ukrainian People's Republic (1917–20), the exclusively Ukrainian identity of Gogol was foregrounded in Mykola Sadovs´kyi's translation of *Taras Bulba* published in 1918. Known better as a theatre director and actor, Sadovs´kyi did not follow the principle of fidelity in his ideological translation. He replaced all instances of "russkii" with either "Ukrainian" or "Cossack" and eliminated the last paragraph about the tsar altogether. His use of ethnonyms reflected some important changes in the Ukrainian historiographical discourse that had been introduced by Hrushevs'kyi in his *History of Ukraine-Rus'* (1898–1937). The scholar replaced the previously used ethnonyms of "russki" and "malorossiskii" with "Ukrainian," and "Rus'" with "Ukraine-Rus'." Likewise, Sadovs'kyi's replaced "Russia" with "Ukraine-Rus'" and "Russian" with "Ukrainian" everywhere in his translation.

The ambitious project of a five-volume edition of Ukrainian translations of Gogol's works was launched in the late 1920s by the collaborative efforts of the Ukrainian modernists.[31] The translators were grouped around the translator and scholar Volodymyr Derzhavyn, who developed the method of stylized ("pereklad–stylizatsiia") or reverse translation ("zvorotnii pereklad"). Independently from Bakhtin's idea of dialogical discourse, the translators proclaimed an orientation toward "the discourse of the other" ("chuzhemovnist'"). They believed that a translator is not confined by the style of the source text but instead can make it more archaic or modern by expanding the resources of the target language and by introducing elements of "another national colouring" ("inshyi natsional'nyi koloryt").[32] To do so, a translator has to deviate from the "correct" literary idiom and explore non-standard and archaic stylistic elements.[33] If translators need to, they may correct a writer's stylistic inconsistencies as dissonant with the overall tone of the work. The stylized translation, therefore, can reproduce not only the meaning of the source text but also the linguistic and stylistic peculiarities of the cultural epoch during which the original text was created. Thus, the translators rejected the principle of "fidelity" and poeticized Gogol's language with uniquely Ukrainian locutions. One of the translators, the leading Ukrainian neoclassical poet Maksym Ryl's'kyi, tried not only to find the closest equivalents to Gogol's original expressions in Ukrainian but also to convey the expressivity and intonation of his idiosyncratic discourse. Andrii Nikovs'kyi made the translation of *Taras Bulba* in this edition. He stylized the original text with archaic Ukrainian expressions peculiar to the landowners' milieu of Gogol's time. He took these language elements from Gogol's draft versions of the tale and from his "Kniga vsiakoi vsiachiny" ("A book of miscellaneous things"). As for the original ethnonyms, Nikovs'kyi was not consistent and in some cases dropped "Russian," in others replaced "Russian" with "Ukrainian," while in others used "Rus'ian."

The editors Ivan Lakiza and Pavlo Fylypovych managed to publish only the first three volumes of Gogol's translated works before almost all of the translators were arrested and executed by the Bolsheviks in the 1930s.[34] The volumes were never reprinted, and all existing copies were confiscated from libraries. This marked the revocation of the "indigenization" policies of the 1920s (during which Ukrainian national culture was revived) and the introduction of the "unified artistic method" of Socialist Realism. Gogol's Ukrainian tales were now viewed as deeply democratic and realistic, which mobilized Russian "progressive writers" to fight against "reactionary Ukrainian nationalists."

Antin Khutorian's post-war translation of *Taras Bulba* (1952) became the first official Soviet version of the tale. It was published two years before the four hundredth anniversary of the Pereiaslav Council (1654), which in Soviet historiography signified the reunification of Russia and Ukraine. In post-war Soviet Ukraine, when the Red Army was still fighting with the remnants of the Ukrainian Insurgent Army, it was important to remind nationalist-minded readers that Ukraine had taken advantage of this historical chance to join the Great Russian civilization. The translator was supposed to incorporate the Cossack myth of Ukraine into the Soviet ideology of the "friendship of brotherly nations" and to demonstrate adherence to the principles of class consciousness and party-mindedness. So, in rendering "Russian," Khutorian followed a selective strategy: he used "rus'kyi" (not "rossiis'kyi," as in accordance with the norms of modern Ukrainian) and translated "Rossiia" as "Rosiia" in the two phrases about "Southern" and "Eastern Russia." The translator also modified Bulba's Ukrainian form of address to the Cossacks, "Proshchaite, panybrat'ia, tovarishchi!" (Farewell, noble brothers, comrades!), to the more ideologically appropriate "Proshchavaite, tovaryshchi!" (Farewell, comrades!), because in the 1950s the very use of the word "pan" (mister) was taken to be a "national-bourgeois" vestige, inadmissible in Soviet society.

In independent post-Soviet Ukraine, translations of Gogol's works remain a highly political enterprise. The most controversial case is the radically re-edited version of Sadovs'kyi's translation of *Taras Bulba* by Ivan Malkovych (first publication in 1998, second edition in 2009).[35] When Malkovych's edition came out without the passage about the "tsar" and the "Rus'ian soul," a prime minister of the Russian Federation, Victor Chernomyrdin, protested, saying that Gogol could have never written this text. Malkovych himself has called his translation a "de-Russification" of Gogol, justifying it on the grounds that Gogol had been forced to "Russify" *Taras Bulba* by the "oppressive ideological climate" of the 1840s.[36] Although Malkovych has asserted that his translation was based on the combination of the 1835 and the 1842 versions, in reality, he only used the 1842 text, having included only one sentence from the earlier edition (about the need to constantly guard the borders from the three hostile nations). Malkovych also replaced "Rossiia" (Russia) and "russkii" (Russian) with "Kozats'ka Zemlia" (Cossack land) and "kozats'kyi" (Cossack) everywhere. He defended this decision by noting that Gogol himself designated Ukraine as "Kozats'ka Zemlia" in his 1836 letter to Jósef Bogdan Zaleski, written in Ukrainian. Therefore, in his combination of the two redactions Malkovych created a third version of *Taras Bulba*, which has irritated Russian readers as a resentful nationalism in its attempts to appropriate Gogol as the exclusively Ukrainian writer.

Recently, Vasyl' Shkliar's translation of the 1835 version of *Taras Bulba* (2006) continued the anti-colonial trend of Malkovych's translation. In the Preface, entitled "The Bulba that was not burnt," Shkliar presented his translation as "the true *Taras Bulba*." He argued that the second edition of the tale was "corrupted" by the "Great Russians and Belinskiis" ("velikorosamy-belins'kymy") and therefore should be rejected as the work's original text.[37] Shkliar has privileged the 1835 redaction as the more authentic text of the tale. He translated all occurrences of "Little Russian" as "Ukrainian," replaced three instances of the word "Russian" with "Muscovite" or with "Orthodox," and "russkoe dukhovenstvo" (Russian clergy) became "pravoslavne dukhovenstvo" (Orthodox clergy). He dropped "Russian" entirely from the phrases "pech' … kak tolstaia russkaia kupchikha" to "iak hladezna perekupka" (a stove … like a fat Russian woman merchant – a stove like a fat merchant).

One cannot entirely discard contemporary Ukrainian translations of *Taras Bulba* as being completely political. To a certain extent, they reflect a general shift in translation studies from using a linguistic-based method to a target-oriented approach.[38] The role of the context has also changed: if early translations were mostly concerned with equivalence, fidelity, and accuracy of the source text and its epoch, in modern translation studies knowledge of the receiving culture and its context has become more important in shaping meaning. The trend to ground translation in a specific sociopolitical and cultural context has persisted in the 2000s, endowing the translator with a new agency as a "subversive scriber."[39] In the postcolonial context of contemporary Ukraine, removing the hybrid nature of Gogol's original text can free it from the restrictions imposed on it by the original context of its publication. Seeking an "adequate" Ukrainian translation of Gogol's works, the reprint of the Ukrainian translations published in the seven-volume edition of *Povne zibrannia tvoriv u semy tomakh* (2007) exemplifies a peculiar case of "non-retranslation." The editors assembled these volumes from the translations made during the 1930s–1950s, which have been recognized by the scholarly community as artistically innovative and ideologically neutral.

The lack of retranslations of Gogol's works into Ukrainian may be seen in a positive light "as a desire to keep stock of works available for readers."[40] If retranslation brings something new to culture, the reprinting of previous translations preserves something old. We often think of retranslations in terms of linear progress from a first "inadequate" translation to a more accurate one that finally reveals the essence of the original text.[41] In one way or another, the idea of progress in translation studies implies a certain refinement of discursive tools. This does not mean, however, that the new retranslation is objectively superior to previous ones, but that it may be more refined in terms of style and discourse.[42] Some scholars question the very idea of "progress" in translation because translation "cannot be reduced to a simple question of stylistic updating. Enduring translations are those that express a successful pact, a 'fit' between sensibilities and styles."[43] The ultimate goal of retranslation, according to Siobhan Brownlie, is "to keep the memory of [a] source text alive, contributing to its canonization in cultural memory."[44]

With regard to translations and retranslations of Gogol's works, in post-Soviet Ukraine the choice of one or another ethnic modifier reflects an adherence to one or another national project. Malkovych's translation clearly represents the tradition of the so-called Galician nationalism, which reconstructs the history of the Ukrainian nation as a continuous and uninterrupted process. The proponents of the "Galician nationalism" view Western Ukraine as an agent of national unity and keeper of the country's true faith.[45] This is why Malkovych eliminates any references to "Russianness" and the passage about the tsar. Khutorian's translation echoes the ideas of the "Kyivan nationalism." Rooted in Kyivan rather than Galician political tradition, it presents a Ukrainian identity that has a shared East Slavic origin and targets a substantial middle group of bilingual and bicultural Ukrainians.[46] The formation of a middle-ground ideological position is palpable in the contemporary audience's attitude to Gogol. The results of the national survey conducted by the Research&Branding Group a week before Gogol's bicentennial in 2009 demonstrated the rather controversial attitude of the Ukrainians toward the publication of Gogol in Ukrainian.[47] Although Gogol's texts translated into Ukrainian are more comprehensible to

Western Ukrainians, they are lost for the 30–35% of the Russian speakers. Overall, 53% of Ukrainians did not approve of translating Gogol into Ukrainian; 17% thought that the translation of Gogol was timely and necessary for society, while about 70% said that reading Gogol in either Russian or Ukrainian could unite the nation. The results of the survey also signalled the awareness of contemporary readers that modern retranslations of Gogol's tales have been ideologically manipulated and that the original texts in hybrid Russian-Ukrainian provide a more aesthetically satisfying experience.

In post-Euromaidan Ukraine, Ukrainian translations of Gogol have received wide public acceptance and have been included in the school curriculum. In order to compensate for reduced time dedicated to Gogol in the course of "World Literature," teachers of "Ukrainian Literature" now offer Gogol's "Ukrainian tales" in Ukrainian translations. In the entire twelve-year school curriculum, four academic hours are devoted to teaching Gogol's works. Only three of Gogol's texts are required in the program: *Taras Bulba* and "St John's Eve" are offered in Ukrainian translation in the course "Ukrainian Literature," while "Nose" (or the first chapter of *Dead Souls*, if the teacher chooses) is taught in "World Literature." This artificial division of Gogol's oeuvre further promotes his ambiguous status in Ukrainian culture. Upon the recommendation of the Ministry of Education and Science of Ukraine, Malkovych's "hybrid" translation of *Taras Bulba* is being taught to ninth graders. The textbook authors recommend that students find the original 1842 edition of *Taras Bulba* and compare it to the 1835 version – something that Ukrainian teenagers can hardly be expected to do.[48]

The history of the Ukrainian translations of *Taras Bulba* demonstrates how problematic a translator's unambiguous position vis-à-vis ideology can be. Translators are expected to be on one or the other side of the divide but very often exhibit dual allegiance. This is exactly the same type of problem that Gogol had to deal with in the Russian Empire – how to present the myth of Cossack Ukraine to the imperial audience without jeopardizing the memory of the heroic epoch preserved by the Ukrainian gentry. At the same time, Ukrainian translations of his texts inevitably place Gogol in several literary traditions – the imperial, the Russian, and the Ukrainian national, which reveals the cultural clash that Ukraine has experienced since 1991. Because many passages and speeches of the characters in Gogol's *Evenings* and *Mirogord* are written in Ukrainian and sound like the Kiyvan-Poltavan dialect (which laid the foundation for the literary Ukrainian language in the nineteenth century), it could be said that Gogol's bilingual and hybrid discourse has participated in shaping the Ukrainian literary and cultural tradition.

Another argument in support of Gogol's biculturality is that the classic Ukrainian poet Taras Shevchenko also created his works in two languages and contributed to the development of two Ukrainian literary traditions in Ukrainian (his poems) and in Russian (his prose fiction, which constitutes two-thirds of his creative output). Ukrainian translations of Gogol's works thus serve to assimilate his legacy into Ukrainian national culture and to shape post-Soviet Ukrainian identity as hybrid.

Afterword

No matter how fervently Gogol tried to persuade his contemporaries of his patriotic feelings, they never stopped questioning his loyalty to the empire. After the satirical portrayal of Russian society in *Dead Souls*, Gogol was accused of faking "Russianness,"[1] pretty much in the same way as he was criticized by Polevoi for being a "forger" of Little Russianism after the publication of *Evenings*.[2] In 1844, Smirnova voiced the collective concern with Gogol's demonstrative lack of patriotism and, on behalf of high society, demanded that the writer clarify his allegiance to Russian national identity. A native Ukrainian, Smirnova strove to come to terms with her own place in imperial society. In a famous letter of 3 November 1844, she confronted Gogol with the question that probably bothered her as well: "Reach into the depths of your soul and ask yourself, are you really a Russian, or are you a *khokhlik* [pejorative for a Little Russian]?" Gogol avoided a direct answer, replying:

> I myself do not know what kind of soul I have: *khokhlatskaia* [i.e., pejorative for "Little Russian"] or Russian. I know only that I would grant primacy neither to a Little Russian one over a Russian one nor to a Russian over a Little Russian one. Both natures are too generously endowed by God, and as if on purpose, each of them in its own way includes in itself that which the other lacks …[3]

Gogol asked Smirnova to read his response publicly at Countess Rostopchina's salon in front of those society people who had accused him of lacking Russianness. His response has been typically interpreted as a demonstration of a "deep-seated insecurity" about his national identity.[4] However, if one keeps in mind that Gogol and Smirnova were the closest of friends and did not keep secrets from each other, the writer's recognition of his dual identity acquires additional shades of meaning other than insecurity. Smirnova had been involved in all of Gogol's problems, including financial. She remained his confidante throughout his entire life. In the fall of 1844, Gogol had asked Smirnova to plead with Nicholas I to give him an imperial stipend so that he could work on the sequel to *Dead Souls*, which he believed would reform Russia's social ills. Considering Gogol's need for government financial support, the question arises: what precluded Gogol from reaffirming his Russian identity to his most intimate friend? I think that Gogol's response was a sincere declaration of his unique *in-betweenness* that cannot be grasped in either ethno-national or imperial terms. Even the word "khokhlatskaia," which Gogol used to characterize his soul, did not indicate submission to the imperial view of him as a Russian, because Gogol was mimicking Smirnova's own wording in her question from the preceding letter ("are you really a Russian, or are you a *khokhlik*?"). Gogol's game with national identification in the letter was another trick he played on a Russian society which wanted him to proclaim his Russian identity forthrightly, but instead received his avowal of having a hybrid identity.

In this book, I have situated Gogol within the practices, institutions, and beliefs that constituted imperial culture and gave impetus to emerging national Ukrainian literature. I have examined how his self-fashioning, hybrid language, and multiple versions of his texts entailed remaking of his national identity. The synthesis of cultures and ethnicities in Gogol's texts produced difference without assuming a hierarchy among imperial, national, and regional cultures. By comparing and juxtaposing Gogol's different redactions and drafts, we can unpack the complexities of his hybrid language and identity. Interpreting Gogol's revised texts is both a methodological and a theoretical problem, since the external reasons for making changes in the earlier versions of his texts were often inseparable from the internal ones. On the one hand, the prescriptive regulations of nineteenth-century imperial ideology assigned linguistically correct and proper norms, condemning all hybrid elements as "contaminated" by Ukrainian influence. Under the banner of regulating Gogol's language, editorial acts were essentially in the service of protecting Russian national identity. But, on the other hand, Gogol himself was preoccupied with refining his literary language and style with each new edition, which resulted in textualization of his identity. This ability to produce a new text was facilitated by the internalization of revision and change. Gogol always revised his texts to refine his language and style, but he did so with the goal of improving his own personality. This can be interpreted as prioritizing the procedural means over the textual ends. He wanted to produce a better text, so he kept revising it, so that he could produce a better self. Revising turned into a habit of his soul. In social terms, revision of a text operates as a social interaction: anticipating responses of the audience, the writer creates a textualized tension between intention and socialization – both imply recursive processes of alteration and reconsideration. Thus, revision became part of the structure of Gogol's thought; it implied the incompleteness of the self, as well as a conscious effort to become a better, fuller person.

I have also tested the idea of Gogol's hybridity with computer-assisted analysis. In order to situate Gogol in the imperial literary tradition, I have created a corpus of all works of prose fiction written in Russian by Ukrainian (Shevchenko, Hrebinka, Kvitka-Osnov'ianenko, Somov, Narizhnyi, Gogol, Kukol'nyk), Russian (Pushkin, Lermontov, Bestuzhev, Odoevskii, Zagoskin, Vel'tman, Pogorel'skii, Lazhechnikov, Sollogub), and Polish (Bulgarin and Senkovskii) writers during the first half of the nineteenth century and performed the PCA (see Appendix 4 for an explanation of the method). This graph (Figure 8) shows that Gogol's works are literally located *in-between* the Russian and Ukrainian traditions and are equally close to those of the Ukrainian, Russian, and Polish writers in the database, which reinforces my argument of his cultural and language hybridity.

It would be an oversimplification to present postcolonial hybrids as spaces of harmonious existence devoid of power, tension, and competition. However, the hybrid performative language of Gogol and of other Ukrainian intellectuals of the period gave the culture a strong jolt toward innovation, openness, and cultural change. Barriers were crossed and aesthetic tastes modernized, which moderated the polarization and dichotomization of Ukrainian society into "us" and "them."

Until today, the centres, both in Russia and in Ukraine, keep defining their national codes in strict ethnic-linguistic categories, showing little interest toward regional identification and hybrid cultures and languages. The situation can be rectified with the advancement of postcolonial and decolonial studies within the Slavic literary field. A strong school of postcolonial and decolonial criticism has not yet developed in the post-Soviet republics, for different reasons.[5] There are two dominating trends in studying Gogol in Russia: "Orthodox Gogol scholarship" ("pravoslavnoie gogolevedenie") and "liberal Gogol scholarship,"[6] on the one hand, and "theological" and "aesthetically oriented Gogol scholarship," on the other.[7] The former scholars are engaged in canonizing Gogol as a staunch monarchist and an Orthodox Christian – an approach articulated by Vladimir Voropaev, an editor-in-chief of the 2009 *Complete Works* of Gogol. For the first time, an academic edition of Gogol's works has included his theological texts and translations from the early Church Fathers. Voropaev has claimed that there is only one

Figure 8. PCA of Gogol's prose fiction in the literary tradition of the first half of the nineteenth century

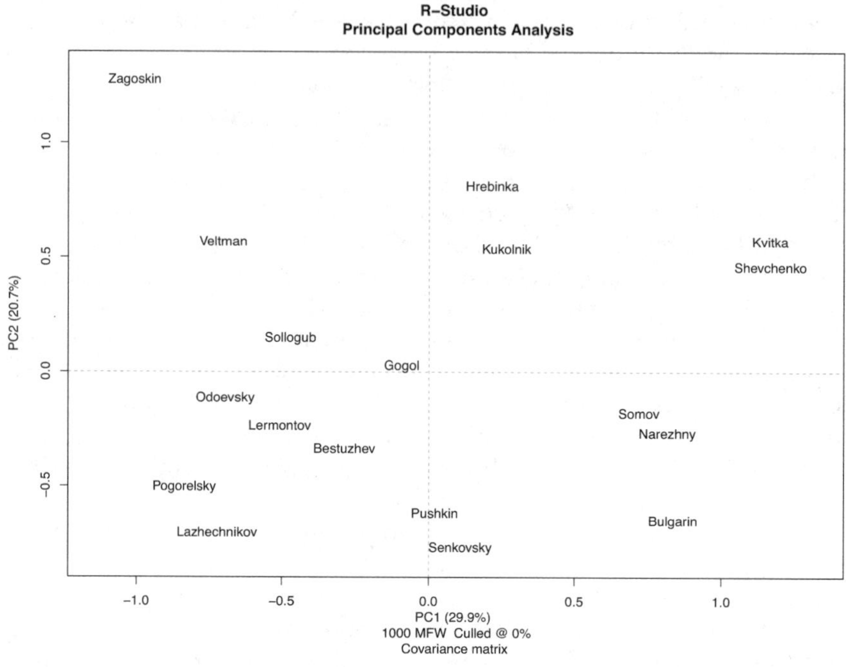

aspect of a writer's works and personality worth studying: "the Orthodox one, taken from the Gospels ... In Gogol scholarship, this criterion can best open Gogol up to readers, can help them comprehend their own lives and the spiritual path of Russia, and solidify their faith."[8] The so-called liberal Gogol scholars apply various methods – psychoanalytical, lingua-poetic, literary historical, comparative – to analyse Gogol's texts and contexts. Since 2001, Russian scholars present their studies at the annual conference "Readings of Gogol" ("Gogolevskie chteniia") in Moscow and publish them in its proceedings. During recent years, more and more emphasis has been placed on Gogol's embeddedness in the European or Slavic tradition,[9] resulting in a proliferation of metaphors concerning "the centre vs the periphery" or "West vs East." This view of the Russian cultural field generally presupposes a version of history that locates the empire or Europe at the centre of modern history. It rejects the culture and history of native peoples as worth studying on their own terms or downgrades them to the realm of folklore and myth.

Thus, the generally negative attitude to the Russian Empire's colonial past and the appropriation of the literature of its ethnic minorities as "Russian" produce a sanitized version of Russian culture and of Gogol as a paragon of the Orthodox tradition. Enriching Gogol scholarship with a postcolonial approach and "decolonial" thinking may reinscribe the tradition in a way that is productive for the present and beneficial for the future, revaluing what the empire devalued in the process of annihilating the differences.

In Ukrainian literary scholarship, the dominant tendency is an anti-colonial reading of Gogol, which identifies the colonizer with Russian culture and views Gogol as a "secret agent" undermining the imperial centre.[10] The danger of the anti-colonial nationalist approach to Gogol is in labelling everything associated with the imperial culture as oppressive and in presenting the relationship between Russian and Ukrainian cultures in binary oppositions. It is important to demarcate "postcolonial" from "colonial" and "anti-colonial," as Marko Pavlyshyn has suggested: "The postcolonial is that which embodies or points toward a supersession of the opposition and traumas inherited from the period of colonial domination. It is unhelpful to conflate it with the anticolonial, which, while endeavoring to demolish colonial structures of dominion, erects alternatives ones."[11] Myroslav Shkandrij also claims that anti-colonialism cannot be a productive strategy because it does not account for the significant cultural, religious, and lingual diversity in Ukraine and does not transcend the claims of both imperial and national myths to embrace such transnational phenomena as border literature, hybrid identities, and cultures in-between. "Elements of hybridity, marginality such as '*surzhyk*' ... or the *maloros* [Little Russian] complex ... have often been defined in Ukrainian literature as scourges ... To the 'anti-colonialists' hybridity damages the idea of a core tradition."[12] It seems that some Gogol scholars in Ukraine have tried to assume the official normative power of Soviet ideology, imposing their own national cultural values in place of the former colonial canon and reversing previous imperial reading practices.[13] The natural reason for this is the anti-colonial resistance to Russia's military aggression since 2014. Nevertheless, the study of Gogol's hybridity can provide an alternative way of resisting Russian political and cultural domination. The annexation of Crimea and occupation of Eastern Ukraine in 2014 took place under the banner of protecting the rights of the russophone population in Ukraine. If Ukrainian academics were to embrace the "border" cultural phenomena as part of their own culture, there would be fewer arguments for Putin's Russia to interfere in Ukraine's affairs. Recently, a Ukrainian scholar, Mykola Riabchuk, and a russophone Ukrainian writer, Andrei Kurkov, have talked about an urgent need to include literature created in Russian by Ukrainian writers in the rubric of Ukrainian culture. Riabchuk has emphasized that "the Ukrainian culture [created in Russian] was not merely a minority culture within the Russian and, eventually, Soviet empires. It was – and still remains, to a certain degree – a sort of diaspora culture."[14] Andrei Kurkov has proposed a more radical measure for reappropriating the Ukrainian version of the Russian language – to establish an academic institute of the Russian language of the russophone diaspora of Ukraine, which would study and protect the cultural heritage created in that language as part of Ukrainian culture.[15] Establishing a status of Russian language and culture as diasporic in Ukraine could serve as a vehicle of ideological and political resistance to the anti-Ukrainian discourse produced in and transmitted from Putin's Russia.

In the epigraph of this book, I quoted J. Hillis Miller, who claimed that the performative aspect of a text shapes our reading practices. If J. Hillis Miller is correct and we presume that a literary text written in the border of two or more traditions lacks any fixed univocal meaning, then Gogol's multiple textual versions exhibit his identity as a work in progress. In this sense, we have expanded the view of a text as an isolated, ahistorical entity and suggested that Gogol's hybrid language practices have had a lasting impact on contemporary Russian and Ukrainian culture and ideology. In cultural materialist studies, ideology and power do not exist in an unshaken continuum, as Michael Foucault and Louis Althusser argued, but coincide with subordinate, residual, emergent, and oppositional cultural forces.[16] Gogol's case has clearly demonstrated that the hegemony of imperial Russian culture was not a passive form of dominance; it was continually resisted, limited, challenged, and modified by pressures from the marginalized. As I have suggested, the study of Gogol's hybridity can deconstruct the Russocentric canon of the nineteenth-century literary tradition. The dense, interlayered structure of Gogol's text and identity can also help us rethink the ethnic communitarian and civil liberal traditions not as opposed but as inseparable phenomena in modern nation-building.

Appendices

A Stylometric Analysis of the Corpus of Gogol's Letters

"Stylometric analysis" was originally developed for forensic author-ship attribution and has recently been applied to the "distant reading"[1] of various literary corpora. Obviously, many aspects of style are con-scious and deliberate, and as such they can be easily imitated. Compu-tational stylometry, however, prioritizes subconscious elements, which are more difficult to imitate because they belong to the deep structures of language. The individual style of an author, or his/her "stylistic fin-gerprint," can be captured with several quantitative criteria, or discrim-inators – whether they are identified with most unusual words, with function words, or even with sentence type. In my application of the method to Gogol, I used the "bag of words" approach and selected all words except for function words, which were excluded from the corpus. First, I manually divided Gogol's epistolary legacy by each individual correspondent and by three periods: early letters (1820–35), mid-life let-ters (1836–46), and late letters (1847–52). Such periodization tallies with the accepted classification of Gogol's oeuvre into an early period before his emigration to Europe in 1836; a mid-life period, during which he wrote his major plays, most of the Petersburg tales, and *Dead Souls*; and a late period, during which he wrote *Selected Passages* and Volume 2 of *Dead Souls*. Second, I created a "Term Document Matrix" of the most frequent words (MFW) of Gogol's letters. Given the relatively small size of the epistolary corpus, the most frequent words present the most reli-able stylistic features[2] because they are considered to be topic-neutral.[3] I have chosen the first 100 MFW for Gogol's early letters and the first 200 MFW for his mid-life and late letters,[4] and used Eder's Delta, which is the most commonly used measurement of distance for highly inflected languages like Russian, because it gives more weight to frequent fea-tures and rescales less frequent ones to avoid random infrequencies. I used the package "stylo" to visualize the results in colourful clustering

Figure 9. The clustering dendrogram of Gogol's early letters

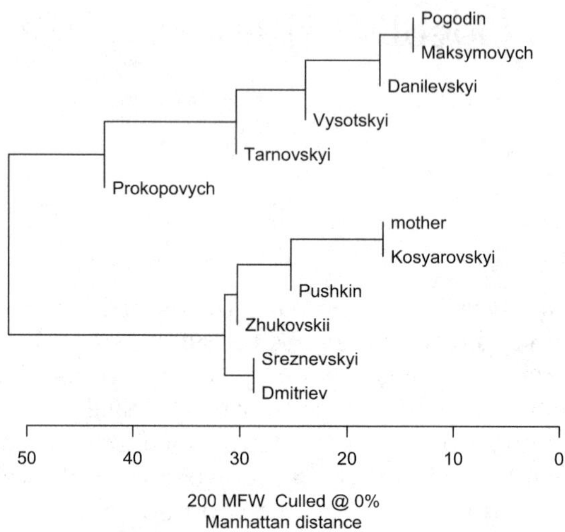

Figure 10. The clustering dendrogram of Gogol's mid-life letters

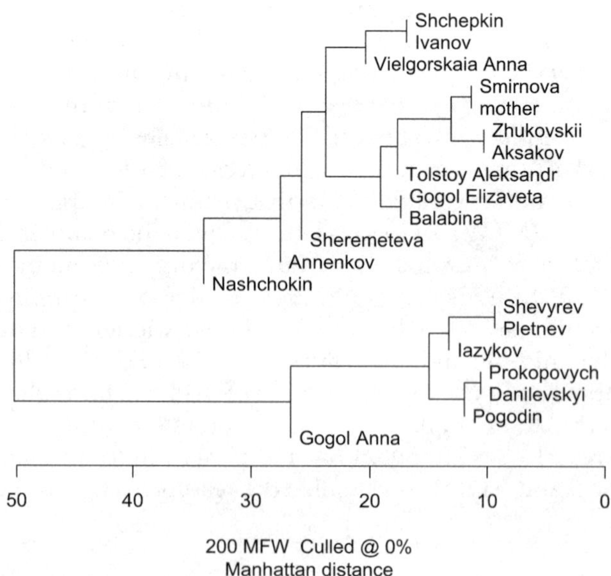

Figure 11. The clustering dendrogram of Gogol's late letters

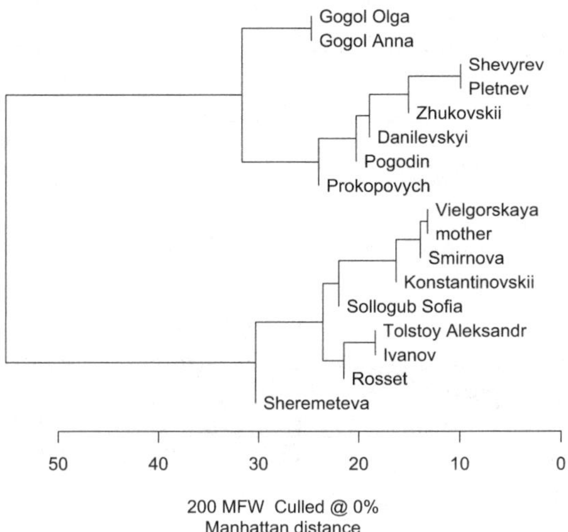

dendrograms for each period of his epistolary output. The arrangements of the "leaves" among the "clades" in the dendrogram exhibit similarities; the width differences between clades measure the degree of likeness: the closer to "0" the clade's position, the lesser degree of likeness it exhibits with others. Finally, I have closely examined the shared stylistic features in each group of letters defined by digital means in order to verify the accuracy of this method of identifying style. The results of hierarchical clustering are presented in Figures 9, 10, and 11.

The Macro Changes to the Plot
of the 1842 Redaction of *Taras Bulba*

Chapter 1: Gogol inserted a passage on the significance of the Ukrainian folk songs, an explanation of the emergence of Cossackdom, and a passage about the negative influence of Polish customs on the "Russian nobility"; changed the dating of the origin of Cossackdom, tracing it back to the fifteenth century (by postponing the origin of the Cossack state to more modern times, Gogol relied on the study by Polish historian Maciej Stryjkowski, which polemicized with the dating established by Nikolai Karamzin); eliminated references to the Polish king Stephan Báthory and Taras Bulba's service to him (because the temporal scope was extended from the sixteenth century in the 1835 redaction to the fifteenth century in the 1842 one); eliminated some demeaning characteristics of Bulba's personality and accentuated his heroism. The narrative mode shows more epic objectivity compared to the rhetorically adorned style of the 1835 redaction.

Chapter 2 did not undergo any significant transformation of the content.

Chapter 3: Gogol increased the number of the *kurens* to "sixty-something"; added more details to the descriptions of Cossacks' customs (shared property, strict punishment of criminals, and recreation during peacetime).

Chapter 4 is a new chapter in the 1842 redaction, which depicts the *koshevoi*'s elections. It concludes with an ardent *koshevoi*'s speech on the need for a new military campaign to protect Ukraine from the harmful influences of Jews and Poles.

Chapter 5 is a modification of chapter 4 of the 1835 version with the following additions: the barbarian characteristics of the Cossacks living in "the semi-wild century"; Cossacks' ferocity in their treatment of enemies; altered descriptions of Cossacks' martial arts and their campground, and of the beginning of a siege of Dubno; underscoring of the

Cossacks' connection with Mezhigorsky Kyiv Monastery, which sent the Cossacks two cypress crosses as their blessing on the war with the infidels.

Chapter 6 (a modification of chapter 5 in the 1835 version) offers a significantly extended depiction of Andrii's betrayal: his contemplation of the starry sky, his conversation with the Tatar woman, his oath to the Polish princess, a flashback to his first meeting with the Polish princess in Kyiv, a seductive image of the Polish girl that sparkled in his mind, his search for food, his threats to kill Ostap, his underground journey to the besieged town; the dialogue between Andrii and the Polish princess was doubled in length; Gogol also added new descriptions of the Catholic church and streets of Dubno.

Chapter 7 (a modification of chapter 5 in the 1835 redaction) begins with a new episode about the captivity of the Pereiaslavsky *kuren'*, which fell asleep after the binge, and the following council of the Cossacks debating how to rescue the comrades. Gogol also added more details to the conversation between Bulba and Yankel, making this episode 60% longer than in the 1835 version. The following battle between Cossacks and Poles is written anew, with the episode of Andrii's execution deleted from the chapter. In the description of the battle, Gogol contrasted the affluent garments and ammunition of the Poles with simple Cossack attire to underscore the class differences between the oppressors and the oppressed. The new details about some Cossacks' view of a battle as a means of profiteering are added to demonstrate that their death was a punishment for their cupidity. A beheaded ataman, Borodatyi, is replaced by Ostap Bulba.

Chapter 8 is a reduced version of chapter 6 of the 1835 redaction. Gogol cut the final episode of the battle, during which Ostap was taken prisoner and Taras was wounded. A scene of the divide between the Cossacks who stayed with Taras Bulba to release the captured Cossacks and the Cossacks who joined the *koshevoi* to defend the Host from Tatars is more elaborated, with thirty new personalized profiles of the Cossacks. Bulba's famous speech about comradeship is deleted from the chapter and moved to chapter 9.

Chapter 9 (chapter 7 in the 1835 redaction): Gogol extended Bulba's speech on comradeship in order to provide a psychological justification for his filicide. The "holy ties of comradeship" emphasized kinship of the Cossacks by spirit, not by blood. The mechanics of war between Cossacks and Poles is now based on acts of personal retaliation, rather than on religious antagonism: Dehtiarenko kills Poles and is murdered later, Mosii Shilo kills Dehtiarenkos's slayer and is killed by the slayer's servant, etc. The depiction of the final battle was altered too. The final attack of the Polish army led by Andrii was absent in the 1835 redaction. Andrii's appeal to the Polish soldiers to help him avoid his father's revenge is deleted from the 1842 edition. Andrii is described as a delinquent student who does not utter a word in the entire chapter, which makes him look humbler in accepting retaliation.

Chapter 10 (chapter 7 in the 1835 redaction) received a new description of Iankel's business in Uman', his commentary about the Cossacks' treatment of Jews. Gogol added a new passage about Taras's comrade Tovkach curing him with a potion obtained from a Jewish healer.

Chapter 11 (chapter 8 in the 1835 redaction): Gogol modified the episode of Ostap's execution by making the Christological motifs more pronounced.

Chapter 12 (chapter 9 in the 1835 redaction) ends with a new monologue by Bulba about the war to defend the Rus'ian faith and his prophecy about the emerging of "our own tsar." In the 1835 redaction, Taras is tied to the log with his right arm nailed to it, whereas in the 1842 version, he is tied to a tree with both hands nailed. Gothic elements are replaced with Christian.

The Draft and Final Version of Taras Bulba's Speech about Comradeship in a Side-by-Side Juxtaposition Using Beyond Compare

Beyond Compare intelligently picks the best way to compare and display differences. Text files (uploaded in .txt format) can be viewed and edited with syntax highlighting and comparison rules. Specific differences are marked with red text, and the entire line is given a light red background to indicate the presence of a difference. The text on the left side is taken from the final version of the 1842 redaction of the tale and compared to the earlier draft version of the same passage about comradeship. In the sentences which were slightly altered, we can immediately see the insertions of new sentences, inversions, new parallelism, substitutions of characteristic words, and simpler syntax and sentence structures – all these stylistic and rhetoric changes demonstrate Gogol's meticulous work on creating the powerful effect of Taras's speech on the Cossacks and, consequently, on the readers.

Хочется мне вам сказать, панове, что такое есть наше товарищество.	=	Хочется мне вам сказать, панове, что такое есть наше товарищество.
Вы слышали от отцов и дедов, в какой чести у всех была земля наша: и грекам дала знать себя, и с Царьграда брала червонцы, и города были пышные, и храмы, и князья, князья русского рода, свои князья, а не католические недоверки.	<>	Вы слышали от отцов и дедов, в какой чести у всех была земля наша: и грекам дала знать себя, и с Царьграда брала червонцы, и города были пышные, и храмы, и князья, князья русского рода, свои князья, а не католические недоверки.
	=	
Все взяли бусурманы, все пропало.		Все взяли бусурманы, все пропало.
Только остались мы, сирые, да, как вдовица после крепкого мужа, сирая, так же как и мы, земля наша!	<>	Только остались мы, сирые, да, как вдовица после крепкого мужа, сирая, так же как и мы, земля наша!
	=	
Вот в какое время подали мы, товарищи, руку на братство!	<>	Вот в какое время подали мы, товарищи, руку на братство!
	=	
Вот на чем стоит наше товарищество!	<>	Вот на чем стоит наше товарищество!
	=	
Нет уз святее товарищества!	<>	Товарищество, которое и без того уже святое дело.
	=	
Отец любит свое дитя, мать любит свое дитя, дитя любит отца и мать.	<>	Нет сильнее уз товарищества.
	=	
Но это не то, братцы: любит и зверь свое дитя.	<>	Любовь материнская, отцовская – все не то: и зверь любит дитя свое.
	=	
Но породниться родством по душе, а не по крови, может один только человек.	<>	Но выбрать себе родство по душе, а не по крови, может только один человек.
	=	
Бывали и в других землях товарищи, но таких, как в Русской земле, не было таких товарищей.	<>	Везде, во всякое время, и во всякой земле, водились товарищи; но таких товарищей, как в Русской земле, таких нет; есть, да не такие.
	=	
Вам случалось не одному помногу пропадать на чужбине; видишь -- и там люди!	<>	
также божий человек, и разговоришься с ним, как с своим; а как дойдет до того, чтобы поведать сердечное слово, -- видишь: нет, умные люди, да не те; такие же люди, да не те!		Может быть, случалось вам пропадать на чужбине, в плену или так, <по> своей воле, - видишь: и там тоже люди, сначала свыкнешься с ними, а как разговоришься о том, о чем бы хотелось разговориться в сердечную минуту.
	=	
	<>	- видишь: нет, умные люди, да не те; такие же люди, да не те!
Нет, братцы, так любить, как русская душа, -- любить не то чтобы умом или чем другим, а всем, чем дал бог, что ни есть в тебе, а...		Нет, братцы, так любить, как русская душа, - любить не то чтобы умом или чем другим, а всем, чем дал бог, что ни есть в тебе, а...
	=	
-- сказал Тарас, и махнул рукой, и потряс седою головою, и усом моргнул, и сказал: -- Нет, так любить никто не может!	<>	- сказал Тарас, и махнул рукой, и потряс седою головою, и усом моргнул, и сказал: - Нет, так любить никто не может!

Знаю, подло завелось теперь на земле нашей; думают только, чтобы при них были хлебные стоги, скирды да конные табуны их, да были бы целы в погребах запечатанные меды их.	<>	Знаю, подло завелось теперь на земле нашей; думают только, чтобы при них были хлебные стоги, скирды да конные табуны их, да были бы целы в погребах запечатанные меды их.
	=	
Перенимают черт знает какие бусурманские обычаи; гнушаются языком своим; свой с своим не хочет говорить; свой своего продает, как продают бездушную тварь на торговом рынке.	<>	Перенимают черт знает какие бусурманские обычаи; гнушаются языком своим; свой с своим не хочет говорить; свой своего продает, как продают бездушную тварь на торговом рынке.
	=	
Милость чужого короля, да и не короля, а паскудная милость польского магната, который желтым чеботом своим бьет их в морду, дороже для них всякого братства.	<>	Милость чужого короля, да и не короля, а паскудная милость польского магната, который желтым чеботом своим бьет их в морду, дороже для них всякого братства.
	=	
Но у последнего подлюки, каков он ни есть, хоть весь извалялся он в саже и в поклонничестве, есть и у того, братцы, крупица русского чувства.	<>	Но у последнего подлюки, каков он ни есть, потерявшего имя человека в низкопоклонничестве, есть и у него, — будь только он русского рода, а не какая чуждая примесь, — есть чувство в душе.
	=	
И проснется оно когда-нибудь, и ударится он, горемычный, об полы руками, схватит себя за голову, проклявши громко подлую жизнь свою, готовый муками искупить позорное дело.	<>	Хоть что хочь говори, а я стою, что есть русское чувство и когда-нибудь да проснется оно, схватит он, горемычный, обеими руками себя за голову и вскрикнет и проклянет он всю подлую жизнь, готовый смертью и муками искупить покрытые позором дела свои.
	=	
Пусть же знают они все, что такое значит в Русской земле товарищество!	<>	Так пусть же теперь знает все бусурманство, что такое значит товарищество в Русской земле и как стоят в ней брат за брата.
	=	
	<>	Если уже умирать, так пусть они придут посмотрят, как мы будем умирать.
Уж если на то пошло, чтобы умирать, -- так никому ж из них не доведется так умирать!..		Да никому же из них не доведется и во сне не приснится так умирать, как станем умирать.
	=	
Никому, никому!..	<>	Никому!
	=	
Не хватит у них на то мышиной натуры их!	<>	Никому! Пусть они и не думают о том, и в мысль пусть о том не приходит то нестаточ- ное для всякого другого. Нечеловеческих сил ему нужно для того. Нет! не доведется никому так умирать, как русскому, никому! никому!

Principal Component Analysis

PCA (Principal Component Analysis) is a multivariate ordination statistical procedure that compares the variability in the corpora of the selected writers. The total variability is always 100% and all the PCs (PC1 + PC2 + PC3 + ...) give a sum of 100%. However, one cannot represent in two dimensions more than four axes; for this reason, one typically deals only with the PC1 and PC2 (represented in the axes x and y). PCA is based on the term-covariance matrix. Let's imagine that instead of x1, x2, ... and y1, y2, ... one has words that are assembled in the matrix, with numbers standing for the number of times these words co-occurred.

	x1	x2	x3	x4
y1	1	1	0	1
y2	1	1	1	0
y3	1	1	0	0
y4	1	1	1	1

I have chosen 1000 MFW (most frequently used words) across the corpora, given the large size of each writer's corpus. This method allows us to see as much variance among texts as possible, based on how words are used at different rates by each author. The proximity of the authors to each other in one or the other corner of the x/y axes is based on the number of shared words in the matrix. All writers of Ukrainian and Polish origins are grouped on the right side (top or bottom), whereas all the Russian ones are on the left.

Notes

Introduction

1 Miller, *Hawthorne and History*, 152–3.
2 "If my work is ever to be published, it will be in a *foreign language*; and I need to be even more precise in order that I not distort the [characteristic] noun[s] [*nomen substantivum*] of the nation with incorrect naming" (*PSS X*, 150). Unless otherwise indicated, *PSS* stands for *Polnoe sobranie sochinenii v chetyrnadtsati tomakh* (Moscow: Izd-vo Akademii nauk SSSR, 1937–52). *PSS* (2001–) refers to *Polnoe sobranie sochinenii i pisem v dvadtsati trekh tomakh* (Moscow: "Nauka," IMLI RAN, 2001–). All translations from Gogol are mine unless stated otherwise.
3 See Gogol's famous letter to Aleksandra Smirnova, 24 December 1844: "I myself do not know what soul I have: *khokhlatskaia* [a derogatory term for "Ukrainian"] or Russian. I know only that I would grant primacy neither to a Ukrainian over a Russian nor to a Russian over a Ukrainian. Both natures are too generously endowed by God, and as if on purpose, each of them in its own way includes in itself that which the other lacks" (*PSS XII*, 419).
4 Koropeckyj and Romanchuk, "Ukraine in Blackface," 539.
5 For instance, in the title of *Vybrannye mesta iz perepiski s druz'iami* (Selected passages from correspondence with friends), "vybrannye" (selected) is a Ukrainiainism; the Russian word would be "izbrannye." In the texts of Gogol's late works, Ukrainian elements penetrate not only the Russian lexicon ("надыхаться," "завгодно," "досягнул," "накласть," "мармор," "схватился со стула," etc.) but also its grammar ("послать по художнику" instead of "послать за художником" and "сшил с него мундир" instead of "сшил из него мундир," etc.). Iosif Mandel'shtam was the first scholar who identified and described the penetration of Ukrainian grammatical elements into Gogol's early and late texts. See his examples in *O kharaktere gogolevskogo stilia*, 207–41.

6 Bakhtin, *The Dialogic Imagination*, 360.
7 In his fundamental work, Glissant illustrates the idea of resistance through language by employing the metaphor of an archipelago ("la pensée archipélique") and detour: "Archipelagic thought is well suited to the ways of our worlds. It adopts their ambiguity, their fragility, their derivation [dérivé]. It accords with the practice of the detour, which is not the same as flight or resignation" (*Traité du Tout-Monde*, 31).
8 Fanon, *Black Skin, White Masks*, 111.
9 Bhabha has described the process as follows: "The question of identification is never the affirmation of a pre-given identity, never a self-fulfilling prophecy – it is always the production of an 'image' of identity and the transformation of the subject in assuming that image. The demand of identification – that is, to be *for* an Other – entails the representation of the subject in the differentiating order of Otherness. Identification … is always the return of an image of identity which bears the mark of splitting in that 'Other' place from which it comes" (*The Location of Culture*, 64).
10 Ashcroft, Griffiths and Tiffin, *Post-Colonial Studies*, 119.
11 Mizutani, "Hybridity and History," 44.
12 Loomba, *Colonialism/Postcolonialism*, 178.
13 For a critique of this kind of transcendentalism, see Eagleton. *The Ideology of the Aesthetic*, 382.
14 Chow has claimed that Bhabha's view of hybridity "ultimately makes it unnecessary to come to terms with the subaltern since she has already 'spoken,' as it were, in the system's gaps." See her book *Writing Diaspora*, 35.
15 McClintock, *Imperial Leather*, 64. For a similar critique, see Larsen, *Determinations*, 36–43.
16 Mizutani, "Hybridity and History," 46.
17 Ibid.
18 As it was formulated in the social theory of the 1960s, internalization is based not on a generalized, symbolic procedure but on day-to-day interaction in society, mediated by language (Berger and Luckmann, *The Social Construction of Reality*). In the 1980s, this theory was revised by Varelas and Becker, who described the process of internalization as a shift from what they call a "sign-empirical-referent dimension" to the "sign-sign" dimension. What this means in practical terms is that while internalizing a certain social identity, individuals are engaged in knowing and doing, i.e., in epistemic and sociocultural processes. It is not a "passive process of receiving and mimicking inside what is going on outside" but rather "the inward movement of the meaning of signs from more empirical referents to more mental referents" ("Internalization of Cultural Forms of Behavior," 217). Therefore, it is not signs but their

meaning that is being internalized. But because signs belong both to the external (sign form) and internal (meaning) world, the process of internalization runs parallel to the process of externalization (218).

19 As Etkind argues in his monograph *Internal Colonization*, Russia colonized itself, or rather, its Westernized upper class enserfed the peasants, whose ethnic background was either secondary or insignificant. The end result of internal colonization was populating, not acquiring new lands, because the Russian Empire always strove to "give economic and political privileges to its colonies, creating opportunities for them for self-rule and self-preservation" (Etkind, "Fuko i tezis vnutrennei kolonizatsii").

20 Groys, "Imena goroda," 358.

21 Rohdewald, "'Vneshniaia kolonizatsiia vnutrennego' i 'vnutrenniaia kolonizatsiia vneshnego.'

22 Etkind, "Russkaia literatura, XIX vek."

23 Hrytsak, "The Postcolonial Is Not Enough," 733–4.

24 Khodarkovsky notes that in the mid-sixteenth century Russia embarked on its own imperialistic mission along the fluid borders of the steppe – a huge swathe of land that covers Eastern Europe in the west through Central Asia to Mongolia and China in the east. See his essay "From Frontier to Empire."

25 Polevoi, quoted in *Moskovskii telegraf* 35 (17) (1830), 85–6.

26 Grabowicz, "Ukrainian Studies," 678.

27 Etkind describes Russian cultural practice: "The main paths of Russian colonization were aimed not outside, but at the interior of the metropolis: not into Turkey, not into Poland, and not even at Siberia, but into the villages of Tula, Pomerania, and Orenburg. Here the state distributed landed estates and subdued uprisings. Here community was discovered, and folklore was recorded. Ancient customs and strange religions were studied here. From here the capital's collections obtained deformities and rarities" (*Internal Colonization*, 3).

28 See Ovsianiko-Kulikovskii, "Gogol," 148.

29 Trubetskoi, "The Ukrainian Problem," 251.

30 See Erlich, *Gogol* (1969); Nabokov, *Nikolai Gogol* (1944); Setchkarev (1965); and others.

31 Mann, "Gogol," 370.

32 Voropaev, "Gogol' i 'russko-ukrainskii vopros,'" 15.

33 Fanger, *The Creation of Nikolai Gogol*, 89.

34 Gasparov, "Alienation and Negation," 114–15.

35 Lounsbery, *Thin Culture, High Art*, 39.

36 Barabash, "'Svoego iazyka ne znaet … ,'" 36–7.

37 Luckyj, *Between Gogol' and Ševčenko*, 127.

38 See chapter 4, "Mizh dvokh stykhii," in Holubenko's *Ukraina i Rosiia u svitli kul'turnykh vzaemyn*, 244–330.

39 Luckyj, *The Anguish of Mykola Hohol a.k.a. Nikolai Gogol*; Bojanowska, *Nikolai Gogol.*

40 Grabowicz, "Hohol i mif Ukrainy," 77.

41 See Ilnytzkyj, "Cultural Indeterminacy in the Russian Empire."

42 See Sawczak, "'Noch pered Rozhdestvom' Mykoly/Nikolaia Gogolia."

43 Piksanov, "Ukrainskie povesti Gogolia," 47.

44 See Koropeckyj and Romanchuk's recent article, "Harkusha the Noble Bandit," and Romanchuk's paper "Mother Tongue."

45 Derrida, *Specters of Marx*, 34.

1. The Negotiation of Ukrainian Identities in the Russian Empire

1 Detailed discussion of the issue can be found in Velychenko, "Empire Loyalism and Minority Nationalism in Great Britain and Imperial Russia, 1707 to 1914"; Berger and Miller, eds., *Nationalizing Empires*, vol. 3; and Kappeler, "Mazepintsy, Malorossy, Khokhly."

2 Miller, "Rossiia i rusifikatsiia Ukrainy v XIX veke."

3 For further reading about the official ideology of "Orthodoxy, Autocracy, Nationality," see Zorin, "Ideologiia 'pravoslaviia-samoderzhaviia-narodnosti.'"

4 For further discussion of Prokopovych's biography, see Plokhii's "The Two Russias of Teofan Prokopovych."

5 An important addition to the Ukrainian political vocabulary of the seventeenth and eighteenth centuries, the concept of "fatherland" originated in the Latin equivalent to the Polish "ojczyzna" and shared a number of features with it. The fatherland was understood as quite independent from its ruler; its good was the highest value and object of loyalty (Tairova-Iakovleva, *Inkorporatsiia*, 21; Plokhii, "The Two Russias of Teofan Prokopovych," 352). In exchange for their service, "fatherland" guaranteed its subjects certain rights ("wolność"). As Tairova-Iakovleva's analysis of Cossack documents of the time has demonstrated, the notion of loyalty to "ojczyzna" only proves the fact that the rights that registered Cossacks shared with Polish gentry were expected to be maintained and expanded (*Inkorporatsiia*, 15). Even fifty years after incorporation into the Russian empire, Ukrainian political leaders and historiographers applied the term "fatherland" to the Polish Commonwealth, not the Russian Empire, which they called the "state."

6 See more on this issue in Kohut, "The Ukrainian Elite in the Eighteenth Century and Its Integration into Russian Nobility"; Kharlampovich, *Malorossiiskoe vliiannie na velikorusskuiu tserkovnuiu zhizn* (Kazan, 1914).

7 See Greenfeld, *Nationalism*, 238–9.

8 Plokhii, *Ukraine and Russia*, 35.

9 Velychenko, "Empire Loyalism and Minority Nationalism in Great Britain and Imperial Russia, 1707 to 1914," 421; Saunders, *The Ukrainian Impact on Russian Culture, 1750–1850*, 68.

10 In general, Pushkin approved of keeping the distinction between classes in Russian society and questioned the value of social mobility: for example, his statement on this topic on 22 December 1834 at Khitrovo's salon: "The nobility ... should be limited and inaccessible [to others] ... If any other class can join the nobility, climbing from one rank to another ... then soon it will cease to exist" (Modzalevskii et al., *Dnevnik A.S. Pushkina*, 24).

11 *Surzhyk* (literally meaning "bread made from a mixture of rye and wheat flour") is a macaronic sociolect of the Russian and Ukrainian languages, used predominantly in Left-Bank Ukraine for communication between peasant Ukrainians and members of the Russified elite.

12 Kohut, *The Question of Russo-Ukrainian Unity and Ukrainian Distinctiveness in Early Modern Ukrainian Thought and Culture*, 15.

13 Miller, *The Ukrainian Question*, 29.

14 Subtelny, *Ukraine*, 3.

15 Geraci, *Window on the East*, 9.

16 Plokhii, *Ukraine and Russia*, 43.

17 Sverbyhuz, *Starosvits'ke panstvo*, 166.

18 Tolochko, "Fellows and Travelers," 154.

19 Iurii Mann in his 2012 monograph *Gogol. Kniga pervaia. Nachalo 1809–1835* has investigated Gogol's genealogy and clarified many details in the history of the noble status of the writer's family. For further discussion, see the chapter "Rod Gogolia."

20 Ibid., 18.

21 *PSS XIV*, 106.

22 Myronchuk, "Vasyl' Kapnist – ukrains'kyi avtonomist," 231–2.

23 Ohloblyn, *Liudy staroi Ukrainy*, 88.

24 "Whenever I direct my eyes, / Washed by torrents of tears, / Everywhere I see my motherland / Like a grieving widow: / Rural pleasures, gay playfulness, dances, / Laughter had disappeared. / ... Golden fields are deserted / Fields, forests, meadows are becoming empty / Sorrow, like a storm-cloud, fell on them ... / Look on those people / Where slavery oppresses them; / Where there is no freedom, / And the sound of chain sounds: / The mortals are born to live in misery, / To be condemned to disparagement, / They drink a cup of ills. / Under the heavy yoke of the state / They shed their bloody sweat / And live a life worse than death" (Kapnist, "Oda na rabstvo," *Sobraniie sochinenii v 2-kh tomakh*, vol. 1, 88–9).

25 Kapeller, "Mazepintsy, Malorossy, Khokhly," 126.
26 Kohut, *The Question of Russo-Ukrainian Unity and Ukrainian Distinctiveness in Early Modern Ukrainian Thought and Culture*, 17.
27 See Bakhtin, "Rable i Gogol'," *Tvorchestvo Fransua Rable i narodnaia kul'tura srednevekov'ia i Renessansa* (Moscow: Khudozhestvennaia literatura, 1990), 486.
28 *Vesel'ie* is transliterated as the Ukrainian *vesillia* (wedding) by means of Russian orthography.
29 "In his story, Mr Narezhnyi employs so many words and expressions pertaining to the regional Little Russian dialect as to be almost incomprehensible to Great Russians. I open at random some of Bursak's books and find, for example, 'krik i gomon razbudili menia' (shouting and noise woke me up). 'Gomonit'' (to vociferate) in Ukrainian means to make noise, whereas in Russian it has the meaning 'to pacify'; see *Dictionary of the Academy of Sciences*, Part 1, page 1179. No Russian would say: 'pod vecher ia ukradus'' iz dvortsa (toward evening I steal out of the palace)." See *Literaturnye Listki* 4 (1824): 50.
30 In Narizhnyi's language, the use of the infinitive "imet'" (to have) is governed by Ukrainian, not Russian, grammar. It is employed not only to indicate possession, but in phrases "there is/are": "zdanie vperedi imelo pustyr'" (the building had a vacant lot in front) instead of "vperedi zdaniia byl pustyr'" (there was a vacant lot in front of the building). In the text of *Two Ivans* the more typical Russian construction "to be" appears only eleven times, whereas the Ukrainian structure "to have" appears more than fifty times. In most cases, "to have" is used idiomatically to mark the bureaucratic mode of speech: "veleli tsyganu imet' popechenie o loshadiakh" (the gypsy was ordered to take care of the horses), or "imet' ego v pochtenii" (to hold him in respect). Sometimes it functions as the auxiliary verb "must" ("ostavshiisia rubl' imeet byt' vydan panu Ivanu" [the remaining ruble ought to be given to Mister Ivan]), which in Narizhnyi's original Russian sounds awkward but which translated into Ukrainian becomes grammatical ("mae buty vydanyi"); at other times, it has idiomatic connotations, as in "oni imeli glaza" (they were surprised), which when translated into Ukrainian sounds more appropriate than in Russian. Beyond the interference of Ukrainian morphology and syntax, new lexemes created as a result of semantic calquing also make Narizhnyi's language hybridized: "dostatochnaia nevesta," that is, "nevesta s dostatkom" (a wealthy bride), or "nekoshtovnye pany," that is, "pany bez koshtiv" (gentlemen without money).
31 Recently, Svitlana Krys has tried to "decolonize" the interpretative lens usually applied to Somov's oeuvre and to approach him from three angles: as a Ukrainian author in the Russian Empire who created in

Russian but who thematically and publicly showed allegiance to Ukraine; as an ethnographer who strove to collect and preserve Ukrainian folklore for future generations; and as "the initiator of the indigenous literary tradition of the Gothic in the Ukrainian literary canon." See Krys, "The Unknown Ukrainian."

32 John Mersereau discusses Somov's engagement with Ukrainian society in St Petersburg in *Orest Somov*, 26–36.

33 Bhabha, *The Location of Culture*, 9.

34 "Сколько различных народов слилось под одно название русских, или зависят от России, не отделяясь ни пространством земель чужих, ни морями далекими! Сколько разных обликов, нравов и обычаев представляется испытующему взору в одном объеме России совокупной! Не говоря уже о собственно-русских, здесь являются малороссияне, с сладостными их песнями и славнями воспоминаниями; там воинственные сыны тихого Дона и отважные переселенцы Сечи Запорожской: все они, соединяясь верою и пламенною любовью к Отчизне, – носят черты отличия в нравах и наружности. Что же, если мы окинем края России, обитаемые пылкими поляками и литовцами, народами финского и скандинавского происхождения, обитателыми древней Колхиды, потомками переселенцев, видевших изгнание Овидия, остатками некогда грозных России татар, многоразличными племенами Сибири и островов, кочующими поколениями монгольцев, буйными жителями Кавказа, северными лапонцами и самоедами?" (Somov, *O romanticheskoi poezii*, 86–7; translation by Mersereau, *Orest Somov*, 31).

35 In a letter from 1829, Somov referred to Baiskii as his fellow townsman who was currently engaged in the publication of his own almanac in Volchans'k (Somov's hometown near Kharkiv). In another letter, Baiskii emerges as a fellow writer who was finishing a novel on Ukrainian Cossack history titled "Gaidamak." See Somov's letter to Maksymovych (23 June 1829), *Russkii arkhiv* 10 (1908): 257.

36 Ibid., 262–3.

37 Such terms as "bandura," "batog," "oseledets," "svitka", "iatka," etc., will also appear in Gogol's "Lexicon of Little Russian Words" appended to his *Evenings*.

38 Koropeckyj and Romanchuk, "Harkusha the Noble Bandit and the 'Minority' of Little Russian Literature," 303.

39 "По грязным улицам тянулись длинные обозы; чумаки с батогом на плече шли медленным шагом подле волов своих … Русские извозчики без пощады погоняли усталых лошадей, суетились около телег, навьюченных московскими товарами, кричали и ссорились. В ятках на площади толпились веселые казаки в красных и синих жупанах и те беззаботные головы, кои, уставши чумаковать, пришли

к ярманке на родину попить и погулять; одни громко рассуждали о старой гетманщине, другие толковали про дальние свои чумакованья на Дон за рыбою и в Крым за солью. Крик торговок и крамарей, жиды с цимбалами и скрыпками; цыгане с своими песнями, плясками и звонкими ворганами, слепцы-бандуристы с протяжными их напевами – везде шум и движение, везде или отголоски непритворной радости, или звуки поддельного веселья. Огромные груды арбузов, дынь, яблок и других плодов, коими небо благословило Малороссию и Украину, лежа рядами на подстилках по обе стороны площади, манили взор и вкус и свидетельствовали о плодородии края" (Somov, "Gaidamak. malorossiiskaia byl," 748–9).

40 The bandura is a plucked-string folk instrument, like a lute in appearance; it is considered the Ukrainian national musical instrument.

41 "Он [Пан Ладович] ввел в гостиную слепца-бандуриста … и вежливо пригласил гостей своих послушать веселых дедовских песен и стародавних былей … Певец повествовал о быстром набеге гетмана Хмельницкого на союзную Польше Молдавию … и заключил песнь свою обращением к славе Гетманщины:

В той час була честь, слава,
Войсковая справа!
Сама себе на смих не давала,
Неприятеля пид ноги топтала.

Громкие знаки одобрения и восторга раздались по светлице. Между ними прорывались и вздохи на память старой Гетманщине, временам Хмельницкого, временам истинно героическим, когда развившаяся жизнь народа была в полном соку своем, когда закаленные в боях и взросшие на ратном поле казаки бодро и весело бились с многочисленными и разноплеменными врагами, и всех их победили; когда Малороссия почувствовала сладость свободы и самобытности народной и сбросила с себя иго вероломного утеснителя, обещавшего ей равенство прав, но тяжким опытом доказавшего, что горе покоренным!" (Somov, "Gaidamak. malorossiiskaia byl," 756–7).

42 "В городе Глухове собрался народ около старца бандуриста и уже с час слушал, как слепец играл на бандуре. Еще таких чудных песен и так хорошо не пел ни один бандурист. Сперва повел он про прежнюю гетьманщину, за Сагайдачного и Хмельницкого. Тогда иное было время: козачество было в славе; топтало конями неприятелей, и никто не смел посмеяться над ним" (*PSS I*, 279).

43 Petrunina has identified the affinity between the plots of Gogol's "Ivan Fedorovich Shpon'ka and His Auntie" and Somov's "Matchmaking"

and "Mother and Son" ("Orest Somov i ego proza"). Mann argues that Somov's *A Living in the Abode of Eternal Bliss* provided an inspiration for Gogol's *Dead Souls* (*Poetika Gogolia*, 405).

44 In one of the footnotes to "A Fairy-Tale about Treasures," Somov writes: "Readers, of course, have understood that the purpose of this story is to collect as many folk traditions and beliefs as possible that are common in Little Russia and Ukraine among the common people, so that they may not be completely lost for future archaeologists and poets. [...] The writer, familiar with the customs and habits of the region, collected as many of these folktales as he could, and, not wanting to make a special anthology [slovar'] of them, decided to disperse them in various of his own tales" (Petrunina, "Orest Somov i ego proza," 217).

45 Strano, *Gogol' (ironia, polemica, parodia)*, 56.

46 Drahomanov, *Perepyska Mykhaila Drahomanova z Melitonom Buchyns'kym 1871–1877* (Lviv, 1910), 68. For Maksymovych, aquaintance with Pushkin opened the door to imperial literary salons, while collaboration with the conservative Sergei Uvarov secured him a position as the first rector of the University of St Volodymyr in Kyiv. At same time, he was in close personal and professional relationship with both social democrats (Herzen, Stankevich, and Ogarev) and Slavophiles (Aksakov and Khomiakov).

47 "І могили мої милі/Москаль розриває ... / Нехай риє, розкопує, / Не своє шукає, / А тим часом перевертні / Нехай підростають / Та поможуть москалеві / Господарювати, / Та з матері полатану / Сорочку знімати / Помагайте, недолюдки, / Матір катувати" (Shevchenko, *Zibrannia tvoriv v 6-ty tomakh*, vol. 1, 253).

48 Shevchenko, *Zibrannia tvoriv*, vol. 6, 84.

49 Shevchenko, *Zibrannia tvoriv*, vol. 1, 131.

50 The Brotherhood of Saints Cyril and Methodius was a secret political society that existed in Kyiv during 1845–7 and that sought to revive the ideals of Christian brotherhood and establish a free and equal Slavic federation. The society was quickly suppressed by the tsarist government in March 1847, with most of the members punished by exile or imprisonment.

51 For example, Amvrosii Metlyns'kyi's *Iuzhno-russkie narodnye pesni* (South Russian Folk Songs) was held up by the censors for seven years before it was finally published in 1854. His *Almanakh* (Almanac), a collection of Ukrainian writers' poetry and prose, was under the censors' review for three years before it was returned with half the text crossed out because the writers used too many problematic words like "Ukraine," "freedom," "free will," etc. (More details can be found in Fabrikant's article, cited in the following note.)

52 Fabrikant, "A Brief Outline of the History of the Treatment of Ukrainian Literature by the Russian Censorship Laws (1905)," 156.

53 Ibid.

54 Ilnytzkyj, "'Imperial Culture' and Russian-Ukrainian Unity Myths," 66.

55 A native of the Russian province of Voronezh, Kostomarov was born out of wedlock, the son of an impoverished Russian noble and a Ukrainian peasant. His parents married when Kostomarov turned one, but, according to the law of the Russian Empire, he remained a serf of his own father. His father's sudden death in 1828 left Kostomarov without the legal right to inherit the family estate. His father's relatives became the legal heirs, leaving the young man without means of subsistence. Kostomarov linked the national victimization of Ukraine to his own experience of social victimization and believed that national equality was subordinate to social equality.

56 Kostomarov emphasized the messianic role of the Ukrainian people in the process of salvation. Once Christ came to earth, the nations received a chance for redemption, but most of them succumbed to the misrule of ambitious kings and defied Christian ethics. Only the Slavic tribes "had neither kings nor masters and all were equal and there were no idols among them." When "the Great Russian people lost their senses and fell into idolatry because they called the tsar the earthly god," Ukrainians alone maintained a democratic order. "Ukraine loved neither the tsar nor the Polish lord and established the Cossack Host among themselves, i.e. a brotherhood in which each upon entering was a brother of the others" (*Books of Genesis of the Ukrainian People*, 38–40).

57 Sokhan' et al., eds., *Kyrylo-Mefodiivs'ke tovarystvo*, vol. 1, 299.

58 That Kostomarov had to conceal his real political views was evident from his correspondence with the dissident Russian writer in exile Alexander Herzen, who published a letter from Kostomarov under the headline "Ukraine" in the January 1860 issue of *The Bell* in London. Kostomarov's letter was a commentary on the growing role of the Ukrainian people in the Polish-Russian relationship; it also confirmed his belief in the national distinctiveness of Ukrainians: "The majority of the Great Russian and Polish public became accustomed not to think of us [Ukrainians] as a separate people … Let neither Great Russians nor Poles call their own the lands settled by our [Ukrainian] people" ("Ukraina").

59 Saunders, "Mykola Kostomarov (1817–85) and the Creation of a Ukrainian Ethnic Identity"; Bilenky, ed., *Fashioning Modern Ukraine*, xlii; Pavlyshyn, "For and against a Ukrainian National Literature," 203.

60 Quoted in Petrov, *Panteleimon Kulish u p'iatdesiati roky*, 243.

61 Kostomarov, "Mysli o federativnom nachale v drevnei Rusi."

62 A nationalist-minded Ukrainian critic, Serhii Efremov, defined Kulish
as "two persons in one, some kind of walking contrast, a two-faced
Janus, an unresolved puzzle not only for his contemporaries but for his
descendants" (*Istoriia ukrains'koho pys'menstva*, 285). Dmytro Chyzhevs'kyi
discerned in Kulish's oeuvre an internal conflict, typical for a Romantic
writer who constantly sought movement and change (*Narysy z istorii
filosofii na Ukraini*, 161). Victor Petrov explained Kulish's internal
contradictions by the duplicity of his social position: being a lower
middle-class landowner, he combined Populist ideology with *raznochinets*
progressiveness and petty bourgeois aesthetic tastes. Evhen Malaniuk
was one of the first who explained Kulish's constant re-evaluation and
shifting position regarding the Ukrainian national project by his desire to
mask his lack of national consciousness.

63 Despite a strong friendship between Kulish and Pletnev, Kulish
recognized colonial undertones in their relations: "He [Pletnev]
considered my Ukrainian studies [ukrainstvovanie] as one of my
flaws, maybe the major one, and, naturally, persuaded me to become
a Russian cosmopolitan … Only my Little Russian origin impeded
our intimacy … For my propensity to Ukrainianism he looked at
me if I was a half-monster [poluurod]" ("Vospominaniia o Nikolae
Ivanoviche Kostomarove," 66). Pletnev's Russian friend Iakov Grot
warned him about being too fascinated with Kulish, pointing at the
latter's suspicious Ukrainian origin: "It isn't exactly to my liking that
you opened your heart to Kulish, without having figured him out
completely. It seems that this goes against prudence. Little Russians
are cunning people, masters of pretending." (*Perepiska Ia. K. Grota s
P.A. Pletnevym*, vol. 2, 632–3).

64 When Kulish experienced problems with censorship while trying to
publish his six-volume edition of Gogol's works, high-ranking Russian
officials (Aleksandr Tolstoy, Dmitry Obolenskii, Grigorii Shcherbatov)
interceded for him, and Kulish's edition of Gogol's *Complete Works* was
published in 1857.

65 Neiman, "Kulish i Valter Skott," 135; Zadorozhna, "Khudozhnia
kontseptsiia istorii v romani P. Kulisha "Mykhailo Charnyshenko," 153);
Nakhlik, *Ukrains'ka romantychna proza 20–60kh rokiv XIX stolittia*, 101.

66 In a letter to Sreznevs'kyi (10 January 1846), entirely written in Russian,
Kulish assessed his language proficiency and preferences: "I want to
write *Black Council* in Ukrainian. I know Ukrainian so much better than
Russian, at least in prose. Poetry is another question. What would you
say about this? There are some people who rebuke me for this intention.
But I feel that the Russian language is foreign to me" (*Povne zibrannia
tvoriv*, vol. 1, 67).

67 Expressing his gratitude to the author, Taras Shevchenko underscored the superiority of the Ukrainian version of the novel: "Thank you and God, my dear and magnificent friend, for your great gifts, and especially thank you for *Black Council*. I have read it twice already and will read it for a third time … It is very, very good that you published *Black Council* in our language [Ukrainian]. I have also read it [the Russian version] in *Russian Conversation*, and liked it too, but in our language it is better" (*Zibrannia tvoriv*, 145).

68 Zerov, "Kulish," vol. 2, 197.

69 Kulish, "Ob otnoshenii malorossiiskoi slovesnosti k obshcherusskoi (epilog k 'Chernoi rade')," 124.

70 In his letter to Grabowski, Kulish wrote: "I wish, therefore, to let my voice be heard, so that the Russians [moskali] do not make too much noise with their nationality, which stands out like a prickly pine … It would be good to show to the Rus world the Polish nationality, with its luxuriant beauty, so that the Muscovites do not hide themselves in their dense forests and snow; but their faces will smile when they see the native beauty of the southern man. Perhaps God will help us, in time, to bring together all three peoples which now stand back to back looking far ahead but not looking behind their backs" (Petrov, *Panteleimon Kulish u p'iatdesiati roky*, vol. 1, 182).

71 In the essay that accompanied the collection, "Zazyvnyi lyst do ukrainskoi inteligentsii" (A Letter of Appeal to the Ukrainian Intelligentsia), Kulish accused the Ukrainian elite of "forsaking its own people … to adopt the culture and identity of politically powerful overlords – either Polish or Russian."

72 Kulish, cited in *Chervonyi shliakh* 8 (1925), 192.

73 Shkanrdij, *Russia and Ukraine*, 177.

74 Zborovs'ka, *Kod ukrainskoi literatury*, 164.

75 Freud, *A General Introduction to Psychoanalysis*, 309.

76 See, for further reading, Korostelina, *Constructing the Narratives of Identity and Power*, and Leith, *Political Discourse and National Identity in Scotland*.

77 Koznarsky, "Obsessions with Mazepa," 579.

78 See the detailed analysis of the folk Ukrainian narrator in Shevelyov, "Kulishevi lysty i Kulish u lystakh," 21 and Grabowicz, "Semantyka kotliarevshchyny," 316–32.

79 Herzen, quoted in Kotov and Poliakov, eds., *Gogol' v russkoi kritike (sbornik statei)*, 435.

80 Bhabha, *The Location of Culture*, 94.

2. Gogol's Self-Fashioning and Performance of Identity in the 1830s

1 Greenblatt, *Shakespearean Negotiations*, vol. 4, 147.

2 Greenblatt, *Renaissance Self-Fashioning*, 9.

 3 Bhabha, *The Location of Culture*, 89, 90.
 4 Belyi, "Gogol'," 70.
 5 Erlich, *Gogol*, 218.
 6 MacLean, "Gogol's Retreat from Love," and Karlinsky, *The Sexual Labyrinth of Nikolai Gogol*.
 7 Iryna Kolesnyk has studied Gogol's networks in her monograph *Gogol: Merezhi kulturno-intelektualnykh komunikatsii*.
 8 "It was sheer accident that hindered him from establishing a relationship with Pushkin earlier. Gogol himself described his first meeting with Pushkin in a story that became perpetuated in his biographical legend. In the fall of 1828, upon his arrival in St Petersburg, Gogol turned up on the great poet's doorstep to introduce himself. He approached Pushkin's house in trepidation, having first stopped at a tavern to bolster his courage. When Gogol finally made it to the door, a servant greeted him with the news that his master was still asleep. It was late in the afternoon. 'Evidently, he was working all night?' Gogol asked with deep sympathy. 'What do you mean by "working"? He was playing cards,' answered the servant." (See Pavel Annenkov, *Materialy dlia biografii A.S. Pushkina* [Moscow: "Sovremennik," 1984], 332.)
 9 *PSS X*, 139.
10 In the 1830s, St Petersburg witnessed many young Ukrainians who found employment in imperial institutions. The Ukrainian poet and author of the famous romance "Black Eyes," Evhen Hrebinka, shared his impressions of the omnipresence of fellow Ukrainians in Petersburg's institutions in a 1834 letter to Nikolai Novitskii: "Petersburg is a colony of intelligent Ukrainians. All institutions, academies, and the university are full of our fellow-countrymen. Applying for a job a Ukrainian candidate compels everyone's attention as a *homme d'esprit*" (quoted in Malaniuk, "Hohol – Gogol," 62).
11 Suproniuk, *N.V. Gogol i ego okruzheniie v Nezhinskoi gimnazii* and *Literaturnaia sreda rannego Gogolia*.
12 Vatsuro analysed this topic in his "Pushkin i literaturnoie dvizheniie ego vremeni" and *Mitskevich i russkaia literaturnaia sreda 1820-kh (razyskaniia)*, and in Vatsuro et al., eds., *Pushkin v vospominaniiakh sovremennikov*.
13 See Liubych-Romanovych's recollection in Igor Vinogradov, *Gogol' v vospominaniiakh, dnevnikakh, perepiske sovremennikov*, vol. 1, 558.
14 See Annenkov's recollection in *Literaturnye vospominaniia*, 24.
15 The literary tastes of Gogol's classmates were carefully studied by Suproniuk in *Literaturnaia sreda rannego Gogolia*.
16 Vinogradov, *Gogol' v vospominaniiakh*, vol. 3, 978. The Third Department was the secret police; hence the degree of Gogol's involvement is controversial.

17 The fact is impossible to verify, since all files of the Third Department were destroyed during a fire. Many Gogol scholars (D. Zolotusskii, M. Gillelson, V. Manuilov, V. Stepanov, S. Mashinskii) argue that Bulgarin made up this "legend" after Gogol's death to discredit the writer. In the 1930s, Vasilii Gippius took Bulgarin's claim seriously, analysed Gogol's correspondence and records from his other position at the Department of Crown Lands, and came to the conclusion that "Bulgarin probably did offer to set Gogol up in the Third Department, but Gogol had no desire to heed his advice" (*PSS X*, 422). Recently, Abram Reitblat has verified the accuracy of Bulgarin's version by comparing it with Gogol's letters to his mother from the same months in which the latter discussed his future position in some department, presumably the Third Department. In the chapter "Gogol i Bulgarin: k istorii literaturnykh vzaimootnoshenii," Reitblat argues that Gogol indeed asked Bulgarin for assistance with a job application in the fall of 1829 and that he was hired by the Third Department but did not work there and soon recalled his application ("Gogol i Bulgarin," 196).

18 Frazier, *Romantic Encounters*, 174.

19 Ibid., 174–6.

20 Gogol comically described this name-changing practice among Ukrainians who strove to Russify their peculiar ethnic names by adding the letter "v" to the Ukrainian suffix "-ko" (for example, Stepanen*ko* became Stepanen*kov*). In "Old-World Landowners," Gogol's narrator mocks name changing: "In them [Afanasii Ivanovich and Pul'kheriia Ivanovna, characters in the tale] you could read the entire story of their lives, the cloudless and tranquil existence of the old landed gentry, simple-hearted but wealthy folk, not to be likened to those mean Little Russians who begin as tar merchants and hawkers, droves of whom can be found in council chambers and government offices, who squeeze every kopeck they can out of their fellow countrymen, flood St Petersburg with denunciations, finally amass a fortune and solemnly add to their surnames ending in 'o' the letter 'v.' No, like all true members of the old landed classes of Little Russia, they were not to be compared with these wretched and despicable creatures" (*PSS II*, 15).

21 Nestor Kukol'nyk left a curious record of Gogol's change of name: "By the way, in the lyceum (both among the friends and in papers) Gogol was not called 'Gogol,' but 'Ianovskii.' Once in St Petersburg, in front of me, one of my friends asked Gogol: 'Why did you change your last name?' – 'No, I did not.' – 'You are Ianovskii.' – 'And Gogol as well.' – 'What does it mean "gogol"?' – 'A drake,' Gogol replied reservedly and changed the topic of the conversation." (Vinogradov, *Gogol' v vospominaniiakh*, vol. 1, 551).

22 *PSS X*, 219.

23 Vinogradov, *Gogol' v vospominaniiakh*, vol. 1, 645.

24 *PSS X*, 196.

25 For further discussion of this issue, see Todd's *Fiction and Society in the Age of Pushkin*.

26 Leaving aside the history of interactions between Pushkin and Gogol, I only want to emphasize that there was no close friendship between the two. They were connected mostly by professional interests and a common vision of the development of Russian literature. Gogol's dependence on Pushkin's help has been exaggerated by scholars. For further discussion of Pushkin and Gogol's relationship, see Petrunina and Fridlender, "Pushkin i Gogol' v 1831–1836 godakh," and Debreczeny, *Social Functions of Literature*.

27 See *Istoricheskii vestnik* 1 (1881): 136–8.

28 See *Russkaia starina* 4 (48) (1888): 333.

29 *PSS XII*, 433.

30 Holquist, "The Tyranny of Difference," 127.

31 Letter to Pogodin of 28 November 1836 (*PSS XI*, 78).

32 For further discussion, see Grabowicz's article, "Between Subversion and Self-Assertion."

33 Pavlyshyn, "The Rhetoric and Politics of Kotliarevsky's *Eneïda*," 23–4.

34 Moeller-Sally views Gogol's use of pseudonyms in 1830–1 as a revelation of the author's anxiety "after the embarrassingly poor reception" of his first work, *Hanz Kuechalgarten* (1829). See "0000; or, The Sign of the Subject in Gogol's Petersburg," 325–6.

35 Vinogradov, *Gogol' v vospominaniiakh*, vol. 1, 704.

36 See A.I. Markevich, "Zametka o psevdonime N.V. Gogolia 'Rudyi Pan'ko'" on the formation of Ukrainian names and, particularly, Gogol's family name.

37 *PSS I*, 103.

38 See the analysis of the *suplika* as an expression of Ukrainian identity in Grabowicz, "Toward a History of Ukrainian Literature," 476–7. See also Pavlyshyn, "Experiments with Audiences: the Ukrainian and Russian Prose of Kvitka-Osnovianenko," and Koropeckyj and Romanchuk, "Ukraine in Blackface."

39 Koropeckyj and Romanchuk, "Ukraine in Blackface," 542.

40 The cultural anthropologist Roger Caillois has claimed that the very "fascination with the Other" inherent in disguise reveals a fundamentally existential desire: being outside or beside oneself provides an inestimable source of psychic pleasure and nourishment (*The Mask of Medusa*, 87).

41 Foucault, "What Is an Author?"

42 Quoted in Chicherin, "Neizvestnoe vyskazyvanie V.F. Odoevskogo o Gogole," 72.

43 Quoted in Dmitrieva, "Pozhiv v takoi tesnoi sviazi s ved'mami i koldunami (Ob osobennostiakh gogolevskogo folklorizma 'Vechera na khutore bliz Dikan'ki')," 138.

44 Koropeckyj and Romanchuk have made an interesting comparative analysis of the role of the patron in American blackface performances with that of Gogol's implicit Russian metropolitan audience that functions as a collective "patron" in *Evenings*: "Although the elite patron must be kept at a distance for the minstrel performance to have its effect, his impotent gaze nonetheless is the place from where the performance must be viewed. Gogol's Russian public feels this gaze, it hears this voice clucking in disapproval, and acts out, snorting and giggling, forging an imaginary identification with the romantically exotic characters and with Pan'ko himself. And the latter encourages just such an identification at every turn" ("Ukraine in Blackface," 541).

45 "Poltava," *Otechestvennye zapiski* 120 (April 1830): 31–2.

46 Quoted in Gippius, ed., *N.V. Gogol*, vol. 1, 170.

47 The idea of Gogol "stealing" from Pushkin appears in two different sources. First, in his memoirs of 1841, Annenkov quoted Pushkin saying that he needed to be "careful with that Little Russian [Gogol]" who "kept fleecing" him. Annenkov in his recollections presented Pushkin's view of the fact of "stealing": "It is known that Gogol borrowed from Pushkin the idea of *The Inspector General* and *Dead Souls*, but it is less known that Pushkin gave him his property [dostoianiie] [i.e., the plots of the above works] not quite willingly. However, in his family circle, Pushkin said, laughing: "I should be careful [dealing] with this *maloross*: he robs me without scruple [chto i krichat' nel'zia]" (Vinogradov, *Gogol' v vospominaniiakh*, vol. 3, 433). Then, in Pushkin's sister's memoirs, the poet is quoted as complaining to his wife, Natalia Goncharova, that the "sly Little Russian [Gogol] used his plot." "My tongue is my enemy. Gogol is a sly *maloross*; he took advantage of my plot" (quoted in Mashinskii, ed., *Gogol v vospominaniiakh sovremennikov*, 630).

48 Vinogradov, *Gogol' v vospominaniiakh*, vol. 1, 717.

49 Pushkin's associate Pavel Nashchokin, for example, emphasized Pushkin's patronage, saying that he "set Gogol up in the world," fostering Gogol's professional development and promoting him as a writer (Vinogradov, *Gogol' v vospominaniiakh*, vol. 2, 550).

50 Quoted in Shenrok, *A.O. Smirnova i N. V. Gogol' v 1829–1852 godakh*, 52.

51 See excerpts from Smirnova's diary in ibid.; for example: "Sverchok [Pushkin's nickname] is very kind, he immediately tamed a poor *khokhol* [Gogol])" (54); "They [Pushkin and Zhukovskii] teased Gogol so much for his wildness and shyness that he eventually stopped being shy" (55);

"The Grand Prince [Mikhail] talked with me about Gogol; he called him 'a *maloross* [a Ukrainian] tamed by donna Sol [Smirnova's nickname]'" (84).

52 Ibid., 46–8.

53 Sarra Zhitomirskaia studied Smirnova's papers and established that Smirnova had worked on her memoirs about Gogol since the 1840s, and more systematically in 1852–4, right after Gogol's death, but she never completed her text. She was writing simultaneously two different memoirs, and although the plotline of the same events remained stable across the two texts, the treatment of one or another literary figure generated different associations in her account ("A.O. Smirnova-Rosset i ee memuarnoe nasledie," 617).

54 Vinogradov, *Gogol' v vospominaniiakh*, vol. 1, 726.

55 Vinogradov, *Gogol' v vospominaniiakh*, vol. 3, 646–7.

56 See Aksakov's account of Gogol's forty-first birthday party, celebrated in 1850, which discloses overt racism in his description of three "khokhols" – Gogol and his two friends Maksymovych and Bodians'kyi – in whose behaviour Aksakov perceives a resemblance to Asiatic (i.e., uncultured or barbarian) subjects (Vinogradov, *Gogol' v vospominaniiakh*, vol. 2, 614).

57 Aksakov, *Istoriia moego znakomstva s Gogolem*, 26.

58 Todd, *Fiction and Society*, 44.

59 Iurii Lotman wrote that Pushkin excelled at switching from one behavioural code to another, from the norm of the *honnête homme*, whose repertoire of genres and styles depended on his audience, to the role of Romantic hero, and finally to the role of a dandy, who resisted society by shocking it by means of dress, actions, and opinions (*Aleksandr Sergeevich Pushkin*, 53–4).

60 *PSS X*, 102–3.

61 Annenkov, "N.V. Gogol v Rime letom 1841 goda," 14–15.

62 Quoted in Kulish, *Zapiski o zhizni Gogolia*, 360.

63 As Olga Vainshtein notes in her comprehensive study of dandyism, Russian dandies of the time usually had at least three different frock coats whose use depended on the social occasion: a green one for morning outings and meetings; an indigo or *azur de Naples* one for afternoon outings; and finally a black one for evening events, such as balls, familiar gatherings, etc. (*Dendi*, 492).

64 Pushkin, as a titular counsellor in government administration, was compelled to wear a *mundir* decorated with galloons inside and outside of court, but often violated this code, wearing a frock coat in society. Ivan Panaev, another contemporary of Gogol's, abandoned a uniform at the workplace and wore fashionable trousers underneath his official uniform. It is curious how other civil servants reacted to Panaev's experiments with fashion. He reported: "Once I came to the department in a uniform but wearing plaid trousers [underneath] which just had appeared in St

Petersburg. I was one of the first who put on such trousers and wanted to show off in front of the department. The effect that my trousers produced surpassed my expectations. When I was passing through the line of rooms toward my division, the staff interrupted their work, tapped each other smiling and pointed at me" (*Literaturnye vospominaniia*, 61).

65 Quoted from *The Collected Tales of Nikolai Gogol*, trans. Pevear and Volokhonsky, 249.

66 *PSS III*, 265.

67 The tension between the self-assertion of the Ukrainian gentry and their obedience to the imperial dress code is thoroughly analysed by Tamara Hundorova in her book *Kitch i literatura*.

68 *PSS I*, 234.

69 Potemkin asks the Cossacks in Russian: "Are you all here?" ("Все ли вы здесь"?). The Cossacks reply in Ukrainian: "Yes, Father!" ("Та вси, батьку!") (*PSS I*, 235). Similarly, in the scene with the Catherine they speak Ukrainian "Thank you, Mother!" ("Та спасиби, мамо!"); "Judge for yourself, Mother!"("Як же, мамо!") (*PSS I* 236, 238) or use the Ukrainian forms (the vocative case, absent in Russian) speaking in Russian ("ведь человеку [in Ukrainian "cholovik" refers to a gendered man and a husband, while in Russian it is genderless, meaning "a human being"] сама знаешь, без жинки нельзя жить" [Man cannot do without a wife] [*PSS I*, 238]).

70 *PSS X*, 236.

71 *PSS I*, 238.

72 *PSS II*, 111–12.

73 Ibid., 160.

74 Boris Floria has examined the origin and evolution of the *khokhol*. According to him, the term had entered Russian political discourse in the early seventeenth century during the Time of Troubles when the army of the Polish-Lithuanian Commonwealth occupied Moscow. The typical hairdo of the Polish army (among which were several thousand Ukrainian Cossacks) was a tuft of hair on the top of the shaven head, which Russians called *khokhol* and associated with Catholicism, in whose name her enemies fought against Orthodox Russia. So, when in 1634 Ukrainian Cossacks led by Hetman Tymofii Orendarenko came to Smolensk to subjugate a popular uprising of Russians, the term *khokhlach* (a modified version of *khokhol*) was applied to any Ukrainian living under Polish rule ("O znachenii termina 'khokhol' i proizvodnykh ot nego v russkikh istochnikakh pervoi poloviny XVII v.," 16–19).

75 Vinogradov, *Gogol' v vospominaniiakh*, vol. 1, 645.

76 Vinogradov, *Gogol' v vospominaniiakh*, vol. 3, 434.

77 Aksakov, *Istoriia moego znakomstva s Gogolem*, 10.

78 Ibid.

79 Gregg, "The Writer and His Quiff," 66.

80 See, for example, the recollections of Gogol's teacher Ivan Kul'zhynskii (Vinogradov, *Gogol' v vospominaniiakh*, vol. 1, 426) and classmate Vasilii Liubych-Romanovich (ibid., 557).

81 Vinogradov, *Gogol' v vospominaniiakh*, vol. 2, 552.

82 Vinogradov, *Gogol v vospominaniiakh*, vol. 1, 645.

83 Ibid., 647.

84 One of the points of the Slavophiles' ideological program was to heal the breach between the elite and the peasantry, and to this end they proposed that the elite should wear less fashionable attire. Konstantin Aksakov, for example, wore traditional Russian dress in salons in order to demonstrate his rejection of Westernization and his solidarity with the people. See Ruane, "Subjects into Citizens."

85 "A whole hour was devoted just to examining his face in the mirror. Attempts were made to confer on it a number of different expressions: grave and dignified, or respectful with a slight smile, or simply respectful with no smile; a number of bows were performed toward the mirror accompanied by vague sounds, in part resembling French, although Chichikov did not know a word of French. He even gave himself numerous pleasant surprises, raising an eyebrow, curling a lip, going so far as to try a few tricks with his tongue" (*PSS VI*, 161).

86 Todd, *Fiction and Society*, 172–3.

87 Quoted in Vikentii Veresaev, *Gogol' v zhizni*, 134.

88 Panaev mentioned how "Gogol's Ukrainian oral tales … made a strong impression on Belinskii" (quoted in Mashinskii, ed., *Gogol' v vsopominaniiakh sovremennikov*, 218).

89 See, for example, the variation on Gogol's anecdote about Khodzha Nasreddin recorded by Vladimir Sollogub (*Povesti*, 551–2).

90 See A.F. Afanas'ev's recollection in Vinogradov, *Gogol' v vospominaniiakh*, vol. 3, 23.

91 See Fedor Chizhov's memoir in ibid., 47.

92 See, for example, Gogol's joke about a brothel, which he related to a stern lady, Louisa Karlovna Vielgorskaia, née Princess Biron, pretending that it was appropriate in a serious conversation about spiritual-mythical issues. The whole episode is recorded in Sollogub, *Povesti*, 441–2.

93 Kurganov, "Gogol as a Narrator of Anecdotes," 30.

94 Sollogub, *Povesti*, 441–2.

3. Hybrid Language and Narrative Performance in *Evenings on a Farm near Dikan'ka*

1 See Pushkin's letter to A. Voeikov of 21 August 1831. See also Vladimir Dal''s letter to M.P. Pogodin, 1 April 1842 (Vinogradov, *Gogol' v vospominaniiakh*, vol. 1, 725).

2 Dmitrieva and Argent, "The Coexistence of Russian and French in Russia in the First Third of the Nineteenth Century."

3 *PSS X*, 80.

4 There was no normative orthography for Ukrainian at this time. Whatever was permitted to be published in Ukrainian was to be transcribed in the *iaryzhka*, in which the characteristic Ukrainian vowels were replaced by Russian equivalents to make the language font look similar to Russian.

5 It is important to pinpoint the differences in the orthographical principles of Russian and Ukrainian. Russian orthography, quite phonemic in practice, is based mostly on morphology (the spelling of prefixes, suffixes, and endings varies significantly from their pronunciation and grammar (it specifies conventional orthographic forms to mark grammatical distinctions, gender, and participles vs adjectives) rather than on phonetic principles. Ukrainian orthography, however, is phonemic (all morphemes are written as they are pronounced in isolation, without vowel reduction) and morphemic, although some historical forms unrelated to its phonemic and morphemic structures have been retained.

6 The absence of vowel reduction in unstressed positions is what differentiates Ukrainian phonology from Russian in which the vowel [o] is reduced in unstressed positions to [ə] or to [ɐ].

7 Vinogradov, *Gogol' v vospominaniiakh*, vol. 3, 825.

8 Vinogradov, *Gogol' v vospominaniiakh*, vol. 2, 552.

9 Because it is not one of the sounds Russian uses to convey meaning, [ɦ] sounds unnatural to native speakers and often becomes the object of jokes about uneducated Ukrainians' inability to pronounce [g] correctly.

10 In modern sociolinguistics, a bilingual is viewed not as a mere sum of two monolinguals, but rather a unique and specific linguistic configuration. According to Grosjean and Soares, "bilingual language processing will often be different from that of the monolingual; one language is rarely totally deactivated when speaking or listening to the other (even in completely monolingual situations) and in a mixed language mode, where the two languages interact simultaneously, bilinguals have to use specific operations and strategies rarely, if ever, needed by the monolingual" ("Processing Mixed Languages," 179).

11 Belyi, *Gogol's Artistry*, 230.

12 The "minor" use of language was theorized by Deleuze and Guattari in their study of Franz Kafka's position within the German literary canon. The "minor" status of such writers as Kafka, Joyce, and Beckett, who were the subjects of Deleuze and Guattari's analysis, was determined by the secondary status of their mother tongues in the situations of bilingualism or multilingualism in which they wrote. Instead of writing

their literary works in the languages of their ethnic groups, these writers wrote in the "major languages" of their empires but inscribed a certain foreignness within those "major languages." As Deleuze wrote about the "minor" writer, he "carves out a nonpreexistent foreign language *within* his own language" (*Essays Critical and Clinical*. Trans. Daniel W. Smith and Michael A. Greco [London: Verso, 1998], 110).

13 Vinogradov, *Gogol' v vospominaniiakh*, vol. 1, 557.

14 In his *Distinction*, Bourdieu theorizes the concept of "habitus," that is, a system of dispositions, or acquired systems of perception, thought, and experiences, which the individual develops in response to objective conditions. However, Bourdieu does not take into account specific practices having to do with gender, class, age, and other factors, in which individual agents engage and which help form the habitus.

15 Although Bourdieu later recognized the political dimension and subversive potential of regional discourse, he nevertheless remained sceptical about speakers' ability to "do style" (*Pascalian Meditations*, 176–7).

16 Butler, *Excitable Speech*, 161.

17 Terts, *V teni Gogolia*, 322.

18 *PSS X*, 150. For the nineteenth-century definition of "существенное имя" as *nomen substantivum* I have used the index to Jagic's *Codex slovenicus rerum grammaticarum*, 776, s.v.

19 *PSS XI*, 320.

20 *PSS X*, 233–4.

21 For further reading, see Pennycook, "Global Englishes, Rip Slyme, and Performativity," and Lee, "Linguistic Hybridization in K-Pop."

22 Chaudenson, *Des îles, des hommes, des langues*, and Mufwene, "Pidgin and Creole Languages."

23 These examples are quoted from the first edition of *Vechera na khutorie bliz Dikanki: poviesti: Pervaia knizhka* (1831).

24 All the examples of Gogol's misspelling have been compared with the entries in *Slovar' Akademii Rossiiskoi* (1806–22), which codified the new morphemic spelling.

25 *PSS I*, 181.

26 *PSS I*, 187.

27 *PSS I*, 190.

28 *PSS I*, 138.

29 *PSS I*, 128.

30 *PSS I*, 160–1.

31 This problem has been studied by V. Vinogradov in *Gogol' i natrual'naia shkola* (1925); Gukovskii in *Realizm Gogolia* (1959); Mushchenko in "Skazovoe povestvovanie u N.V. Gogolia" (1972); and Fanger in

The Creation of Nikolai Gogol (1979). This approach is still popular in contemporary Russian Gogol studies. The articles on Gogol's *Evenings* in *Gogol' i narodnaia kul'tura: Materialy dokladov i soobshchenii mezhdunarodnoi nauchnoi konferentsii* (2008) analyse the tales from the point of view of the opposition between the oral and written word, or literary and folk traditions. See Sapchenko, "Literaturnaia i fol'klorno-mifologicheskaia traditsii v *Vecherakh na khutore bliz Dikanki*," and Shraga, "Bylichka i svetskii razgovor kak strukturnaia osnova prozaicheskoi tsiklizatsii."

32 Koropeckyj and Romanchuk, "Ukraine in Blackface," 539.

33 Ibid., 545.

34 The authorship of the epigraphs in "Sorochintsy Fair" is usually attributed by scholars to Makar Nazarovich, which is viewed as a sign of his literariness and belonging to the high (Russian) culture. However, the cycle of the tales is compiled by the fictitious editor-narrator Pan'ko, placing the epigraphs into the extradiegetic domain. By blurring the boundary between the diegetic fiction and extradiegetic elements (such as epigraphs) in the framed narration, Gogol played with the status of Makar Nazarovich as a Little Russian gentleman-ethnographer who is cut from the same cloth as Orest Somov's Porfirii Baiskii.

35 Bojanowska, *Nikolai Gogol*, 49.

36 Ibid., 50.

37 Bhabha, *The Location of Culture*, 139.

38 As Anne Lounsbery has demonstrated, while the distinction between oral and written is clear-cut in *Evenings*, the construction of "orality" and "literacy" as opposites seems rather problematic because this division is often blurred in the tales (*Thin Culture, High Art*, 38–9).

39 Threadgold, "Performing Theories of Narrative," 265.

40 Since Smith's application of Austin's speech act theory to the reading of prose narrative, many scholars have attempted to study narrative as intrinsically context bound. See for example Shoshana Felman, *The Literary Speech Act: Don Juan with J.L. Austin, or Seduction in Two Languages* (1983); Susan Lanser, *The Narrative Act: Point of View in Fiction* (1981); Chambers, *Story and Situation*.

41 Smith, "Narrative Versions, Narrative Theories," 221.

42 Such variables as "the narrator's motives for telling the tale and all the particular interests, desires, expectations, memories, knowledge, and prior experiences … that elicited his telling it on that occasion, to that audience, and that shaped the particular way he told it" (ibid., 222).

43 See the works of Vladimir Propp, Algirdas Greimas, Claude Bremond, Tzvetan Todorov, Gerald Prince, and others.

44 In his article "Gogol and His Reader," Donald Fanger has noted that Gogol always treated his readers as concrete people, which affected his attitude toward his texts and authorship.

45 Eikhenbaum, "How Is Gogol's 'The Overcoat' Made," 259.

46 Adopted and translated by Karamzin from French sources, particularly from Jean-François Marmontel, the genre of *vechera* became very popular in the 1810–1820s (e.g., Narizhnyi "Slavenskiie vechera"; Pogorel'skii "Dvoinik, ili moi vechera v Malorossii"; Odoevskii, "Russkiie Noch'i"; Levshin "Vechernie sny, ili drevnie skazki slavian drevlianskikh"; Zhukova, "Vechera na Karpovke," etc.). The cyclization of stories suggested by the genre was a first step toward the development of large prose forms.

47 Koropeckyj and Romanchuk, "Ukraine in Blackface," 527.

48 Ibid., 527.

49 "Бывало соберутся, *накануне* праздничного дня, добрые люди в гости в пасечникову лачужку, усядутся за стол, – и тогда прошу только слушать" (On the eve of a holiday, the locals would gather at my little beekeeper's hut, take their places around the table, and the stories would just tumble out, one after another) (*PSS I*, 104).

50 "Да вот было и позабыл самое главное: как будете, господа, ехать ко мне, то прямехонько берите путь по столбовой дороге на Диканьку" (Do you know, I've gone and forgotten the most important thing: if you should be coming to visit me, my good sirs, what you must do is take the high road straight to Dikan'ka) (*PSS I*, 106).

51 Koropeckyj and Romanchuk, "Ukraine in Blackface," 542.

52 In "Maiskaia noch'," each chapter is titled either by the personages' names (for instance, "Ganna," "Golova," "Neozhidannyi sopernik," and "Utoplennitsa") or by the main action ("Parubki guliaiut").

53 This is especially visible at the end of chapter 4 of ""Maiskaia noch'," when the headman's threat is followed by the author's remark (*PSS I*, 173).

54 *PSS I*, 159.

55 Ibid., 181.

56 Ibid., 139.

57 Ibid., 309.

58 Ibid., 148.

59 Ibid., 151.

60 Ibid.

61 Ibid., 141.

62 See Pomerantseva, *Mifologicheskie personazhi v russkom fol'klore*, 22.

63 The strange things in "Vecher nakanune Ivana Kupala" are seen by all of the villagers: "еще бы ничего, если бы одному, а то именно всем" (and it wouldn't be worth the mentioning if only one had seen it, but they all saw it) (*PSS I*, 151).

64 Bhabha, "DissemiNation," 303.

65 *PSS I*, 106.

66 Pan'ko's promise in his preface to Book One to publish two of his own tales in the next book supports this suggestion. Clearly, when Gogol published Book One of the tales in 1831, Pan'ko functioned as one of the ethnic narrators, but later, during his work on Book Two, Gogol began to develop a unified narration and Pan'ko could not fulfil this task anymore.

67 *PSS I* (2001–), 442.

68 In his preface, Pan'ko swears that he would not dare "to stick his nose out into the great world" ("высунуть нос из своего захолустья в большой свет").

69 *PSS I* (2001–), 485.

70 Natalie Kononenko has studied the history of bandura performances in depth in her monograph *Ukrainian Minstrels*.

71 In this seemingly biblical myth about Cain and Abel, Gogol incorporated actual historic figures (the Hetmans Sagaidachnyi and Kmel'nitskii, the Polish King Stephan Báthory), battles (the battle of Sivash, when Cossacks went to war against the Crimean Khanate in 1620), and documents (the Brest Union), as well as concrete national Ukrainian toponyms (Kyiv, Lemberg [L'viv], Glukhov, Zadneprov'e, the Carpathian Mountains, etc.).

72 Danilo complains that "порядку нет в Украйне: полковники и есаулы грызутся, как собаки, между собою. Нет старшей головы над всеми. Шляхетство наше все переменило на польский обычай, переняло лукавство … продало душу, принявши унию" (there is no order in Ukraine: the lieutenants and *esauls* fight among themselves like dogs. There is no superior authority. Our nobility has gone over to Polish customs, taken up trickery … sold its soul, accepted the Uniate religion) (*PSS I*, 266).

73 *PSS I*, 279.

74 Adrianova-Perets, ed., *Slovo o polku Igoreve*, 10. The English translation by Nabokov is quoted from *The Song of Igor's Campaign*.

75 *PSS I*, 279.

76 Ibid., 279.

77 Ibid., 282.

78 Kononenko, *Ukrainian Minstrels*, 13.

79 I. Sen'ko, *Hoholivs'ka Dikan'ka na istorychnykh perekhrestiakh*, 55.

80 *PSS I*, 284.

81 Bojanowska, *Nikolai Gogol*, 62.

4. Heteroglossia, Speech Masks, and the Synthesis of Languages

1 Scholars have hypothesized that Gogol might have read the works of the German Romantic philosophers that were subscribed to and

popularized among the students at the Nizhyn Lyceum. The influence
of German Romanticist aesthetics on Gogol has been studied by
Fusso, *Designing Dead Souls*; Jenness, *Gogol's Aesthetics Compared
to Major Elements of German Romanticism*; Shults, "Gogol' i Novalis";
Shults, "Gogol' i Shelling o dushe"; Frazier, *Frames of the Imagination*;
Peace, *The Enigma of Gogol*; and Mikhailov, "Gogol v svoei literaturnoi
epokhe."

2 Schleiermacher, *Hermeneutik und Kritik*, 171.

3 See Gogol's essay "The Textbook of Philology for the Russian Youth"
(*PSS VIII*), 471–2.

4 Herder, *Sprachphilosophische Schriften*, 33–4.

5 In the theory of performativity, Judith Butler and Lois McNay claim
that ethnic and gendered discourses have the potential for speech
performance and can break with the social contexts in which they
occur. They believe that reflexivity emerges at the moment when the
discrepancy between habitus and field becomes so strong that it causes
actors to experience a state of dissonance and to become reflexively aware
of their relation to social structures.

6 Bakhtin, *Polnoie sobranie sochinenii v 7-mi tomakh*, vol. 3, 78.

7 Ibid., vol. 4 (2), 495.

8 Ibid., 515, 519.

9 Spitzer, *Die wortbildung als stilistisches mittel exemplifiziert an Rabelais*, 75.

10 Bakhtin, *Polnoie sobranie sochinenii*, vol. 3, 446.

11 Ibid., vol. 4 (2), 528.

12 The stenogram of his doctoral dissertation defence is published in Isupov,
ed., *Bakhtin: Pro et Contra*, vol. 1, 325–90.

13 See the chapter "The Social Text: Bakhtin and Arendt" in Bhabha, *The
Location of Culture*.

14 "Разноголосные речи потопляют друг друга, и ни одно слово
не выхватится, не спасется от этого потопа; ни один крик не
выговорится ясно" (*PSS I*, 115).

15 *PSS VI*, 162.

16 "Или же, зажмурив вовсе глаза и приподняв голову кверху, к
пространствам небесным, представлял он [Tentetnikov] обонянью
впивать запах полей, а слуху поражаться голосами воздушного
певучего населения, когда оно отовсюду, от небес и от земли,
соединяется в один звукосогласный хор, не переча друг другу"
(*PSS VII*, 21).

17 Yiddish was often called a dialect, or "Jewish jargon," and depicted
comically in the texts of Russian literature. For example, in Bulgarin's
picaresque novel *Ivan Vyzhigin*, the narrator encounters three Jews: the
leaseholder Movsha and his wife, Rifka, whose distorted Russian speech

is transcribed phonemically and interspersed with Yiddish expressions, and their son-in-law, Iosel, who does not speak in the novel. "Молци, гой! Вы все только и думаете, *цтоб* есть и пить, а не думаете, цто *каздая* кроха стоит денег: надобно деньги *берец,* теперь худыя времена! … Герш-ту? … Разве ты видал и *сцитал наси* деньги? Герш-ту! Ах ты хомут! Ах ты *дуга!*" Dostoevsky reproduced the speech of his Jewish characters in a supposedly funny manner: "А-зе, сто-зе вам и здеся на-а-до?" a Jewish fireman asks Svidrigailov in *Crime and Punishment.* In *Notes from a Dead House,* Dostoevsky created a gallery of political prisoners in Omsk exile, among whom a Jewish prisoner, Isai Fomich, emerges as the only humorous and humane character and whose funny Jewish accent illuminates the gloomy reality of prison ("Не то нельзя будет зениться, – сказал он мне однажды, – а я непременно хоцу зениться") In "The Hard Year," Saltykov-Shchedrin created a gallery of comic Jewish characters, all with peculiar speech and manners ("По царке! По две царки на каздого ратника зертвую! За веру!" – провозглашает в патриотическом восторге откупщик, "перекрест из жидов").

18 Dubnow, *History of the Jews in Russia and Poland,* vol. 2, 138–9; Zaslavskii, "Evrei v russkoi literature," 60, 65; Gorev, "Russkaia literatura i evrei," 6; Nakhimovsky, *Russian-Jewish Literature and Identity,* 6.

19 Livak, *The Jewish Persona in the European Imagination,* 106.

20 Katz, *Neither with Them, nor without Them,* 8.

21 Rosenshield, *The Ridiculous Jew,* 28.

22 *PSS II,* 79.

23 *PSS X,* 80.

24 *PSS II,* 111.

25 Ibid., 159.

26 Ibid., 155. All translated passages of *Taras Bulba* are taken from the 2003 translation by Peter Constantine (here 123–4).

27 Ibid., 124–5.

28 *PSS III,* 44.

29 "Обе особы говорили на немецком языке … Впрочем, слова Шиллера заключались вот в чем. 'Я не хочу, мне не нужен нос! … У меня на один нос выходит три фунта табаку в месяц. И я плачу в русский скверный магазин, потому что немецкий магазин не держит русского табаку, я плачу в русский скверный магазин за каждый фунт по сорок копеек … Шесть да четырнадцать – двадцать рублей сорок копеек на один табак. Это разбой! Я спрашиваю тебя, мой друг Гофман, не так ли?' Гофман, который сам был пьян, отвечал утвердительно. 'Двадцать рублей сорок копеек! Я швабский немец; у меня есть король в Германии. Я не хочу носа! режь мне нос! вот мой нос!'" (Both men were talking in German … However, what Schiller said amounted to this: "I don't want it, I

have no need of a nose! … I use three pounds of snuff a month on my nose alone. And I pay in a dirty Russian shop, for German shops do not keep Russian snuff. I pay in a dirty Russian shop forty kopeks a pound … Six plus fourteen that makes one ruble twenty kopeks, twelve times one ruble twenty kopeks, that makes fourteen rubles forty kopeks. This is robbery! I ask you my friend Hoffmann, right?" Hoffman, who himself was drunk, answered in the affirmative: "Twenty rubles and forty kopeks! Damn it, I am a Swabian! I have a king in Germany. I don't want a nose! Cut off my nose! Here is my nose") (*PSS III*, 37).

30 Ibid., 38.
31 Ibid., 40.
32 *PSS VIII*, 177.
33 *PSS IV*, 317.
34 Ibid., 13.
35 Bakhtin, *The Dialogic Imagination*, 368, 369.
36 See the comprehensive analysis of the cultural-linguistic debates of the period in Liudmila Chapaeva's *Kul'turno-iazykovaia situatsiia v 1830kh–1840kh v kontekste sporov slavianofilov i zapadnikov* (2014).
37 Kiukhel'beker, "O napravlenii nashei poezii, osobenno liricheskoi, v poslednee desiatiletiie," 237.
38 Zhivov, *Language and Culture in Eighteenth-Century Russia*, 355–6.
39 Nikolai Grech wrote: "It is desirable that respected inhabitants of the provinces, especially the country clergy and nobles who withdraw themselves from the vanity of society to their country estates, begin to observe and collect regional dialects, special expressions, unusual grammatical forms, proverbs and other unique linguistic elements in the various regions of vast Russia … By doing this, they will help to compile first a review, then a dictionary and a comparative grammar of Russian provincialisms" (*Syn Otechestva* 61 [1820]: 269–71).
40 Moeller-Sally, *Gogol's Afterlife*, 21.
41 Nadezhdin, "Review of *Vechera na khutore bliz Dikan'ki*, vol. 1."
42 Ibid., 561.
43 Koznarsky, "Neither Dead nor Alive," 7.
44 In his article, Koznarsky closely analyses the debate between Ukrainian scholars and writers and Russian ones over Ukrainian's right to serve as a literary language. Those who defended the status of Ukrainian included Sreznevs'kyi, who insisted on Ukrainian as a "a legitimate medium of literary enterprises" in his piece "Vzgliad na pamiatniki Ukrainskoi narodnoi Slovesnosti"; Metlyns'kyi, who defined Ukrainian as an ancient language spoken in the entire territory of Little Russia in his introduction to a collection of his poems (Kharkiv, 1839); Bodians'kyi, who also claimed the antiquity of the Ukrainian language in his review of

Malorossiiskie povesti (1834); and Kostomarov, who defended the "natural right" of millions of Ukrainians to have their own language and culture created in that language in "A Survey of Works Written in the Little Russian Language" (1843).

45 Polevoi, "Review of *Chary, ili neskol'ko stsen iz narodnykh bylei i rasskazov ukrainskikh by Kyrylo Topolia*," 72.

46 Polevoi, "Review of *Kobzar* by Taras Shevchenko," 836.

47 In his *Opyt kratkoi istorii russkoi literatury* (An Attempt at a Concise History of Russian Literature) (1822), Nikolai Grech wrote: "The Little Russian dialect originated from the lasting dominion of the Poles in south-west Russia and may be called a regional Polish dialect" (12–13).

48 S. Shevyrev's review of Maksymovych's collection of *Little Russian Songs* in *Moskovskii vestnik* 23 (1827), 310–17.

49 See Levshin, "Otryvki iz pisem o Malorossii."

50 In "Stat'i o narodnoi poezii," Belinskii wrote: "The literary language of Ukrainians should be the language of their educated society: the Russian language. If a great poet can emerge in Ukraine at all, then it will only be under the condition that he will be a Russian poet … A tribe can only have folk songs but cannot have poets, and especially great ones. Great poets appear only in great nations, and what sort of a nation is it if it does not have great, independent political significance? … [Gogol's] poetry features many purely Ukrainian elements which do not and cannot exist in Russian, but who would call him a Ukrainian poet?" (*Sobraniie sochinenii V*, 330).

51 Senkovskii attacked philo-Ukrainian attitudes on the grounds that Ukraine's history was one of stubborn resistance to all forms of legitimate political authority. In his 1836 review of Gogol's *Evenings*, the critic sharply rebuked the author for his Ukrainian plebeian theme. For Senkovskii, Ukrainian culture and history had no value, being merely a history of anarchic resistance to authority ("Istoriia Malorossii, Nik. Markevicha"). Even liberal critics, such as Pletnev, expressed doubts about the appropriateness of the Ukrainian literary language for educated society. In his review of Izmail Sreznevs'kyi's *Ukrainskii sbornik* (The Ukrainian Collection) (1838), Pletnev asserted that Ukrainian is a provincial dialect, inappropriate for the educated classes of imperial society ("Ukraiinskii sbornik I. Sreznevskogo," 31).

52 Polevoi asserted that it is awkward to say in Russian "*через трубу повалил дым*" and that one should say instead "*из трубы повалил дым*." Other examples of "bad" Russian, according to Polevoi, included "удивительно видеть чорта, пустившегося и себе туда же" and "очи твои так угрюмо надвинулись бровями" (1832 "Review of *Vechera na khutore bliz Dikan'ki*, vol. 2," 266–7). In his other articles, Polevoi

continued seeking out non-Russian expressions in Gogol's texts. See his lists of Gogol's alleged mistakes in *Dead Souls* published in 1842 in *Russkii vestnik* ("Pokhozhdeniia Chichikova, ili mertvye dushi. Poema N. Gogolia").

53 Osip Senkovskii, "Review of *Pokhozhdeniia Chichikova, ili Mertvye dushi* (1842) by N. Gogol."

54 Bulgarin, "Nastoiashchii moment i dukh nashei literatury," 48. See also Bulgarin's critical remarks on Gogol's language in his reviews of *The Inspector General* ("Rezko otritsatel'naia otsenka siuzheta, iazyka, dostovernosti p'esy") and of *Dead Souls* ("Review of *Mertvyie dushi*").

55 Quoted in Tikhonravov, "Zametki o slovare, sostavlennom Gogolem," 198.

56 Dal', letter to M.P. Pogodin, 1 April 1842, in Vinogradov, *Gogol' v vospominaniiakh*, vol. 1, 725.

57 These continuous attacks on Gogol's language gradually resulted in the claim that, inasmuch as Gogol was ignorant of the rules of Russian grammar, he was unfamiliar with real life in Russia. Reviewing Gogol's *Selected Passages*, Bulgarin wrote: "Gogol has a very poor knowledge of the Russian language, he writes in the provincial idiolect which he admitted himself in his last book ... he does not know Russia at all and finally there are only depraved pictures [of Russia] in his works" ("Felieton," 389).

58 *PSS IV*, 233.

59 "Письма Гоголя вводят нас в громадный, запутанный лабиринт: какое удивительное соединение в них самой задушевной искренности, непосредственности, с явными признаками природной хитрости, – хитрости, скрывающейся еще в детстве, вместе с странной преждевременной практичностью и ранним уменьем играть на самых затаенных струнах человеческой души! В них и искательность, преклонение пред сильными – и гордость гениальной натуры, уверенность в себе и сознание своего высокого назначения ..." (Kallash, in Gogol, *Sochineniia i pis'ma N.V. Gogolia*, 9 vols.).

60 Hale and Whitlam, *Impact and Influence*, 135–6.

61 Argyle and Kendon, "The Experimental Analysis of Social Performance"; Bauman, "Verbal Art as Performance"; Jaffe, "Measurement of Verbal and Vocal Behavior"; Matarazzo, Weitman, and Saslow, "Interview Content and Interviewee Speech Durations."

62 For example, Pushkin's speech masks in his correspondence have been studied as a positive phenomenon by Dmitrieva, "Stilisticheskiie funktsii iazyka v perepiske Pushkina i ego poezii"; Kaizer, "Rechevoi etiket v pis'makh A.S. Pushkina"; Maimin. "Druzheskaia perepiska

Pushkina s tochki zreniia stilistiki"; Malakhovskii, "Iazyk pisem Pushkina"; Modzalevskii, "Epistoliarnoe naslediie Pushkina"; Stepanov, "Druzheskoe pis'mo nachalo XIX veka"; Todd, *The Familiar Letter as a Literary Genre in the Age of Pushkin*; and Vol'pert, *Pushkin v roli Pushkina*.

63 Gogol's copying the language of the authorities has been studied by William Todd. In his analysis of Gogol's epistolary writing, the scholar asks: "does the writer alter his letters for different correspondents, or does he direct his entire arsenal of styles and subjects at any one of them?" ("Gogol's Epistolary Writing," 53). Answering this question, Todd classifies Gogol's letters into two categories: "humorous or objective" and "subjective"; the latter are based on "emotionally heightened self-dramatization."

64 He also used the epistolary form in his literary texts to impart verisimilitude to the fictitious situations. Thus, the part of the story "Ivan Fedorovich Shpon'ka and His Auntie" in *Evenings* is structured as the exchange of letters between the protagonist Ivan Fedorovich and his aunt, Vasilisa Kashporovna, who is trying to set up her nephew's marriage. *The Inspector General* begins and ends with reading a letter, which frames the entire play as the classic plot of mistaken identity. Letters abound in Gogol's other works ("Nose," "A Diary of a Madman," *Marriage, Dead Souls*, and *Selected Passages from the Correspondence with Friends*) and play a crucial role in developing the plot, and, more importantly, in establishing a dialogue between the artistic and epistolary legacy of the writer.

65 I have summarized the method of stylometric analysis and presented the dendrograms in Appendix 1.

66 For example, also from the letters: "it was precisely in Simbirsk Governorate at Sofron Ivanovich Bezpechnyi's, where his daughter Adelaide Sofronovna with three sisters-in-law Marya Gavrilovna, Alexandra Gavrilova and Adelgeida Gavrilovna were then" (*PSS X*, 32).

67 *PSS X*, 55.

68 On Gogol's mistakes in his early correspondence, see further Tikhonravov, "Zametki o slovare, sostavlennom Gogolem," 197–8.

69 Some examples include "выключая" (seven times), "переторжники," "переуверит," "печатлеется," "поиспортилось," "поиспытал," "понаберешься," "пообтерся," "поражену," "порасстроило," "поцалуйте," "пощечиться," "для прочета," "размашками рук," "разочли," "разрознении," "разрозниться," "план рушенным," "рясных," "сбыточности," "смушевую," "щекатурка."

70 Among very few examples there are "кохти," "крехтя," "потребна," "переждутся," "обнадеживательно," "до беспамяти."

71 *PSS X*, 274.

72 For example, "Нет, ты будешь совершенный лошадиный помет, если
всё это не подействует на твою вялую душу. Тогда можно будет
решительно сказать, что весь мозг из головы твоей перешел в ту
неблагородную часть тела, которою мы имеем обыкновение садиться
на стуле и даже на судне, а всё содержимое в этой непозволительной
и мало употребляемой в разговоре части поднялось в голову"
(Well, you will be real horse manure if all these won't influence your
languid soul. Then, one could definitely say that all of your brains have
transferred from your head to that indelicate part of body which we
typically use to sit on a chair or even on a toilet, and all the contents of
that improper and rarely-mentioned-in-conversation body part have risen
into your head) (*PSS X*, 235).

73 *PSS X*, 366.

74 *PSS XI*, 60.

75 Ibid., 102.

76 Ibid.

77 *PSS X*, 316–17.

78 Pushkin, *Sobranie sochinenii v 10-ti tomakh*, vol. 10, 180.

79 Lotman, "Dekabrist v povsednevnoy zhizni."

80 *PSS XI*, 67–71.

81 "If you have difficulty writing to me, I can give you a brief model. You
can write in such a manner: 'Dear Sir, respectable Nikolai Vasilievich!
I had the honour to receive your letter from this October, such and
such date. I cannot express to you, dear Sir, all of the feelings that
excited my soul. I poured tears in hearty emotion. Where did you
master the great art to speak so comprehensibly to heart and soul? I
would die to have your skilful pen in order to be able to express in
such words my grateful and excited appreciation.' And then you can
write: 'your obedient [servant], ready to render all kinds of service,'
or something like that … and the letter, I assure you, will be good"
(ibid., 70–1).

82 "Cosi a voi vi si rapresenta forse il mio naso, lungo e simile a quello degli
uccelli (o dolce speranza!). Ma lasciamo in pace i nasi; questa una materia
delicata e tratandosi di questa, si puo facilmente restare con un palmo
di naso" (Perhaps, you imagine my long, bird-like nose in the same way
(oh sweet hope!). But let's leave my nose alone; this is a delicate subject,
and while talking about it, one can easily be fooled [lit., left with a nose])
(ibid., 127).

83 Ibid., 130.

84 Todd, "Gogol's Epistolary Writing," 75.

85 Olson and Worsham. "Staging the Politics of Difference," 374.

86 *PSS VI*, 71.

87 "В картишки играл он не совсем безгрешно и чисто, зная много разных **передержек** и других тонкостей и потому игра весьма часто оканчивалась другою игрою: или поколачивали его сапогами, или же задавали **передержку** его густым и очень хорошим бакенбардам" (He played cards in neither a faultless [or sinless] nor an overly clean [i.e., honest] way, since he knew many various tricks [ways to cheat] and other subtleties, and therefore the game often ended in another kind of sport: either he received a good kicking, or his thick and very handsome whiskers were given a good pull) (ibid., 70).

88 Ibid., 22.

89 *PSS VII*, 30.

90 Ibid., 214.

91 *PSS VI*, 42.

92 All translated passages of *Dead Souls* are taken from the 2004 translation by Robert A. Maguire (here 165).

93 Ibid., 106.

94 Ibid., 171.

95 Ibid., 116.

96 Iurii Barabash in his *Pochva i sud'ba* and Gavriel Shapiro in his *Nikolai Gogol and the Baroque Cultural Heritage* analyse Gogol's engagement with the Ukrainian polemical and baroque traditions.

97 Serebrennikov, *Kratkoie rukovodstvo k Oratorii rossiiskoi, sochinennoie v Lavrskoi seminarii v pol'zu iunoshestva, krasnorechiiu obucheiushchegosia.*

98 *PSS VIII*, 276. Repetition of a key word for an emphatic purpose is already evident in his *Arabesques* (1836). While describing his exaltation in front of Briullov's painting *The Last Day of Pompeii*, Gogol used the verb "to breathe" four times within a short passage to express his aesthetic excitement. In his *Selected Passages*, however, this principle was taken to an extreme and used as a means of direct polemics with his contemporaries.

99 *PSS VIII*, 105.

100 Ibid., 88.

101 Ibid., 276.

102 Ibid., 233.

103 "Всякому теперь кажется, что он мог бы наделать много добра на месте и в должности другого, и только не может сделать его в своей должности. Это причина всех зол. Нужно подумать теперь о том всем нам, как на своём собственном месте сделать добро" (*PSS VI*, 142).

104 See Nimchuk, *Movoznavstvo na Ukraini v XIV–XVII stolittia*, 72.

105 In Kotliarevs'kyi's comedy *Natalka-Poltavka*, dialogues between a poor Ukrainian girl, Natalka, and a Russianized rich suitor, pan vozny Tetervakovs'kyi, are conducted in two languages.

106 See Ivan Matviias's article "Rol' slobozhans'koho hovoru v movotvorchosti
 Hryhoriia Kvitky-Osnov'ianenka" and "Ukrains'ka literaturna mova i
 teritorial'ni dialekty v ikh vzaiemodii na riznykh istorychnykh etapakh."

107 Ibid., 25.

108 The original meaning of *surzhyk* was a mixture of rye and oats, resulting
 in low-quality bread. In the early twentieth century, it referred to a person
 of mixed Russian-Ukrainian origin. In modern usage, it lost the previous
 meanings, but not its significance as a sociolinguistic phenomenon.
 Although there has yet to be developed a definition that would cover
 all of the linguistic and sociocultural connotations of the term, one of
 the main characteristics of *surzhyk* is associated with its violation of the
 norms of standard Ukrainian as well as of Russian and with the lack of
 education and culture on the part of its speakers.

109 The Ukrainian sociolinguist Larysa Masenko dates the emergence of
 surzhyk as a linguistic phenomenon separate from Ukrainian and Russian
 back to the seventeenth–eighteenth centuries ("Surzhyk").

110 The history of *surzhyk* has been studied by Masenko, "Surzhyk"; Flier,
 "Surzhyk or Surzhyks?"; and Stavytska and Trub, "Surzhyk."

111 *PSS VIII*, 233.

112 *PSS VIII*, 184–5.

113 Tomlinson, "Globalization and Cultural Identity," 273.

5. Gogol's Texts as Palimpsest: *Taras Bulba* and *Dead Souls*

  1 Gukovskii, *Realizm Gogolia*, 522.

  2 *PSS VIII*, 14.

  3 Gogol's historical essays in *Arabesques* have been discussed by scholars
 in the context of Romantic aesthetic ideas and of Hegelian dialectics.
 Sven Spieker emphasized the importance of the middle/medium, as
 developed by Novalis and Schelling, in Gogol's "non-linear, cyclical
 view of history" ("The Centrality of the Middle," 464). Iurii Mann
 considered Gogol a pioneer of the dialectical method ("Gogol – kritik i
 publitsist," 459). Mikhail Vaiskopf discerned in Gogol's essays ideas "at
 least superficially directed toward a positive solution of the problem of
 synthesis" (*Siuzhet Gogolia*, 191).

  4 See Belinskii's essay "On the Russian Tale and the Tales of Mr. Gogol,"
 Sobranie sochinenii, vol. 1, 138–84; and Bulgarin's "Review of *Vechera na
 khutore bliz Dikanki*, 2nd ed."

  5 *PSS X*, 311–12.

  6 "Do me a favour, look it through and if there are some [mistakes], correct
 them in ink right away ... Do not hold back your indignation when you
 see mistakes" (*PSS X*, 346–7).

7 For example he replaced "пьяненек" with "пьянехонек," "анбар" with "амбар," "чудеса деются" with "чудеса делаются," "чего ж вы перепугались" with "чего ж вы испугались," "посереди" with "посреди," "сткло" with "стекло," etc.

8 *PSS XII*, 84–5.

9 For example, Vakula in "Christmas Eve" tries to speak Russian: "Но Боже мой, от **чево** она так чертовски хороша" (Oh my God, why does she have to be so devilishly pretty?); Prokopovych corrected one word, "чево," replacing it with "чего," but the comic effect of Rudy Pan'ko's ignorance of Russian grammar was lost. Similarly, in "May Night," a village clerk reads a letter from the district commissioners: "приказываю тебе сей же час … подчинить мосты на столбовой дороге" (I forthwith direct you … to subjugate the bridges on the highway). Prokopovych thought that this was one of Gogol's blunders and replaced "подчинить" (to subjugate) with "починить" (to repair), which sounded more logical, but which destroyed the clerk's ridiculous bureaucratic manner of speech.

10 All nouns ending in -ць were replaced with -ц ("голодрабець" – "голодрабец," "оселедець" – "оселедец," "хлопець" – "хлопец"); noun endings ("Купала" – "Купалы," "Галю" – "Галя"), Ukrainian adverbs and prepositions ("по-за селом" – "за селом," "по-над самым провалом" – "над самым провалом") were replaced with their Russian counterparts.

11 Prokopovych used Russian words: "хилый" instead of the original Ukrainian "тендитный и маленький"; "среда" instead of "середа"; "за ужином" instead of "за вечерею"; "изготовленного" instead of "сготовленного"; "фартуками" instead of "фартухами."

12 Thus he changed original Ukrainian grammatical forms to Russian ones: "и то хорошо" instead of "и то хороше"; "мешков" instead of "мешечков"; "шнурочки" instead of "шнуречки"; "маленькие, низенькие" instead of "маленьки, низеньки"; changed the plural form of the following words: "младенцы," "воробушки," "поросята" (instead of "ребенки," "воробьенки," "поросенки"); and he corrected the nominal case in idiomatic expressions (for example, "не в состоянии повернуть языком" instead of "не в состоянии повернуть языка").

13 For example, "ярмарке" instead of "ярманке"; "кофе" instead of "кофий"; "закусывал" instead of "закушивал"; "простолюдины" instead of "простолюдимы"; "английских" instead of "англинских"; "блюдо" instead of "кушанье."

14 Shenrok, *Materialy dlia biografii Gogolia*, 370.

15 *PSS V*, 472.

16 "Элтажах" was replaced with "этажах," "сподтишка" with "исподтишка," "сенахтор" with "сенатор," "губернахтор" with

"губернатор," "аглицкие" with "английские," "острамишься"
with "осрамишься," "звестно" with "известно," "физиогномия"
with "физиономия," "прибыточный" with "прибыльный,"
"попоглядистее" with "попригляднее," etc.

17 Shenrok, *Materialy dlia biografii Gogolia*, 54.

18 Aleksandr Slonimskii traced Belinskii's influence on Prokopovych's editing of Gogol's texts. See "Voprosy gogolevskogo teksta."

19 *PSS XII*, 215–16.

20 Vinogradov, *Gogol' v vospominaniiakh*, vol. 3, 649.

21 Such as "ни с сего, ни с того" – "ни с того, ни с сего," "цаловать" – "целовать," "околоток" – "околодок"; as well as Ukrainianisms, such as "спознается" – "зазнается," "скирды" – "стога," "секира" – "топор."

22 The historical sources that Gogol used in his tale are thoroughly analysed in *Taras Bul'ba. Avtografy, prizhiznennyie izdaniia*, ed. Vinogradov.

23 By the fifteenth century, Byzantium had finally lost its political influence, and the Mongols stopped terrorizing the Eastern Slavs. In the last third of the fifteenth century, the Crimean Tatars began to raid the Rus' lands, which prompted the Cossacks to mobilize as a group and repulse the Tatars' attacks. See Serhii Plokhii's analysis of the emergence of the Cossacks in chapter 1 of his monograph *The Cossacks and Religion in Early Modern Ukraine*.

24 Scott's advertisement was published in the *Quarterly Review* (London, 1816), 125.

25 See, for example, Markevych's five-volume *History of Little Russia* (1842–3).

26 Pogodin, *Issledovaniia, zamechaniia i lektsii o russkoi istorii*, vol. 7.

27 See Pavlo Mykhed's investigation of Gogol's interaction with Polish intellectuals in his papers "Gogol' i pol's'ka literatura 30-kh–40-kh rokiv XIX st. (problema vyvchennia)" and "Mykola Hohol i poliaky (deiakyi aspekty doslidzhennia)."

28 The Polish state had disappeared with the third partition in 1795, although it briefly reappeared during the Napoleonic period as the Duchy of Warszawa in 1807–15. Poland conclusively became part of the Russian Empire after the November Uprising of 1830–1. This led to the exile of the above-mentioned intellectuals.

29 See Mickiewicz's *Forefathers' Eve* (part 3), *The Book of the Polish Nation* (1832), and the essays published in the émigré magazine *The Polish Pilgrimage* (1833).

30 This public attitude of the Slavophiles to Gogol was captured by Khomiakov's sister, E.M. Khomiakova, who wrote to her brother, offended by Kireevsky's evaluation of Gogol: "Among them the one

who does not shout is a fool" ("У них, кто не кричит, тот и глуп")
(Khomiakov, *Polnoe sobranie sochinenii*, vol. 8, 106).

31 See Yoon, "Transformation of a Ukrainian Cossack,'" 439–40.

32 *PSS XI*, 98.

33 Quoted in Gippius, ed., *Gogol'*, 167.

34 Vinogradov, *Gogol' v vospominaniiakh*, vol. 1, 729.

35 In the draft excerpt to chapter 7 of the 1842 *Taras Bulba*, material from
the burnt drama can be detected in the story about Demid Popovich,
who escaped captivity and ran to the Sich with a "blackened head
and burnt moustaches" ("с обсмоленною головою и выгоревшими
усами"). The image of Demid Popovich also demonstrates the
humiliation of Cossack dignity. In the first draft of the tale, the Polish
side threatens the Cossacks: "We will cut your ears off, dogs … We'll
shave your beards" ("Будете вы с обрезанными ухами, собаки …
Побреем бороды"). In the intermediary draft, the Poles threaten:
"'Just you wait, we'll cut your forelocks off!' they shouted from the top.
'I'd like to see how they cut off our forelocks!' – said Popovich" ("Вот
погодите, поотрежем мы чубы вам!" – кричали сверху. "А хотел бы
я поглядеть, как они нам поотрезывают чубы!" – говорил Попович)
(*PSS II*, 409). Compare this to the same episode in the final version:
"'Just you wait, we'll cut your forelocks off!'" they shouted from the
top. 'I'd like to see how they cut off our forelocks!' – said Popovich,
turning in front of them on the horse" ("Вот, погодите, обрежем мы
вам чубы!" – кричали им сверху. "А хотел бы я поглядеть, как они
нам обрежут чубы!" – говорил Попович, поворотившись перед
ними на коне) (*PSS II*, 116).

36 *PSS II*, 540.

37 "And the most important thing: in the current copy the word 'I hear
you' [slyshu] uttered by Taras during Ostap's execution is replaced with
'chuiu' [the Ukrainian form of "I hear you"]. Leave it as it was before:
'Bat'ko, where are you? Can you hear this?' – 'I hear' ["Батько, где
ты? Слышишь ли ты это?" – "Слышу"]. I completely overlooked the
fact that the readers have already got used to it [the Russian form] and
therefore they will be dissatisfied with the change, no matter how much
better it is than the original expression" (*PSS XII*, 85).

38 In the second redaction, Gogol inserted new, peculiar idiomatic
expressions ("ка зна що," "чорта с два," "что байрак, то козак,"
"моргнуть усом" – used four times in different episodes); added more
uses of the Cossack lexicon "кошевой" (26/62) "куренной атаман"
(4/26), "курень" (3/62), "рада" (4/8), "очкур" (3/5); and replaced
the Russian transcription of "Сечь" or "Сеча" with the Ukrainian
transcription "Сичь" (Zaporozhian Host).

39 Ilnytzkyj, "Is Gogol's 1842 Version of *Taras Bulba* Really 'Russified'?"
    51–4.

40 *PSS II*, 165–6.

41 Gogol, *Taras Bulba*, trans. Constantine, 134–5.

42 Ibid., 270.

43 "The history of *Southern Russia* amazes everyone with its adventures and
    semi-fictional heroes; those people are incredibly original, their land is
    beautiful. And all these remain unrepresented in the eyes of the educated
    world, although *Little Russia* has long had its own composers, artists, and
    poets. I don't know what they were interested in, having forgotten their
    own culture; as for me, even if my homeland were the poorest and most
    insignificant in the world, it would seem to me more beautiful than any
    Switzerland or Italy. Those who have once seen our country say that they
    would like to live and die in its most beautiful fields. What should we say
    to her children? One should love and be proud of their beautiful mother.
    I, as a member of her great family, serve her, if not for substantial benefit,
    then at least for the glory of the name of *Ukraine*. Being trained a little in
    painting, I undertook this edition called *Colourful Ukraine*" (Shevchenko,
    Zibrannia tvoriv, vol. 6, 31–2; emphasis added).

44 Bojanowska, *Nikolai Gogol*, 266.

45 Kornblatt, *The Cossack Hero in Russian Literature*, 40.

46 "Еще солнце не дошло до половины неба, как все запорожцы
    собрались в круги. Из Сечи пришла весть, что татары во время
    отлучки козаков ограбили в ней все, вырыли скарб, который
    втайне держали козаки под землею, избили и забрали в плен всех,
    которые оставались, и со всеми забранными стадами и табунами
    направили путь прямо к Перекопу ... В подобных случаях водилось
    у запорожцев гнаться в ту ж минуту за похитителями, стараясь
    настигнуть их на дороге, потому что пленные как раз могли
    очутиться на базарах Малой Азии, в Смирне, на Критском острове,
    и бог знает в какие местах не показались бы чубатые запорожские
    головы. Вот отчего собрались запорожцы" (The sun had not yet
    reached the middle of the sky when all the Zaporozhians gathered into
    a circle. Word had come that during their absence the Tatars had raided
    the Sech, dug up the treasures the Cossacks had hidden, slaughtered and
    taken captive all who had remained behind, and set out to Perekop with
    the herds of horses and cattle they had rounded up ... When marauders
    raided the Sech, the Cossacks always charged after them right away in
    an effort to catch up with them, as the captives were usually sold in the
    bazaars of Asia Minor, Smyrna, and the island of Crete, and God knew
    where else the forelocked heads of the Zaporozhians might end up. This
    was why the Zaporozhians had now gathered in a cricle) (Gogol, *Taras*

Bulba, trans. Constantine, 89–90. This and all subsequent quotes from *Taras Bulba* are taken from this translation).

47 Ibid., 100–1.
48 Dibrova, "What Are We to Make of Gogol's Nationality?" 250.
49 *PSS II*, 172.
50 Gogol, *Taras Bulba*, trans. Constantine, 140–1.
51 Ilnytzkyj, "Is Gogol's 1842 Version of 'Taras Bulba' Really 'Russified'?" 55.
52 Grabowicz, "Three Perspectives on the Cossack Past," 189.
53 Shkanrdij, *Russia and Ukraine*, 107.
54 Bojanowska, *Nikolai Gogol*, 256.
55 Ilnytzkyj, "Is Gogol's 1842 Version of 'Taras Bulba' Really 'Russified'?" 55.
56 Barabash, *Pochva i sud'ba*, 141.
57 http://old-ru.ru/02-2.html.
58 Pavlyshyn, "Writing in Ukraine and European Identity," 129.
59 Markevich, *Ukrainskie melodii*, 121.
60 "заговоривши про Малоросію мовою, загально прийнятною для обох племен, з одного боку, показав своєму рідному племені, що у нього є й було прекрасного, а з іншого – відкрив для великоросів своєхарактерний і поетичний нарід, знаний доти в літературі тільки з карикатур" (Kulish, *Vybrani tvory*, 485–6).
61 Gogol, *Polnoe sobranie sochinenii i pisem v semnadtsati tomakh*, vol. 2, 469.
62 Kornblatt, *The Cossack Hero in Russian Literature*, 44.
63 Yoon, "Transformation of a Ukrainian Cossack into a Russian Warrior," 431.
64 Bojanowska, *Nikolai Gogol*, 267.
65 The first redaction included a rough "autograph 1" (incomplete chapters 2, 3, 5, 6), dated the beginning of 1839–April of 1840, and a rough "autograph 2" (incomplete chapter 8) dated summer–autumn of 1836; presumably, this was the chapter that Gogol read to Pushkin, evoking his famous reaction, "how sad is our Russia!" The second redaction consists of fourteen rough drafts, most dated autumn 1840, covering material from chapters 9 and 11.
66 Annenkov, *Literaturnye vospominaniia*, 80–2.
67 *PSS VII* (2) (2001–), 316.
68 See Koropeckyj and Romanchuk's article "Harkusha the Noble Bandit and the 'Minority' of Little Russian Literature" about the impact of the legend of Harkusha on preserving the Ukrainianness of the Cossacks' descendants in the empire under the mask of popular folklore. The scholars claim that "already during his lifetime Harkusha's name became synonymous with righteous banditry, and stories about his exploits, hypertrophied to sometimes fantastic proportions – he was a sorcerer, a werewolf, a lover, a sensitive sage who liked to quote Latin proverbs and

play on the bandura – spread throughout Little Russia, striking fear into the hearts of the rich and powerful and offering vicarious satisfaction to the poor and exploited. As the anonymous N.N. remarks in the introduction to his collection of anecdotes about Harkusha, among the common folk 'stories about the bandit were enlivened by a very specific kind of gaiety, as if they liked his conduct, as if they were actually taking part in his exploits'" (298).

69 *PSS VII* (2) (2001–), 492.
70 *PSS XII*, 54.
71 Ibid., 40.
72 *PSS VI*, 71.
73 Ibid., 20–1.
74 Ibid., 26.
75 Ibid., 150–1.
76 Ibid., 164–5.
77 Ibid., 182–3.
78 Ibid., 198.
79 Nikolai Grech, Faddei Bulgarin, and Osip Senkovskii criticized Gogol's novel for its caricature of Russia and its "barbaric," "non-Russian" language; see Grech, "Review of *Pokhozhdeniia Chichikova, ili Mertvye dushi* (1842), by N. Gogol," *Severnaia pchela* 137 (1842): 546–7; Bulgarin's reviews in his regular column "Zhurnal'naia vsiakaia vsiachina" in *Severnaia pchela* 135 (1843); 274 (1843); 288 (1846); 261 (1845); and Senkovskii's "Review of *Pokhozhdeniia Chichikova, ili Mertvye dushi* (1842), by N. Gogol," 32). Nikolai Polevoi reproached Gogol for attributing the vices of his personages to the Russian national character; his review appeared in *Russkii vestnik* 5–6 (1842).
80 *PSS X*, 375.
81 Nabokov, *Nikolai Gogol*, 71.
82 *PSS X*, 74.
83 *PSS VI*, 17, 139, 220, 220, 221, 244, 247, 247.
84 Ibid., 17.
85 Ibid., 221.
86 Ibid., 244.
87 Ibid., 43, 49, 70, 94, 109, 109, 117, 120, 150, 164, 166, 190, 191, 231.
88 This is evident, for example, in the description of Russian churches: "Just as a countless multitude of churches, of monasteries with cupolas, domes and crosses is scattered across holy, pious Rus' …" (*PSS VI*, 109); in the description of the Woodenware Market in Moscow: "barrels, compartmented casks, tubs, buckets, jugs with spouts and without spouts, honeypots, punnets, hampers into which peasant women put their flax and other such rubbish … and much else that serves the needs

of Rus', rich and poor" (*PSS VI*, 117); and in statements like "Such is the situation of the writer in Rus'!" (*PSS VI*, 164), "in Rus' everything likes to issue forth on a broad scale, everything without exception" (*PSS VI*, 166).

89 For example, in the following passages: "such sports of nature do occur in paintings on historical subjects that have been brought to our Russia, who knows when, whence, or by whom" (*PSS VI*, 9); "once one had finished reading … one could turn again to the card table, the solace of Russia" (*PSS VI*, 243); "in a certain remote little corner of Russia lived two ordinary citizens" (*PSS VI*, 243); "But Chichikov merely said that such an undertaking, or negotiation, would in no way be incompatible with the civil decrees and future prospects of Russia" (*PSS VI*, 35).

90 Lotman, "Khudozhestvennoe prostranstvo v proze Gogolia," *V shkole poeticheskogo slova: Pushkin, Lermontov, Gogol. Kniga dlia uchitelia* (Moscow: Prosveshcheniie, 1988), 288.

91 *PSS VI*, 120.

92 Ibid., 246–7.

93 Konstantin Aksakov, one of the leading Slavophiles of the time, discerned in the troika passage the novel's patriotic message. As a Slavophile, he believed that, by describing the proper relationship between the empire and its many peoples and nations, Gogol transformed Russia from an imperial polity into a unified Russian nation ("Neskol'ko slov o poeme Gogolia: 'Pokhozhdeniia Chichikova' ili 'Mertvye dushi,'" *Estetika i literaturnaia kritika*).

94 Bojanowska, *Nikolai Gogol*, 231.

95 "Спасите меня! возьмите меня! дайте мне тройку быстрых, как вихорь, коней! Садись, мой ямщик, звени, мой колокольчик, взвейтеся, кони, и несите меня с этого света! Далее, далее, чтобы не видно было ничего, ничего. Вон небо клубится передо мною; звездочка сверкает вдали; лес несется с темными деревьями и месяцем; сизый туман стелется под ногами; струна звенит в тумане; с одной стороны море, с другой Италия; вон и русские избы виднеют" (Save me! Carry me away! Give me three steeds swift as the wind! Mount your seat, coachman, ring bells, gallop, horses, and carry me straight out of this world! Farther, ever farther, till nothing more is to be seen, nothing! The sky swirls before me; a little star glimmers in the distance; the forest with its dark trees in the moonlight rushes past; a bluish mist floats under my feet; a string pings in the fog; on the one side is the sea, on the other, Italy; beyond Russian peasant huts also become visible) (*PSS III*, 214).

96 In the chapter "Rodina-ved'ma: ironiia stilia u N. Gogolia," Epshtein writes: "Russia is peering into Gogol with the same incandescent gaze

that the socerers and witches [from his texts] peer into their victims."
(*Ironiia ideala*, 33).

97 Smolikowski, *Historya Zgromadzenia Zmartwychwstania Pańskiego*, vol. 2,
134.

98 Letter to F. Chizhov, October 1845, in Botkin, ed., *Aleksandr Andreevich
Ivanov*, 198.

99 *PSS VIII*, 221–2. The passage goes: "звуки ее взялись из сокровенных
сил нашей русской породы нам общей, по которой я близкий
родственник вам всем."

6. The Posthumous Publications and Translations of Gogol's Texts

1 Gogol's doctor Tarasenkov left an account of Gogol's rewriting activity:
"During the last months of his life Gogol worked with love and
passionately, almost from every morning to dinner time (around 4 p.m.),
only taking breaks to go for a walk for fifteen minutes, and right after
dinner he … returned to his room to work. He had already prepared a
clean copy of 'The Divine Liturgy' and *Dead Souls* [Volume 2], written
in his own hand, clearly penned. He did not give his works to others
to copy; and how could anybody decipher his manuscripts when there
were so many revisions … He had many notebooks in which long
excerpts from his different works were written out in his own hand …
And he postponed giving the clean copies of his works to the censors,
explaining that he wished to correct passages which seemed to him not
fully comprehensible" (quoted in Mashinskii, ed., *Gogol' v vospominaniakh
sovremennikov*, 513–14).

2 Tikhonravov in Gogol, *Sochineniia N.V. Gogolia*, vol. 1, xviii.

3 See Korobka's introduction to Gogol, *Polnoe sobranie sochinenii N.V. Gogolia*.

4 See the editors' note in Gogol, *Sochineniia v trekh tomakh*, vol. 1, 416.

5 *PSS I* (2001–), 499.

6 See the editors' note in Gogol, *Polnoe sobranie sochinenii i pisem v dvadtsati
trekh tomakh*, vol. 1, 621–6.

7 Ibid., 625.

8 Ibid., 84, 96.

9 Discussed by Shenrok in *Ukazatel' k pis'mam Gogolia, zakliuchaiushchim v
sebe ob'iasneniie initsialov i drugikh sokrashchenii v izdanii Kulisha*.

10 Ibid., 89.

11 "Главной нашей задачей есть представить все возможные материалы,
которые собраны по крупицам и общую картину представят только
после действительного приятия и проникновения главной идеей
Гоголя, состоящей, по мнению издателя, в поиске истины и
совершенства" (*Sochineniia i pis'ma N.V. Gogolia*, ed. Kulish, 4).

12 *PSS XIII*, 218–19.

13 *PSS XII*, 248.

14 *PSS X*, 284.

15 Ibid., 288.

16 For further reference, see Iurii Venelin's programmatic essay "O spore mezhdu iuzhanami i severianami naschet ikh rossizma" (1827).

17 *PSS X*, 301.

18 See Marcus Levitt's analysis of Pushkin's posthumous reputation and the bowdlerization of his oeuvre in *Russian Literary Politics and the Pushkin Celebration of 1880*, 68. In contemporary popular literary studies, uncensored letters and diaries have been collected and published by Pavel Fokin in the series of publications *Pushkin bez gliantsa* (Unvarnished Pushkin) (2007), *Gogol bez gliantsa* (Unvarnished Gogol) (2008), *Lermontov bez gliantsa* (Unvarnished Lermontov) (2008), etc.

19 In the introduction to her translation of Gogol's Ukrainian tales, Olena Pchilka wrote that "it is difficult to say what develops the language more, translations or original texts" (*Pereklady z M. Hoholia [dva rozmaitykh zrazky] Oleny Pchilky* [Kyiv, 1881], 30). Mykhailo Drahomanov called Gogol's *Taras Bulba* the best and the only Ukrainian national epic ("V spravi rozvytku ukrains'koi literatury," *Lysty na Naddniprians'ku Ukrainu*, 112).

20 The characters of Taras and Ostap Bulba were held to typify civic models of Ukrainianness. Mikhail Pogodin, for example, opened his public letter "To the Galician Brothers" (1866) with a lengthy quote from the tale, comparing Ostap's suffering and heroic deeds with those of the Galician Ukrainians ("K galitskim brat'iam," *Moskovskie vedomosti* no. 200, 24 September 1868).

21 For further information about the Ruthenian Triad and its activities, see Kozik, *The Ukrainian National Movement in Galicia, 1815–1849* and Wendland, *Die Russophilen in Galizien*.

22 Nina Pashaeva has identified the role of the Russian historian Mikhail Pogodin in the debates of Galician Ukrainians about the Ukrainian literary language. In the 1840s, he visited Eastern Galicia and met with Iakiv Holovat'skyi and other Ukrainian intellectuals. From Moscow, Pogodin sent Russian books and periodicals to them, which could have informed their negative view of the possibility of making vernacular Ukrainian a literary language. Holovats'kyi had admitted that he did not abandon his native language, but he believed that it was only suitable for popular literature which could be understood by an "illiterate or semi-literate peasant." But the education of the people, he thought, should be conducted exclusively in "Slavic-Russian" ("slaveno-russkii") or the "all-Russian" ("obshcherusskii") language. For further analysis, see Pashaeva, *Ocherki istorii russkogo dvizheniia v Galichine v XIX–XX vekov*.

23 *Taras Bulba. Povest' iz Zaporozhskoi stariny, sochinenie N. Gogolia na galitsko-ruskii iazyk*, trans. Holovats'kyi (1850), 11, 171.

24 "Poliahla kozats'ka, molodets'ka holova, / Iak ot vetru u stepu trava! / Slava ne vmre, ne poliazhe, / Rytsarstvo kozats'ke vsiakomu rozkazhe!" (A young Cossack head fell / Like steppe grass from the wind! / Glory will not die, not perish, / The Cossack knighthood will pass it to the next generations!) (ibid., 172).

25 *Taras Bulba: vyklad Hoholiv*, trans. Loboda (1874).

26 For further detail, see Miiakovs'kyi, "Iuvilei tsenzurnoho aktu 1876 roku."

27 It is interesting that Lobodovs'kyi's colleague Mykhailo Drahomanov, who had the reputation of a cosmopolitan intellectual among emerging Ukrainian nationalists, was critical of this loose translation of *Taras Bulba* mostly because he would have preferred a closer, non-ideological translation of Gogol's work. Relying on Yuzefovych's (inaccurate) accusation, Drahomanov wrote: "For example, Dr Loboda, a translator of *Taras Bulba*, audaciously added entire new tirades to Gogol's text. Many people examined this translation, but nobody noticed that it is anti-literary" (*Lysty na Naddniprians'ku Ukrainu*, 115).

28 Hrushevs'kyi, "Iuvilei Mykoly Hoholia," 378.

29 Shchurat, *Ukrains'ki povisti M. Hoholia*, iv.

30 Ibid., 18.

31 The history of publication is discussed in Kal'nychenko and Kal'nychenko, "'Taras Bulba' v ukrains'kykh shatakh."

32 Zerov, *Ukrains'ke pys'menstvo*, 766.

33 Derzhavin, "Review of Hohol. M. 'Tvory.' Vol. 2. (Myrhorod, Kyiv: Knyhospilka, 1930)."

34 Out of the seven translators of this edition (Mykola Zerov, "Ivan Fedorovich Shpon´ka ta ikh titon'ka"; Andrii Nikovs'kyi, "Zahublena hramota," "Taras Bulba"; Dmytro Revuts´kyi, "Vechir proty Ivana Kupala"; Maksym Ryl's'kyi, "Mais'ka nich, abo Utoplena," "Nich proty Rizdva"; Serhii Taranenko, "Zacharovane mistse"; Antin Kharchenko, "Sorochyns'kyi iarmarok," "Strashna pomsta" and Hryhorii Kosynka, "Mertvi dushi"), only Maksym Ryl's'kyi survived Stalin's purges.

35 See Romanchuk, "Mother Tongue," for a discussion of Malkovych's editing practice.

36 Ivan Malkovych, "Vid redaktora: dekil'ka zauvah shchodo perekladu 'Tarasa Bul'by'" in http://ababahalamaha.com.ua/uk/ІВАН_МАЛКОВИЧ._Від_редактора:_декілька_зауваг_щодо_перекладу_«Тараса_Бульби».

37 Shkliar, "Bulba, iakyi ne zhoriv," 7.

38 As Brian James Baer and Susanna Witt have noted, "[m]oving away from the context of the original was an important stage in dismantling the

model of translation as mimesis, which inevitably cast translations as pale copies of their originals" (Introduction to *Translation in Russian Context: Culture, Politics, Identity*, 2).

39 See the contributions in the collected volume edited by Wolf and Fukari, *Constructing a Sociology of Translation*; Angelelli, "The Sociological Turn in Translation and Interpreting Studies"; and Levine, *The Subversive Scribe*.

40 Paloposki and Koskinen, "Reprocessing Texts," 34.

41 One of the first retranslation hypotheses was articulated by Antoine Berman, who suggested that a "great translation" could only be produced after numerous rounds of translation. Berman's hypothesis is based on the idea of domestication of the original text, which inevitably results in gaps and inconsistencies on a textual level, thus creating the need for new translations (see "La retraduction comme espace de la traduction," 4–6). Drawing on Berman, Andrew Chesterman hypothesizes that first translations are always target-oriented, while retranslations are source-oriented ("Hypotheses about Translation Universals," 8).

42 Thus, Lawrence Venuti has developed the idea of retranslation as a challenge, because retranslations try to "justify themselves by establishing their differences from one or more previous versions" ("Retranslation: The Creation of Value," *Translation Changes Everything*, 96).

43 Simon, *Translating Montreal*, 207.

44 Brownlie, *Mapping Memory in Translation*, 78.

45 Yaroslav Hrytsak has summarized the ideas of political and cultural autonomy of Galician Ukraine popularized by Viacheslav Chronovil, leader of the Ukrainian Rukh Party in the early 1990s, as presented to Andrii Sadovyi, mayor of Lviv and currently leader of the "Self-Help" Party, in *Strasti za natsionalizmom*.

46 For further discussion of the competing projects of nationalism in contemporary Ukraine, see Wilson, "Elements of a Theory of Ukrainian Ethno-National Identities"; Kas'ianov, *Teorii natsii ta natsionalizmu*; Petro Tolochko, *Vid Rusi do Ukrainy*; and Kulyk, *Ukrains'kyi natsionalizm u nezalezhnii Ukraini*.

47 The results of the poll were presented in "Ukraintsy schitaiut Gogolia 'svoim' pisatelem," published on https://rian.com.ua/culture_society /20090326/78124188.html.

48 See Ukrainian textbooks with excerpts from Malkovych's translation and interpretations of Gogol's bi-national identity, which closely relate to Edyta Bojanowska's arguments: Oleksandr Avramenko, *Ukrainian Literature 9th Grade* (Kyiv: Vydavnytstvo "Hramota," 2017), 133–91; Liudmyla Kovalenko and Bernads'ka N., *Ukrainian Literature 9th Grade* (Kyiv: UOVTs "Orion," 2017), 203–17. Olena Mishchenko, *Ukrainian*

Literature 9th Grade (Kyiv: "Heneza," 2017), 171–9. O.V. Sloniovs'ka et al. *Ukrainian Literature 9th Grade* (Kyiv: Litera LTD, 2017), 149–60.

Afterword

1 Nikolai Grech condemned the novel in *Severnaia pchela* for these reasons. See his "Review of Pokhozhdenia Chichikova, ili Mertvye dushi (1842) by N. Gogol" in *Severnaia pchela* 137 (1842): 546. Bulgarin reproached Gogol for his ignorance of Russian life, which he ascribed to the fact that Gogol, being a Ukrainian, could not know it (*Severnaia pchela* 135 [1843]; 274 [1843]; 288 [1846]). Senkovskii accused Gogol of piling "tons of excess filth ... against Russian civil servants," in which the critic discerned Gogol's allegiance to the burlesque tradition of Little Russian literature ("Review of *Pokhozhdenia Chichikova, ili Mertvye dushi* (1842) by N. Gogol," 32).

2 Polevoi, "Review of *Vechera na khutore bliz Dikan'ki* vol. 1."

3 *PSS XII*, 419.

4 Bojanowska, *Nikolai Gogol*, 1.

5 In Western Slavic studies, there were also a handful of works in the field of postcolonial studies: Thompson, *Imperial Knowledge*; Layton, *Russian Literature and Empire*; and Shkandrij, *Russia and Ukraine*.

6 V. Voropaev, "Poltora veka spustia. Gogol v sovremennom literaturovedenii," http://www.domgogolya.ru/science/researches/1687.

7 Kalmykova, "Gogolevedeniie 'chistoe' i 'nechistoe.'"

8 Voropaev, "Poltora veka spustia."

9 The titles of recent "Readings of Gogol" include "Gogol's Art in the Context of European Cultures: A Glance from Rome" (2017), "N.V. Gogol and the Slavic World" (2016), "Gogol Days in Vienna" (2015), "Gogol's Art in the Dialogue of Cultures" (2014).

10 This results in studying the "Gogolian myth of St. Petersburg" by Vira Aheeva (*Sorochyns'kyi iarmarok na Nevs'komu prospekti*, 2003), "the world of Gogol" by Myroslav Popovych (*Narys istorii kul'tury Ukrainy*, 1998); and "the secret agent Mykola Hohol'" by Petro Kraliuk (*Taemnyi ahent Mykola Hohol'*, 2016).

11 Pavlyshyn, "'The Tranquil Lakes of the Transmontane Commune,'" 59.

12 Shkandrij, "The Postcolonial Moment in Ukrainian Writing," *Postcolonial Europe*, 29 April 2009. http://www.postcolonial-europe.eu/pl/studies /70-the-postcolonial-moment-in-ukrainian-writing.html.

13 Ibid.

14 Riabchuk, "Ukrainian Culture after Communism," 340.

15 Kurkov, "Ukraine Should Make Russian Language Its Cultural Property."

16 Williams, *Marxism and Literature*, 9.

Appendices

1 "Distant reading" (as opposed to close reading) is a concept proposed by Franco Moretti to understand literature not only by studying particular texts, but also by aggregating and analysing large amounts of data.
2 Burrows, "'Delta'"; Hoover, "Corpus Stylistics, Stylometry, and the Styles of Henry James"; Eder, "Mind Your Corpus"; Eder and Rybicki, "Deeper Delta across Genres and Languages"; and Eder and Rybicki, "Do Birds of a Feather Really Flock Together, or How to Choose Training Samples for Authorship Attribution."
3 Burrows, "'Delta'"; Juola and Baayen, "A Controlled-Corpus Experiment in Authorship Identification by Cross-Entropy"; and Holmes, Gordon, and Wilson, "A Widow and Her Soldier."
4 A description of the method can be found in Evert et al.: "The starting point for the document representation [i.e., the creation of a dendrogram] is a 'bag of words' model of the text, i.e. we count how often each word form occurs in each document. The word counts are then transformed to relative frequencies to compensate for different text lengths. For further processing, the n most frequent different words over the whole corpus ... are chosen. In the vector space model, each different word corresponds to a different dimension. The word frequencies of all documents can now be arranged in a documents x words matrix ... Given the normalized document vectors, there are ... different standard ways to calculate the distance between two documents" ("Understanding and Explaining Delta Measures for Authorship Attribution," 116).

Bibliography

Primary Sources

Gogol, Nikolai Vasil'evich. *The Collected Tales of Nikolai Gogol*. Trans. Richard Pevear and Larisa Volokhonsky. New York: Pantheon Books, 1998.
– *Dead Souls*. Translated by Robert A. Maguire. London: Penguin Classics, 2004.
– *Pereklady z M. Hoholia (dva rozmaitykh zrazky) Oleny Pchilky*. Kyiv, 1881.
– *Polnoe sobranie sochinenii i pisem v dvadtsati trekh tomakh*. Ed. Iu. Mann. Vol. 1. Moscow: Nauka: IMLI RAN, 2001–.
– *Polnoe sobranie sochinenii i pisem v semnadtsati tomakh*. Editor in chief I.A. Vinogradov. Moscow: Izdatel'stvo Moskovskoi Patriarkhii, 2009.
– *Polnoe sobranie sochinenii v chetyrnadtsati tomakh*. Moscow: Izd-vo Akademii nauk SSSR, 1937–52.
– *Polnoe sobranie sochinenii N.V. Gogolia*. 12 vols. Ed. N.I. Korobka. St Petersburg: Russkoe knizhnoe t-vo "Deiatel'," 1900.
– *Sochineniia i pis'ma N.V. Gogolia*. Ed. P. Kulish. St Petersburg: Russkoe knizhnoe t-vo "Deiatel'," 1857.
– *Sochineniia i pis'ma N.V. Gogolia v 2-kh tomakh*. Ed. V.V. Kallash. St Petersburg: Tip. "Samoobrazovaniie," 1896.
– *Sochineniia i pis'ma N.V. Gogolia*. 9 vols. Ed. V.V. Kallash. St Petersburg: Tipo-lit. t-va "Prosveshcheniia," 1907–9.
– *Sochineniia N.V. Gogolia*. Ed. Nikolai Tikhonravov. Moscow: Izdanie knizhnogo magazina V. Dumnova, 1889.
– *Sochineniia v trekh tomakh*. Moscow, Leningrad, 1928.
– *Taras Bulba*. A new translation by Peter Constantine. Introduction by Robert D. Kaplan. New York: Modern Library, 2003.
– *Taras Bul'ba. Avtografy, prizhiznennyie izdaniia. Istoriko-literaturnyi i tekstologicheskii kommentarii*. Ed. I.A. Vinogradov. Moscow: IMLI RAN, 2009.

– *Taras Bul'ba. Povest' iz Zaporozhskoi stariny, sochinenie N. Gogolia na galitsko-ruskii iazyk.* Trans. P. Holovats'kyi. Lviv: Cherenkami Instituta Stavropygians'kogo, 1850.
– *Taras Bulba. Povist'.* Trans. V. Shchurat. Lviv: Nakladom M. Iatskova i S-ky Druk. Vil'hel'ma Tsukerkandlia v Zolochevi, 1900.
– *Taras Bul'ba: vyklad Hoholiv.* Trans. M. Loboda. Kyiv: Tip. M.P. Fritsa, 1874.
– *Vechera na khutore bliz Dikan'ki: povesti/Pervaia knizhka.* St Petersburg: Tip. dep. narod. prosveshcheniia, 1831.
Pushkin, A.S. *Sobranie sochinenii v desiati tomakh.* Moscow: Khudozh. lit., 1959–62.
Shevchenko, Taras Hryhorovych. *Zibrannia tvoriv.* 6 vols. Ed. M. Zhulyns'kyi. Kyiv: Naukova dumka, 2003.
The Song of Igor's Campaign. Trans. V. Nabokov. London: Weidenfeld & Nicolson Ltd, 1961.

Secondary Sources

Adrianova-Perets, V.P., ed. *Slovo o polku Igoreve.* Moscow, Leningrad: Akademiia nauk SSSR. Literaturnye pamiatniki, 1950.
Aheeva, V.P., ed. *Sorochyns'kyi iarmarok na Nevs'komu prospekti: Ukrains'ka retseptsiia Hoholia.* Kyiv: Fakt, 2003.
Agha, Asif. *Language and Social Relations.* Cambridge, New York: Cambridge University Press, 2007.
Aizenshtok, I. Ia. "Khronologiia napisaniia 'Vecherov na khutore bliz Dikan'ki'." *Izvestiia akademii nauk SSSR. Otdelenie literatury i iazyka* 21 (3) (1962): 252–62.
Akimova, N. "Bulgarin i Gogol': literaturnaia biographiia i literaturnaia reputatsiia." *Russkaia literatura* 3 (1996): 3–18.
Aksakov, K.S. *Estetika i literaturnaia kritika.* Moscow: Iskusstvo, 1995.
Aksakov, S.T. *Istoriia moego znakomstva s Gogolem. Akademia nauk SSSR. Literaturnye pamiatniki.* Moscow: Izd-vo Akademii nauk SSSR, 1960.
Altshuller, M. "The Walter Scott Motifs in Nikolai Gogol's Story 'The Lost Letter.'" *Oxford Slavonic Papers* 22 (1989): 81–8.
Aman, Robert. *Impossible Interculturality?: Education and the Colonial Difference in a Multicultural World.* Diss. Linköping University Electronic Press, 2014.
Andriewsky, O. "The Russian-Ukrainian Discourse and the Failure of the 'Little Russian Solution,' 1782–1917." *Culture, Nation, and Identity: The Ukrainian–Russian Encounter (1600–1945).* Ed. Andreas Kappeler et al. Edmonton: Canadian Institute of Ukrainian Studies Press, 2003. 182–214.
Angelelli, Claudia V. "The Sociological Turn in Translation and Interpreting Studies." *Translation and Interpreting Studies* 7 (2) (2012): 125–8.
Annenkov, Pavel. *Literaturnye vospominaniia.* Leningrad: Academia, 1928.

– *Materialy dlia biografii A.S. Pushkina.* Moscow: "Sovremennik," 1984.

– "N.V. Gogol' v Rime letom 1841 goda." *Gogol' v vospominaniiakh sovremennikov.* Moscow: Gosud. izd. khudozh. literatury, 1952.

Argyle, Michael, and Adam Kendon. "The Experimental Analysis of Social Performance." *Advances in Experimental Social Psychology.* Vol. 3. Academic Press, 1967. 55–98.

Arsen'iev, K. *Statisticheskiie ocherki Rossii.* St Petersburg, 1848.

Ashcroft, B., G. Griffiths, and H. Tiffin. *The Empire Writes Back: Theory and Practice in Post-Colonial Literatures.* 2nd ed. London, New York: Routledge, 2007.

– *Post-Colonial Studies: The Key Concepts.* 2nd ed. London, New York: Routledge, 2007.

Austin, John. *How to Do Things with Words.* Oxford: Oxford University Press, 1962.

Baer, B.J., and S. Witt. *Translation in Russian Context: Culture, Politics, Identity.* New York: Routledge, 2018.

Bahri, Deepika. "Hybridity, Redux." *PMLA* 132 (1) (2017): 142–8.

Bahrii Pikulyk, Romana. *Shliakh sera Val'tera Skotta na Ukrainu.* Kyiv: Vsesvit, 1993.

– "Taras Bulba and The Black Council: Adherence to and Divergence from Sir Walter Scott's Historical Novel Pattern." PhD dissertation, University of Toronto, 1978.

Bakhtin, M.M. *The Dialogic Imagination: Four Essays.* Trans. M. Holquist, and C. Emerson Austin: University of Texas Press, 1981.

– *Polnoie sobranie sochinenii v 7-mi tomakh.* Moscow: "Russkiie slovari," 1996–2012.

– "Rable i Gogol' (Iskusstvo slova i narodnaia smekhovaia kul'tura)." *Voprosy literatury i estetiki.* Moscow: Khudozh. lit-ra, 1965.

– *Tvorchestvo Fransua Rable i narodnaia kultura srednevekov'ia i Renessansa.* Moscow: Khudozhestvennaia literatura, 1990.

Bantysh-Kamenskii, D. *Istoriia Maloi Rossii so vremen prisoedineniia onoi k rossiiskomu gosudarstvu pri Tsare Aleksee Mikhailoviche.* 2 vols. Moscow: Tip. S. Selivanovskogo, 1822.

Barabash, Iu. *Pochva i sud'ba: Gogol' i ukrainskaia literatura.* U istokov. Moscow: Nasledie, 1995.

– "'Svoego iazyka ne znaet …' ili Pochemu Gogol' pisal po-russki?" *Voprosy literatury* 1 (2001): 36–58.

Barker, C. *The Sage Dictionary of Cultural Studies.* Thousand Oaks, CA: Sage, 2004.

Baudrillard, J. *The System of Objects.* London, New York: Verso, 2005.

Bauman, Richard. "Verbal Art as Performance." *American Anthropologist* 77 (2) (1975): 290–311.

Beliakov, Sergei. *Ten 'Mazepy. Ukrainskaia natsiia v epokhu Gogolia.* St Petersburg: Izdatel' stvo AST, 2016.

Belinskii, V. *Sobranie sochinenii v deviati tomakh.* 9 vols. Moscow: Khud. literatura, 1976–82.

Belyi, A. "Gogol'." *Vesy* 4 (1909).

– *Gogol's Artistry.* Trans. Christopher Colbath. Evanston, IL: Northwestern University Press, 2009.

Bene, C., and Gilles Deleuze. *Superpositions.* Paris: Minuit, 1979.

Benjamin, W. *Das Passagen-Werk.* Frankfurt: Suhrkamp, 1982.

Berehulak, A. "Gogolian Myth and the Colonial Ethos." *Journal of Ukrainian Studies* 20 (1–2) (1995): 33–42.

Berger, Peter, and Thomas Luckmann. *The Social Construction of Reality: A Treatise in the Sociology of Knowledge.* Garden City, NY: Anchor Press, 1967.

Berger, Stefan, and Alexei Miller, eds. *Nationalizing Empires.* Vol. 3. Budapest: Central European University Press, 2015.

Berman, Antoine. "La retraduction comme espace de la traduction." *Palimpsestes. Revue de traduction* 4 (1990): 1–7.

Bhabha, Homi. "Culture's In-Between." *Questions of Cultural Identity.* Ed. Stuart Hall and Paul Du Gay. London: Sage, 1996. 53–60.

– "DissemiNation: Time, Narrative, and the Margins of the Modern Nation." *Nation and Narration.* London: Routledge, 1990. 291–322.

– *The Location of Culture.* 2nd ed. London: Routledge, 2004.

– "The Other Question." *Contemporary Postcolonial Theory: A Reader.* Ed. Padmini Mongia. London, New York, Sydney, Auckland: Arnold, 1996. 37–54.

– "Remembering Fanon: Self, Psyche and the Colonial Condition." *Colonial Discourse and Post-Colonial Theory.* Ed. P. Williams and Laura Chrisman. New York: Columbia University Press, 1994. 112–23.

Bhatia, T.K., and W.C. Ritchie. *The Handbook of Bilingualism.* Malden, MA: Blackwell Publishing, 2004.

Bilaniuk, Lada. *Contested Tongues: Language Politics and Cultural Correction in Ukraine.* Ithaca: Cornell University Press, 2005.

Bilenky, Serhiy. *Romantic Nationalism in Eastern Europe: Russian, Polish, and Ukrainian Political Imaginations.* Stanford: Stanford University Press, 2012.

Bilenky, Serhiy, ed. *Fashioning Modern Ukraine: The Writings of Mykola Kostomarov, Volodymyr Antonovych and Mykhailo Drahomanov.* Edmonton and Toronto: Canadian Institute of Ukrainian Studies Press, 2013.

Bodians'kyi, Osyp. (pseud. I. Mastak). "Review of *Malorossiiskie povesti* by Grigorii Kvitka-Osnov'ianenko." *Uchenye zapiski Imperatorskogo Moskovskogo Universiteta* 5 (1834): 287–313.

Bojanowska, Edyta M. *Nikolai Gogol: Between Ukrainian and Russian Nationalism.* Cambridge, MA: Harvard University Press, 2007.

Botkin, M., ed. *Aleksandr Andreevich Ivanov. Ego zhizn' i perepiska 1806–1858*. St Petersburg: Tip. M.M. Stasiulevicha, 1880.

Bourdieu, Pierre. *Distinction: A Social Critique of the Judgement of Taste*. Trans. Richard Nice. Cambridge, MA: Harvard University Press, 1984.

– *Pascalian Meditations*. Trans. Richard Nice. Stanford: Stanford University Press, 2000.

Brownlie, Siobhan. *Mapping Memory in Translation*. New York: Springer, 2016.

Bulgarin, F. "Felieton." *Severnaia pchela* 98 (1847).

– "Nastoiashchii moment i dukh nashei literatury." *Severnaia pchela* 12 (16 January 1836).

– "Review of *Mertvyie dushi*." *Severnaia pchela* 119 (1842).

– "Review of *Vechera na khutore bliz Dikan' ki*, 2nd ed." *Severnaia pchela* 26 (1836).

– "Rezko otritsatel'naia otsenka siuzheta, iazyka, dostovernosti p'esy." "Review of *Revizor*." *Severnaia pchela* 98 (1836).

– *Sochineniia*. Vol. 6. St Petersburg: Tip. N. Grecha, 1830.

Burke, L., T. Crowley, and A. Girvin. *The Routledge Language and Cultural Theory Reader*. London: Routledge, 2000.

Burrows, John. "'Delta': A Measure of Stylistic Difference and a Guide to Likely Authorship." *Literary and Linguistic Computing* 17 (3) (2002): 267–87.

Bushkovitch, P. "The Ukraine in Russian Culture, 1790–1860: The Evidence of the Journals." *Jahrbucher für Geschichte Osteuropas* 39 (3) (1991): 339–63.

Butler, Judith. *Excitable Speech: A Politics of the Performative*. New York: Routledge, 1997.

– *Gender Trouble: Feminism and the Subversion of Identity*. London: Routledge, 1990.

Caillois, R. *Man, Play and Games*. Trans. Meyer Barash. Urbana: University of Illinois Press, 2001.

– *The Mask of Medusa*. New York: C.N. Potter, 1964.

Chambers, R. *Story and Situation: Narrative Seduction and the Power of Fiction*. Minneapolis: University of Minnesota Press, 1984.

Chapaeva, Liudmila. *Kul'turno-iazykovaia situatsiia v 1830kh–1840kh v kontekste sporov slavianofilov i zapadnikov*. Saarbrücken: Palmarium Academic Publishing, 2014.

Chaplenko, V. "Ukrainizmy v movi M. Hoholia." *Slavica. Pratsi Instytutu slovianoznavstva*. Vol. 2. Augsburg: Ukrainska vil'na akademiia nauk, 1948.

Chaudenson, Robert. *Des îles, des hommes, des langues: essais sur la créolisation linguistique et culturelle*. Paris: L'Harmattan, 1992.

Chertoryz'ka, T. "Ukrains'ke slovo v tvorchosti M.V. Hoholia." *Movoznavstvo* 3 (105) (1984): 10–17.

Chesterman, A. "Hypotheses about Translation Universals." *Claims, Changes and Challenges in Translation Studies*. Amsterdam: John Benjamins Publishing Company, 2004. 1–13.

Chicherin, A.V. "Neizvestnoe vyskazyvanie V.F. Odoevskogo o Gogole." *Trudy kafedry literatury L'vovskogo gos. un-ta. Literaturovedeniie* 2 (1958): 72.

Chow, Rey. *Writing Diaspora: Tactics of Intervention in Contemporary Cultural Studies*. Bloomington and Indianapolis: Indiana University Press, 1993.

Chyzhevs'kyi, D. *Narysy z istorii filosofii na Ukraini*. Kyiv: Vyd-vo Orii, 1992.

– "The Unknown Gogol'." *Slavonic and East European Review* 30 (75) (1952): 476–93.

Comaroff, J. "The Empire's Old Clothes: Fashioning the Colonial Subject." *Cross-Cultural Consumption: Global Markets, Local Realities*. Ed. David Howes. London, New York: Routledge, 1996. 19–38.

Cooper, F., and A.L. Stoler. *Tensions of Empire: Colonial Cultures in a Bourgeois World*. Berkeley: University of California Press, 1997.

Dal´, Vladimir. *Tolkovyi slovar' zhivogo velikorusskogo iazyka*. St Petersburg, 1880.

Davis, F. *Fashion, Culture, and Identity*. Chicago: University of Chicago Press, 1992.

Debreczeny, P. "Nikolai Gogol and His Contemporary Critics." *Transactions of the American Philosophical Society* 56 (3) (1966): 5–68.

– *Social Functions of Literature: Alexander Pushkin and Russian Culture*. Stanford: Stanford University Press, 1997.

Deleuze, G. *Essays Critical and Clinical*. Trans. Daniel W. Smith and Michael A. Greco. London: Verso, 1998.

Deleuze, G., and F. Guattari. *Kafka: Toward a Minor Literature*. Trans. Dana Polan. Minneapolis: University of Minnesota Press, 1986.

– *A Thousand Plateaus: Capitalism and Schizophrenia*. London, New York: Continuum International Publishing Group, 2004.

Derrida, J. *L'Écriture et la difference*. Paris: Éditions du Seuil, 1967.

– *Specters of Marx: The State of the Debt, the Work of Mourning and the New International*. Trans. Peggy Kamuf. New York and London: Routledge, 1994.

Derzhavin, V.M. "Review of Hohol. M. 'Tvory.' Vol. 2. (Myrhorod, Kyiv: Knyhospilka, 1930)." *Chervonyi shliakh* 3 (1931): 220.

Dibrova, Volodymyr. "What Are We to Make of Gogol's Nationality?" *Hoholeznavchi studii* 18 (2009): 247–63.

Dmitrieva, E.E. "Pozhiv v takoi tesnoi sviazi s ved'mami i koldunami (Ob osobennostiakh gogolevskogo folklorizma *Vechera na khutore bliz Dikan'ki*)." *N.V. Gogol' i mirovaia kul'tura: Vtoryie Gogolevskiie chteniia. Sbornik dokladov*. Moscow, 2003.

– "Stilisticheskiie funktsii frantsuzskogo iazyka v perepiske Pushkina i ego poezii." *Problemy sovremennogo pushkinovedeniia*. Leningrad: Mezhvuzovskii sbornik nauchnykh trudov LGPI im. A.N. Gertsena, 1981. 58–65.

Dmitrieva, E.E., and I.U. Mann, eds. *Gogol' kak iavlenie mirovoi literatury: po materialam mezhdunarodnoi nauchnoi konferentsii, posviashchennoi 150-letiiu so dnia smerti N.V. Gogolia, 31 oktiabria–2 noiabria 2002 g.* Moscow: IMLI RAN, 2003.

Dmitrieva, N., and G. Argent. "The Coexistence of Russian and French in Russia in the First Third of the Nineteenth Century: Bilingualism with or without Diglossia?" *French and Russian in Imperial Russia*. Vol. 1. Edinburgh: Edinburgh University Press, 2015. 228–42.

Drahomanov, M.P. *Lysty na Naddniprians'ku Ukrainu*. Kolomyia: Vyd. Red. "Naroda," 1894.

– *Perepyska Mykhaila Drahomanova z Melitonom Buchyns'kym 1871–1877*. Lviv: Naklad NTSh, 1910.

Dubnow, Simon. *History of the Jews in Russia and Poland: From the Earliest Times until the Present Day*. Philadelphia: Jewish Publication Society of America, 1920.

Eagleton, Terry. *The Ideology of the Aesthetic*. Cambridge, MA: Basil Blackwell, 1990.

Eder, Maciej. "Mind Your Corpus: Systematic Errors in Authorship Attribution." *Literary and Linguistic Computing* 28 (4) (2013): 603–14.

Eder, Maciej and Jan Rybicki. "Deeper Delta across Genres and Languages: Do We Really Need the Most Frequent Words?" *Literary and Linguistic Computing* 26 (3) (2011): 315–21.

– "Do Birds of a Feather Really Flock Together, or How to Choose Training Samples for Authorship Attribution." *Literary and Linguistic Computing* 28 (2) (2013): 229–36.

Efimenko, A. "Natsional'naia dvoistvennost' v tvorchestve Gogolia." *Vestnik Evropy* (June 1902): 229–44.

Efremov, S. *Istoriia ukrains'koho pys'menstva*. St Petersburg: Ukrainskii uchitel', 1903.

Egerton, W.B. "Laying a Legend to Rest: The Poet Kapnist and Ukraino-German Intrigue." *Slavic Review* 30 (3) (1971): 551–60.

Eikhenbaum, B. "How Is Gogol's 'The Overcoat' Made." *Gogol from the Twentieth century: Eleven Essays*. Ed. and transl. Robert Maguire. Princeton: Princeton University Press, 1974.

– *Lermontov*. Moscow, Leningrad: Akademiia nauk, 1961.

– *O literature*. Raboty raznykh let. Moscow: Sovetskii pisatel', 1987.

– *O proze*. Leningrad: Izd-vo "Khudozhestvennaya literatura," 1969.

Epshtein, Mikhail. *Ironiia ideala: paradoksy russkoi literatury*. Moscow: Novoe literaturnoe obozreniie, 2015.

Erlich, V. *Gogol*. New Haven: Yale University Press, 1969.

Etkind, A. "Fuko i tezis vnutrennei kolonizatsii: postkoloniial'nyi vzgliad na sovetskoe proshloe." *Novoe literaturnoe obozrenie* 49 (2001). https://magazines.gorky.media/nlo/2001/3/fuko-i-tezis-vnutrennej-kolonizaczii.html.

– *Internal Colonization: Russia's Imperial Experience*. Cambridge: Polity, 2011.
– "Russkaia literatura, XIX vek: Roman vnutrennei kolonizatsii." *Novoe literaturnoe obozreniie* 59 (2003). http://magazines.russ.ru/nlo/2003/59 /etk.html.
Evert, Stefan, et al. "Understanding and Explaining Delta Measures for Authorship Attribution." *Digital Scholarship in the Humanities* 32.suppl_2 (2017): ii4–ii16.
Fabrikant, Nik. "A Brief Outline of the History of the Treatment of Ukrainian Literature by the Russian Censorship Laws (1905)." *East/West: Journal of Ukrainian Studies* 4 (2) (2017): 153–72.
Fanger, D. *The Creation of Nikolai Gogol*. Cambridge, MA: Belknap Press of Harvard University Press, 1979.
– "Gogol and His Reader." *Literature and Society in Imperial Russia, 1800–1914*. Eds. R.L. Belknap and W.M. Todd. Stanford: Stanford University Press, 1978. 61–95.
Fanon, F. *Black Skin, White Masks*. Trans. Charles Lam Markmann. London: Pluto Press, 1986.
Felman, Shoshana. *The Literary Speech Act: Don Juan with J.L. Austin, or Seduction in Two Languages*. Ithaca: Cornell University Press, 1983.
Fishman, Joshua A., and Ofelia Garcia. *Handbook of Language and Ethnic Identity*. 2nd ed. New York: Oxford University Press, 2010.
Flier, Michael. "Surzhyk or Surzhyks?" *Belarusian Trasjanka and Ukrainian Surzhyk: Structural and Social Aspects of Their Description and Categorization*. Ed. Gerd Hentschel and Siarhiej Zaprudski. Oldenburg: BIS-Verlag der Carl von Ossietzky Universitaet Oldenburg, 2008. 39–56.
Floria, B.H. "O znachenii termina 'khokhol' i proizvodnykh ot nego v russkikh istochnikakh pervoi poloviny XVII v. (epizod iz istorii russko-pol'sko-ukrainskikh kontaktov)." *Studia Polonica. K 60-letiiu Viktora Aleksandrovich Khoreva*. Moscow: Institut slavianovedeniia i balkanistiki RAN, 1992. 16–20.
Foucault, M. "What Is an Author?" Trans. D.F. Bouchard and Sh. Simon. *Language, Counter-Memory, Practice: Selected Essays and Interviews*. Ithaca: Cornell University Press, 1977. 113–38.
Frazier, M. *Frames of the Imagination: Gogol's Arabesques and the Romantic Question of Genre*. New York: Peter Lang, 2000.
– *Romantic Encounters: Writers, Readers, and the Library for Reading*. Stanford: Stanford University Press, 2007.
Freud, Sigmund. *A General Introduction to Psychoanalysis*. New York: Horace Liveright, 1920.
Fusso, Susanne. *Designing Dead Souls: An Anatomy of Disorder in Gogol*. Stanford: Stanford University Press, 1993.

Fylypovych, P. "Ukraïns'ka stykhiia v tvorchosti Hoholia." *Sorochyns'kyi iarmarok na Nevs'komu prospekti: Ukraïns'ka retseptsiia Hoholia.* Ed. V.P. Ageeva. Kyiv: Fakt, 2003.

Gasparov, B. "Alienation and Negation: Gogol's View of Ukraine." *Gogol: Exploring Absence: Negativity in 19th Century Russian Literature.* Bloomington, IN: Slavica, 1999. 113–23.

Geraci, Robert. *Window on the East: National and Imperial Identities in Late Tsarist Russia.* Ithaca: Cornell University Press, 2001.

Gippius, V.V. *"Vechera na khutore bliz Dikan'ki* Gogolia." *Trudy otdela novoi russkoi literatury In-ta literatury (Pushkinskii dom) AN SSSR* 1. Leningrad: Izdatel', 1948. 9–38.

Gippius, V.V., ed. *Gogol': vospominaniia, pis'ma, dnevniki.* Moscow: Agraf, 1999.

– ed. *N.V. Gogol': materialy i issledovaniia.* Vol. 1. Moscow, Leningrad: Izdatel'stvo Akademii nauk SSSR, 1936.

Giuliani, Rita. *Rim v zhizni i tvorchestve Gogolia, ili Poteriannyi rai: Materialy i issledovaniia.* Trans. M. Iampol'skii. Moscow: Izd-vo Novoe literaturnoe obozreniie, 2009.

Glissant, Édouard. *Traité du Tout-Monde.* (Poétique IV). Paris: Gallimard, 1997.

Gorev, Boris. "Russkaia literatura i evrei." *Russko-evreiskaia literatura.* Ed. V. Lvov-Rogachevskii. Moscow: Moskovskoe otdelenie gosudarstvennogo izdatel'stva, 1922. 5–29.

Grabowicz, G. "Between History and Myth: Perceptions of the Cossack Past in Polish, Russian and Ukrainian Romantic Literature." *International Congress of Slavists.* Vol. 2. Ed. Paul Debreczeny. Kyiv, 1983. 173–88.

– "Between Subversion and Self-Assertion: The Role of *Kotliarevshchyna* in Russian-Ukrainian Literary Relations." *Culture, Nation, and Identity: The Ukrainian-Russian Encounter (1600–1945).* Edmonton: Canadian Institute of Ukrainian Studies Press, 2003. 215–28.

– "Hohol' i mif Ukrainy." *Suchasnist'* 9–10 (1994): 77–92, 137–49.

– "Semantyka kotliarevshchyny." *Do istorii ukrains'koi literatury: Doslidzhennia, ese, polemika.* Kyiv: Osnovy, 1997. 316–32.

– "Three Perspectives on the Cossack Past: Gogol', Shevchenko, Kulish." *Harvard Ukrainian Studies* 5 (2) (1981): 171–94.

– "Toward a History of Ukrainian Literature." *Harvard Ukrainian Studies* 1 (4) (1977): 407–523.

– "Ukrainian-Russian Literary Relations in the Nineteenth Century: A Formulation of the Problem." *Ukraine and Russia in Their Historical Encounter.* Ed. P.J. Potichnyj et al. Edmonton: Canadian Institute of Ukrainian Studies Press, 1992. 214–44.

– "Ukrainian Studies: Framing the Contexts." *Slavic Review* 54 (3) (1995): 674–90.

Grech, N. *Opyt kratkoi istorii russkoi literatury*. St Petersburg: Tip. N. Grecha, 1822.

– "Review of *Pokhozhdeniia Chichikova, ili Mertvye dushi* (1842), by N. Gogol." *Severnaia pchela* 137 (1842): 546–7.

– *Sochineniia*. Vol. 3. St Petersburg: Tip. Ia. Treia, 1855.

Greenblatt, S. *Renaissance Self-Fashioning*. Chicago: University of Chicago Press, 1984.

– *Shakespearean Negotiations: The Circulation of Social Energy in Renaissance England*. Vol. 4. Berkeley: University of California Press, 1988.

Greenfeld, L. *Nationalism: Five Roads to Modernity*. Cambridge, MA: Harvard University Press, 1992.

Greenleaf, M., and S. Moeller-Sally, eds. *Russian Subjects: Empire, Nation, and the Culture of the Golden Age*. Evanston, IL: Northwestern University Press, 1998.

Gregg, R. "The Writer and His Quiff: How Young Gogol' Sought to Shape His Public Image." *Russian Review* 63 (1) (2004): 63–9.

Grosjean, F., and C. Soares. "Processing Mixed Languages: Some Preliminary Findings." *Language Processing in Bilinguals: Psycholinguistic and Neuropsychological Perspectives*. Ed. J. Vaid. Hillsdale, NJ: Lawrence Erlbaum, 1986. 145–79.

Grot, Ia. *Perepiska Ia. K. Grota s P.A. Pletnevym*. 3 vols. St Petersburg: Tipografiia Ministerstva Putei Soobshcheniia, 1896.

Groys, Boris. "Imena goroda." *Utopiia i obmen*. Moscow: Znak, 1993. 357–65.

Gukovskii, G.A. *Realizm Gogolia*. Leningrad: Gos. izd-vo khudozh. lit-ry [Leningradskoe otd-nie], 1959.

– "*Vechera na khutore bliz' Dikan'ki*." *Vestnik Leningradskogo universiteta* 3 (1948): 98–117.

Hale, Richard, and Peter Whitlam. *Impact and Influence: Tools and Techniques for Creating a Lasting Impression*. London: Kogan Page, 1999.

Hammarberg, G. "Sartor Resartus: Gogol's Overcoats." *Russian Review* 67 (3) (2008): 395–414.

Herder, Johann. *Sprachphilosophische Schriften*. Hamburg: Meiner, 1975.

Hester, S., and W. Housley. *Language, Interaction and National Identity: Studies in the Social Organization of National Identity in Talk-in-Interaction*. Burlington, VT: Ashgate Publishing Company, 2002.

Hoisington, S. "Pushkin's Belkin and the Mystifications of Sir Walter Scott." *Comparative Literature* 33 (4) (1981): 342–57.

Holden, P. *Imagined Individuals: National Autobiography and Postcolonial Self-Fashioning*. Singapore: Asia Research Institute, National University of Singapore, 2003.

Holmes, David I., Lesley J. Gordon, and Christine Wilson. "A Widow and Her Soldier: Stylometry and the American Civil War." *Literary and Linguistic Computing* 16 (4) (2001): 403–20.

Holquist, M. "The Tyranny of Difference: Gogol and the Sacred." *Gogol: Exploring Absence: Negativity in 19th-Century Russian Literature*. Bloomington, IN: Slavica Publishers, 1999. 125–37.

Holubenko, Petro. *Ukraina i Rosiia u svitli kul'turnykh vzaemyn*. New York, Paris, Toronto: Vydavnytstvo "Ukrains'ke slovo," 1987.

Hoover, David. "Corpus Stylistics, Stylometry, and the Styles of Henry James." *Style* 41 (2) (2007): 174–203.

Hosking, G. *Russia: People and Empire, 1552–1917*. Cambridge, MA: Harvard University Press, 1997.

Howes, D. *Cross-Cultural Consumption: Global Markets, Local Realities*. London, New York: Routledge, 1996.

Hrushevs'kyi, Mykhailo. "Iubilei Mykoly Hoholia." *Tvory in 50 vols*. Ed. P. Sokhan, Ia. Dashkevych, I. Hyrych, et al. Vol. 2. Lviv: Vydavnytstvo "Svit," 2005. 378–81.

Hryniov, Volodymyr. *Nova Ukraina, iakoiu ia ii bachu*. Kyiv: Abris, 1995.

Hryshko, W. "Nikolai Gogol' and Mykola Hohol'." *Annals of the Ukrainian Academy of Arts and Sciences in the United States* 12 (1–2) (1969): 113–42.

Hrytsak, Yaroslav. "The Postcolonial Is Not Enough." *Slavic Review* 74 (4) (2015): 732–7.

– *Strasti za natsionalizmom: stara istoriia na novyi lad. Esei*. Kyiv: Krytyka, 2011.

Huggan, G. *The Postcolonial Exotic: Marketing the Margins*. London, New York: Routledge, 2001.

Hundorova, T. *Kitch i literatura. Travestiï*. Kyiv: Fakt, 2008.

– "'Vechory na khutori bilia Dykan'ky': dyiavol'skyi kontrakt i kul'turna initsiatsiia. Vstupne slovo." *Vechory na khutori bilia Dykan'ky. Taras Bul'ba. Vii: Povisti*. Ternopil', Kyiv: B-ka "Svitovyd," 2004.

Ilnytzkyj, O. "Cultural Indeterminacy in the Russian Empire: Nikolai Gogol as a Ukrainian Post-Colonial Writer." *A World of Slavic Literatures: Essays in Comparative Slavic Studies in Honour of Edward Mozejko*. Ed. Paul Duncan Morris. Bloomington, IN: Slavica, 2002. 153–71.

– "'Imperial Culture' and Russian-Ukrainian Unity Myths." *Ukraine, the EU and Russia*. London: Palgrave Macmillan, 2007. 52–69.

– "Is Gogol's 1842 Version of 'Taras Bulba' Really 'Russified'?" *Journal of Ukrainian Studies* 35–6 (2010): 51–8.

– "Modeling Culture in the Empire: Ukrainian Modernism and the Death of the All-Russian Idea." *Culture, Nation, and Identity: The Ukrainian-Russian Encounter (1600–1945)*. Ed. A. Kappeler et al. Edmonton: Canadian Institute of Ukrainian Studies Press, 2003. 298–324.

Isupov, K.G., ed. *Bakhtin: Pro et Contra*, 2 vols. St Petersburg: Izdatel'stvo Russkogo Khristianskogo instituta, 2001.

Ivanitsky, A.I. "Iazyk 'Vybrannykh mest …' v kontekste russkoi publitsisticheskoi traditsii (Gogol i Avvakum)." *Vestnik Moskovskogo universiteta. Seriia 10. Zhurnalistika* 2 (1988).

Jaffe, Joseph. "Measurement of Verbal and Vocal Behavior: Verbal Behavior Analysis in Psychiatric Interviews with the Aid of Digital Computers." *Association for Research in Nervous and Mental Disease* 42 (1964): 389–99.

Jagic, V. *Codex slovenicus rerum grammaticarum*. Berlin, 1896. Repr. as Slavische Propylaen 25. Munich: Fink, 1968. 776.

Jenness, Rosemarie K. *Gogol's Aesthetics Compared to Major Elements of German Romanticism*. New York: Peter Lang, 1995. 57–83.

Joseph, John. *Language and Identity: National, Ethnic, Religious*. New York: Palgrave Macmillan, 2004.

Juola, Patrick, and Harald Baayen. "A Controlled-Corpus Experiment in Authorship Identification by Cross-Entropy." *Literary and Linguistic Computing* 20 (suppl) (2005): 59–67.

Kaizer, L. "Rechevoi etiket v pis'makh A.S. Pushkina." *Kul'tura i tekst 99. Pushkinskii sbornik*. St Petersburg, Samara, Barnaul: Rossiiskii gos. pedagogicheskii universitet im. A.I. Gertsena, Samarskii gos. pedagogicheskii universitet, Barnaul'skii gos. pedagogicheskii universitet, 2000. 47–60.

Kalmykova, Vera. "Gogolevedeniie 'chistoe' i 'nechistoe.' V Gogolevskiie chteniia (Moscow, spring of 2005)." *Novoe literaturnoe obozreniie* 76 (2005). http://magazines.russ.ru/nlo/2005/76/ka35.html.

Kal'nychenko, O.A., and N.M. Kal'nychenko. "Taras Bulba' v ukrains'kykh shatakh: pereklad ta formuvannia natsional'noi svidomosti." *Visnyk Kharkivs'koho natsional'noho universytetu im. V.N. Karazina* 69 (2012): 137–46.

Kamanin, I.M. "Nauchnyie i literaturnyie proizvedeniia N.V. Gogolia po istorii Malorossii." *Pamiati Gogolia: Nauchno-Literaturnyi Sbornik* 1 (1902): 75–132.

Kapnist, Vasily. "Oda na rabstvo." *Sobraniie sochinenii v 2-kh tomakh*. Vol. 1. Moscow, Leningrad: AN SSSR In-t rus. literatury (Pushkinskii dom), 1960.

Kappeler, Andreas. "Mazepintsy, Malorossy, Khokhly: Ukrainians in the Ethnic Hierarchy of the Russian Empire." *Culture, Nation, and Identity: The Ukrainian-Russian Encounter (1600–1945)*. Edmonton: Canadian Institute of Ukrainian Studies Press, 2003. 125–44.

Karlinsky, Simon. *The Sexual Labyrinth of Nikolai Gogol*. Cambridge, MA: Harvard University Press, 1976.

Karpov, A.A., and M.N. Virolainen, eds. *Perepiska N.V. Gogolia*. Vol. 2. Moscow: Khudozh. lit-ra, 1988.

Karpuk, P.A. "Gogol's Research on Ukrainian Customs for the Dikan'ka Tales." *Russian Review* 56 (2) (1997): 209–32.

Kas'ianov, Heorhii. *Teorii natsii ta natsionalizmu*. Kyiv: Lybid', 1999.

Katz, Elena M. *Neither with Them, nor without Them*. Syracuse, NY: Syracuse University Press, 2008.

Kharlampovich, K. *Malorossiiskoe vliiannie na velikorusskuiu tserkovnuiu zhizn*. Kazan: Izdanie kn. mag. M.A. Golubeva, 1914.

Khodarkovsky, Michael. "From Frontier to Empire: The Concept of the Frontier in Russia, Sixteenth–Eighteenth Centuries." *Russian History* 19 (1–4) (1992): 115–28.

Khomiakov, A.S. *O starom i novom. Stat'i i ocherki.* Moscow: Sovremennik, 1988.

– *Polnoe sobranie sochinenii.* 8 vols. Moscow: Univ. tip., 1900.

Kirby, Vicki. *Judith Butler: Live Theory.* London, New York: Continuum, 2006.

Kiselev, V. "'Arabeski' Gogolia i traditsii romanticheskoi tsiklizatsii." *Izvestiia RAN. Seriia literatury i iazyka* 63 (6) (2004): 16–17.

Kiukhel'beker, V. "O napravlenii nashei poezii, osobenno liricheskoi, v poslednee desiatiletie." *Pushkin v prizhiznennoi kritike, 1820–1827.* St Petersburg: Gosudarstvennyi pushkinskii teatral'nyi tsentr, 1996. 236–8.

Knight, N. "Ethnicity, Nationality and the Masses: *Narodnost'* and Modernity in Imperial Russia." *Russian Modernity: Politics, Knowledge, Practices.* Ed. David L. Hoffmann and Yanni Kotsonis. New York: St Martin's Press, 2000. 41–64.

Kohut, Z. "The Development of a Little Russian Identity and Ukrainian Nation-Building." *Harvard Ukrainian Studies* 6 (3–4) (1986): 559–76.

– *The Question of Russo-Ukrainian Unity and Ukrainian Distinctiveness in Early Modern Ukrainian Thought and Culture.* Washington, DC: Kennan Institute, 2001.

– *Russian Centralism and Ukrainian Autonomy: Imperial Absorption of the Hetmanate, 1760s–1830s.* Cambridge, MA: Harvard Ukrainian Research Institute, 1988.

– "The Ukrainian Elite in the Eighteenth Century and Its Integration into Russian Nobility." *The Nobility in Russia and Eastern Europe.* Ed. I. Banac and P. Bushkovitch. New Haven: Slavica Publishers, 1983. 65–97.

Kolesnyk, Iryna. *Gogol': Merezhi kulturno-intelektualnykh komunikatsii.* Kyiv: Instytut istorii Ukrainy NAN Ukrainy, 2009.

Komarov, A. "Ukrainskii iazyk, fol'klor i literatura v russkom obshchestve nachala 19-go veka." *Uchenye zapiski Leningradskogo gosudarstvennogo universiteta* 47 (1939): 138–41.

Kononenko, N.O. *Ukrainian Minstrels: And the Blind Shall Sing.* Armonk, NY, London: M.E. Sharpe, 1998.

Kornblatt, Judith. *The Cossack Hero in Russian Literature: A Study in Cultural Mythology.* Madison: University of Wisconsin Press, 1992.

Koropeckyj, R., and R. Romanchuk. "Harkusha the Noble Bandit and the 'Minority' of Little Russian Literature." *Russian Review* 76 (2) (2017): 294–310.

– "Ukraine in Blackface: Performance and Representation in Gogol's 'Dikan'ka Tales,' Book 1." *Slavic Review* 62 (3) (2003): 525–47.

Korostelina, Karina. *Constructing the Narratives of Identity and Power: Self-Imagination in a Young Ukrainian Nation*. Lanham, MD: Lexington Books, 2013.

Kostomarov, M. *Books of Genesis of the Ukrainian People*. New York: Research Program on the USSR, 1954.

– *Istoricheskie proizvedeniia. Avtobiografia*. 2nd ed. Kyiv: Lybid', 1990.

– "Mysli o federativnom nachale v drevnei Rusi." *Osnova* 1 (March 1861): 121–58.

– "Ukraina. Pis'mo k izdateliu "Kolokola." *Kolokol. Pribavochnye listy*. Letter 61 (15 January 1860).

Kotov, A., and M. Poliakov, eds. *Gogol' v russkoi kritike (sbornik statei)*. Moscow: Gosudarstvennoe izdatel'stvo khudozhestvennoi literatury, 1953.

Kozik, Jan. *The Ukrainian National Movement in Galicia, 1815–1849*. Ed. Lawrence D. Orton. Trans. Andrew Gorski and Lawrence D. Orton. Edmonton: Canadian Institute of Ukrainian Studies, 1986.

Koznarsky, T. "Neither Dead nor Alive:" Ukrainian Language on the Brink of Romanticism." *East/West: Journal of Ukrainian Studies* 4 (2) (2017): 7–37.

– "Obsessions with Mazepa." *Poltava 1709: The Battle and the Myth*. Ed. Serhii Plokhii. Cambridge, MA: Distributed by Harvard University Press for the Ukrainian Research Institute, Harvard University, 2012. 569–615.

Kraliuk, P. *Taemnyi ahent Mykola Hohol'*. Lviv: Vydavnytstvo Staroho Leva, 2016.

Krutikova, N. Ie. *Hohol' ta ukrains'ka literatura*. Kyiv: Derzhavne vydavnytstvo khudozhnioi literatury, 1957.

Krys, S. "The Unknown Ukrainian: Orest Somov's Prose as a Window to Early Nineteenth-Century Ukraine." *Kyivan Witches and Other Gothic Tales of Horror: Selected Works by Orest Somov*. Lidcombe, Australia: Sova Books, 2016.

Kulish, P. "Ob otnoshenii malorossiiskoi slovesnosti k obshcherusskoi (epilog k "Chernoi rade")." *Tvory v 2-kh tomakh*. Vol. 2. Kyiv, 1989.

– *Povne zibrannia tvoriv. Lysty*. Vol. 1. Kyiv: Krytyka, 2005.

– "Vospominaniia o Nikolae Ivanoviche Kostomarove." *Nov'* 4 (1885): 61–75.

– *Vybrani tvory*. Kyiv: Vydavnytstvo khudozhnioi literatury "Dnipro," 1969.

– *Zapiski o zhizni Nikolaia Vasil'evicha Gogolia: sostavlennye iz vospominanii ego druzei i znakomykh i iz ego sobstvennykh pisem*. 2 vols. Vol. 1. Moscow: IMLI RAN, 2003.

– "Zazyvnyi lyst do ukrains'koi inteligentsii." *Khutorna poeziia*. Lviv: Z drukarni Tovarystva imeny Shevchenka, 1882. 117–32.

Kulyk, Volodymyr. *Ukrains'kyi natsionalizm u nezalezhnii Ukraini*. Kyiv: Vydavnychyi dim "Kyevo-Mohylians'ka Akademiia," 1999.

Kunitz, Joshua. *Russian Literature and the Jew: A Sociological Inquiry into the Nature and Origin of Literary Pattern*. New York: Columbia University Press, 1929.

Kurganov, E. "Gogol as a Narrator of Anecdotes." *Reflective Laughter: Aspects of Humour in Russian Culture*. Ed. Lesley Milne. London: Anthem Press, 2004. 27–36.

Kurkov, Andrei. "Ukraine Should Make Russian Language Its Cultural Property." Interview with Delovaia Stolitsa (10 January 2018). https://www.dsnews.ua/politics/andrey-kurkov-putinu-ne-vazhno-chto-dumayut-ukrainskie-russkie-02012018220000.

Lacan, J. *The Four Fundamental Concepts of Psychoanalysis*. Trans. Alan Sheridan. New York: Norton, 1978.

Lanser, Susan. *The Narrative Act: Point of View in Fictio*. Princeton: Princeton University Press, 1981.

Larsen, Neil. *Determinations: Essays on Theory, Narrative and Nation in the Americas*. London, New York: Verso, 2001.

Layton, Susan. *Russian Literature and Empire: Conquest of the Caucasus from Pushkin to Tolstoy*. Cambridge, New York: Cambridge University Press, 2005.

Lee, J.S. "Linguistic Hybridization in K-Pop: Discourse of Self-Assertion and Resistance." *World Englishes* 23 (3) (2004): 429–50.

Lefevere, André. *Translating Literature: Practice and Theory in a Comparative Literature Context*. New York: Modern Language Association of America, 1992.

Leith, M.S. *Political Discourse and National Identity in Scotland*. Edinburgh: Edinburgh University Press, 2012.

Levine, Suzanne. *The Subversive Scribe: Translating Latin American Fiction*. St Paul, MN: Graywolf Press, 1991.

Levitt, Marcus. *Russian Literary Politics and the Pushkin Celebration of 1880*. Ithaca: Cornell University Press, 1989.

Levshin, A. "Otryvki iz pisem o Malorossii." *Ukrainskii vestnik* 4 (1816): 35–47.

Livak, Leonid. *The Jewish Persona in the European Imagination: A Case of Russian Literature*. Stanford: Stanford University Press, 2010.

Lockridge, K.A. "Colonial Self-Fashioning: Paradoxes and Pathologies in the Construction of Genteel Identity in Eighteenth-Century America." *Through a Glass Darkly: Reflections on Personal Identity in Early America*. Chapel Hill: University of North Carolina Press, 1997. Pp. 279–87.

Loomba, Ania. *Colonialism/Postcolonialism*. London, New York: Psychology Press, 1998.

Lotman, Iu. M. *Aleksandr Sergeevich Pushkin*. Leningrad: Prosveshchenie, 1982.

– "Dekabrist v povsednevnoi zhizni: Bytovoe povedenie kak istoriko-psikhologicheskaia kategoriia." *Izbrannyie stat'i*. 3 vols. Vol. 1. Tallinn: Aleksandra, 1992. 296–336.

– "Khudozhestvennoe prostranstvo v proze Gogolia." *V shkole poeticheskogo slova: Pushkin, Lermontov, Gogol'. Kniga dlia uchitelia*. Moscow: Prosveshcheniie, 1988.

– "Theatre and Theatricality in the Order of Early Nineteenth-Century
Culture." *Semiotics and Structuralism: Readings from the Soviet Union.* New
York: International Arts and Sciences Press, 1976.

Lounsbery, A. *Thin Culture, High Art: Gogol, Hawthorne, and Authorship in
Nineteenth-Century Russia and America.* Cambridge, MA: Harvard University
Press, 2007.

Loxley, R. "Roles of the Audience: Aesthetic and Social Dimensions of the
Performance Event." *Literature in Performance* 3 (1) (1983): 40–4.

Luckyj, G. *The Anguish of Mykola Hohol a.k.a. Nikolai Gogol.* Toronto: Canadian
Scholars' Press, 1998.

– *Between Gogol and Ševčenko: Polarity in the Literary Ukraine: 1798–1847.*
Munich: W. Fink, 1971.

– *Panteleimon Kulish: A Sketch of His Life and Times.* New York: East European
Monographs, 1983.

Macherey, P. "Creation and Production." *Authorship: From Plato to the
Postmodern.* Edinburgh: Edinburgh University Press, 1995.

MacLean, Hugh. "Gogol's Retreat from Love: Towards an Interpretation
of *Mirgorod*." *American Contributions to the Fourth International Congress of
Slavistics.* The Hague: Mouton & Co., 1958. 225–45.

Maguire, R.A. *Exploring Gogol.* Stanford: Stanford University Press, 1994.

Maimin, E. "Druzheskaia perepiska Pushkina s tochki zreniia stilistiki."
Pushkinskii sbornik. Pskov, 1962. 77–87.

Maksymovych, M.A. *Sobranie sochinenii v 3-kh tomakh.* Kyiv: Tip. M.P. Fritsa,
1876–7.

Malakhovskii, V. "Iazyk pisem Pushkina." *Izvestiia AN SSSR. Otd. obshchestv.
nauk* 2–3 (1937): 503–5.

Malaniuk, Ie. "Hohol – Gogol." *Ukrainian Review* 14 (3) (1967): 55–69.

Mandel'shtam, I. *O charaktere gogolevskogo stilia: glava iz istorii russkago
literaturnogo iazyka.* St Petersburg: Gel'singfors, 1902.

Mann, Iu. "Gogol." *Istoriia vsemirnoi literatury v 8-mi tomakh.* Vol. 6. Moscow:
AN SSSR, Institut mirovoi literatury im. A.M. Gor'kogo. 369–84.

– *Gogol'. Kniga pervaia. Nachalo 1809–1835.* Moscow: RGGU, 2012.

– "Gogol' – kritik i publitsist." *Sobranie sochinenii v 7-mi tomakh.* Vol. 6.
Moscow: Khud. lit., 1978. 469–89.

– *Gogol': trudy i dni: 1809–1845.* Moscow: Aspekt Press, 2004.

– *Poetika Gogolia: Variatsii k teme.* Moscow: Coda, 1996.

Markevich, A.I. "Zametka o psevdonime N.V. Gogolia 'Rudyi Pan'ko.'"
Izvestiia otdeleniia russkogo iazyka i slovesnosti Imperatorskoi Akademii nauk 3 (4)
(1898): 1270–2.

Markevich, N. *Istoriia Malorossii.* 5 vols. Moscow: V tip. Avgusta Semena,
1842–3.

– *Ukrainskie melodii.* Moscow: V tip. Avgusta Semena, 1832.

Markovskii, M.N. "Istoriia vozniknovenia i sozdania 'Mertvykh dush.'" *Pamiati Gogolia. Nauchno-literaturnyi sbornik, izdannyi Istoricheskim Obshchestvom Nestora-letopistsa*. Ed. N.P. Dashkevich. Kiev: Tip. R.K. Lubkovskogo, 1902. 133–226.

Masenko, Larysa. "Surzhyk: Istoria formuvannia, suchasnyi stan, perspektyvy funktsionuvannia." *Belarusian Trasjanka and Ukrainian Surzhyk: Structural and Social Aspects of Their Description and Categorization*. Ed. Gerd Hentschel and Siarhiej Zaprudski. Oldenburg: BIS-Verlag der Carl von Ossietzky Universitaet Oldenburg, 2008. 1–34.

Mashinskii, S.I., ed. *Gogol' v vospominaniiakh sovremennikov*. Moscow: Gos. izd-vo khudozh. lit-ry, 1952.

– *Istoricheskaia povest' Gogolia*. Moscow: "Sovetskii pisatel'," 1940.

Matarazzo, Joseph D., Morris Weitman, and George Saslow. "Interview Content and Interviewee Speech Durations." *Journal of Clinical Psychology* 19 (4) (1963): 463–72.

Matviias, I. "Rol' slobozhans'koho hovoru v movotvorchosti Hryhoriia Kvitky-Osnov'ianenka." *Instytut ukrains'koi movy NAN Ukrainy. Kul'tura movy na shchoden'*. http://kulturamovy.univ.kiev.ua/KM/pdfs /Magazine70–2.pdf.

– "Ukrains'ka literaturna mova i teritorial'ni dialekty v ikh vzaiemodii na riznykh istorychnykh etapakh." *Ukrains'ka literaturna mova v ii vzaiemodii z teritorial'nymy dialektamy*. Kyiv: Naukova dumka, 1977. 5–31.

McClintock, Anne. *Imperial Leather: Race, Gender, and Sexuality in the Colonial Contest*. London, New York: Routledge, 1995.

Megill, Allan. "Historical Representation, Identity, Allegiance." *Narrating the Nation: Representations in History, Media and Arts*. Ed. Stefen Berger, Linas Eriksonas, and Andrew Mycock. New York, Oxford: Berghahn Books, 2008. 19–34.

Mel'nyk, L. *Osyp Bodians'kyi (1808–1877). 200 rokiv vid dnia narodzhennia*. Nizhyn: PP Lysenko M.M., 2008.

Mersereau, J. *Orest Somov: Russian Fiction between Romanticism and Realism*. Woodstock, NY: Ardis Publishing, 1989.

Miiakovs'kyi, V. "Iuvilei tsenzurnoho aktu 1876 roku." *Bibliolohichni visti* 3 (1929): 62–73.

Mikhailov, A.V. "Gogol' v svoei literaturnoi epokhe." *Gogol': istoriia i sovremennost'*. Moscow: Sov. Rossiia, 1985.

– "Poetika barokko: zavershenie istoricheskoi epokhi." *Iazyki kul'tury: uchebnoe posobie po kul'turologii*. Moscow: Iazyki russkoi kul'tury, 1997. 112–75.

Miller, A. "Rossia i rusifikatsia Ukrainy v XIX veke." *Rossiia-Ukraina: istoriia vzaimootnoshenii*. Moscow: Iazyki russkoi kul'tury, 1997. 145–55.

– *The Ukrainian Question: The Russian Empire and Nationalism in the Nineteenth Century*. Budapest: Central European University Press, 2003.

Miller, D. "Ocherki is istorii i iuridicheskogo byta staroi Malorossii: Prevrashchenie malorusskoi starshiny v dvorianstvo." *Kievskaia starina* 1 (1897): 1–31.

Miller, J.H. *Hawthorne and History: Defacing It.* Oxford: Blackwell, 1991.

Mink, L.O. "Narrative Form as a Cognitive Instrument." *The Writing of History: Literary Form and Historical Understanding.* Madison: University of Wisconsin Press, 1978. 129–49.

Mizutani, Satoshi. "Hybridity and History: A Critical Reflection on Homi K. Bhabha's Post-Historical Thoughts." *Ab Imperio* 4 (2013): 27–48.

Modzalevskii, B.L., et al. *Dnevnik A.S. Pushkina: 1833–1835.* Moscow: Izd-vo "Tri veka," 1997.

Modzalevskii, L. "Epistoliarnoe naslediie Pushkina." *Izvestiia AN SSSR. Otd. obshchestv. nauk* 2–3 (1937): 230–5.

Moeller-Sally, S. "0000; or, the Sign of the Subject in Gogol's Petersburg." *Russian Subjects: Empire, Nation, and the Culture of the Golden Age.* Ed. Monika Greenleaf and Stephen Moeller-Sally. Evanston, IL: Northwestern University Press, 1998. 325–46.

– *Gogol's Afterlife: The Evolution of a Classic in Imperial and Soviet Russia.* Evanston, IL: Northwestern University Press, 2002.

Motorin, A. "K voprosu o nauchnom izdanii sochinenii Gogolia." *N.V. Gogol' i russkaia literatura XIX veka: mezhvuzovskii sbornik nauchnykh trudov.* Ed. Ia. S. Bilinkis, E.I. Annenkova and S.A. Goncharov. Leningrad: Leningradskii gos. pedagog. in-t im. A.I. Gertsena, 1989. 103–21.

Mufwene, Salikoko. "Pidgin and Creole Languages." *International Encyclopedia of the Social and Behavioral Sciences.* Vol. 18. Ed. James D. Wright. Oxford: Elsevier, 2015. 133–45.

Mushchenko, Ie. G. "Skazovoe povestvovanie u N.V. Gogolia: (Iz nabliudenii za poetikoi 'Vecherov na khutore bliz Dikan'ki')." *Voprosy poeticheskoi literatury i fol'klora.* Voronezh: Voronezhskii gos. pedagogicheskii universitet, 1972. 62–72.

Mykhed, P. "Gogol' i pol's'ka literatura 30-kh–40-kh rokiv XIX st. (problema vyvchennia)." *Hoholeznavchi studii* 4 (21) (2014): 87–98.

– "Mykola Hohol' i poliaky (deiaki aspekty doslidzhennia)." *Slovo i chas* 5 (2008): 3–11.

– "Privatizatsiia Gogolia? Vozvrashchaias' k russko-urkainskomu voprosu." *Voprosy literatury* 3 (2003): 94–112.

Myronchuk, A. "Vasyl' Kapnist – ukrains'kyi avtonomist." *Podvyzhnyky i metsenaty: Grets'ki pirpryemtsi i diiachi v Ukraini XVII–XIX st. Istoryko-biohrafichni narysy.* Ed. V. Smolii. Kyiv: National Academy of Sciences. Institute of Ukraine's History, 2001.

Nabokov, V. *Nikolai Gogol.* Norfolk, CT: New Directions Books, 1944.

Nadezhdin, N. "Review of *Vechera an khutore bliz Dikan'ki*, vol. 1." *Teleskop* 5 (1831): 558–63.

Nakhimovsky, Alice Stone. *Russian-Jewish Literature and Identity: Jabotinsky, Babel, Grossman, Galich, Roziner, Markish*. Baltimore: Johns Hopkins University Press, 1992.

Nakhlik, Yevhen. *Ukrains'ka romantychna proza 20–60kh rokiv XIX stolittia*. Kyiv: Naukova dumka, 1988.

Nechiporenko, Iu. D. "Iarmarka u Gogolia." *Zhertvoprinoshenie: ritual v iskusstve i kul'ture ot drevnosti do nashikh dnei*. Ed. L.I. Akimova. Moscow: Iazyki russkoi kul'tury, 2000.

Neiman, B. "Kulish i Valter Skott." *Panteleimon Kulish: Zbirnyk prats' komisii dlia vydavannia pam'iatok novitn'ioho pys'menstva*. Kyiv, 1927. 127–56.

Nimchuk, V. *Movoznavstvo na Ukraini v XIV–XVII stolitti*. Kyiv: Naukova dumka, 1985.

Ohloblyn, Oleksander. "Ancestry of Mykola Gogol (Hohol)." *Annals of the Ukrainian Academy of Sciences in the U.S.* 12 (1969–73): 3–43.

– *Liudy staroi Ukrainy*. Munich: "Dniprova khvylia," 1959.

Oksman, Iu. "Sozhzhennaia tragediia Gogolia iz proshlogo Zaporozh'ia." *Atenei: istoriko-literaturnyi vremennik*. Edited by B.L. Modzalevskii and Iu. G. Oksman. Vol. 3. Leningrad: Puskinskii dom Akademii nauk SSSR, 1926. 46–58.

Olson, Gary A., and Lynn Worsham. "Staging the Politics of Difference: Homi Bhabha's Critical Literacy." *Journal for Advanced Composition* 18 (3) (1998): 361–91.

Ovsianiko-Kulikovskii, Dmitrii. "Gogol'." *Sobranie sochinenii v deviati tomakh*. Vol. 1. St Petersburg: Prometei, 1910.

Paloposki, Outi, and Kaisa Koskinen. "Reprocessing Texts. The Fine Line between Retranslating and Revising." *Across Languages and Cultures* 11 (June 2010): 29–49.

Panaev, I.I. *Literaturnye vospominania*. Moscow: Pravda, 1988.

Parker, A., and E.K. Sedgwick. *Performativity and Performance*. New York: Routledge, 1995.

Pashaeva, N.M. *Ocherki istorii russkogo dvizheniia v Galichine v XIX–XX vv.* Moscow: "Imperskaia traditsiia," 2007.

Pavlyshyn, M. "Experiments with Audiences: The Ukrainian and Russian Prose of Kvitka-Osnovianenko." *Slavic and East European Journal* 58 (2) (2014): 197–216.

– "For and against a Ukrainian National Literature: Kostomarov's *Sava Chalyi* and Its Reviewers." *Slavonic and East European Review* 92 (2) (2014): 201–27.

– *Literatura, natsiia, modernist'*. Lviv: Tsentr humanitarnykh doslidzhen', Kyiv: Smoloskyp, 2013.

– "The Rhetoric and Politics of Kotliarevsky's *Eneïda*." *Journal of Ukrainian Studies* 10.1 (1985): 9–24.

– "'The Tranquil Lakes of the Transmontane Commune': Literature and/ against Postcoloniality in Ukraine after 1991." *Postcolonial Slavic Literatures After Communism*. Ed. K. Smola and D. Uffelmann. New York: PL Academic Research, 2016. 59–82.

– "Writing in Ukraine and European Identity." *Australian Slavonic and East European Studies* 21 (1–2) (2007): 125–42.

Peace, R. *The Enigma of Gogol: An Examination of the Writings of N.V. Gogol and Their Place in the Russian Literary Tradition*. Cambridge, New York: Cambridge University Press, 1981.

Pêcheux, M. *Language, Semantics, and Ideology*. Trans. Harbans Nagpal. Basingstoke: Macmillan, 1982.

Pennycook, Alastair. "Global Englishes, Rip Slyme, and Performativity." *Journal of Sociolinguistics* 7 (4) (2003): 513–33.

Perets, V. "Gogol' i malorusskaia literaturnaia traditsiia." *Rechi posviashchennye ego pamiati*. St Petersburg: Tip. Imperskoi Akademii Nauk, 1902. Pp. 47–55.

Petrov, V. *Panteleimon Kulish u p'iatdesiati roky. Zhyttia, ideolohiia, tvorchist'*. Vol. 1. Kyiv: Z drukarni Vseukrains'koi Akademii Nauk, 1929.

Petrunina, N. "Orest Somov i ego proza: vstup. stat'ia." *Somov O.M. Byli i nebylitsy*. Moscow: Sovetskii pisatel', 1984.

Petrunina, N., and G. Fridlender. "Pushkin i Gogol' v 1831–1836 godakh." *Pushkin: Issledovaniia i materialy, vol. 6. Realizm Pushkina i literatura ego vremeni*. Leningrad: Nauka, 1969.

Pieters, J. *Moments of Negotiation: The New Historicism of Stephen Greenblatt*. Amsterdam: Amsterdam University Press, 2001.

Piksanov, N.K. "Ukrainskie povesti Gogolia." *O klassikakh*. Moscow: Moskovskoe t-vo pisatelei, 1933. 43–148.

Pletnev, P. "Ukraiinskii sbornik I. Sreznevskogo." *Sovremennik* 14 (1839): 31–2.

Plokhii, Serhii. *The Cossacks and Religion in Early Modern Ukraine*. New York: Oxford University Press, 2002.

– "The Two Russias of Teofan Prokopovych." *Mazepa and His Time: History, Society, Culture*. Ed. G. Siedina. Alessandria: Edizioni dell'Orso, 2004. 333–66.

– *Ukraine and Russia: Representations of the Past*. Toronto: University of Toronto Press, 2008.

Pogodin, M.P. *Issledovaniia, zamechania i lektsii o russkoi istorii*. Vol. 7. Moscow: Univ. tip., 1856.

Polevoi, N.A. "Pokhozhdeniia Chichikova, ili mertvye dushi. Poema N. Gogolia." *Russkii vestnik* 5–6, otd. III (1842).

– "Review of *Chary, ili neskol'ko stsen iz narodnykh bylei i rasskazov ukrainskikh* by Kyrylo Topolia." *Biblioteka dlia chteniia* 25 (1837): 51–72.

– "Review of *Kobzar* by Taras Shevchenko." *Syn Otechestva* 2 (8) (1840): 836–7.
– "Review of *Vechera na khutore bliz Dikan'ki* vol. 1." *Moskovskii telegraf* 41 (17) (1831): 91–5.
– "Review of *Vechera na khutore bliz Dikan'ki* vol. 2." *Moskovskii telegraf* 44 (6) (1832): 262–7.
Pomerantseva, E.V. *Mifologicheskiie personazhi v russkom fol'klore*. Moscow: Nauka, 1975.
Popovych, Myroslav. *Narys istorii kul'tury Ukrainy*. Kyiv: "ArtEk," 1998.
Pratt, M.L. *Imperial Eyes: Travel Writing and Transculturation*. New York: Routledge, 1992.
Prymak, Thomas M. *Mykola Kostomarov: A Biography*. Toronto, Buffalo, London: University of Toronto Press, 1996.
Pumpianskii, L.V. "Gogol'." *Klassicheskaia traditsiia: sobranie trudov po istorii russkoi literatury. Iazyk, semiotika, kul'tura*. Moscow: Iazyki russkoi kul'tury, 2000.
Radkovskaia, E.V. "Ukrainskie motivy poeticheskoi antropologii rannikh povestei N. Gogolia." *Voprosy literatury narodov SSSR* 15 (1989): 169–77.
Ram, H. *The Imperial Sublime: A Russian Poetics of Empire*. Madison: University of Wisconsin Press, 2003.
Rebecchini, D. "Kak krest'iane chitali Gogolia: popytka rekonstruktsii retseptsii." *Novoe literaturnoe obozreniie* 49 (2001): 508–25.
Reitblat, A. "Gogol' i Bulgarin: k istorii literaturnykh vzaimootnoshenii." *Faddei Bulgarin: ideolog, zhurnalist, konsul'tant sekretnoi politsii. Stat'i i materialy*. Moscow: Novoe literaturnoe obozrenie, 2016.
– *Ot Bovy k Bal'montu: ocherki po istorii chteniia v Rossii vo vtoroi polovine XIX veka*. Moscow: Izd-vo MPI, 1991.
Riabchuk, Mykola. "Ukrainian Culture after Communism: Between Post-Colonial and Neo-Colonial Subjugation." *Postcolonial Europe? Essays on Post-Communist Literatures and Cultures*. Ed. Dobrota Pucherová and Róbert Gáfrik. Leiden, Boston: Brill Rodopi, 2015. 337–55.
– *Vid Malorossii do Ukrainy: parodoksy zapizniloho natsietvorennia*. Kyiv: "Krytyka," 2000.
Riasanovsky, N.V. *Nicholas I and Official Nationality in Russia, 1825–1855*. Russian and East European Studies. Berkeley: University of California Press, 1959.
Rohdewald, Stefan. "'Vneshniaia kolonizatsiia vnutrennego' i 'vnutrenniaia kolonizatsiia vneshnego': Oppozitsionnye elity stolits vs. loialnye elity Zapadnogo kraia, 1830–1910 gody." *Tam, vnutri: Praktiki vnutrennei kolonizatsii v kul'turnoi istorii Rossii*. Moscow: Novoe literaturnoe obozrenie, 2012. 518–51.
Romanchuk, Robert. "Mother Tongue: Gogol's *Pannochka*, Pogorel'skii's *Monastyrka*, and the Economy of Russian in the Little Russian Gothic." *Slavic and Eastern European Journal* 62 (2) (2018): 272–92.

Rosenshield, Gary. *The Ridiculous Jew: The Exploitation and Transformation of a Stereotype in Gogol, Turgenev, and Dostoevsky*. Stanford: Stanford University Press, 2008.

Rowe, W.W. *Through Gogol's Looking Glass: Reverse Vision, False Focus, and Precarious Logic*. New York: New York University Press, 1976.

Rozov, V.A. "Traditsionnye tipy malorusskogo teatra XVII–XVIII v. i iunosheskie povesti N. V. Gogolia." *Pamiati N.V. Gogolia. Sbornik rechei i statei, izdannyi Imperatorskim universitetom Sv. Vladimira*. Kiev, 1911. 99–169.

Ruane, C. "Subjects into Citizens: The Politics of Clothing in Imperial Russia." *Fashioning the Body Politic: Dress, Gender, Citizenship*. Ed. Wendy Parkins. Oxford, New York: Berg, 2002. 49–70.

Rudnytsky, I.L., and P.L. Rudnytsky. *Essays in Modern Ukrainian History*. Edmonton: Canadian Institute of Ukrainian Studies Press, 1987.

Russett, M. *Fictions and Fakes: Forging Romantic Authenticity, 1760–1845*. Cambridge, New York: Cambridge University Press, 2006.

Rutherford, A. "Vissarion Belinskii and the Ukrainian National Question." *Russian Review* 54 (4) (1995): 500–15.

Safran, Gabriella. *Rewriting the Jew: Assimilation Narratives in the Russian Empire*. Stanford: Stanford University Press, 2000.

Said, E.W. *Culture and Imperialism*. London: Chatto & Windus, 1993.

– *Orientalism: Western Conceptions of the Orient*. London: Penguin, 1978.

Samyshkina, A. "K probleme gogolevskogo fol'klorizma (Dva tipa skaza i literaturnaia polemika v *Vecherakh na khutore bliz Dikan'ki*)." *Russkaia literatura* 3 (1979): 61–80.

Sapchenko, L. "Literaturnaia i fol'klorno-mifologicheskaia traditsii v *Vecherakh na khutore bliz Dikan'ki*." *Gogol' i narodnaia kul'tura: materialy dokladov i soobshchenii mezhdunarodnoi nauchnoi konferentsii. Sed'mye gogolevskie chteniia*. Moscow: CheRo, 2008. 123–31.

Saunders, D. "Mykola Kostomarov (1817–85) and the Creation of a Ukrainian Ethnic Identity." *Slavonica* 7 (1) (2001): 7–24.

– *The Ukrainian Impact on Russian Culture, 1750–1850*. Edmonton: Canadian Institute of Ukrainian Studies, University of Alberta, 1985.

Sawczak, Peter. "'Noch' pered Rozhdestvom' Mykoly/Nikolaia Gogolia: k voprosu o 'maloi literature.'" *Russian Literature* 49 (2001): 259–70.

Schilder, P. *The Image and Appearance of the Human Body*. New York: International Universities Press, 1970.

Schleiermacher, Freidrich. *Hermeneuptik und Kritik*. Frankfurt: Suhrkamp, 1977.

Schöch, Christof. "Beyond the Black Box, or: Understanding the Difference between Various Statistical Distance Measures." (2012). http://dragonfly.hypotheses.org/101.

Sen'ko, I. *Hoholivs'ka Dikan'ka na istorychnykh perekhrestiakh*. Uzhhorod: Uzhhorods'kyi Natsional'nyi Universytet, 2003.

Senkovskii, O.I. "Istoriia Malorossii, Nik. Markevicha." *Biblioteka dlia chteniia* 56 (1843): 1–46.

– "Review of *Pokhozhdeniia Chichikova, ili Mertvye dushi* (1842), by N. Gogol'." *Biblioteka dlia chteniia* 53 (1842): 24–54.

– "Review of *Vechera na khutore bliz Dikan'ki*, 2nd edition." *Biblioteka dlia chteniia* 15 (1836): 3–4.

Serebrennikov, Amvrosii. *Kratkoie rukovodstvo k Oratorii rossiiskoi, sochinennoie v Lavrskoi seminarii v pol'zu iunoshestva, krasnorechiiu obucheiushchegosia.* Moscow: Tip. pri teatre u Khr. Klaudiia, 1791.

Setchkarev, V. *Gogol: His Life and Works.* New York: New York University Press, 1965.

Shapiro, G. *Nikolai Gogol and the Baroque Cultural Heritage.* University Park: Pennsylvania State University Press, 1993.

Shchurat, Vasyl'. *Ukrains'ki povisti M. Hoholia.* Lviv, 1900.

Shelukhin, S. "Gogol' i malorossiiskoe obshchestvo." *Sbornik, izdavaemyi Novorossiiskim universitetom po sluchaiu 100–letiia so dnia rozhdeniia N.V. Gogolia.* Odessa, 1909.

Shenrok, V.I. *A.O. Smirnova i N.V. Gogol' v 1829–1852 gg. Russkaia starina 4,* 1888.

– *Materialy dlia biografii Gogolia.* Moscow: Tip. A.I. Mamontova, 1892.

– *Ukazatel' k pis'mam Gogolia, zakliuchaiushchim v sebe ob'iasneniie initsialov i drugikh sokrashchenii v izdanii Kulisha.* Moscow: Tip. T. Ris, 1886.

Shevelyov, G. "Kulishevi lysty i Kulish u lystakh." *Vybrani lysty Panteleimona Kulisha ukrainskoiu movoiu pysani.* Ed. Yu. Lutskyi. New York: Ukr. vilna akademiia nauk u SShA, 1984.

– *The Ukrainian Language in the First Half of the Twentieth Century (1900–1941): Its State and Status.* Cambridge, MA: Harvard University Press, 1989.

Shkandrij, M. *Russia and Ukraine: Literature and the Discourse of Empire from Napoleonic to Postcolonial Times.* Montreal: McGill-Queen's University Press, 2001.

Shkliar, V. "Bulba, iakyi ne zhoriv." *Mykola Hohol'. Taras Bulba.* Trans. V. Shkliar. Kyiv: "Dnipro," 2003.

Shraga, E. "Bylichka i svetskii razgovor kak strukturnaia osnova prozaicheskoi tsiklizatsii: *Vechera an khutore bliz Dikan'ki* v kontekste traditsii." *Gogol' i narodnaia kul'tura: materialy dokladov i soobshchenii mezhdunarodnoi nauchnoi konferentsii. Sed'myie gogolevskiie chteniia.* Moscow: CheRo, 2008. 267–74.

Shults, Sergei. "Gogol' i Novallis." *Russkaia literatura* 3 (2005): 99–107.

– "Gogol' i Shelling o dushe." *Chelovek* 1 (2016): 155–63.

Shvedova, N. Yu. "Printsipy istoricheskoi stilizatsii v iazyke povesti Gogolia 'Taras Bul'ba.'" *Materialy i issledovaniia po istorii russkogo literaturnogo iazyka.* Vol. 3. Moscow: Izd-vo Akademii Nauk SSSR, 1953. 45–67.

Simon, Sherry. *Translating Montreal: Episodes in the Life of a Divided City.*
    Montreal: McGill-Queen's University Press, 2006.
Siniavskii, Andrei: *see* Terts
Slocum, J.W. "Who, and When, Were the Inorodtsy? The Evolution of the
    Category of 'Aliens' in Imperial Russia." *Russian Review* (1998): 173–90.
Slonimskii, A. "Voprosy gogolevskogo teksta." *Izvestiia AN SSSR. Otd. lit. i iaz.*
    12 (5) (1953): 401–16.
Slovar' Akademii rossiiskoi po azbuchnomu poriadku razpolozhennyi. St Petersburg,
    Imperatorskaia Akademiia Nauk, 1806–22.
Smirnova-Rosset, A.O. *Dnevnik, vospominaniia.* Moscow: Nauka, 1989.
– "Letter to Gogol of 11 January 1847." *Russkaia starina* 67 (1890): 282–4.
– "Letter to Gogol of 11 March 1845." *Severnyi vestnik* 1 (1893): 246–50.
– "Letter to Gogol of 6 May 1844." *Russkaia starina* 58 (1888): 603–7.
– "Letter to Gogol of 26 September 1844." *Russkaia starina* 59 (1888): 57–60.
Smith, B.H. "Narrative Versions, Narrative Theories." *On Narrative.* Ed. W.J.T.
    Mitchell. Chicago: University of Chicago Press, 1981. 209–32.
Smola, Klavdia, and Dirk Uffelman, eds. *Postcolonial Slavic Literatures after
    Communism.* New York: PL Academic Research, 2016.
Smolikowski, Paweł. *Historya Zgromadzenia Zmartwychwstania Pańskiego.*
    Vol. 2. Kraków: Księg. Spółki Wydawniczej Polskiej, 1892.
Sokhan', P., et al., eds. *Kyrylo-Mefodiivs'ke tovarystvo. U triokh tomakh.* 3 vols.
    Vol. 1. Kyiv: Naukova dumka, 1990.
Sokolov, B.V. *Gogol': entsiklopediia.* Moscow: Algoritm, 2003.
Sollogub, V.A. *Povesti. Vospominaniia.* Moscow: Khudozhestvennaia literatura,
    1988.
Somov, Orest. "Gaidamak. malorossiiskaia byl'." *Poliarnaia zvezda izdannaia A.
    Bestuzhevym i K. Ryleevym.* Ed. V. Arkhipov, V. Bazanov, and Ia. Levkovich.
    Moscow, Leningrad: Izdatel'stvo Akademii Nauk SSSR, 1960. 748–65.
– *O romanticheskoi poezii. Opyt v trekh statiiakh.* St Petersburg: Tip. Imp.
    Vospitatelnogo Doma, 1823.
Spieker, Sven. "The Centrality of the Middle: On the Semantics of the
    Threshold in Gogol's 'Arabeski.'" *Slavonic and East European Review* 73 (3)
    (1995): 449–69.
Spitzer, Leo. *Die wortbildung als stilistisches mittel exemplifiziert an Rabelais.*
    Halle: A.S. Verlag von Max Niemeyer, 1910.
Sreznevskii, Izmail. "Vzgliad na pamiatniki Ukrainskoi narodnoi Slovesnosti.
    Pis'mo k Professoru I. M. Snegirevu." *Uchenye zapiski Imperatorskogo
    Moskovskogo universiteta* 4 (1834): 134–50.
Stavytska, Lesia, and Volodymyr Trub. "Surzhyk: Mif, mova, komunikatsia."
    Ukrains'ko-rosiis'ka dvomovnist'. Ed. Lesia Stavytska. Kyiv: Pulsary, 2007. 31–121.
Stepanov, N.L. "Druzheskoe pis'mo nachala XIX veka. Pis'ma Pushkina kak
    literaturnyi zhanr." *Poety i prozaiki.* Moscow: Khudozh. lit-ra, 1966. 66–100.

– *N.V. Gogol': Tvorcheskii put'*. 2nd ed. Moscow: Gosudarstvennoe izdatel'stvo khudozestvennoi literatury, 1959.

Stilman, L. *Gogol*. Tenafly, NJ: Hermitage Publishers, 1990.

Storozhenko, A. [signed A. Tsarynnyi]. "Mysli Malorossiianina po prochtenii povestei pasichnika Rudogo Pan'ka." *Syn Otechestva* 25 (1832): 41–9, 101–15, 59–64, 223–42, 288–312.

Strakhovsky, Leonid I. "The Historianism of Gogol." *American Slavic and East European Review* (1953): 360–70.

Strano, Giacomo. *Gogol' (ironia, polemica, parodia)*. Soveria Mannelli: Rubbettino Edittore, 2004.

Stromecky, Ostap. "Ukrainian Elements in Mykola Hohol''s 'Taras Bul'ba.'" *Ukrainian Quarterly* 15 (4) (1969): 350–61.

Subtelny, O. *Ukraine: A History*. Toronto: University of Toronto Press, 2000.

Sullivan, H. *The Work of Revision*. Cambridge, MA: Harvard University Press, 2013.

Suproniuk, O.K. "Literaturnaia sreda rannego Gogolia." *Izvestiia AN SSSR. Ser. lit. i iazyka* 50 (1) (1991): 58–68.

– *Literaturnaia sreda rannego Gogolia*. Kyiv: Akademperiodika, 2009.

– *N.V. Gogol' i ego okruzheniie v Nezhinskoi gimnazii. Bibliograficheskii slovar'*. Kyiv: Akademperiodika, 2009.

Sverbyhuz, V. *Starosvits'ke panstvo*. Warsaw, 1999.

Szporluk, R. "Ukraine: From an Imperial Periphery to a Sovereign State." *Russia, Ukraine, and the Breakup of the Soviet Union*. Stanford: Hoover Institution Press, 2000. 361–94.

Tairova-Iakovleva, T. *Inkorporatsiia: Rossiia i Ukraina posle Pereiaslavskoi rady (1654–1658)*. Kyiv: Vydavnytstvo "Klio," 2017.

Terts, A. *V teni Gogolia*. Moscow: Agraf, 2001.

Teslia, A. "'Ukrainophil' v 'obshcherusskom kontekste:' publitsistika N.I. Kostomarova 1861–1883 godov." *Novoe literaturnoe obozrenie* 2 (144) (2017): 137–53.

Ther, Philipp. "Caught in Between: Border Regions in Modern Europe." *Shatterzone of Empires: Coexixtence and Violence in the German, Habsburg, Russian, and Ottoman Borderlands*. Ed. Omer Bartov and Eric D. Weitz. Bloomington: Indiana University Press, 2013. 485–502.

Thompson, E.M. *Imperial Knowledge: Russian Literature and Colonialism*. Westport, CT: Greenwood Press, 2000.

Threadgold, T. "Performing Theories of Narrative: Theorizing Narrative Performance." *The Sociolinguistics of Narrative*. Ed. J. Thornborrow and J. Coates. Amsterdam: John Benjamins Publishing Company, 2005.

Tikhonravov, N. "Zametki o slovare, sostavlennom Gogolem." *Sbornik Obshchestva liubitelei rossiiskoi slovesnosti na 1891 god*. Moscow: Tipo-lit. I.N. Kushnerev, 1891. 196–208.

Todd, W.M. *The Familiar Letter as a Literary Genre in the Age of Pushkin.* Evanston, IL: Northwestern University Press, 1999.

– *Fiction and Society in the Age of Pushkin: Ideology, Institutions, and Narrative.* Cambridge, MA: Harvard University Press, 1986.

– "Gogol's Epistolary Writing." *Columbia Essays in International Affairs: The Dean's Papers* 5 (1969): 51–76.

– "A Russian Ideology." *Stanford Literature Review* 1 (1984): 85–117.

Tolochko, Oleksiy. "Fellows and Travelers: Thinking about Ukrainian History in the Early Nineteenth Century." *A Laboratory of Transnational History: Ukraine and Recent Ukrainian Historiography.* Ed. Philipp Ther and H.V. Kasianov. Budapest: Central European University Press, 2009. 149–68.

Tolochko, Petro. *Vid Rusi do Ukrainy.* Kyiv: Abrys, 1997.

Tolz, V. Russia: *Inventing the Nation.* London: Arnold, 2001.

Tomachinsky V.V. "Sintez vmesto khaosa. 'Vybrannyie mesta iz perepiski s druz'iami' kak stilisticheskaia programma Gogolia." *Evangel'skii tekst v russkoi literature XVIII–XX vekov: tsitata, reministsentsiia, motiv, siuzhet, zhanr. Sbornik nauchnykh trudov Petrozavodskogo gosudarstvennogo universiteta* 6 (2001): 250–76.

Tomlinson, John. "Globalization and Cultural Identity." *The Global Transformations Reader: An Introduction to the Globalization Debate.* Ed. D. Held and A. McGraw. Cambridge: Polity Press, 2000.

Tretiakova, N.P. "Rabota Gogolia nad iazykom i stilem 'Tarasa Bul'by' (sopostavlenie raznykh redaktsii povesti)." *Materialy i issledovaniia po istorii russkogo literaturnogo iazyka.* Vol. 3. Ed. V. Vinogradov. Moscow: Izd-vo Akademii Nauk SSSR, 1953. 68–106.

Trubetskoi, N. "The Ukrainian Problem." *The Legacy of Genghis Khan and Other Essays on Russia's Identity.* Ann Arbor: Michigan Slavic Publications, 1991. 245–67.

Tynianov, Iurii. "Dostoevsky and Gogol': Towards a Theory of Parody. Part One: Stylization and Parody." *Dostoevsky and Gogol: Texts and Criticism.* Ed. Priscilla Meyer and Stephen Rudy. Ann Arbor, MI.: Ardis, 1977. 101–17.

Ungurianu, Dan. *Plotting History: The Russian Historical Novel in the Imperial Age.* Madison: University of Wisconsin Press, 2007.

Ushakov, V.A. "Review of *Vechera na khutore bliz Dikan'ki* vol. 1." *Severnaia pchela* 219, 220 (1831).

Uspenskii, B.A. "Spory o iazyke v nachale XIX veka kak fakt russkoi kul'tury." *Izbrannye trudy.* Moscow: Gnozis, 1994. 331–467.

Vainshtein, O. *Dendi: moda, literatura, stil' zhizni.* Moscow: Izd-vo Novoe literaturnoe obozrenie, 2006.

Vaiskopf, M. *Siuzhet Gogolia: Morfologiia, Ideologiia, Kontekst.* Moscow: Radiks, 1993.

Varelas, Maria, and Joe Becker. "Internalization of Cultural Forms of Behavior: Semiotic Aspects of Intellectual Development." *Sociogenetic Perspectives*

on Internalization. Ed. Brian D. Cox and Cynthia Lightfoot. Mahwah, NJ:
Lawrence Erlbaum Associates, 1997. 203–19.

Vatsuro, V.E. *Mitskevich i russkaia literaturnaia sreda 1820-kh (razyskaniia).*
Moscow: Iazyki slavianskoi kul'tury, 2004.

– "Pushkin i literaturnoie dvizhenie ego vremeni." *Novoe literaturnoe obozrenie*
59 (2003): 307–32.

Vatsuro, V.E., et al., eds. *Perepiska N.V. Gogolia.* 2 vols. Moscow:
Khudozhestvennaia literatura, 1988.

– *Pushkin v vospominaniiakh sovremennikov.* 2 vols. St Petersburg:
Gumanitarnoe agentstvo "Akademicheskii proekt," 1998.

Velychenko, S. "Empire Loyalism and Minority Nationalism in Great Britain and
Imperial Russia, 1707 to 1914: Institutions, Law, and Nationality in Scotland
and Ukraine." *Comparative Studies in Society and History* 39 (3) (1997): 413–41.

Velychko, Samiilo. *Litopys.* Trans. Valerii Shevchuk. Vol. 1. Kyiv: Dnipro, 1991.

Venelin, Iurii. "O spore mezhdu iuzhanami i severianami naschet ikh
rossizma." *Istoki Rusi i slavianstva.* Ed. O. Platonov. Moscow: Institut russkoi
tsivilizatsii, 2011. 789–804.

Venuti, Lawrence. *Translation Changes Everything: Theory and Practice.* New
York: Routledge, 2013.

Veresaev, V.V. *Gogol' v zhizni: sistematicheskii svod podlinnykh svidetel'stv
sovremennikov.* Moscow: Moskovskii rabochii, 1990.

Viazemskii, P. *Ostaf'evskii arkhiv kniazei Viazemskikh.* Vol. 1. St Petersburg, 1899.

Vikulova, V.P., ed. *Gogol' i narodnaia kul'tura: materialy dokladov i soobshchenii
mezhdunarodnoi nauchnoi konferentsii.* Moscow: CheRo, 2008.

Vinogradov, I.A. *Gogol' v vospominaniiakh, dnevnikakh, perepiske sovremennikov.*
3 vols. Moscow: IMLI RAN, 2011.

Vinogradov, V.V. *Etiudy o stile Gogolia.* Leningrad: Academia, 1926.

– *Gogol and the Natural School.* New York: Ardis, 1987.

– *Gogol' i natrual'naia shkola.* Leningrad: Kul'turno-prosvetitel'noe trudovoe
tovarishchestvo "Obrazovanie," 1925.

– *The History of the Russian Literary Language from the Seventeenth Century to the
Nineteenth.* Madison: University of Wisconsin Press, 1969.

– "Iazyk Gogolia i ego znachenie v istorii russkogo iazyka." *Materialy i
issledovaniia po istorii russkogo literaturnogo iazyka.* Vol. 3. Moscow: Izd-vo
Akademii Nauk SSSR, 1953. 4–44.

Voloshinov, V.N. *Marxism and the Philosophy of Language.* Trans. L. Matejka and
I.R. Titiunik. New York: Seminar Press, 1973.

Vol'pert, L.I. *Pushkin v roli Pushkina.* Moscow: Iazyki slavianskoi kul'tury, 1998.

Voropaev, V.A. "Gogol' i 'russko-ukrainskii vopros.'" *Moskovskii zhurnal* 1
(2002): 12–15.

– "Poltora veka spustia. Gogol' v sovremennom literaturovedenii." http://
www.domgogolya.ru/science/researches/1687/.

258   Bibliography

Wachtel, A. "Translation, Imperialism, and National Self-Definition in Russia."
     Public Culture 11 (1) (1999): 49–73.
Watts, Richard J. *Packaging Post/Coloniality: The Manufacture of Literary Identity
     in the Francophone World.* After the Empire: The Francophone World and
     Postcolonial France. Lanham: Lexington Books, 2005.
Wendland, Anna V. *Die Russophilen in Galizien. Ukrainische Konservative
     zwischen Oesterreich und Russland, 1848–1915.* Vol. 27. Österreichische
     Akademie der Wissenschaften, 2001.
White, H. "The Narrativization of Real Events." *Critical Inquiry* 8 (1981):
     793–8.
Williams, Raymond. *Marxism and Literature.* Oxford: Oxford University Press,
     1977.
Wilson, Andrew. "Elements of a Theory of Ukrainian Ethno-National
     Identities." *Nations and Nationalism* 8 (1) (2002): 31–54.
– *The Ukrainians: Unexpected Nation.* New Haven: Yale University Press, 2002.
Wolf, Michaela, and A. Fukari, eds.*Constructing a Sociology of Translation.*
     Philadelphia: John Benjamins Publishing, 2007.
Wortman, R.S. *Scenarios of Power: Myth and Ceremony in Russian Monarchy.*
     Princeton: Princeton University Press, 1995.
Yekelchyk, Serhiy. *Ukraine: Birth of a Modern Nation.* Oxford: Oxford University
     Press, 2007.
Yoon, Saera. "Transformation of a Ukrainian Cossack into a Russian Warrior:
     Gogol's 1842 'Taras Bulba.'" *Slavic and East European Journal* 49 (3) (2005):
     430–44.
Zadorozhna, Lyudmyla. "Khudozhnia kontseptsiia istorii v romani P. Kulisha
     'Mykhailo Charnyshenko.'" *Literaturoznavchi studii* 29 (2010): 153–9.
Zaslavskii, Dmitrii. "Evrei v russkoi literature." *Evreiskaia letopis': sbornik.* 4
     vols. Ed. L.M. Kliachko. Petrograd, Moscow: Izdatel'stvo "Raduga," 1923.
     Vol. 1. Pp. 59–86.
Zborovs'ka, Nila. *Kod ukrains'koi literatury. Proekt psykhoistorii novitn'ioi
     ukrains'koi literatury.* Kyiv: Akademvydav, 2006.
Zerov, Mykola. "Kulish: 'Chorna rada.'" *Tvory v dvokh tomakh.* Vol. 2. Kyiv:
     Dnipro, 1990. 196–203.
– *Ukrains'ke pys'menstvo.* Ed. M. Sulyma. Kyiv: Vyd-vo Solomii Pavlychko
     Osnovy, 2002.
Zhitomirskaia, S. "A.O. Smirnova-Rosset i ee memuarnoe nasledie." *A.O.
     Smirnova-Rosset. Dnevnik. Vospominaniia.* Moscow: "Nauka," 1989. 579–631.
Zhivov, V.M. *Iazyk i kul'tura v Rossii XVIII veka.* Moscow: Shkola "Iazyki
     russkoi kul'tury," 1996.
– *Language and Culture in Eighteenth-Century Russia.* Trans. Marcus Levitt.
     Boston: Academic Studies Press, 2009.

Zorin, A. "Ideologiia 'pravoslaviia-samoderzhaviia-narodnosti': opyt
rekonstruktsii (Neizvestnyi aftograf memorandum S.S. Uvarova Nikolaiu I)."
Novoe literaturnoe obozrenie 26 (1997): 71–104.

Zviniatskovskii, V. "Istoricheskoe iadro 'Mirgoroda' v svete
khudozhestvenno-mifologicheskikh ustanovok XVIII–pervoi treti XIX
i dokumentirovannoi istorii Ukrainy: 'Taras Bul'ba' i 'Istoria russov.'"
*Fenomen Gogolia. Materialy Iubileinoi mezhdunarodnoi nauchnoi konferentsii,
posviashchennoi 200-letiiu so dnia rozhdeniia N.V. Gogolia.* Ed. M.N. Virolainen
and A.A. Karpova. St Petersburg: Petropolis, 2011. 289–307.

– *Nikolai Gogol': tainy natsional'noi dushi.* Kyiv: Likei, 1994.

– "V chem zhe nakonets sushchestvo 'ukrainstva' Gogolia i v chem ego
osobennost.'" *Gogol' i narodnaia kul'tura: materialy dokladov i soobshchenii
mezhdunarodnoi nauchnoi konferentsii. Sed'mye gogolevskie chteniia.* Moscow:
CheRo, 2008. 41–50.